park
planning
handbook

park planning handbook

FUNDAMENTALS OF
PHYSICAL PLANNING
FOR PARKS AND
RECREATION AREAS

MONTY L. CHRISTIANSEN
Associate Professor

Recreation and Park Program
and
Department of
Landscape Architecture
The Pennsylvania
State University
University Park,
Pennsylvania

Illustrations by
James R. DeTuerk
Associate Professor

Department of
Landscape Architecture
The Pennsylvania
State University

JOHN WILEY & SONS
New York
Santa Barbara
London
Sydney
Toronto

Library of Congress Cataloging in Publication Data:

Christiansen, Monty L   1941–
  Park planning handbook.

  Includes bibliographies and indexes.
  1. Parks—Planning.   2. Recreation areas—Planning.
I. Title.

SB481.C53   711′.558   76-51844
ISBN 0-471-15619-1

Printed in the United States of America

10 9 8 7 6 5 4 3 2 1

dedication

TO MY WIFE
CONNIE
AND MY DAUGHTERS
CHARISSE AND ERIKA

preface

Park planning is a process designed to provide recreational experiences in designated settings using human and physical resources and support services.

This book was written primarily as a textbook for students of recreation and park administration who will have park planning as an important responsibility in their future professional roles. This book covers the total park planning process, including the predesign, design, development, and actualization phases, with a special emphasis on physical planning for support facilities. There are many good sources of detailed information about physical planning for specific sports and recreational activities. Entire books have been written about swimming pools, campgrounds, marinas, sports fields, and the various other activity areas. These are excellent references for activity facility planning. However, these books have not presented, in a comparable comprehensive manner, any of the support elements that unify and service each of various activity areas of a park. This book provides the basic planning considerations necessary to form a collection of activity facilities into a complete park. It is intended to complement texts in general administration, program development, personnel management, budgeting, facility operations and maintenance, and leadership.

Because park planning in this book is treated as an interdisciplinary team process, rather than the exclusive function of single specialists, students and practitioners of all the contributory fields gain a broader understanding of park planning and recognize the significance that their contributions and participation have on this total process. A variety of professions may be involved in the physical aspects of park planning: public administration, landscape architecture, engineering, resource management, forestry, public health services, wildlife management, physical education, recreation planning, and programming are some obvious examples.

Besides serving as a park planning textbook, this book is a useful desk reference and sourcebook for park planning consulting firms, public, private and commercial park agencies, schools, park board members, and other decision makers in the various levels of government providing parks and recreation facilities.

Park Planning Handbook is organized into two parts:

Part 1 gives a detailed description of the process of park planning, phase by phase, explaining the functions, roles, contributions, and responsibilities of the many members of the park planning team, from predesign conceptualization to actualization of the recreation experience.

Part 2 contains a comprehensive explanation of each of the major support requirements for a park. Each chapter in Part 2 is dedicated to one specific supportive element of a park: circulation, lighting, water, wastewater, solid waste, and health, safety, and emergency provisions.

Each chapter of Part 2 may be read separately and was intended to be an authoritive unit independent of other chapters. Because of the interrelationships of many of these physical planning considerations, appropriate cross references to other chapters have been included where it was deemed useful to the reader. The reading order of the materials in Part 2 should correspond to the reader's needs or concerns of the moment.

The appendices contains numerous examples and information sources for park planners, including special periodicals, lists of helpful governmental agencies, and special interest organizations with expert advice for park agencies, consultants, and individuals.

Monty L. Christiansen
University Park, Pennsylvania

acknowledgments

I am indebted to many people, including former students, colleagues, and professionals in the field who provided the inspirations for my effort. While most of these individuals must accept my expression of deepest appreciation in anonymity, I especially thank the individuals mentioned below.

Fred M. Coombs, Professor Emeritus, and the late **Wayne H. Wilson** who, as Chairmen of the Recreation and Parks Program and Department of Landscape Architecture at The Pennsylvania State University, together fostered a philosophy of inter-disciplinary cooperative park planning and who supported my efforts by providing a unique intercollege joint appointment with their two departments.

Tony A. Mobley and **David L. Young**, Chairmen of the above departments during the preparation of this book, who offered just the right words of support and encouragement at critical periods.

James R. DeTuerk, whose outstanding graphics communicate so well what could not be expressed in mere words.

I am indebted to the following colleagues who read early drafts of certain chapters of the manuscript and provided advice and constructive criticism, checking for technical accuracy in their special field of expertise:

Professor **David A. Long**, Department of Civil Engineering, The Pennsylvania State University, for his excellent contribution to those chapters covering physical planning for park water, wastewater, and solid waste systems.

Professor **Donald V. Joyce**, Recreation and Parks Program, the Pennsylvania State University, for his recommendations and reactions to the chapters on park planning as part of the park administration processes and actualization.

Professor **Donald W. Leslie**, Department of Landscape Architecture, The Pennsylvania State University, for his review and suggestions for the chapter on park circulation.

State College Health Officer **Mark S. Henry**, for his help with the chapter on health, safety, and emergency provisions.

Former graduate students **William W. Davis** and **James A. Burkhart**, who reviewed the manuscript from the perspective of the new professional, offering many valuable suggestions for general readability and clarity of concept for students and practitioners alike.

Three scholars of park planning were selected by John Wiley & Sons to provide academic reviews and critiques. Their input resulted in changes that improved the final text immeasurably:

Professor **Walter H. Bumgardner**, Department of Landscape Architecture and Regional Planning, University of Massachusetts.

Professor **Robert D. Greenleaf**, Recreation and Parks Program, University of New Hampshire.

Professor **Jesse H. Grove**, Department of Recreation and Park Administration, Clemson University.

My sincere appreciation is also extended to my typist, **Mrs. Jane Windom**, who very ably transformed my original holograph into the final, typed manuscript.

M. L. C.

contents

park
planning
handbook

part one the park planning process

A park is a miniature community, with all a community's characteristic complexities. Park planning shares these inherent qualities. Because of this complexity, there is often a tendency to disavow any role in park planning by many individuals who could make valuable contributions.

Much of this hesitancy is caused by misconceptions about park planning and an impression that it is an inscrutable discipline understood and practiced only by inventive but often impractical theorists. Much criticism has been directed to "those planners": "It may have looked good on paper, but it sure doesn't work." Admittedly some of this criticism has been justified, but as many cases, plans for parks have been prepared in vacuums, with no contributions by those who were often best qualified to do so.

Part One of this volume offers the concept that park planning is a process, not a role. It involves everyone who has a vested interest in the ultimate provision of recreational experiences. A broad overview of the separate phases of park planning is presented here to help all members of the park planning team see the entire process in logical progression.

We must all be park planners to achieve success from the perspective of park visitors.

1
park planning: part of the park administration processes

"A recreational service agency principally provides recreational experiences and support services to its clientele. It does not matter whether the agency (defined here as a recreational service agency) is a public, quasi-public, or private organization, as long as provision of opportunities for recreational experiences is its primary goal.

For our purposes, any recreation service agency that has the provision of physical areas and facilities as one of its methods to fulfill this goal is generically defined as a park department (park agency). Use of the descriptor *park department* is intended only to connote the special physical recreation resource management responsibilities inherent in such an agency. It is not intended to designate an organization whose *exclusive* role is resource and facility development and maintenance, but signifies that this role may parallel comparable program and operation services as well. Many municipal recreation service agencies are combined recreation and park departments. Here such combination agencies as well as private or commercial parks are broadly called park agencies.

THE PARK ADMINISTRATION PROCESSES

It is an acknowledged fact that administration of recreation service agencies has a common root in general administration or

3

Table 1.1
Chronological list of administration processes described by
representative authorities of general administration/management
and administration of recreation services

Date	Authorities	Administration Processes
	Group One: General Administration/Management Authorities	
1929	Henri Fayol	Planning, organizing, commending, coordinating, controlling[a]
1937	Luther Gulick and Lyndall Urwick	Planning, organization, staffing, directing, coordinating, reporting budgeting[b]
1944	Lyndall Urwick	Planning, coordination, control[c]
1950	William H. Newman	Planning, organizing, assembling resources, directing, controlling[d]
1950	Jess B. Sears	Planning, organizing, directing, coordinating, controlling[e]
1961	W. Warren Haynes and Joseph L. Massie	Decision making, organizing, planning, directing, controlling, staffing, co-ordinating, communicating, motivating, evaluating[f]
1968	Ray A. Killian	Planning, organizing, administering, controlling[g]
1971	James H. Donnelly, Jr., James L. Gibson, and John M. Ivancevich	Planning, organizing, controlling[h]
1974	Don Hellriegel and John W. Slocum, Jr.	Designing, planning, controlling, decision making[i]
1975	Dale Carnegie & Associates	Planning, organizing, directing, coordinating, controlling[j]
	Group Two: Recreation Services Administration Authorities	
1964	Lynn S. Rodney	Planning, organizing, staffing and resourcing, directing, coordinating, controlling, evaluating[k]

management—"the guiding of human and physical resources
into dynamic organization units which obtain their objectives to
the satisfaction of those served and with a high degree of morale
and sense of attainment on the part of those rendering the
service."* It is not difficult to project this broad interpretation of
management into the specific scope of recreational services
administration. This has been defined as the process of mo-

* Lawrence A. Appley, President of the American Management Association,
quoted by Ray A. Killian: *Managing by Design . . . for Maximum Executive
Effectiveness,* American Management Association, 1968, p. 5.

Table 1.1 (Continued)

Date	Authorities	Administration Processes
1969	Harold D. Meyer, Charles K. Brightbill, and H. Douglas Sessoms	Plan, organize, manage, direct, supervise, operate, evaluate[l]
1972	George Hjelte and Jay S. Shivers	Cooperation, coordination, control[m]
1973	James F. Murphy, John G. Williams, E. William Niepoth, and Paul D. Brown	Planning, organizing, staffing, directing, controlling[n]
1973	Richard G. Kraus and Joseph E. Curtis	Planning, organizing, controlling[o]
1973	James A. Peterson and Michael F. Pohlen	Planning, organizing, motivating, controlling[p]

[a] James H. Donnelly, Jr., James L. Gibson, and John M. Ivancevich, *Fundamentals of Management,* Business Publications, Inc., Austin, Tx. 1971, p. 45.

[b] Lynn S. Rodney, *Administration of Public Recreation,* Ronald Press Co., New York, 1964, p. 29.

[c] James H. Donnelley, et al., *op. cit.,* pp. 49–54.

[d] Lynn S. Rodney, *op. cit.,* p. 29.

[e] Jess B. Sears, *The Nature of the Administrative Process,* McGraw-Hill, New York, 1950, p. ix.

[f] W. Warren Haynes and Joseph L. Massie, *Management: Analysis, Concepts and Cases,* Prentice-Hall, Englewood Cliffs, N. J., 1961, pp. 11–12.

[g] Ray A. Killian, *Managing by Design . . . for Maximum Executive Effectiveness,* American Management Association, New York, 1968, p. 12.

[h] James H. Donnelly, et al., *op. cit.,* p. 22.

[i] Don Hellriegel and John W. Slocum, Jr. *Management: A Contingency Approach,* Addison-Wesley, Reading, Mass. 1974, p. 92.

[j] Dale Carnegie and Associates. *Managing Through People,* Simon and Schuster, New York, 1975, p. 18.

[k] Lynn S. Rodney, *op. cit.,* pp. 27–28.

[l] Harold D. Meyer, Charles K. Brightbill, and H. Douglas Sessoms, *Community Recreation: A Guide to Its Organization.* 4th Ed., Prentice-Hall, Englewood Cliffs, N. J. 1969, p. 398.

[m] George Hjelte and Jay S. Shivers, *Public Administration of Recreational Services,* Lea & Febiger, Philadelphia, 1972, p. 4.

[n] James F. Murphy, John G. Williams, E. William Niepoth, and Paul D. Brown, *Leisure Service Delivery System: A Modern Perspective,* Lea & Febiger, Philadelphia, 1973, p. 107.

[o] Richard G. Kraus and Joseph E. Curtis, *Creative Administrations in Recreation and Parks,* C. V. Mosby Co., Saint Louis, 1973, pp. 17–18.

[p] James A. Peterson and Michael F. Pohlen in Sidney G. Lutzin and Edward H. Storey (Eds.). *Managing Municipal Leisure Services,* International City Management Association, Washington, D. C., 1973, p. 45.

bilizing, organizing, and applying the resources directed toward providing recreation opportunities for people. Note that administrative processes are functions within agency, not the role of an individual with a title of administrator. The administrator's role is one of executive leadership to insure that these processes are efficiently and effectively incorporated.

Administrative techniques have been described, developed, and studied by numerous scholars over the years. There is no uniformly accepted single formula of common management, or administration, processes. Table 1.1 is an abridged chronological list of previous attempts to identify these various modes of administrative operation. Notice the constant inclusion of *planning* as an integral part of the administration processes by the management scholars for almost 50 years.

PARK PLANNING AND PARK ADMINISTRATION

Planning may be the first step of management at any level of a recreation service agency. Planning not only involves predetermining a course of action to be taken, relative to a known event, but it includes mentally searching for possibilities of future problems that might appear.*

Planning is described as:

☐ Identification of a need or reflection of a stimulus.

☐ Accumulation of information.

☐ Relating of bits of information and beliefs.

☐ Establishing objectives.

☐ Establishing premises.

☐ Forecasting future conditions.

☐ Structuring alternative chains of actions based on sequential decisions.

☐ Ranking or selecting total plans that will achieve the best balance of ultimate objectives and subsidiary objective.

☐ Establishing policies.

☐ Establishing standards and means for measurement of adherence to the plan of action.†

Planning should be performed by all the various people who have vested interest in the ultimate results: administrators, staff, consultants, park board members, advisory committees, and participants.

TYPES OF PLANNING. There are six main classifications of planning. Each may require some special competency or expertise. Large park departments may designate special divisions within the administrative organization to perform one particular function. This is done by *organizational planning.* The grouping of roles, such as recreation program services, design and construction, maintenance, interpretation, special facilities, and ranger services, is a typical example of organizational planning for a park department.

Financial planning is concerned with the budgetary control of the park department, including allocations, fees and charges,

* Joseph L. Massie, *Essentials of Management,* 2nd Edition, Prentice-Hall, Inc., Englewood Cliffs, N.J., 1971, p. 83.
† Robert G. Murdick, "Nature of Planning and Plans," *Advanced Management Journal,* 30:4, October, 1965, p. 37.

grants, donations and other revenue, purchases, amortization schedules, wages and salaries, capital development costs, and related operating expenses.

Physical planning is concerned primarily with the spatial arrangement of recreation areas and facilities, ranging from basic sports field or court layout to complex general development planning requiring the skills of competent site designers.

Program planning involves the integrated schedules, services, and events that are packaged (for instruction, competition, interpretation, or general recreation) for special events or other series of corresponding planned recreational experiences. Program planning might be thought of as process planning.

Functional planning is directed toward regularly continuing tasks and services performed by the department. This includes preparation of operations manuals, in-service safety and training manuals, labor relations and employee benefits plans, quality control standards, and other day-by-day operational concerns.

General planning is a combination of all the previous types of planning. It is the "master planning" or "general management planning" process that provides for the realization of the agency's purpose for each park, including management, protection, interpretation, use, and development.* It is in this sense that general planning is defined here as park planning.

Park general management planning (simply called park planning) is a special type of planning and a vital part of the park administrative function. It is essential to the success of the agency, just as any of the other park administration processes are, and, like these other processes, it requires participation from numerous individuals—from policy-making board members to field managers and program supervisors to special consultants to park users.

Park planning is too complex to be delegated exclusively to a division or special branch of the park department. It is a process, not a role; an essential function of overall park administration, not an assignment.

The real nature of the recreation service function can be made clearer by drawing an analogy between the work of recreational service systems and that of school systems. The paramount function of the school system is not to build schools and maintain grounds and buildings, but to provide activities that will contribute to the children's growth and development. Similarly, the effectiveness of a recreational service system is to be judged not so much from the standpoint of the material facilities it provides (playgrounds, swimming pools, tennis courts, baseball diamonds, auditoriums, stadiums, and the like) and the manner

* In recognition of the limited interpretation of "Master Plan", the National Park Service discontinued use of that term in 1975. It has been replaced by the term "General Management Plan." U.S. Department of the Interior, National Park Service *Management Policies of the National Park Service,* April, 1975, p. II-2.

in which the properties are maintained, but from the activities and other opportunities it carries on, sponsors, or coordinates and their contribution to individual satisfaction, enjoyment, personal growth, social objectives, and whatever distinct values may be derived by the individual.*

THE PARK PLANNING PROCESS

The purpose of park planning is to ensure the necessary means, including human and physical resources and support services, to provide an established recreational experience.

The process described here is site specific. That is, it is directly applicable to a new park site or new project site within an established park. It has been assumed that the park agency already exists and is viable. Basic department goals and objectives are also assumed to exist. There are four major phases to park planning: predesign, design, development, and actualization. Each is meant to accomplish the goals and objectives set forth by the park department.

The *predesign phase* describes the goals of the park in experiential and physical terms. Each proposed activity is carefully analyzed to determine what environmental conditions must be provided; what type and extent of development is required; what program, operations and maintenance support personnel, facilities and services are necessary; and what use-effectiveness control and evaluation provision must be present to maintain an acceptable experience level. The predesign phase is the basis for the other phases of park planning. It is described in detail in Chapter 2.

The next two phases of the park planning process follow chronologically after the predesign phase and represent the physical area and facility aspects of the process.

Design is the basis for all development in a park. Because of the major financial commitments required in construction, it is essential that designers obtain all relevant information about the activity and agency program and service plans as soon as possible. Too frequently, nondesign professionals and support personnel do not provide recommendations prior to development, only to find unsatisfactory conditions in a new facility. For this reason, emphasis is placed on the physical aspects of the park plan in this volume. All members of the park planning team, designers as well as nondesigners, must be aware of certain major park design considerations and how these should be incorporated into the design phase. Chapter 3 contains a full discussion of park design.

The *development phase* has three distinct steps: preconstruction documentation, construction contracting, and project

* George Hjelte and Jay S. Shivers, *Public Administration of Recreational Services,* Lea & Febiger, Philadelphia, 1972, pp. 52–53.

construction. Public park agencies must conform to specific policies, regulations, and procedures during development. These have been explained, with examples, in Chapter 4.

Actualization occurs several times during the various stages of park planning, from predesign to postdevelopment. Actualization is the preparation of essential use effectiveness controls and other necessary plans (e.g., program, financial, functional, and organizational plans) important to the success of the total planning effort for the recreational experiences intended. It is a dynamic measure that, unlike design or development, is not culminated in a final product, but produces interim instruments that are applied, revised, and modified in a constant process of evolution based on the needs of the park visitor. Chapter 5 describes the various elements of the actualization phase.

MEMBERS OF THE PARK PLANNING TEAM

The park planning team is not an inflexible working group of the same individuals or even of individuals with the same skills. Instead, it should be a changing, task-oriented team of specialists and nonspecialists who conceive and provide a good recreational experience together. As the process begins, continues, and passes through certain stages, the team membership changes. Their skills, knowledge, and input are drawn on as required. At one time one area of expertise will be dominant; at another time a different specialty will be more important. The team leader ("park planner") must direct the overall efforts of the team; he must identify and utilize the team's input resources to the utmost; and he must control the total process. To accomplish this, he must be a skilled organizer and synthesizer of input from others.

In the past, park teams have been grouped according to their predevelopment and postdevelopment specialities. The predevelopment team included the designers (landscape architects, architects, and engineers, for instance) and builders. The postdevelopment team included maintenance and operations people and face-to-face park leaders. However, visualization of the park team in such a polarized manner created a problem: there was often little crossover of input during the planning process; in fact planning was frequently considered to be a predevelopment process only.

If park planning is viewed as an ongoing dynamic process of conceiving, directing, and providing park experiences, it cannot be limited to facility design and development. Park planners should be experience directed, not development directed. The development of park facilities provides only the setting for recreational experiences. This complete role should be reflected in the park planning process.

When members of the park planning team are grouped according to their primary contribution toward the provision of recreational experiences, it is then possible to classify them within four areas: participant, activity, facility, and support-oriented task groups.

PARTICIPANT-ORIENTED TASK GROUP

This is the most significant group within the park planning team, and is the least-structured and planning-oriented one. Since it is impossible to plan a park by involving everyone who would use it, the participant is often represented by proxy: planners, use needs, preferences studies, user profiles, and other data. Many recreationists are becoming organized into visible organizations (such as citizen's advisory task forces or committees for individual parks) that are valuable resources for planning input, and large park agencies now have sociologists as well as program specialists on their staff. The use of participant-oriented imput into the park planning process is essential; the degree and sophistication of the input depends on the complexity of the problem.

ACTIVITY-ORIENTED TASK GROUP

These specialists include professional sportsmen, athletes, coaches, and sometimes outstanding amateurs and local advocates. National activity organizations (such as Little League, United States Tennis Association, National Rifle Association, and Trout Unlimited) provide information about specific activities. The activity-oriented task group is important before and after facility construction, and it is uniquely experience oriented— thus ideally suited for the park planning process.

FACILITY-ORIENTED TASK GROUP

The term "facility" applies to all of the physical resources that are utilized during the recreational experience, and it includes the man-made elements of the park as well as the natural environment.
Physical designers such as landscape architects, architects, and engineers are major members of the task group. Other possible contributors include ecologists, foresters, horticulturists, soil scientists, wildlife specialists, archeologists, and historians. The facility-oriented task group has resource data gathering and synthesis capabilities.

The physical design members are a dominant force during the design and construction phases of park planning. Unfortunately, because they are so specialized, they are often excluded from other phases of the process. This most often occurs if they are consultants who are hired only for their expertise in its narrowest sense. Staff designers have a greater opportunity than consultants to become involved in the total park planning process, which includes follow-up of design to evaluate and modify when necessary to complement the rest of the recreational experience considerations.

SUPPORT-ORIENTED TASK GROUPS

The support services that are important to the provision of recreational experiences are primary and secondary support services, which are described below.

PRIMARY SUPPORT SERVICES.   Primary services are provided by the park agency or the commercial or private enterprise that offers the recreation experience directly to the recreationist for his convenience, comfort, and welfare. The basic recreation activity does not require these support services, but they sustain the experience standard established during the planning process.

Maintenance is the daily and recurrent care, cleaning, re-plenishment, and grooming of activity apparatus, areas, and facilities, and its level should be consistent with the experience and development norms set by the park planners. Maintenance is performed by building custodians, field maintenance men, contract landscape and cleaning services firms, and other specialists.

Operations includes fee collection, reservations, control and manipulation of technical processing equipment, and support supplies. The more complex the physical plant (or the greater capacity of the facility), the more complex will be the operations services. Examples of operations specialists are clerical and equipment technicians.

Programming services involve the organization and direction of participant activities, including instruction, scheduling, competitive seeding, tournaments, special events, leadership, and supervision.

Safety and security services are concerned with the welfare of the park user as well as the protection of personal and public property; they are provided by lifeguards, emergency first aid and medical personnel, and security officers (rangers, park police, fish and game wardens, and Coast Guard, for example).

Refreshment and supply services, which are conveniences for the recreationists, are services that provide the food, beverage, and activity supplies consumed by park users. These services are frequently provided by concessionaires.

SECONDARY SUPPORT SERVICES.   These external services are conveniences provided for recreationists at the park as a subgroup of a community, and they are provided to all of the community instead of just to park users. The services (such as fire protection, water purification and supply, sanitation collection, treatment and disposal, health protection, power and light, emergency and medical services, public protection, telephone, and transportation) provide the support structure that makes recreation opportunities possible by getting the most out of human support efforts. Some very large or isolated recreation areas (e.g., National or State Parks, resorts, and large recreation complexes) must supply some or all of these services as primary support. Whenever possible, the available services should be utilized without duplication or waste.

ROLES OF PARK PLANNING TEAM INDIVIDUALS

Large, well-staffed park departments have professional park planners who organize and coordinate the planning process. Frequently, however, the role is assigned to a member of the planning team who is usually a specialist in either design or administration. A park planner must be goal oriented, and he may relinquish the team-leader role after his significant contributions are complete.

For large new projects, many park departments and commercial enterprises wisely select their key personnel—park superintendents, special facility directors (e.g., aquatic directors, tennis center managers, interpretive center directors, and golf course managers), and activity programmers—at the beginning of the planning process. Thus these individuals are involved in the predesign, development, and operation of the park, and they do not have to adapt to or modify the project after it is constructed.

Park planning cannot be an egalitarian process because complete equality of responsibility and authority in planning is undesirable and nonproductive. Although each group within the park planning team should be represented in each phase of the planning process, its role will change with each phase. The following roles are typical of the various groups during the activity predesign, design, development, and actualization phases of park planning from the experience base: establish objectives, supply information, formulate alternatives, evaluate, and make recommendations.

Notice that the park planners were not given the role of major decision making. This role must be reserved for the executive administrator or policy-making body of the agency, since it carries with it the responsibility to make decisions in a logical and timely manner that will not impede the progress of the park planning team.

SUMMARY

Planning is an intrinsic part of park administration. Park planning is a combination of several types of planning: organizational, financial, physical, program, and functional. Its purpose is to insure the means, including all necessary resources and support service, to provide an established recreational experience.

There are four major phases to park planning: predesign, design, development, and actualization. Each phase requires contributions from a number of multidisciplinary professionals, support personnel, and the public to achieve the desired level of recreational experiences.

GLOSSARY OF TERMS

Administration
Guiding human and physical resources into dynamic organization units that obtain their objectives to the satisfaction of these served and with a high degree of morale and a sense of attainment on the part of those rendering the service.

Financial Planning
Budgetary determination and allocation of park agency revenue and expenses.

Functional Planning
Systematic provision of regular, continuing tasks and services performed by the park agency.

General Planning
The overall management planning required for the success of a park; see Park Planning.

Organizational Planning
The grouping of roles to achieve efficient performance of special functions of the park agency.

Park Department (Park Agency)
A recreational service agency that has the provision of physical areas and facilities as one of its methods to provide opportunities for recreation experiences.

Park Planning
A type of management planning applied to ensure the necessary means, including human and physical resources and support services, to provide recreational experiences.

Park Planning Team
All the individuals who make contributions to the park planning process.

Park Planner
A professional who organizes and coordinates the park planning process; (broadly) any member of the park planning team.

Physical Planning
The spatial arrangement of recreational areas and facilities.

Planning
A process of determining future action based on systematic review of objectives and pertinent facts.

Program Planning
The determination of schedules, services, and events needed for structured recreation activities.

Recreational Services Administration
A type of administration specifically directed toward providing recreational opportunities.

Recreational Service Agency
A public, quasi-public, or private agency primarily providing recreational activities and helping services to its clientele.

Support Services
Services provided to park users for convenience, comfort, and welfare; amenities not essential to the basic provision of an activity.

BIBLIOGRAPHY

Dale Carnegie & Associates. *Managing Through People.* Simon & Schuster, New York, 1975.

Davis, Albert. "Planning—Elements and Problems," *Advanced Management Journal,* 32:3, July, 1967, pp. 39–44.

Donnelly, James H., Jr., James L. Gibson, and John M. Ivancevich. *Fundamentals of Management.* Business Publications, Inc., Austin, Texas, 1971.

Haynes, W. Warren and Joseph L. Massie. *Management: Analysis, Concepts and Cases.* Prentice-Hall, Englewood Cliffs, N.J., 1961.

Hellriegel, Don and John W. Slocum, Jr. *Management: A Contingency Approach.* Addison-Wesley, Reading, Mass., 1974.

Hjelte, George and Jay S. Shivers. *Public Administration of Recreational Services.* Lea & Febiger, Philadelphia, 1972.

Killian, Ray A. *Managing by Design . . . for Maximum Executive Effectiveness.* American Management Association, New York, 1968.

Kraus, Richard G. and Joseph E. Curtis. *Creative Administration in Recreation and Parks.* C. V. Mosby Co., Saint Louis, 1973.

LeBreton, Preston P. and Dale A. Henning. *Planning Theory.* Prentice-Hall, Englewood Cliffs, N.J., 1961.

Lutzin, Sidney G. and Edward H. Storey (Editors). *Managing Municipal Leisure Services.* International City Management Assoc., Washington, D.C., 1973.

Massie, Joseph L. *Essentials of Management,* Second Edition. Prentice-Hall, Englewood Cliffs, N.J., 1971.

Meyer, Harold D., Charles K. Brightbill, and H. Douglas Sessoms. *Community Recreation, A Guide to Its Organization.* Fourth Edition, Prentice-Hall, Englewood Cliffs, N.J., 1969.

Murdick, Robert G. "Nature of Planning and Plans," *Advanced Management Journal,* 30:4, October, 1965, pp. 36–46.

Murphy, James F., John G. Williams, E. William Niepoth, and Paul D. Brown. *Leisure Service Delivery System: A Modern Perspective.* Lea & Febiger, Philadelphia, 1973.

Rodney, Lynn S. *Administration of Public Recreation.* Ronald Press Co., New York, 1964.

Sears, Jess B. *The Nature of the Administrative Process.* McGraw-Hill, New York, 1950.

United States Department of the Interior, National Park Service. *Management Policies of the National Park Service.* Washington, D.C., April, 1975.

2
the
predesign
phase

Each of the four major phases in the park planning process—predesign, design, development, and actualization—has one or more objectives. Predesign and actualization are concerned with all the park planning aspects. Predesign is the basis for design and development that are essentially physical planning oriented. It is often difficult to systemize and itemize in order all the various steps of a flexible process such as park planning because not all steps are always necessary nor do they always have to occur in the same order. The process depends on the experience and orientation of the planning team and the complexity of the problem.

PREDESIGN OBJECTIVE

Before the physical plan for the park can be prepared, several planning considerations must be determined. These considerations are essential to all members of the planning team for direction and guidance. The major objective of the predesign phase is to prepare a design program (sometimes called a design directive), which describes the objectives of the park plan in experiential and physical terms.

STEPS OF THE PREDESIGN PHASE

Usually the following predesign steps are necessary to prepare a good design program:

Step 1.   Determine activities to be offered.

Step 2.   Consider activity experience orientation for each activity.

Step 3.   Prepare activity analysis for each activity.

Step 4.   Prepare synthesis of complete predesign package.

Step 5.   Document into organized design program.

Each of these steps are explained in detail below. The predesign phase is the basis for all the other phases; it must be very carefully executed.

DETERMINATION OF ACTIVITIES TO BE OFFERED

The importance of this step in the predesign phase cannot be overemphasized. Mistakes made at this step cannot easily be rectified and can be very costly in terms of wasted resources (land, capital, and labor). All too often this decision is made quickly, so that park planners can proceed with subsequent phases.

There are two basic alternative approaches to the determination of activities to be provided. The first approach is to select these activities prior to any resource allocations—including natural, human, and fiscal resources. This is perhaps the most unrestricted opportunity for the park planning team to recommend activities to be offered in this project. With each resource allocation, the restrictions are more definitive.

PRE-RESOURCE ALLOCATION ACTIVITY DETERMINATION.   To aid the planners, many agencies utilize survey and sampling techniques to determine the people's needs, desires, and expressed and latent wants and preferences. In some park planning situations, the activities that must be offered at the parksite are known. They may have been specified in a well prepared comprehensive communitywide recreation plan or state comprehensive outdoor recreation plan. Other agencies obtain quite satisfactory results by accepting expert opinion. Using a process explained later in this chapter, a series of activity analyses are made to determine which site characteristics are essential for the selected activities. These characteristics are used to select the best parksite.

DETERMINATION BY NATURAL RESOURCE ACTIVITY.   The second approach to activity determination is based on available resources. Occasionally a site (natural resource) has already been selected or donated to the agency. Then it is best to have a competent site designer prepare a site analysis to determine what recreational activities the site is best suited for or if certain needed activities could be provided there. This approach must be carefully balanced against known needs to prevent over supply just because the natural resources were appropriate to certain activities not in demand.

ACTIVITY DETERMINATION BY HUMAN RESOURCES.   The opportunity to utilize special human resources also influences the selection of activities. The offer of special interest groups to instruct, program, or maintain facilities provided for certain activities is a factor that is important in activity selection.

ACTIVITY DETERMINATION BY FISCAL RESOURCES.   When fiscal resources are readily available and specifically earmarked for certain activities, their provision is greatly enhanced. Capital development grants for outdoor recreation have supported the provision of facilities for swimming, camping, tennis, picnicking, and other outdoor activities. A direct gift or bequest is often earmarked for a certain activity.

ACTIVITY EXPERIENCE ORIENTATION

When preparing a design directive for the physical designer, two preliminary considerations must be examined: experience opportunities and experience/development norms.

EXPERIENCE OPPORTUNITIES.   There are six role experiences inherent in every recreational activity.* These different ways to enjoy an activity are all valid experiences. Park planners must carefully consider each opportunity when providing an activity. Not all experiences are necessary for every activity or for every park; some experiences will be predominant, others subordinate. Inadequate considerations of any of these could limit the ultimate recreational provisions by oversight and default:

1. *Entry-Level Participation.*   The basic skills of any activity must be mastered at this initial experience role. Every recreational activity has rudimentary skill requisites. Instruction of these skills may be organized, programmed, and structured; it may be casual, informal, and impromptu. Introduction to many activities are done better under carefully planned situations including competent instructors, a thoughtful program of instruction and special equipment, area and facilities for novices. Basic instruction is the most often-provided service of public recreation departments. Examples of

* Monty L. Christiansen, *The Application of a Recreation-Experience Components Concept for Comprehensive Recreation Planning,* Pennsylvania Department of Community Affairs, Harrisburg, Pa. 1974, pp. 8–9.

activities that have special entry-level participation considerations include swimming, skiing, skating, canoeing, mountain climbing, and sailing.

Figure 2.1*a*

Six experience opportunities are inherent in every recreational activity. For example, planning for swimming requires consideration for *entry-level participation,* **where basic swimming skills are mastered.**

2. *Skills-Improvement Participation.* Many recreationists become avid participants who are not satisfied with basic skills and mediocre achievement. Opportunities for skills improvement require special program planning for advanced instruction and practice as well as special or auxiliary areas and facilities for tricks and technique development. Some physical examples of proper planning for this activity experience include golf driving ranges, practice putting greens, tennis practice walls, baseball batting cages, ball-serving machines, ski slope designations according to skill proficiency, golf hole difficulty ratings, video tape or filming equipment used in instruction, and the like.

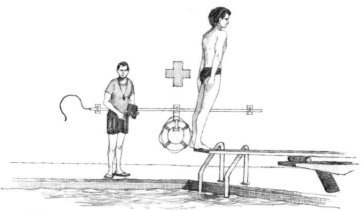

Figure 2.1*b*

Skills-improvement participation, **where advanced instruction, practice, and technique development are important.**

3.   *Programmed Participation.*   In addition to the instructional participation discussed above, many recreationists enjoy a structured opportunity to enjoy an activity. These participants seek regular, scheduled experiences with or without formal organization. The activity may be a habit for these participants. The characteristic of regularity is the primary concern for planners. The complexities of programmed recreation include scheduling, reservation systems and controls, peak and pulsating facility demand times and impact on support facilities. Activities that are popular for programmed participation include dual and team sports (tennis, golf, basketball, handball, etc.), individual and physical fitness activities (swimming, jogging, weight lifting, equestrian events, etc.), and social activities (card playing, choral or instrumental music, dancing, crafts, etc.).

Figure 2.1c

Programmed participation, **such as water ballet or synchronized swimming shown here, or physical fitness programs.**

4.   *Unstructured Participation.*   Some activities are prone to inclination and opportunity. If, for example, a group of people are gathered for a picnic, the activities of volleyball, softball, horseshoes, or others may occur if the minimal area, facilities, and equipment are available. The experience may or may not have been preplanned by the participants. The opportunity of "makeup," sandlot, or similarly named experiences are important considerations for park planners when providing for such catalytic activities as family and group picnicking, swimming, day camping, overnight camping, and other group activities not bound by established playing rules. The *catalytic activity* is the primary reason people are present but it often provides the need for secondary activities because of its inherent casualness, long activity period, and simplicity.

Figure 2.1d

Unstructured participation, **like this impromptu water play.**

5.   *Competitive Participation.*   Many recreationists enjoy an activity because it enables them to compare, compete, and evaluate. This is done individually, with another, or as a member of a competing group. All sports activities are examples of competitive participation. It may be as simple as a golfer trying to improve his low game, a fisherman trying to better his last trophy fish or a canoeist trying to shave off a few minutes from his best time on a measured distance or it may be as complex as the Masters golf tournament, a fly casting competition, or an international whitewater slalom race. Planning considerations include scheduling, seeding, officiating, special apparatus and facility development, maintenance, and provision of adequate and efficient support and auxiliary demands such as suitable accommodations for spectators and the media. The professional and intercollegiate sports stadiums in the United States are excellent examples of planning for the competitive level of participation in selected activities.

Figure 2.1e

Competitive participation, **such as racing, where performances are compared and evaluated.**

6. *Vicarious Participation.*   Enjoyment of a sport, game, or other recreational activity is not limited to the actual participant. Spectators enjoy a recreational experience role that is part of any activity. Competitive sports especially are enjoyed vicariously by spectators. The sports stadiums noted above are usually planned with ample spectator considerations. But many other activities have significant primary orientation to spectators. Examples include attending plays, orchestrations, vocal and other performing arts, fairs, exhibits, and festivals, as well as watching children at play, wildlife, visiting historical, cultural, or natural displays, trails, or demonstrations. Planning for spectators is not an incidental consideration.

Figure 2.1 represents these experience opportunities possible for a single activity.

Figure 2.1*f*

Vicarious participation, **where spectators enjoy the excitement and fun of an activity such as swimming while not actually being involved.**

EXPERIENCE AND DEVELOPMENT NORMS.   Park planners should recognize that there is a range of recreational experience needs. Recreationists have different expectations and real-ize different levels of satisfaction or gratification for activity participation. Some achieve a high level of pleasure at basic, simple, unadored, and uncomplicated levels of participation. This does not imply that their activity competencies are low. Their skill or proficiency may even be adroit. Their experience needs are not dependent on extraneous amenities and re-finements. At the other end of the satisfaction stimulus range are the recreationists who enjoy participation in an activity more when they can indulge themselves in conveniences, embellishments, and extra amenities. The activity is often the vehicle for this simultaneous perceptional "bonus" that increases enjoyment of the activity.*

Activity participation roles have no bearing on the experience satisfaction determinants. One novice skier may only enjoy the activity as "packaged" by luxurious winter resorts; another learns skiing with gusto on an undeveloped slope. Programmed activities occur at lavish community centers, sports complexes, or in old barns and natural clearings. Some spectators enjoy music under the stars while sitting on a blanket; others prefer formal dress and elaborate, acoustically designed music halls.

Each experience level is a valid expression of an activity; one is not always "better." It is important, therefore, that park planners know the prospective recreationists' experience desires.

The extent to which the natural environment is modified for resource-oriented activities, or refinements included for facility-oriented activities, is directly related to experience levels. Recreation experience and development models or norms are useful control guides when physical design concepts, recreationists' desires, agency management policies and fiscal constraints are considered. Tables 2.1 and 2.2 are examples of these experience/development norms.

Figure 2.2 shows an example of a primitive experiment/ development level for camping while Figure 2.3 illustrates a modern example of the same activity.

Many park and recreation agencies have similar experience/ development norms. Some of these are very detailed and are related to specific activities. State parks often have Class 1, Class 2, and Class 3 campgrounds, for example, based on a predetermined experience/development model. Metropolitan recreation and park departments also use experience/development norms in park planning.

Many basic facilities are available as auxiliary activity areas to family picnic grounds. They include ball fields, hard surface courts and lawn game areas. Large departments may provide basic facilities as part of a mobile unit by using portable net standards, goalposts, backstops, and so forth, on closed off streets and vacant lots, as shown in Figure 2.4. The middle norms are commonly used for neighborhood and community facilities. Figure 2.5 shows a refined level of a tennis facility.

It is important to realize that the planning norm is not only a control for development, but for the experience. This requires a comparable control to the established norm for all the supportive services—maintenance, supervision, programming, safety, security, operations, and refreshment provisions— necessary to sustain the predetermined norm. This is the basis for

* Ibid., pp. 9–11.

experience actualization, explained in detail in Chapter 5. Capital funding for a new development as a one-time cost item is often approved without proper consideration for the total, continuing committment necessary to provide the required support.

ACTIVITY ANALYSIS

For each activity to be provided in a new park, a careful predesign analysis must be prepared. This is a study of the various factors to be considered by all members of the planning team. There are three primary functions of the activity analysis: to guide the physical planner, to guide the program and

Figure 2.2

A primitive backcountry camping experience may present a challenge to use simple equipment and what the natural environment provides.

Table 2.1
Recreation experience and environmental modication norms
for resource-oriented activities[a]

Experience/ Development Level	Recreation Experience Norm	Environmental Modication Norm
1 *Primitive*	Primary interest is the feeling of achievement, sense of adventure and challenge to the elements. Small group participation develops comaraderie. Fine opportunities for solitude. Some activities may require a high level of outdoor skills at this level. Outside distractions or influences often very displeasing.	Natural primitive environment is dominant. Minimum site modification. Rustic rudimentary improvements designed for protection of the site rather than comfort of the users. Use of indigenous materials preferred. Water provided by participant. Sanitation provisions spartan. Site maintenance by participants. Minimum controls are subtle. No obvious means of regimentation. Spacing informal and extended to minimize contacts with others. Motorized access not provided or permitted.
2 *Secondary Primitive*	Feeling of accomplishment is important but physical stamina is not essential. Several small groups may socialize briefly, then separate for the majority of the experience. Some activities may require a moderate level of outdoor skills. Outside influences tolerated.	Natural environment is dominant. Little site modification. Rustic or rudimentary improvements designed for protection of the site rather than comfort of the users. Use of synthetic materials avoided. Water and sanitation provisions developed but simple. Site and facility maintenance provided at least seasonally. Minimum controls are subtle. Little obvious regimentation. Spacing informal and extended to minimize contacts with others. Motorized access provided or permitted. Primary access over primitive roads.

25

Table 2.1 (Continued)

Experience/ Development Level	Recreation Experience Norm	Environmental Modification Norm
3 *Intermediate*	A taste of adventure is important, but a sense of security is present. Considerations for convenience and comfort accepted. Some activities may require a moderate level of outdoor skills. Outside influences accepted.	Environment essentially natural. Site modification moderate. Facilities about equally for protection of site and comfort of users. Design of improvements is usually based on use of native materials with contemporary conservation techniques. Water and sanitation provisions adequate and regularly maintained. Inconspicuous vehicular traffic controls usually provided. Roads may be hard surfaced and trails formalized. Primary access to site may be over high standard well traveled roads. Visitor information services, if available is informal and incidental. Security patrols may be made periodically.
4 *Secondary* *Modern*	Experience provides change of routine and surroundings. Apparent opportunities for socializing with others. Provisions for convenience and comfort expected. Willing to pay for extras. May rely on program services for entertainment as much as exposure to the environment. Outside influences present but not regarded as incongruous.	Environment pleasing but necessarily natural. Site heavily modified. Some facilities designed strictly for comfort and convenience of users but luxury facilities not provided. Facility designs may tend toward and incorporate synthetic materials. Extensive use of artificial surfacing of roads and trails. Vehicular traffic controls present and usually obvious. Primary access usually over paved roads.

26

Table 2.1   (Continued)

Experience/ Development Level	Recreation Experience Norm	Environmental Modification Norm
		Plant materials usually native. Visitor information services frequently available. Maintenance and security checks regular and periodic. Some programming services provided.
5 *Modern*	Pleasing environment attractive to the tourist, the novice or highly gregarious recreationist. Opportunity to socialize with others very important. Satisfies need for compensation experiences. Obvious to user that he is in secure situation where ample provision is made for his personal comfort. Expects to be entertained by program services; does not expect to find own amusement. Outside influences considered part of the show.	High degree of site modication. Facilities mostly designed for comfort and convenience of users include flush toilets; may include showers, bath houses, laundry facilities, and electrical hookups. Synthetic materials commonly used. Formal walks or surfaced trails. Regimentation of users is obvious. Access usually by high speed highways. Plant materials may be foreign to the environment. Formal visitor information services usually available. Designs formalized and architecture may be contemporary. Mowed lawns and clipped shrubs not unusual. Maintenance and security forces usually visible. High degree of programming services.

[a] Adapted from ''Recreation Experience Levels'' from U.S. Department of Agriculture, *Forest Service Manual*, 2330.5-3 and ''National Forest Camp and Picnic Site Levels of Environmental Modification and Recreation Experiences'' from *Forest Service Manual*, 2331.11c-3.

Figure 2.3

A modern camping experience provides people a chance to visit new places, make new friends, and enjoy the outdoors on their own terms.

functional planners and support personnel, and to serve as an evaluation instrument to judge the success of a completed activity provision during actualization. It should be a dynamic document but is subject to modification and revision if concepts change. It is the initial control for the total activity delivery package. These are the basic factors to be examined in activity analysis:

ACTIVITY FACTORS

Brief description of activity.

Activity experience opportunities to be provided.

Established rules and regulations—play, conduct, fees and charges, reservations.

Special participant equipment needs.
Length of activity period.
Proposed experience norm.

PARTICIPANT FACTORS

User profile.
Participation rate per activity period.
Daily participation projection patterns.
Seasonal, monthly, weekly peak participation periods.

Figure 2.4

Playing tennis with basic recreational facilities requires only the essential activity provisions with no frills. Often setup and care of the apparatus is part of the experience.

Table 2.2
Recreation experience and facility/support provision norms for
facility-oriented activities

Experience/ Development Norms	Recreation Experience Norms	Facility/Support Provision Norms
1 *Basic*	Primarily interested in physical activity only. Use of activity facility is related to its proximity during free time. Street dress common. Use dependent upon weather; willing to maintain facility. Players will supply all basic equipment. Considers this a physical activity.	Basic activity facilities at minimum level. May not be regulation size. May be multiple use area shared with other activity or other needs. Economy of development of primary importance. No frills or amenities. No attempt to control outside distractions. No special maintenance or other service support.
2 *Modified* *Basic*	Primarily interested in activity. Use of activity facility is related to availability and informal scheduling. Athletic shoes may be worn by some. Use dependent upon weather. Willing to do routine maintenance, appreciate provision of special maintenance. Will supply most equipment.	Activity facilities developed to regulation. May have seasonable multiple use. Water, sanitation provisions available but not convenient. Day use only. Occasional special maintenance. May have voluntary instruction services for short period of use season. No provisions for activity containment.
3 *Intermediate*	Interested in activity and social atmosphere. Use of facility subject to regulated control. Athletic dress common. Use dependent on weather. Does not expect to do any maintenance. Will supply personal equipment. Expects extra services for special events.	Facility for exclusive use for specific activity. General water, sanitation provisions convenient and adequate. May have activity lights for evening use. Regular special maintenance. Programmed use of facility provided. May have some seating for players, spectators. Suitable for sanctioned competition. May have some provisions for activity containment and control of outside distractions.

Table 2.2 (Continued)

Experience/ Development Norms	Recreation Experience Norms	Facility/Support Provision Norms
4 *Modified Intermediate*	Interested in activity at "nice" facility. Expects high level of support services. Enjoys pseudoexclusive atmosphere. May wear special activity clothing; change shoes at center. Considers this a social and athletic event.	Better than adequate activity facility development. Some refinements and extras provided. Separate support facilities (parking, water, restrooms, refreshments, supplies dispersing) convenient and well done. Activity and safety lights provided for night use. Reservation system. Regular special maintenance. Facility is supervised during open hours. Program services available by well developed schedule or special arrangement. Facility is separated from other use areas. May be protected for year-round use.
5 *Refined*	Interested in social ramifications of participation. Activity is part of image. May arrive in sports clothes, change into specialty clothes in locker room, play, shower, and change into other clothes for meal and social activities. Considers this a social status privilege.	Elaborate facility development. Many refinements and extras provided. Exclusive atmosphere. Entire center "well appointed." Activity, safety and aesthetic lighting. Access and reservation controls. Specialized facilities, equipment and services for skills development. Complimentary activities provided, including meal and refreshment service. Center provides year-round use.

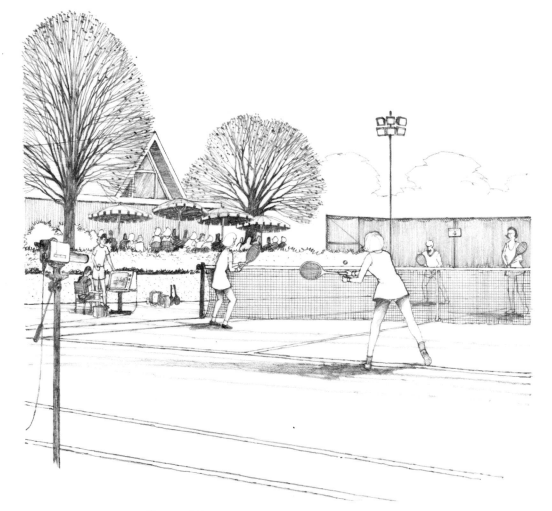

Figure 2.5

Playing tennis at an exclusive refined facility with many special amenities enhances the experience for discriminating players regardless of their competency.

RESOURCE AND FACILITY FACTORS

Special area and facility requirements—size, configuration, orientation, containment.

Development norms.

Special environmental requirements—land, water, vegetation, climate, wildlife.

Utilization externalities—access, proximity, use compatibilities.

SUPPORT FACTORS

Support services:

  Maintenance

  Programming

    Health, safety and emergency
    Operations
    Refreshments and supplies
Support Facilities:
    Circulation and parking
    Power and lighting
    Health, safety, and emergency provisions
    Shelter and park furniture
    Water system
    Wastewater system
    Solid waste system
    Support equipment storage and work areas
    Refreshment and supplies

ACTIVITY FACTORS OF THE ACTIVITY ANALYSIS.   *Activity factors* establish the groundwork for the primary planning objective—to provide a quality recreational experience for the participants. A brief description of the activity is necessary to solidify the various concepts of the activity as individually interpreted by the separate members of the planning team. This orients everyone to one concept.

Experience opportunities.   A consideration of which experience opportunities should be provided and the relative significance of each at this development is necessary before support services, equipment, and facilities can be determined.

Rules and regulations.   Structured activities such as sports and organized games have established rules. These rules may be sanctioned by a national organization or they may be set by local acceptance. Unstructured activities such as picnicking or camping do not have uniform playing rules—many departments do have use regulations for these activity areas, however. These rules and regulations have a direct effect on the development of the activity facilities, support facilities, and program services. Examples include nationally established Little League rules, which define the playing field, physical boundaries, and play, and a local reservation and fee system regulation, which determines contact station development and operations personnel commitments for a campground.

Equipment needs.   It is important to note what activity equipment will be provided by the agency and what will be provided by the participants. This is especially important for large pieces of equipment such as boats, trailers, bicycles, horses, or snowmobiles and other off road vehicles (ORVs), which require substantial care and storage area. A decision whether to simply provide the facility or both facility and equipment (perhaps through a concession or rental system) has a major impact on physical, program, and functional plans.

Activity period.   The length of the activity period also has a direct bearing on the support provision and services. It may indicate possible daily turnover factors for an activity facility. This will affect the amount of parking, sanitation, maintenance, and program scheduling, for example.

Experience norm.   The proposed experience norm is a synergistic product of the participant profile, agency policy, development, and support services budgets.

PARTICIPANT FACTORS OF ACTIVITY ANALYSIS.   Participant factors are essential descriptions of the specific user population for the community or, if the community is large and diversified and the development intended to serve only a portion of the community, for the proposed park. These factors, like the other factors of the activity analysis, are unique to the proposed park. While there may be some correlations between "typical" user groups described in previous national studies and reports, each user group has its own characteristics.

User characteristics.   A brief user profile of the expected participants is very useful. Such a profile might include age distribution, sex, skill levels for the activity if known, disabilities and recreational time patterns. Much of this data is really available in good communitywide comprehensive recreation plans, census data banks, and various sampling techniques.

Participation rates.   Some indications of acceptable participation rates per activity period is necessary to determine the activity area design load, number of facility units, support and services. The design load is frequently expressed as optimum people at one time (PAOT) for the established experience/development norm. In addition to this design load for an area, consideration for the maximum experiental carrying capacity ("psychological carrying capacity") is a factor. Some activities are enhanced by large numbers of people. For example, the pleasure of many spectator events often diminishes with poor attendance. Other activities may decrease in quality if too many people are present. Backcountry hiking and camping, fishing and hunting, nature study, and photography are some activities that can be adversely affected by crowding.

Daily participation projection patterns identify peak demand periods. This may identify physical planning considerations such as lighting, parking, and proper orientation of facilities. An example of how use periods affect development is the adult league softball often played after work or early evening. Use periods also affect functional plans and controls such as main-tenance schedules as well as operational policy. Some peak demand patterns can be readjusted by special programming or by lull time fee discounts.

Seasonal, monthly, and weekly peak participation periods are additional planning factors. Some activities such as fishing and hunting have established regulatory seasons. Others, such as soccer, football, baseball, and picnicking have "traditional" activity seasons. The climatic conditions of these seasons often are not ideal for sustained activity resource management. Significant impact on the wet, soft ground and tender, new vegetation along stream banks and lake shores occur every spring during the first week of fishing season. Other activities require a long activity period to be meaningful. Families camp and tour during weekends or vacations. These varying use fluctuations may require special planning for sanitation facilities and service, refreshments and supplies, and operational considerations.

RESOURCE AND FACILITY FACTORS OF THE ACTIVITY ANALYSIS.   Resource and facility factors are directly related to development and are most significant to physical planners but are also important to any member of the planning team who must use the park resources and facilities to provide the park user with a quality experience.

Special requirements.   Many activities have special area and facility requirements. One important requirement is the spatial size necessary for an activity. Most sports and organized games have areal, or ground space, requirements expressed as square feet, meters, acres, or hectares defined by two-dimensional boundaries. The need for adequate air space for aerial sports such as tennis, baseball, and football is important as well, although not expressed as a volumetric requirement in cubic feet or meters. Tree limbs, power lines, and telephone wires sometime infringe on this air space and detract from the activity. Other activities may not be affected by overhead elements.

The shape or configuration of many activity areas are standardized. A parcel of land may have adequate space for a baseball field, for example, but have an improper shape.

The solar orientation of the critical lines of play varies with the activity, season of predominent play, daily use period, and location in the country. The primary objective is to minimize glare and sun blindness during the most important plays. Sports on basically linear fields (football, soccer, tennis, basketball, etc.) should avoid solar orientation parallel to the length of the playing area. The critical lines of play in baseball and softball are from the pitcher's rubber to home plate and from the pitcher's rubber to first base. Some activities have no designated playing field but still have critical solar orientation considerations. Swimming pools and beaches should be oriented to prevent sun blindness, reflection, and glare in a line between lifeguard chairs (stations) and swimmers and divers. Good campsites are often exposed to morning sun to remove the night chill and dew and are shaded from the hot afternoon sun.

Some activities occur in multiple groups within a single activity area. Each group participates in its own experience without major exchanges with other groups. Examples of this type of parallel participation include picnicking and camping. Each picnic and camp unit is part of the total activity area. Support facilities and services are available to the entire picnic area and campground. Each picnic and campsite has a shared benefit of these supports. Each unit also has its own containment—territory, privacy, and functional activity zone. These are often strengthened by physical separation, visual screening, and accoustical buffers as well.

Development norms.   Development norms are physical expressions of the expected experience levels for the activity. The established development norm must be consistent for the entire activity provision from the facility construction to the operations and maintenance programs.

Environmental requirements.   Resource-oriented activities depend more on the natural conditions of the land, water, vegetation, climate, and wildlife than facility-oriented activities that can usually be provided at predominately man-made centers. The quality of any outdoor recreational activity depends on special environmental characteristics. These characteristics can be classified into three recreational resources categories. The primary group of natural resources is the set of *specific resource requirements* essential for the activity to take place. A second group of natural resources is the *general resource requirements* that have a range of acceptable characteristics or conditions for an activity, with known thresholds at each end of the range. Once conditions exceeded these threshold points, it is not possible to provide the activity without environmental modification. The third category includes natural conditions that do not determine the suitability of an area or feasibility to provide an activity, but which influence the quality of the recreational experience. These have been termed *ranked resource requirements.*

To help you identify possible resource conditions that affect specific activities, a list of natural resource descriptors is shown in Appendix 1. A *natural resource descriptor* is a word or phrase identifying the conditions of a particular characteristic of the natural resource base.

A primary determination of applicability must be made for each descriptor as it affects each activity. There are 77 possible environmental features listed in Appendix 1. Not all of these are applicable to each activity. One activity may have 38 important natural resource considerations; another may have only 16. These considerations should be identified as part of the activity analysis. These will be used directly in the site analysis, evaluation, and selection discussed later in Chapter 3.

Utilization externalities.   In addition to these natural resource conditions, there are other utilization factors that must be considered in the analysis of activity.

One of these externalities is the accessibility of the activity area. Will users be able to really get to the facility? Will it require driving or cycling? Can users conveniently walk to it? Is it accessible to the physically disabled? Another factor is proximity. How close is it to the anticipated user groups?

Use compatibility must also be studied. It has been illustrated that some activities are catalytic. Some activities are complementary. But some activities are incompatible to certain other activities. An exuberant, noisy, strenuous, space-consumptive, large-group activity would distract or disrupt a passive, quiet, reposing, or localized small-group activity. This is why it is important to study the entire recreational experience system for a proposed park as well as a detailed analysis of each activity.

SUPPORT FACTORS OF THE ACTIVITY ANALYSIS. Support factors can be separated into two groups: services and facilities. These provide amenities in addition to the basic activity needs.

Support services. Five support services enhance the provision of a recreational activity in a park. *Maintenance* includes the daily and recurrent care, cleaning, replenishment, and grooming of activity apparatus, areas, and facilities. *Operations* includes fees and charges collection, reservations, control and manipulation of technical equipment (filters, pumps, purification systems, power plants, etc.), and support supplies. *Programming* services provide instruction, scheduling, competitive seeding, special events, leadership, and supervision. *Health, safety, and emergency* services protect the park user as well as personal and public property. Lifeguards, emergency first aid and medical personnel, rangers, park police, security officers, and rescue crews are some examples. *Refreshment and supply* services provide the food, beverage, and activity supplies consumed by park users. These services may range from supplying dispensing machines, operating a refreshment stand or limited menu restaurant, or managing an entire concession to spectators at a sports stadium, a golf or tennis pro shop, or souvenir, crafts, and travel supplies shop. All these support services are important development factors. Consideration for these services must be included in predesign planning for any activity.

Support facilities. Support facilities are used by either the activity participant or support service personnel. *Part 2 of this book provides a detailed explanation of the major park support facilities.*

Circulation and parking systems are usually considered automotive related but other park circulation facilities are provided for bicycle riders, equestrians, and other ORV users as well as pedestrians. *Power* from electricity and other energy sources is needed for park users, maintenance equipment, operations machinery, refreshment coolers, stores, and lights.

Fire, safety, emergency, and communications facilities include hydrants, extinguishers, protective barriers, first aid provisions, and emergency care transportation equipment and telephones, radios, and alarm systems. *Shelter* is not only needed during rainstorms but also as protection from excessive wind, sun and insects. *Park furniture* includes benches, tables, grills, fireplaces, bleachers, seats, storage boxes, and bike racks. *Water* systems are used for drinking, irrigation, maintenance, and sewage disposal. *Sanitation* systems provide solid waste (trash, garage, litter, and rubbish) storage, collection, and disposal as well as liquid waste collection, treatment, and discharge. *Security* facilities include control barriers, alarm systems and lighting. *Support storage and work* areas may range from small program equipment storage boxes to maintenance and storage complexes with supply warehouses, garages, sign shops, repair shops, workshops, and the like.

Too frequently a park superintendent has to construct these support facilities after the park has been "developed" and open for public use. He then has to construct these needed elements in leftover park areas or as an infringement on activity areas in order that the support area be as functional as possible.

Refreshment and supply facilities can range from dispensing machines to indoor or outdoor dining facilities to complete shopping centers within parklands, with grocery stores, crafts and equipment supply shops, and even banks.

It should be apparent that, while the activity analyses form an important component of the design program, its value is not exclusively limited to physical planning and should not be primarily directed to addressing only the design members of the park planning team.

The examples of complete activity analyses in Appendix 2 illustrate the simple process of briefly listing the activity, participant, resource and facility, and support factors important to the activity. The first and second examples are for tennis, a facility-oriented activity; the last example is for beach swimming, a resource-oriented activity.

Note that activity analysis is a process that should be done for *each* activity to be offered at each park. While some portions of the analyses may be similar, it is not recommended that an agency "standard analysis" be utilized for the same activity to be provided at different parksites. To do so would encourage a standardized planning solutions for each unique situation.

SYNTHESIS OF COMPLETE
PREDESIGN PACKAGE

After each activity analysis has been completed as an individual study, they should be reviewed to identify areas of duplication, conflict, omission, and multiple use and synthesize these into a summation for the complete project. This helps put each activity into proper perspective and permits the planning team to look at the complete planning package.

Special agency controls such as policies and regulations not directly related to any one of the activities analyzed but important when planning the park should be detailed at this time. Extra support considerations should be examined as well. Examples of these include possible resident staff provisions, a need for a maintenance center, an internal park communications system, staff lockers, showers, and so on.

AGENCY SPECIFICATIONS.   It is very useful if a park agency or private recreation development can establish departmentwide standards for certain common park items. This is done for "stock items," which are used in all park and recreation areas in the system. This offers the advantages of bulk purchasing and its economies, ease in replacement and repair when necessary, interchangeability between areas, and an "image" of consistent quality equipment. Some of the items that are often standardized for an entire department include picnic tables, benches, drinking fountains, flagpoles, bicycle racks, cooking grills, waste containers, play apparatus, and other manufactured park equipment.

It is common to utilize agency specifications for standard construction items as well as manufactured items. These are often based on municipal, state, or federal specifications that have been developed in conformance to building and safety codes. Some specifications are adapted from national manufacturing associations, professional societies, or the American Society for Testing Materials (ASTM). Examples of these commonly used construction items that are usually part of an agency specification include structural concrete, asphalt paving, sanitary and plumbing equipment, electrical installations, and plant materials.

Agency specifications require continuous evaluation and review. Careful notes during construction or installation and over a long period of use help make revisions, improvements, and corrections to the standard specification possible. Repeated unthinking use of agency specifications from project to project over a long period of time can be a way to compound an uncorrected problem. But if these specifications are kept current, they can be a very valuable control of consistent quality.

Development of agency specifications.   The first step in developing an item standard (e.g., park signs, picnic table, bench, drinking fountain, etc.) is to write a general *performance specification*. This is a brief statement explaining exactly what it is the item is expected to do. Important considerations include use capacity, durability, ease of repair and maintenance, and availability. Next all possible manufacturing sources for the items should be investigated. Check manufacturer and product directories in professional, industry, and trade periodicals.

Write letters of inquiry directly to manufacturers. Discuss these products with other practitioners who have had experience with them. Then prepare a *materials specification* based on the various data sources reviewed. This should describe the materials, sizes and measurements, number of essential pieces, methods of fabrication, preservatives and finish, on-site assemblage details, and other necessary information that describes the item. Be very careful to write this specification in such a way so that several manufacturers can meet these requirements.

Do not use a single "brand specification" as a guide. These are usually written to single out that manufacturer's product from all others. If this is done, other manufacturers or suppliers might not be able to bid against the selected firm's product, thus perhaps increasing costs as well as eliminating alternative sources of supply of items and parts. The specification of trade names or brands without qualification in public works is illegal because it restricts fair trade. Private and commercial recreation projects may do so but should consider the advantages of carefully prepared nonexclusionary specifications.

As a final step in the development of an agency specification, review the materials specifications with the brand specifications of all the products investigated. Maintain a list of acceptable manufacturers and design or model number that comply with the specifications.

Appendix 3 gives an example of an agency specification for one of several types of picnic benches approved for use by a public park department. Following is that an example of an agency park construction specification. Notice that the agency utilizes state highway department specifications for materials and methods that have been tested by engineers and substantial periods of use. Contractors and construction materials suppliers are familiar with state specifications. Concrete and asphalt mixes, as an example, are regularly prepared to these standards.

COMPILATION OF DESIGN PROGRAM

The park design program is sometimes referred to as the design directive because it provides the basic directions for the physical design of the park. Additionally, it will be the criterion by which the design will be evaluated. Because the design program is so important it is understandable that park physical planners prefer a well-prepared design program rather than have to second guess what is expected of the facility. A good design program saves time and efforts by preventing the necessity of redesign time and time again because "That's not exactly what we had in mind."

The park design program has four basic components: objectives, activity conception, design controls, and submission format.

The *program objectives* outline the primary objectives of the project and its relationship to the goals of the total recreation system (usually as developed in the communitywide comprehensive recreation and parks plan or state comprehensive outdoor recreation plan). These statements should be experience oriented rather than facility oriented.

The section on *activity conception* is the area that should offer the most stimulation for creativity to physical planners. It usually consists of all the activity analysis studies and the combined park predesign synthesis. For the activities conceived in each study, the designer creates an appropriate physical setting or facility. *The activity analysis must not be written in a way that would unduly restrict the designer.*

Design controls include all important constraints placed on the design. These are the parameters within which the good designer finds innovative and creative expression. Information for this section is obtained from the pre-design synthesis (e.g., agency regulations, special support considerations, state and local codes, U.S. Department of Labor Occupational Safety and Health Administration (OSHA) regulations, etc.), all pertinent agency standards and specifications, budget ceilings, and description of known site limitations and restrictions.

The manner in which the design is to be presented in its final form is explained in the *submission format*. If the design is desired in two-dimensional graphics, a plan scale or sheet size is specified. The number of copies of the plan and any required narrative is indicated as well. If special techniques are needed, they should be listed in this section of the design directive. This includes mounting of plans on display mats, rendering or coloring of presentation copies, inclusion of models or pictorial conceptions of the project or other special treatment. The method of plan reproduction may be specified in the submission format. These requirements are repeated or referred to in any contract with consultants if the design is not to be done by in-house professional staff.

SUMMARY

During the predesign phase, park planners determine the activities to be offered in the park and identify their essential qualities that are to be provided in physical, programmatic, functional, and operational plans. This requires careful determination of the experience opportunities to be provided for each activity, definition of proposed experience and development norms, and other essential activity, participant, resource, facility, and support factors. This can be accomplished by doing a comprehensive activity analysis for every recreational activity to be provided in the park.

These analyses should be synthesized for the entire park to identify areas of duplication, conflict, omission, and multiple use.

This helps each activity into the complete package and permits the planning team to study the interrelationships.

A design program to provide the basis for physical planning may be compiled from these predesign decisions. If the pre-design steps are done well, the design phase of park planning is apt to be much more successful.

The results of the predesign analyses and other studies also become the basis for program, functional, and operational planning for the park.

GLOSSARY OF TERMS

Activity Analysis
A study of basic considerations that determine the design, development, use, and maintenance of a recreational area or facility.

Agency Specification
An official standard for certain common items or construction techniques used by an agency in the development or management of a park.

Catalytic Activity
An activity that is the basis for other secondary activities because of its inherent casualness, long activity period, and simplicity.

Design Load
The optimum number of people or other units, such as boats or cars, that an area or facility has been designed to physically hold; expressed as PAOT, dock slips, seats, parking spaces, and so on.

Design Directive
The design program.

Design Program
The basic directions for the physical design of a park including project objectives, activity concepts, design controls, and submission format.

Development Norm
The physical development or environmental modification compatable with the proposed experience levels; the amenities, refinements, conveniences, and comforts provided.

Experience Norm
The level of expectations by recreationists for self-sufficiency, exertion, adventure, and solitude (or the opposite extreme of these qualities) in a recreational activity.

Experience Opportunities
The various different ways to participate in and enjoy the same activity.

Natural Resource Descriptor
A word or phrase identifying the conditions of a particular characteristic of the natural environment.

PAOT
People At One Time; a measurement of the design load for a building or other facility of occupancy.

Recreation Resource Requirements
Natural conditions that determine the suitability of an area to provide an activity or the quality of that activity experience at a given site, based on an established activity analysis.

Site Analysis
A study of an area to determine what recreational activities the site is best suited for or if certain needed facilities could be provided there.

Utilization Externality
A situation or condition outside the immediate activity area and its natural environment that affects the use of that area.

BIBLIOGRAPHY

Christiansen, Monty L. *The Application of a Recreation— Experience Components Concept for Comprehensive Recreation Planning.* Pennsylvania Department of Community Affairs, Harrisburg, Pa., 1974.

U.S. Department of Agriculture, Forest Service. *Forest Service Manual.* Washington, D.C.

3
the
design
phase

Design is normally the second phase of the park planning process, following the predesign efforts. This is the basis for all development in the park. Because of the conspicuous costs involved in capital development, major significance is most often placed on this physical planning phase. The result of this phase is a tangible, visible entity easily noticed, appreciated, or criticized by the public.

Because of these elements, design has been disproportionately emphasized in the park planning process in the past. It was sometimes even conceived as being the nucleus if not in fact the sum total, of park planning. This fallacy is now beginning to be recognized and it has come to be accepted as one of the four principal phases of the park planning process.

Park design (physical planning) is the process of conceiving and structuring the physical arrangement of recreational areas and facilities and their necessary functional support elements.

This may require careful consideration of a large number of design factors that will vary depending on the nature of the project. Because of these factors, complexity of the design will directly affect the expertise required for the design. Some basic area designs may require nothing more than careful study and use of reference materials. A park project design requiring more personal and specific knowledge than what is available in general references is best handled by a trained professional park designer. For a comprehensive park project, a designer trained as a landscape architect is best qualified. His training can be supplemented with other design disciplines such as architecture and engineering when necessary.

In fact, during the design phase of park planning, the park designer assumes a dominant role within the planning team. A wise park designer coordinates the design process while utilizing all the necessary expertise available. The physical plan of the park is evolved through an open process of park component analysis and problem solving. It is possible for the park designer to do all this alone for projects of limited complexity if they are within his professional field. Usually the designer becomes the leader of a design group composed of design and non-design specialists. The team contributions are made in the form of design objectives, data input, recommendations, critiques, and evaluations.

It is not the intent of this chapter to train park designers, but to explain the design process and show how the entire park planning team can work with the designer. Only by understanding and respecting the roles and contributions of each other, made in the correct manner and at the right time, can the entire team support the physical planner in this vital phase of park planning.

DESIGN OBJECTIVE

The object of this planning phase is to document the recommended physical arrangement of the park object in conformance with the design program. Because the design is the requisite for the development phase of park planning, this scheme is often termed the *general development plan.*

STEPS OF THE DESIGN PHASE

Design is a process that is not completed in a well-defined series of steps that are completed one by one in chronological order. As the process evolves, there is usually a large degree of retracking, repetition, and ingemination of procedures because of the inherent flux and reflux in design resolution. The following is a peremptory listing of the essential stages of park design in logical, if not actual, order.

Step 1.   Establish design objectives from design program.

Step 2.   Site analysis.

Step 3.   Develop alternative concept plans.

Step 4.   Evaluation of alternatives/recommendation of primary concept plan.

Step 5.   Refinement of concept.

Step 6.   Preparation of general development plan.

ESTABLISH DESIGN OBJECTIVES FROM DESIGN PROGRAM

The design program included activity analyses for all the proposed activities as well as the overall design controls for the project. (See Chapter 2.) Attention must be paid to the approved development norms, special activity, program, and support facility requirements, environmental requirements, and agency standards. The design objectives should be expressed as functional or performance objectives instead of specific physical facilities. An example of part of such a design objective might be: "Boat docking facilities shall be appropriate to the established activity analysis; protected from high waves or rough water; have sufficient draft to permit use by both motorboats and sailboats with submerged centerboards, daggerboards, or keels; capable of adjusting to water elevation fluctuations of up to twelve inches; constructed with a non-slip surface wide enough for three people walking side-by-side; . . . ." This establishes design objectives instead of presenting predesign solutions. It permits the park designer to create areas and facilities that will function as required without restricting the design to a predetermined form at the first step of the design process.

The amount of detail required for the design objectives will depend on the designer. Most staff park designers as well as consultants who have worked on other projects with the park department may be able to work directly from the design program. Other designers work best from physical rather than experiential objectives.

SITE ANALYSIS

The park designer is best qualified to conduct the site analysis. There may be specific detailed information that may require the expertise of a specialist (e.g., soils engineer, forester, geologist, wildlife ecologist, or others), but the park designer determines what information is needed.

The process may be evaluative—comparing several sites to determine which is best suited for the project—or the process may be an assessment of a previously selected site.

The evaluative site analysis stresses identification and evaluation of those known natural conditions that are essential to the proposed recreational activities. The site judged to be best endowed with these resource requirements is then subject to a more detailed assessment analysis.

The resource descriptors discussed in Appendix 1 can be used as the basis for the evaluative analysis instrument. After the appropriate resource descriptors necessary for each activity have been determined from the activity analysis, an identifiable or quantifiable natural condition (requirement) for each descriptor is established. When establishing these resource requirements, the following objectives should be observed.

☐ The criteria should conform to known user preferences for given environmental conditions or situations. Examples include the amount of shade, temperature, natural screening, slope and degree of development refinements desired by participants.

☐ The criteria should be in compliance with established health, sanitary and safety regulations, codes and laws. These factors usually affect support facilities. Examples include health regulations for drinking water, liquid waste disposal and surface water quality.

☐ The criteria should reflect considerations for resource constraints. Examples of this factor include protection of steep slopes and fragile vegetation, soil conservation, and erosion control.

☐ Accepted good design considerations should be an inherent part of the criteria. Good design practices affecting functional relationships of use areas, automobile/pedestrian conflicts, construction considerations and elimination of appropriate architectural barriers are included in this factor.

☐ The criteria should reflect agency policies, capabilities, limitations, and standards for development, use, maintenance, and operations.

(The example evaluative site analysis instrument described in Appendix 4 is based on the activity analysis for beach swimming that precedes it in Appendix 2. Forty of the 77 descriptors were significant to the activity of beach swimming for the project for which the analysis instrument was prepared.)

It is emphasized that the resource requirements for this activity, like the activity analysis itself, are unique to the specific project for which they were prepared. While some natural conditions are universally essential to the activity, most of the criteria are based on the specific activity analysis prepared for the project.

After a site has been selected, a more comprehensive site analysis is made. In addition to a study of natural resources, this analysis includes on-site and off-site cultural, logistical, aesthetic, and socioeconomic determinants.

A trained designer knows the essential details and depth of information necessary to make design decisions. Other individuals play basically a data-gathering role during this stage of the design, which is not actually completed until the final design is accepted. All the remaining stages of the design process generate needs for accurate information. It is impossible to foresee all the information needed to design a park. Much of it must be assembled initially as a preliminary step; additional data will be required as design concepts are refined and developed into the general development plan.

DEVELOP ALTERNATIVE CONCEPT PLANS

The park designer combines, or synthesizes, the design program to the site by using information obtained from the site analysis, a study of spatial requirements and activity area needs for each activity and support facility, and a conceptual functional analysis of all the proposed areas and facilities.

The *site analysis* identifies the portions of the site best suited for each activity; the *space needs schedule* shows how much area is needed for each activity; the *functional analysis* is an abstract study of use relationships.

The combination of these design techniques enables the park designer to conceptually zone the site into activity areas. There may be several possible arrangements that are acceptable at this stage.

These use zones are linked by a circulation infrastructure—a supporting network of roads, walks, and other circulation systems. Circulation planning considerations and patterns are discussed in detail in Chapter 6.

The concept plans show activity and support areas as land use zones of the approximate correct size and form located where they are proposed on the site and connected by a system of circulation corridors. The physical shape and placement of facilities, including buildings, playing fields, courts, or other structures, are not part of the concept plans. Figure 3.1 shows a concept plan for a small urban park.

EVALUATION OF ALTERNATIVES

A concept plan is free from details and complications. It shows how a limited number of the essential, inceptive design considerations were resolved:

☐ Where is the best location for each activity?

☐ How much area is needed for each activity?

☐ Which activities are best located together, adjacent, or separated?

☐ How can the activity areas be linked by public or service circulation systems?

The alternative design concept plans show different design approaches, priorities, compromises, and structure. Each alternative will have its own strengths and weaknesses. Before a development plan can be made, one of these concept plans (or a combination of plans) must be accepted and refined.

It is not practical to have everyone that has an interest in the project review and evaluate the alternative concept plans. All their interests however must be considered. The decision-making authority, whether a board or a park administrative executive, should decide which concept plan is to be refined and developed into a final design. For large agencies this decision is

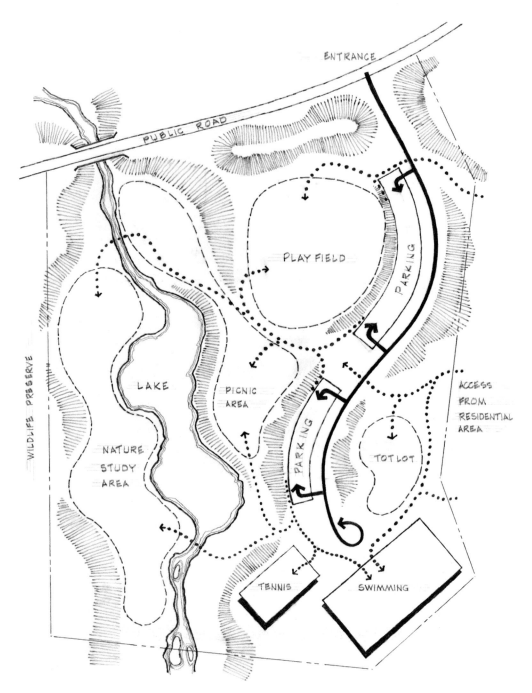

Figure 3.1

A concept plan for an urban park, showing the relationships of activity areas, circulation, and adjacent land use.

49

usually delegated to a professional in charge of park planning. In small agencies the director makes the choice.

CONCEPT REFINEMENT

The internal functional use areas, circulation, buffers, controls, and patterns for each of the site land use or activity zones are studied in detail as the concept is refined. These are carefully positioned in the landscape to utilize the natural resources best suited to the use. Additionally, each activity area is linked to others by incorporating general support systems to area subsystems. The designer will develop the expanded concept plan by a series of studies and revisions.

During this evolutionary process, open communication and cooperation between the designer and individuals knowledgeable in specific aspects of each activity and support service are essential. The information, advice, recommendations, suggestions, and constructive criticism provided by these consulting experts during concept refinement and general development plan preparation are virtually indispensable. During these stages more detailed information is usually required about the site. Data collection, analysis and plan refinement are simultaneous activities.

PREPARATION OF GENERAL
DEVELOPMENT PLAN

There is no distinct separation between concept refinement and general development plan preparation. Parts of the design may be solved in detail while others are still being studied in abstract.

The *general development plan* is a scaled graphic representation of the park project showing the location, form, size, and orientation of all significant activity and support areas and facilities (see Figure 3.2). The plan is the product of the park designer's expertise combined with the technical knowledge of the consulting experts. Staff park designers have the advantage of immediate and convenient contact with most of these individuals. The input process is continuous.

Consultant park designers seek this input during the development of the plan on an informal basis and at specified review periods. At these working sessions, the designer may present a preliminary plan. The agency studies it in detail and offers suggestions for improvement. It is important that the agency is prepared to study the preliminary plan in depth. The review may be completed during a single comprehensive work session or the plans may be left with the agency for several days to allow all functional divisions an opportunity to evaluate and critique them. When the preliminary plan reviews are not carefully done, a most significant opportunity to contribute and possibly improve the design is missed.

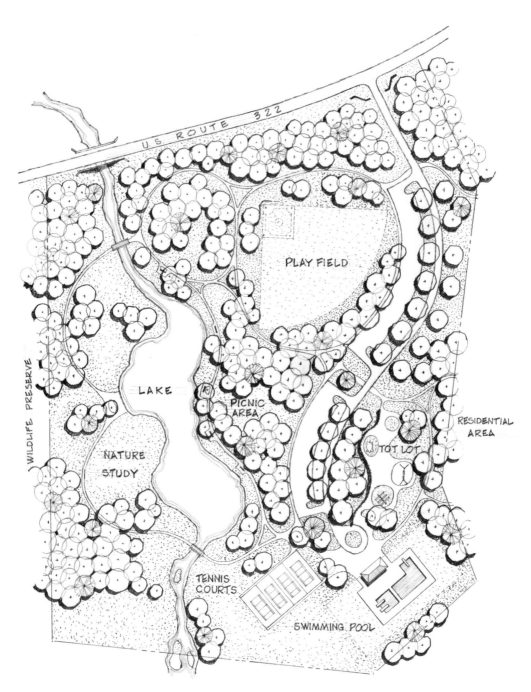

Figure 3.2

A general development plan of a park based on the concept plan shown in Figure 3.1. The true scale and fine details are examples of the accuracy that is typical for this design drawing.

The designer incorporates the suggestions made during the preliminary plan review into the final general development plan. The final plan should be based on the original design program but should reflect acceptable compromises, tradeoffs, and changes that were made during the evolution of the design. Of particular concern is the cost estimate for the capital development. It should be consistent with the original budget in the design program unless written change was approved by the agency. The general development plan must be approved for the agency by the responsible decision maker or board. This plan is the basis for the construction plans, detail drawings, and specifications that are needed for the development phase of park planning.

SUMMARY

Park design is the process of conceiving and structuring the physical arrangement of recreational areas and facilities and their necessary functional support elements. The complexity of the project should be directly correlated with the expertise of the park designer. While simple positioning of a basic sandlot ballfield may be readily accomplished by anyone, even without design training, after a quick check with a general reference, a detailed general development plan or more technical design requires the knowledge and training of specialists.

The design objectives should be based on the program. It is essential that the physical planner work closely with program and functional planners, participants, park agency support personnel, and others to insure that the park design complements their efforts to provide all the necessary element for the recreational experiences intended.

GLOSSARY OF TERMS

Concept Plan
A schematic plan of a proposed park that shows general activity area location, approximate areal requirements, functional relationships, and circulation patterns.

General Development Plan
A scaled plan of a park project showing the specific location, form, size, and orientation of all significant activity and support areas and facilities.

Park Design
The process of conceiving and structuring the physical arrangement of recreational areas and facilities and their necessary functional support elements.

BIBLIOGRAPHY

Douglass, Robert W. *Forest Recreation,* Second Edition. Pergamon Press, New York, 1975.

Fogg, George E. *Park Planning Guidelines.* National Recreation and Park Association, Arlington, Va., 1975.

Lynch, Kevin. *Site Planning,* Second Edition. M.I.T. Press, Cambridge, Mass., 1971.

Planning Facilities for Athletics, Physical Education and Recreation, Revised Edition, American Alliance for Health, Physical Education, and Recreation (AAHPER), Washington, D.C., 1971.

Rubenstein, Harvey M. *A Guide to Site and Environmental Planning.* Wiley, New York, 1969.

Rutledge, Albert J. *Anatomy of a Park.* McGraw-Hill, New York, 1971.

4
the development phase

There are three distinct steps of the development phase of park planning. Of these three, the first step—that of *preconstruction documentation*—is the most vital for park planners. It is during this step that the critical details for the construction of the proposed general development plan are finalized.

The other steps of the park development are the *construction contracting,* which must be done according to proper competitive-bid procedures for public parks, and *project construction,* which is controlled by the contract, construction drawings, and specifications.

PRECONSTRUCTION DOCUMENTATION

Before any project can be built, *construction drawings* and *specifications* are prepared to explain to the contractor what facilities are to be constructed, where they are to be located, what sizes are to be provided, what materials are to be used, the relationships of the various areas and facilities, and what essential construction procedures are to be followed.

This documentation, in graphic and narrative form, is simply a detailed, technical medium of communication between the park designer and the construction contractor. It is a set of directions just as a cookbook or a series of recipes for a banquet is a set of

54

directions. The success of the end result similarly often depends on how well the contractor (chef) understood and followed directions.

This is a continuation of the park planning process based on a series of directives: objective procedures (i.e., design directive) for the general development plan, construction documents for the development phase, and program and other support performance specifications for the actualization phase of the process.

The step of preconstruction documentation, as with the vast majority of the various steps and phases of park planning, is essentially based on appropriate and efficient communications. The construction documents—the drawings and specifications— are the tangible results of a series of discussions, interviews, presentations, reviews, and revisions between the park designer and park support services personnel, activity specialists, and technical specialists. It is essential that all significant members of the planning team be involved in the preparation of these construction documents. It is one of the roles of the park designer to utilize all their input, assimilate it, and draft the directions to the contractor.

To make meaningful contributions to these construction documents, each advisor must understand the "language" used in the drawings and specifications.

THE CONSTRUCTION DRAWINGS

The graphic portion of the construction documents is the set of drawings that show the physical characteristics of the items to be built. Because these drawings are two-dimensional representations of proposed three-dimensional objects, the draftsman uses a graphic shorthand, standardized symbols for various materials (selected symbols commonly found in park drawings are shown in Figure 4.1), consistent labeling techniques, and commonly used graphic depictions of structures (elevations, sections, isometric views, plans, perspectives). To read the drawings, a person must translate this graphic language into a mental version of the real object. Figures 4.2 to 4.6 illustrate use of each of these graphic representations for a small basketball court.

To help the contractor understand what is required to complete the construction project, the drawings are usually prepared as a set of separate sheets. Each sheet shows one phase or portion of the project. Comprehensive park projects usually require these contract drawings:

SITE DRAWINGS

Location Map
Grading Plan
Dimensioning Plan

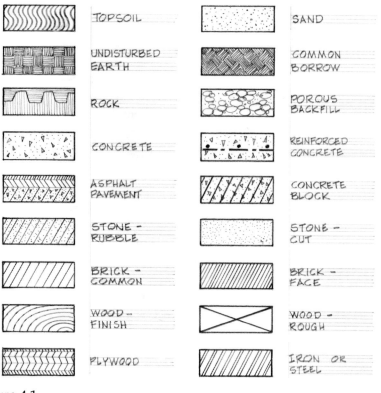

Figure 4.1

Graphic communications in construction drawings are assisted by using standarized symbols for materials commonly used in development.

Profiles (for roads and sewers)
Utilities Location Plan
  Water
  Sanitation
  Electricity
  Telephone
Miscellaneous Detail Drawings
Planting Plan, Details, and Schedule

STRUCTURAL DRAWINGS

Foundation Plan
Superstructure Sections and Details
Roof Framing Plan
Typical Details

ARCHITECTURAL DRAWINGS

Floor Plans
Building Elevations and Sections

Typical Details
  Stairs
  Window and Door Elevations, Details and Schedule

PLUMBING DRAWINGS

Water Distribution Layout
Sanitary System Layout
Valve and Meter Details and Schedule

MECHANICAL DRAWINGS

Heating, Ventilation, Air Conditioning Systems

Figure 4.2

A perspective drawing such as this shows how a facility might look to an observer after construction.

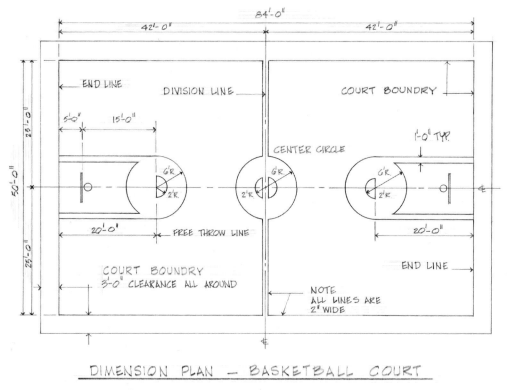

DIMENSION PLAN — BASKETBALL COURT

Figure 4.3

A dimension plan of the full court shown in Figure 4.2. This is useful to the contractor for court layout and marking.

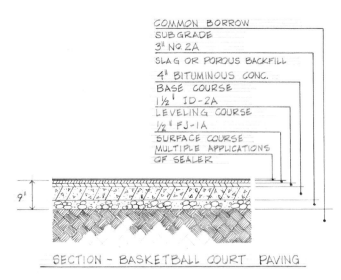

SECTION – BASKETBALL COURT PAVING

Figure 4.4

This section through the basketball court surface illustrates the layered construction, using material symbols shown in Figure 4.1.

58

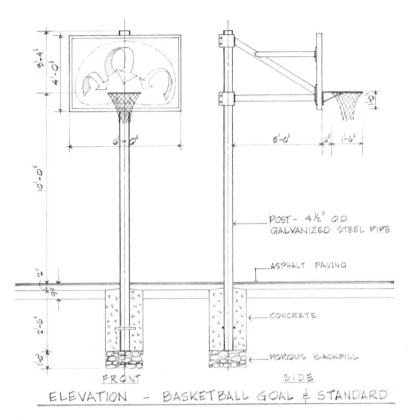

Dimensions and labels in Figure 4.5:
3'-4", 4'-0", 6'-0", 10'-0", 2", 9", 2'-6", 1'-0", 5'-0", 6", 1'-6", 1'-6"

POST - 4½" O.D. GALVANIZED STEEL PIPE

ASPHALT PAVING

CONCRETE

POROUS BACKFILL

FRONT   SIDE

ELEVATION - BASKETBALL GOAL & STANDARD

Figure 4.5

These combined elevation/sections show the basketball goals and standards used in the courts shown in Figure 4.2.

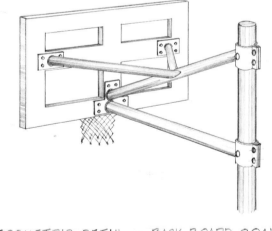

ISOMETRIC DETAIL - BACK BOARD GOAL MOUNTING

Figure 4.6

An isometric drawing such as this is often used to help the contractor fabricate or assemble parts of a facility or piece of equipment.

59

ELECTRICAL DRAWINGS

Electrical Distribution Layout

Lighting and Fixture Details and Schedule

Complex developments may require several sheets for each of these categories; for simple projects it may be possible to incorporate more than one of these items on a single sheet.

The technical accuracy of these drawings are rightly the responsibility of the appropriate design professional—landscape architect, architect, civil engineer, sanitary engineer, architectural engineer, electrical engineer, and mechanical engineer as examples.

The functional efficiency and use performance of the developments proposed in these construction documents are the joint responsibilities of designers as well as nondesigner park planners. It is recommended that all the activity analyses for the project as well as all appropriate agency standards and specifications be reviewed as an initial step of the preparation of the construction documents.

It is particularly important that all the postdevelopment support and service division leaders be capable of interpreting construction drawings and critiquing the functional utility of the proposed developments. These nondesign professionals—such as recreation directors, maintenance superintendents, technical operations specialists, facility directors (aquatic directors, tennis complex directors, golf course operators, etc.), security officers, and chief interpreters—have firsthand working knowledge of innumerible development considerations of which the designer alone cannot possibly be aware.

During this exchange of suggestions, advice and comments, it is important that these individuals be confident that each has an important role in the construction documentation. The wise designer understands that the nondesign input is a compliment to his design skills, not a quibbling criticism of his efforts. Good support services administrators realize it is better (and in the long run, more economical) to help the designers meet their needs before construction than to belatedly complain or work with a poor situation afterward. A common misconception often held by both designer and non designer is that the preparation of the construction drawings and specifications is the sole responsibility of the designer. The designer is actually the contributing editor of these documents. Many other professionals provide him the essential materials to make the ultimate development successful.

SPECIFICATIONS

The other portion of the construction documents is the written directions called *specifications.* These specifications contain descriptions of required workmanship and quality of materials necessary to construct the park project. The specifications are used by the park agency, prospective bidder, and the contractor who is awarded the project. The park agency, as owner, uses the specifications to establish quality controls, maintain continuity within all the units of the park system, and insure completion of the project with minimal disruption of ongoing public use.

Bidders who are preparing proposals to the park agency use the specifications to help prepare cost estimates, determine what subcontractors may be necessary for specialized work, and what additional equipment will be necessary to do the project.

The contractor who is awarded the project uses the specifications to order supplies and materials from suppliers, plan work progress, and direct the efforts of subcontractors.

The drawings and specifications together are used by the contractor and the park agency (or the designer acting as the agency's representative) as the quality control during construction. Each phase of the project is inspected by the agency or its representative to insure that it is in conformance with those construction documents.

SPECIFICATION FORMAT.   The specifications are usually divided into two major provisions:

1.   The *general specifications,* which apply to the overall conditions and provisions of the work.

2.   The *technical specifications,* which describe the construction procedures and materials of the project in the usual order of development.

The general specifications ("general conditions") discuss the responsibilities of all parties and establish working policy for the work. Because these considerations are basic to most types of development, various segments of the construction industry have prepared standardized general conditions. It is a good practice for municipal and state agencies, including park departments, to use a standard set of general specifications for all public works projects.

These conditions are similar to the general conditions of the contract. Even though the construction documents and contract documents are equally binding to both the park agency and the contractor, the contract is often considered to be legally stronger. Many agencies duplicate these conditions in each document—as part of the specifications so that all bidders are aware of the stipulations, as part of the contract so that the winning contractor is legally obligated to them.

The following conditions are typically part of the general specifications:

Definitions.   To avoid misinterpretations, special words or phrases are defined. Examples of commonly defined terms include agency, owner, contracts, project, general contractor, subcontractor, designer, and work.

Contractor's Responsibilities.   The amounts required for bonds, insurance, taxes, permits, fees, and other financial responsibilities are indicated. The adherence to specified construction provisions is emphasized. Progress of work documentation procedures are outlined.

Owner's Responsibilities.   The park agency should indicate its responsibility to contractors. The necessity to control public access and use in parkland affected by the project, to let other contracts, to clean up, and other actions of the agency must be detailed.

Consultant's Responsibilities.   For those circumstances when the consulting designer is acting as an agent of the owner, his role must be specified.

Inspections, Suspensions, and Termination.   The extent and timing of material and workmanship inspections should be clearly indicated. The conditions when it may be necessary to suspend work should be carefully defined. The termination of the contract is permitted only under carefully specified situations.

Payments and Deductions.   The basis and nature of partial payments, standard deductions, and final acceptance and payment is specified.

Work Changes.   The procedure to institute corrections, additions, deletions, or modifications in the original construction documents should be detailed and complete.

Prevailing Minimum Wage Rates.   The Davis-Bacon Act of 1931, as amended in 1955, requires a schedule of wage rates for each federal public works contract. These are provided by the Secretary of Labor for each project and are attached to the general conditions. Most states have similar Prevailing Wage Acts for state-supported contracts.

Equal Employment and Nondiscrimination Provisions.   Federal and state-supported contracts for public works require compliance with national and state human relation laws. This applies to local projects as well, if any financial support is provided by these governments.

STANDARDIZED GENERAL SPECIFICATIONS.   Use of standardized general specifications can have several advantages. They are comprehensive and have application to a wide range of park development projects. They have evolved into an accepted and familiar form, with use over time. Experienced local contractors understand the provisions and their application. They are readily revised if unique situations warrant a special modification.

Small park agencies, or agencies without an ongoing development phase of park planning, may not have a standard general specification for construction. Their consulting designer must assist the agency in the preparation of this portion of the specifications. Many consultants use the *General Conditions of the Contract for Construction* published by the American Institute of Architects* or similar copyrighted general conditions from the American Public Works Association, American Society of Landscape Architects, American Society of Civil Engineers, Consulting Engineers Council, or others as a basis for these one-time provisions. These conditions must be reviewed by the attorney for the park agency and accepted in writing since they are also used as the general conditions of the contract, a realm of the lawyer, not the designer.

An example of a standardized general conditions is included in Appendix 5. Used by the Pennsylvania Department of Environmental Resources, Bureau of State Parks, it is typical of state-level agency general specifications provisions.

The technical specifications are written as each working drawing is done. They must be written with precision and accuracy. Because the designer is liable for the safety and structural soundness of the project, it is he or a specification writer under his control who prepares these specifications.

This does not however preclude any ethical or legal responsibilities of the park agency or owner. Acceptance of the construction documents by the agency, and the subsequent contracting for the project construction, makes the agency legally responsible for any structural failure that was built in accordance with these plans and specifications.

TYPES OF TECHNICAL SPECIFICATIONS. Most capital development specifications for park agencies are *descriptive specifications*. They describe in careful detail the composition and quality of materials, the step-by-step construction process, and the standards of workmanship to be maintained.

Specifications for manufactured equipment such as trucks, tractors, mowers, or other machinery are usually *performance specifications*. This is done to insure satisfactory results while encouraging competitive bidding and economy.

Standard specifications, sometimes called *reference specifications*, are materials or workmanship standards that have been developed by a governmental agency, professional or technical associations, or manufacturing or research institutes. Standard specifications may be developed for intrasystem use such as those discussed in Chapter 2, or they may be used for all materials or construction of that type regardless of the system. Use of standard specifications greatly simplifies the materials and workmanship descriptions necessary. Instead of lengthy, detailed

* *General Conditions of the Contract,*A.I.A. Document A201, 11th Edition, September 1967. The American Institute of Architects, 1735 New York Ave., N.W., Washington, D.C. 20006.

item-by-item descriptions, the specifications can refer to the standard. ". . . park road surface shall conform to the requirements of Pennsylvania Department of Transportation Specification 430 for bituminous surface course FB-2, . . ." or ". . . construction of Tennis Courts shall be in accordance with USTC & TBA Guide Specification VI, ..." Copies of these standard specifications should be kept on file in the agency.

The examples of standard specifications in Appendix 6 illustrate the minute concern for detail contained in them. It also illustrates the economy of time and effort saved when several standard specifications are utilized when a project specification is prepared. It is not uncommon for over several dozen such references to be used in the specifications for a park project requiring the construction of roads, buildings, recreational surfacing, fencing, and utilities.

The completed set of construction drawings and specifications must be reviewed and accepted by the appropriate authorized representative of the park agency before the construction contract may be let.

COMPETITIVE-BID
CONSTRUCTION CONTRACTING

This is the second step of the development phase of park planning. Small or uncomplicated development projects may be done with the agency's own work force. Several of the large, growing park departments in the United States have their own construction divisions that are able to build most of their agencies' projects. But the majority of park and recreation agencies find it more economical to contract for the construction of these developments. All government construction is classified as *public works*.

Private, industrial, and commercial park agencies may negotiate construction contracts with selected contractors. Public park agencies are required to obtain a public works contract through an established *competitive-bid* process. This process is governed by the legislative policy of the particular governmental body or unit involved. It is important that the responsible official of the public park agency follow the policy of the governmental unit concerned. This may be federal, state, or local policies, depending on the agency.

THE COMPETITIVE-BID PROCESS

The process may vary to a small extent between governmental units, but essentially they all follow a standard pattern. The park agency publicly requests interested contractors to submit an offer to build the project for a stated price. The agency publicly selects the offer. A contract is made between that contractor and the agency and the work is done according to that agreement.

This process is used to protect the public from collusion or fraud and to obtain the best value at the lowest possible cost. It insures fair competition and an equal advantage to anyone wishing to do business with the public park agency.

There are five distinguishable steps of the competitive-bid process:

Step 1.   Preparation and publishment of the *advertisement,* or *notice to bidders* by the park agency. It is a solicitation for proposals that has enough information about the project to help a contractor decide if he is sufficiently interested to get additional details.

Step 2.   Study of the *instructions to bidders* and all the contract documents by interested contractors. The instructions, prepared by the park agency, are detailed directions about how bids are to be submitted. The contract documents include the contract, construction drawings and specifications.

Step 3.   Submission of the sealed *proposal* by bidding contractors. The proposal is usually made on a special *bid form* prepared by the park agency to insure uniformity and to make it easier to compare bids.

Step 4.   Public opening and review of the proposals and the qualifications of the bidders, the subsequent tabulation of the bids by the agency, and *notice of award* to the lowest qualified bidder.

Step 5.   Acceptance of the award by the successful bidder, a mutual signing of the contract, and issuance of a formal *notice to proceed* by the agency.

The park agency may have responsibility for the preparation of the precontract documents that are related to the preparation of the bid. These are the *advertisement, instructions to bidders,* and the *bid form.* Large municipalities, states, and the federal government have separate agencies (e.g., Department of Public Works, General State Authority, General Services Administration) that are assigned these tasks. Smaller governmental units may contract with their consulting designer for the preparation of these documents along with the construction documents.

THE ADVERTISEMENT

Besides the obvious purpose of fulfilling legal requirements, the public advertising of a competitive-bid park development contract attempts to interest enough contractors to encourage careful bid preparation and economy of costs.

The contents and publication requirements are usually established by governmental statute or policy. It is important that the requirements be carefully followed.

The advertisement should be placed where the greatest

number of potential bidders will see it. Some agencies post a Notice to Bidders in a prominent location in a public building frequented regularly by construction contractors (e.g., near the municipal engineer's office, bidding permit and inspections office, etc.). Others use the "public notices" section of the classified advertisements of a local newspaper or periodicals published by construction and contractors associations, as well as commercial trade journals or papers. Many of these special periodicals are published in regional or localized editions. Some are published daily; others weekly or biweekly. State and federal park agencies submit their advertisement or notice to bidders to a government information agency which produces a serial report or bulletin. Federal construction advertisements are published in "Commerce Business Daily" by the U.S. Department of Commerce. Most states have similar periodicals that are published weekly or biweekly. Appendix 7 has examples of these advertisements.

The advertisement is usually a concise synopsis of the instruction to bidders. The following items are most frequently included in the advertisement:

1. *Brief description of the work.* This includes all work to be done under the contract and identifies the location of the project site. This is usually emphasized by setting it as a separate heading or by printing it in boldface. This is to attract the attention of those contractors who are able to perform the work required and who are willing to work in the named locale.

2. *The name of the park agency.* This may be the park department or supervisory agency who will be accepting the contractor's work for the public.

3. *An outline of procedures and regulations.* All controls related to bid submission, opening and award of the contract are outlined. This includes address and submission deadline, format requirements, public opening and reading of bidder's qualifications, as well as the right to reject all bids.

4. *Major items of work to be done.* This is usually a listing of those major categories of work that indicates the construction skills and equipment that will be required.

5. *The character of the bids.* This is usually "unit-price" if the project consists of installation or construction of measurable items of development such as areas of clearing, paving, or seeding, installation of water or sewer pipes, fencing, and lighting. "Lump-sum" bids are usually used on projects they do not have identifiable units of work. Most park projects are done on a "unit-price" basis.

6.   *Bond and security requirements.*   A *bid bond,* which is a financial guarantee that the bidder will accept the contract if awarded, and a *performance bond,* which is a financial guarantee that the winning contractor will complete the project as specified in the contract, are the most commonly required.

7.   *Construction documents information.*   The location, availability and cost of drawings and specifications are indicated. It should be clear whether or not these documents are returnable.

Park agencies who have infrequent development projects should have a through advertisement. This insures that contractors are encouraged to make bids on the project even though they are not familiar with the agency. Agencies who have a continuous development program may maintain lists of approved and qualified bidders who regularly submit proposals. The advertisements of these agencies may contain only the essential basics of the particular contract, assuming the bidders are familiar with the normal data and requirements.

THE INSTRUCTIONS TO BIDDERS

Because of space limitations and costs, the advertisement is supplemented by an expanded, detailed explanation of the brief information outlined in the notice to bidders. This amplified explanation is the *instructions to bidders.* Those contractors who have been attracted by the advertisement are able to obtain identical instructions about bid submission procedures, information about contract awarding procedures and specific details about the project.

The instructions are usually accompanied by a bid form and a package of contract documents, i.e., a set of construction drawings and specifications and a copy of the contract. (It has become a common practice to incorporate the instructions to bidders as the first section of the specifications for the work.) These are all available at the location(s) established in the advertisement. Usually this is at the park agency office (or public works office if this separate governmental agency is in charge of all public capital development and acquisitions). Sometimes these materials are also avalilable at the office of the consulting design firm. Many agency policies stipulate that a deposit must be made for any set of bidding materials requested by prospective bidders. This deposit is refunded if the materials are returned in good condition. Because of the preparation and duplication expenses, a nonrefundable charge is often now being made for these materials.

The instructions are often a standardized set of directions and procedural explanations that are used by the park agency (or a coordinating public works agency). The usual items of a standarized set of instructions include guidelines for the bidder and an explanation of the procedures used by the contract-awarding agency. An example of standardized instructions is included in Appendix 8. Special additions to these standard instructions may be prepared for each contract which provide information unique to the project. The following items are most frequently included in the instructions to bidders:

GUIDELINES AND DIRECTIONS FOR BID SUBMISSION

1. *Contract documents* are named to insure that all parties to the contract are aware of their existence. The strongest of these documents, legally, are the contract agreement, specifications and drawings. It is common practice to list the advertisement, instructions to bidders, proposal form (bid), general and special contract conditions as well when naming the entire set of contract documents.

2. *A proposal format* is established to insure that all bids will be evaluated for the same quantities and items of work. A *bid form* is usually prepared by the agency and the project designers to insure that all items are included and that alternatives to certain bid items are presented to all prospective bidders. This prevents confusion, errors, and omissions that might occur if each bidder submitted his bid in his own way.

   The required signatures of the individual(s) with the authority to make the bid must be designated. The laws relating to this are different for corporations and partnerships and vary between states.

3. The *basis for bids* is usually established in the instructions as well as indicated on the bid form. Park construction projects are usually bid on a lump-sum or unit-price basis. *Lump-sum* projects are often used when the construction is standardized or where it is very difficult to break down the project into work units. Examples of common park construction that is often done on a lump-sum basis include building standardized shelters, comfort stations or hard surface court game areas. *Unit-price* bidding is important for projects with large amounts of easily identifiable types of work. This is especially significant when the exact amounts of each work unit cannot be determined in advance of the job. Unit-price bidding is often used when construction conditions, such as the stability of wetland areas within the project boundaries, subsurface rock or other difficulties exist. Unit-price contracts are usually let for extensive clearing and grubbing, regrading, road construction, underground utilities, and similar park construction. See Table 4.1.

Table 4.1

Selected common work items used in park development cost estimates and unit-price bidding

Item of Work	Cost Unit for Estimating and Bidding
Buildings, basic[a]	Each
Clearing and grubbing	Acre
Curbing	Linear foot
Drainage pipe installation	Linear foot per diameter
Embankments	Cubic yard
Excavation	
Common	Cubic yard
Rock	Cubic yard
Unclassified	Cubic yard
Muck or peat	Cubic yard or ton
Borrow	Cubic yard
Fencing	Linear foot per height
Grates	Each
Grading	
Rough	Acre
Fine	Acre or square yard
Landscaping	
Liming, Fertilizing, Seeding, Mulching	Acre
Planting Ground Cover	Square foot
Planting Shrubs	Each per size and species
Planting Trees	Each per size and species
Lighting	
Poles and bases	Each
Luminaires and lamps	Each
Paving	
Limited (asphalt)	Ton or square yard
Limited (concrete)	Cubic yard
Limited sealing or waterproofing	Square yard
Roads	Mile per pavement width or lanes
Play or sport apparatus installation	Each
Prefabricated utility unit installation (manholes, frames, vaults, boxes, grates)	Each
Retaining walls	Square foot of face area or linear foot
Signs	Each
Structural foundations	Linear foot
Tree/stump removal	Each
Underground utility lines (water, electric)	Linear foot per size
Valves, meters, hydrants, fountains	Each

[a] Basic park buildings, such as standardized or "packaged" shelters, cabins, contact stations, booths, comfort stations, pavilions, end pole sheds, are usually estimated as a lump-sum cost and listed as separate unit-price items on the bid form. More complex buildings, such as visitor centers, museums and exhibit buildings, offices, maintenance buildings, restaurants, concession buildings, and others, are usually constructed under a separate contact with possible cost-reducing alternatives for furnishings, materials or equipment.

Not as commonly used as either lump-sum or unit price bases are the cost-plus contracts. A *cost-plus-percentage* contract is sometimes used in emergency situations or in unique situations when construction decisions are made as work processes. A *cost-plus-fixed-fee* contract is preferred by most park agencies under these situations, however, because of the possible waste in materials and labor that would inflate an unscrupulous contractor's profit under a cost-plus-percentage contract.

4.   *Bid bonds* are usually stipulated in the instructions to insure that each bidder is sincere. The bond is a monetary guarantee that, if awarded the contract, the bidder would accept the project as he has bid it. The bid bond is usually based on a percentage of the bid (usually ten percent) or a set amount for small projects.

EXPLANATION OF THE CONTRACT-AWARDING PROCEDURE

1.   *Qualifications of bidders* are often stipulated in the instructions. This requirement is necessary to minimize the possibility of awarding the work to an incompetent or unfit contractor. Large park agencies (or the appropriate coordinating public works agencies) that are involved in large amounts of public construction over time—such as the U.S. government and many of the states—require that contracting firms complete a prequalification form that must be evaluated and approved before the firm is permitted to even submit a bid. This reduces constant and repeated evaluation of bidders' qualifications. Other park agencies, with occasional or infrequent construction contracts to let, require each bidder to submit a form with his bid, which proves that he has the competence to complete the work as specified. Qualification may be evidenced by records of successful completion of similar projects, proof of ownership or availability of special construction equipment needed for the project, records of financial solvency, personnel experience records for key individuals in the firm, as well as other information requested by the agency.

As an additional guarantee, many park agencies will require that all bidders agree to provide a *performance bond or surety* if awarded the contract. Usually obtained from a bonding company, this bond is a guarantee that the contractor will not default on any provisions of the contract.

2.   *Withdrawal of proposals* are sometimes prompted by discovery of numerical errors by the bidder. Park agencies must be fair to all bidders. To insure fairness, a

procedure and deadline for withdrawals are explained in the instructions. Withdrawal of a bid, if done in writing and received prior to the opening of bids, is usually permitted.

3.   *Modification of proposals* are usually accepted when done in writing and received prior to bid opening.

4.   *Bid opening procedures* must be well defined in the instructions. Bids are usually submitted in sealed envelopes labeled "Proposal for _____." This is done to keep each bid secret until all are opened. At the designated time all proposals should be publicly opened and read aloud to let all interested individuals know the results as a matter of public record and to avoid any possibility of collusion between any bidders or any bidder and a public official.

5.   *The contract award* for public works projects must be made to the lowest responsible bidder. If all bidders were approved as qualified as a prerequisite for bidding, the lowest bidder is offered the contract. If the qualifications of the bidders have not been made, an award is often tentatively made to the lowest bidder contingent on his qualifications. This process may take considerable time if the bids were complex (e.g., there are often many alternatives for construction to compare as well as verification of unit-price totals).

6.   *Rejection of bids* should be a stated right of the park agency. Individual proposals may be rejected if the agency is not satisfied with the qualifications of any bidder. All bids may be rejected if they all exceed the agency's cost estimate for the project and it feels it cannot afford the low bid. If this happens, the agency may elect to reject all bids, redesign, or add cheaper alternatives to the project and readvertise for the new project.

INFORMATION ABOUT THE WORK

1.   *A materials and work unit estimate* should be included in the instructions. While these quantities are only approximate and may be slightly more or less than the actual quantities actually used on the project, they do give the bidders a close idea of the amounts of various materials and work units to be used. Unit-price bids are made on the sum per unit cost of each item. The materials and work units are inserted into the bid form for unit-cost proposals.

2.   *The completion date* for the project should be clearly indicated in the instructions. This will help bidders establish prospective work and delivery schedules. This

scheduling is vital to each contractor's profit margin. It will also determine when essential utility connections must be done. Procedures for time extensions should also be described.

3.   *Responsibility for accuracy of data* provided as a basis for the bidding must be indicated in the instructions. Usually the park agency assumes responsibility for the accuracy of core drillings, samples, and tests made prior to the letting of the contract if they are used as a basis for the work unit estimates or design. Unless a disclaimer is stated with the instructions, the agency must rightly accept responsibility for major revisions in the project, including scheduling, due to inaccuracies in this data.

4.   *Clarification or revisions of the plans or specifications* is the responsibility of the park agency. If any bidder notes an error or ambiguity in these documents while preparing his bid and requests an interpretation, the agency must have the designer prepare a clarification or change and notify all bidders in writing so that all bidders have the same information. These changes become part of the contract documents.

5.   *Site conditions* may place constrains on the progress of the project. It should be stated in the instructions that it is the responsibility of the bidders to visit the site and become acquainted with its conditions.

6.   *Additional miscellaneous information* unique to each contract may be included in the instructions. Examples of these items occasionally found in park development projects may include requirements for public access along certain park roads used by contractors in a park improvement or expansion, special phasing or partial project completion and acceptance for public use of portions of the project, temporary sanitation provisions, or other unique requirements. These items are usually detailed in the general conditions of the specifications.

It is important that the park agency carefully review the instructions to bidders before approving the contract documents. Standardized instructions are convenient and are usually suitable for normal situations, but should be relevant to the contract going to bid. Items that are particularly important to each specific contract include the bid basis and bid form, bonding qualifications of bidders, materials and work unit estimate, completion date, changes in the plans or specifications, site conditions and other unique features of the project. An example of a standard instructions to bidders has been included in Apendix 8.

THE PROPOSAL

Each bidder submits a written offer (proposal) to complete the work and supply the materials indicated in the plans and specifications according to the conditions established in the contract. A proposal is also a written promise that the bidder will sign that contract. The park agency (or appropriate public works agency) should prepare a standard proposal form for the work to be contracted and require each bidder to use it. This will insure that all proposals can be evaluated on an equal basis. A standard form prepared by the agency helps bidders avoid oversights and omissions. When properly prepared and submitted it is the result of many hours of study, measurement, calculation, collection of materials, costs, equipment purchase or rental, labor estimates, and overhead by each bidder. The proposal must clearly and fairly state the offer and acknowledge acceptance of the contractual requirements.

There are three major parts to each public works proposal. (1) The agreement to the basic conditions of the proposed contract is usually a brief paragraph or more in which the work to be done, the name of the project, and its location are specifically named; the maximum number of calendar days within which the work will be done is stated; reference is made to an attached cashiers check or for the appropriate bid bond; and promises are made to sign the actual contract and provide the appropriate performance bonds, guarantees, and warranties. (2) The detailed contract cost(s) prepared by the bidder that he offers to accept in payment for his work is compared to and evaluated against other proposals. This portion of the standard proposal (or bid form) must be carefully prepared by the park agency so that the cost comparisions can be made fairly and easily.

These costs may be in the form of a single lump-sum bid cost, several lump-sum costs for a collection of separate construction items whose sum total is the bid cost, or as a schedule of unit-price costs that are multiplied by the agency's (or design consultant's) estimates for each of the required work units, with the sum total on the bid cost. Table 4.1 lists some commonly used units of work in park construction. These are representative of the work units used in cost estimates and unit-price bid forms. This bid basis is established by the park agency, stipulated in the advertisement and instructions, and dictated by this bid form. Each bid basis may include alternative methods, materials, or units of construction. Each alternative must be clearly stated so that the bidder can indicate whether or not an offer is made to substitute the alternative materials or type of work indicated as well as its effect upon the total bid cost.

Part (3) is the identification of the bidding firm and the name, title, and signature of the individual authorized to commit the firm to the contract.

SELECTING THE BEST BIDDER

Because park construction is considered public works, selection of the bidder for the construction job must be carefully done. The object is to obtain the services of the least expensive, qualified firm. To do this, park agencies (or their public works sister agency) must evaluate each bid according to two criteria: qualifications and economy.

DETERMINING WHICH BIDDERS ARE QUALIFIED.   To avoid the consequences of contracting with a firm who is unable to do the work specified, all bidders should be required to show evidence of their ability to do the work. This is usually the first step in selecting the responsible low bidder for the contract. Many park agencies require that only approved firms be permitted to submit bids. This means that only those contracting firms that are on an approved prequalification list may bid. Other park agencies may use the information compiled by the Bureau of Contract Information, Inc. This nonprofit organization, located in Washington, D.C., is supported by the Associated General Contractors of America and the surety companies that provide the contract performance bonds required for most construction projects. Many park agencies—especially those with infrequent development projects requiring a public works contract—review the qualifications of each bidder by evaluating previous construction experience, the talents of key personnel in this firm, availablility of construction equipment needed for the job (which may be owned by the firm or leased especially for the job), and evidence of sufficient capital or financial backing to do the job.

Regardless of whether the qualifications of interested contracting firms are determined as a prerequisite to submitting a bid or are done after bids are made, this step should be done before the bids are publicly opened and disclosed.

BID EVALUATION AND COMPARISON.   All the proposals from qualified bidders are kept in sealed envelopes until the bid opening, which was established in the advertisement and instructions to bidders. No late bids should be accepted. The acceptable bids should be opened one at a time and publicly read aloud. Many agencies post the bids as announced for the benefit of those attending this public meeting. All bids must be included as part of the public record of the meeting.

If the bid form called for lump-sum proposals, the lowest qualified bidder is awarded the contract. If the bid form called for unit-cost proposals, usually only the sum total for all of the separate bid items is announced. All the unit-cost item proposals are included in the written public records. If there are no alternative materials or work items included in the proposal, the bidder with the lowest total bid for the contract is the apparent winner. Before the contract is awarded, all calculations should be checked by multiplying each bidder's unit price by the estimated quantities listed by the agency on the bid form and totaling all these products. If errors are found, these should be noted and the correct results recorded. The revisions should be used in the final determination of the low bid. These verifications may take several days to complete following the bid opening. Appendix 9 shows an example of a bid tabulation sheet for a park construction project.

Occasionally a park agency will include several alternative materials or work items in the bid form. These alternatives are possible substitutions that may reduce construction costs and permit development of a project within a specified budget. Without alternatives in the proposal, many construction projects would have to be canceled and all bids rejected because the budget was exceeded. When this happens, the project is often scaled down and revised to reduce costs only to have the savings lost by inflation during the time spent making new plans and specifications and rebidding the project. Alternatives within the original bid process can save this time and financial setback.

Evaluation and comparison of bids with several alternatives can be difficult unless a consistent procedure is followed. The basic total bid, not including any alternatives, should be examined first. If the low bid does not exceed the agency budget for the project, it is awarded the contract. If no bidder submits a basic total bid within the budget, the proposals which have made bids for the predetermined alternatives are reexamined. *It is important that the bidders know the order of importance for the alternatives prior to bidding.* Each proposal with the first alternative is compared. If the low bid under the terms is within the agency budget, it is awarded the contract. If it is not, proposals with the first and second alternatives are compared. This process continues until a low bid for the work and a set of predetermined rank ordered alternatives is within the budget and is awarded the contract.

NOTIFICATION OF AWARD.   The low bidder should be officially informed of his selction. A written *notice of award* is usually mailed to the contractor describing the construction project, establishing the park agency as the owner, acknowledging the qualifications of the contractor, noting the accepted bid price, and establishing a time and place for the signing of the contract.

Usually it is after the contract is signed that an official *notice to proceed* is sent to the contractor to authorize him to acquire all the required construction permits, licenses, temporary utility hookups, as well as have legal access to the project site and begin work. Sometimes it is important that this construction process begin as soon as possible instead of waiting until the contract is prepared and signed (a formality that may take over a week). If both the contractor and the park agency sign a *letter of intent*—a written agreement to enter into contract—the contractor may begin prior to the actual contract signing.

THE CONTRACT

The advertisement, instructions to bidders, and proposal are precontract documents. They are often bound as part of the specifications however, and are often included in the contract documents by reference. Usually the contract, specifications, and drawings are considered the most important of the contract documents. The *contract agreement* itself is the legal covenant signed by both the contractor and the authorized representative of the park agency. Detailed explanation of the technicalities of contracts is beyond the scope of this book. It is important that construction contracts be reviewed by the counsel for the park agency. There are many standard agreement forms that have been developed over long periods of time. The federal and state governments have standard contract agreements as do many municipalities. Several professional associations have prepared special construction contracts. Most frequently used are those prepared by the American Institute of Architects, the American Society of Landscape Architects, the American Society of Civil Engineers, and the American Public Works Association. It should be noted that standard agreement forms must be used with a complementary set of general conditions in the specifications.

The contract signing concludes the construction contracting step of the development phase of park planning, followed by the project construction that is controlled by the contract documents.

PROJECT CONSTRUCTION

The third step of the development phase is actual project construction. The parties directly involved in this step are the general contractor, his subcontractors, the park agency, and the authorized *construction inspector*. The contractors direct the work; the park agency is the owner and ultimate manager of the project facility; the construction inspector—usually the public works engineer or inspector in large public agencies, often the consulting site designer for park department in small public agencies—approves materials and workmanship, authorizes payments, and resolves problems of plan or specification interpretation.

CONSTRUCTION INSURANCE REQUIREMENTS

Park construction can be hazardous to workmen employed by private contractors, park employees carrying out normal duties, and the public using open portions of the park outside of the construction project limits (as well as people who may be injured while in the construction area by mistake or trespass).

PARK AGENCY INSURANCE PROTECTION.   Because the owner of a construction site can be held liable for certain personal injury and property damage instances, it is important that the park agency obtain insurance to protect its interests. Usually the agency is covered by an umbrella policy for the entire government (i.e., the specific local municipality, county, regional government, state government, etc.) for liability. Many states require additional insurance coverage for fire, vandalism, and malicious mischief as part of a property insurance policy as well.

As a courtesy and protection to all the building and construction contractors, it is a good practice to file a copy of all applicable policy certificates with the general contractor.

PRIVATE CONTRACTOR INSURANCE PROTECTION.   Contractors carry certain liability insurance policies because (1) they are required by law, (2) they are stipulated in the contract, and (3) they protect against financial losses that may incur due to injuries to his employees or damages to his property. The cost of this coverage is, of course, passed to the park agency as part of the contracted price for the project. Usually these policies include contractor's public liability and property damage insurance, builder's risk, fire insurance, contractor's contingent liability insurance, contractual liability insurance, fidelity insurance, workman's compensation insurance, motor vehicle, equipment, and machinery insurance, unemployment insurance, old-age, survivors, and disability insurance as well as group accident and hospitalization (and often life) insurance. A detailed explanation of these coverages has been prepared by Clough.*

It is important that park planners verify public insurance responsibilities as well as those legally required for contractors of public work contracts for the state and municipality where the park development is located.

CONSTRUCTION PROGRESS AND QUALITY CONTROL

The construction inspector (public works engineer, inspector or consulting site designer) is authorized to represent the park agency's interests during construction. It is his responsibility to see that the plans and specifications are followed by the contractor.

APPROVAL OF MATERIAL SUBSTITUTION AND WORK ORDER CHANGES.   All revisions and modifications from the original plan and specification must be authorized in writing by the

* Richard H. Clough, *Construction Contracting*, Second Edition, Wiley-Interscience, New York, 1969.

inspector. If the changes are substantial, the park agency is consulted before a decision is made. All parties receive a copy of the written approval. It is important that all changes be carefully documented to facilitate possible future repair, replacement or service requirements.

INSPECTION, MATERIALS TESTING AND APPROVAL.   As construction progresses, it is important to inspect the work prior to concealment. Reinforcing steel must be examined before concrete is poured, underground utilities (electric lines, sewer and water pipe, for example) and structures must be inspected and tested before they are buried. Building frames, wiring, and plumbing must be approved before walls are enclosed. This requires careful coordination and scheduling between the inspector and the contractor so that work can continue un-interrupted and undelayed. Some construction materials, such as concrete and asphalt, must be sampled and tested for durability, stress, and overall strength. The inspector takes uniform samples during installation in the presence of the contractor's project supervisor and submits the materials to field or laboratory tests to see if they conform to the standards specified. Approval of all inspections and tests should be documented in writing with copies sent to the contractor and the park agency.

DETERMINATION OF WORK COMPLETED AND PAYMENTS. To provide wages, materials, and delivery payments, overhead, and other operating funds, the contractors are typically paid a portion of the contract price periodically throughout the construction project. Usually this is done monthly, however it may be done biweekly on large or rapidly moving projects with a demanding completion deadline. The general conditions of the contract documents usually signify how progress estimates and payments are made. The construction inspector is the usual party given the responsibility and authority to measure or estimate the amount of work completed and recommend payment by the owner.

Unit-price contract payments are based on field measurements of work units completed for work such as clearing and grubbing, excavation, fill, linear installation, and paving. Quantities of specific items such as fountains, benches, lights, play apparatus, and nursery stock are counted as they are delivered to the construction site. Both the inspector and contractor may prepare itemized lists and verify the payment request form which is sent to the park agency.

Lump-sum contract payments are based on the estimated percentage of work completed for the necessary work units. For example, a group picnic shelter being built under a public works contract may have 100 percent of the concrete work, 75 percent of the structural framing, and 50 percent of the electrical work done at the end of the first pay period. The inspector and contractor may make independent progress appraisals and adjust any differences of opinion.

An example of a periodic partial payment form for a park construction project is shown in Appendix 10.

A common practice of payment for park projects is to retain a small percent of each partial payment (usually 5 to 10 percent) as a financial guarantee that the work will be completed and in acceptable condition before final approval and payment is made. These deductions are usually stopped when the amount of money retained by the park agency reaches a specified portion of the contract price. This portion should be low enough that it does not cause undue financial hardship to the contractor but high enough that the contractor is encouraged to correct any inadequacies discovered in the work to obtain the retained payment. Five percent of the contract price is commonly withheld.

FINAL ACCEPTANCE AND PAYMENT.   When the contractor completes construction and cleans the project site of all construction equipment, he requests a final inspection by the inspector. Any discrepancies from the contract requirements, unacceptable materials, or poor workmanship must be corrected before final payment is made. Frequently a preliminary inspection is held to bring to the contractor's attention any inadequacies in the work; a follow-up "official inspection" is made with all parties (park agency, contractor, and construction inspector) present.

Notification of final acceptance is sent to the contractor by the park agency on recommendations of the inspector. Final payment includes the balance of the contract price including all retainage withheld from the contractor.

SUMMARY

The development phase of park planning follows the design phase. There are three major steps in development: preconstruction documentation, contracting for the development, and the actual project construction.

Preconstruction documentation requires very careful preparation of construction drawings and specifications that will be used to guide and control construction. These materials are compiled by the site designer, his specification writers, construction detail specialists, and others under his direction. They are assisted by park superintendents, facility operators, program directors, and maintenance specialists who provide advice and recommendations related to their areas.

There is a common competitive-bid process park agencies use to obtain contracting services. Careful control of contracting procedures will result in a contract letting to a qualified contractor at a reasonable price. Development and use of well-written advertisements for bids, instructions to bidders, proposals, and the contract are parts of the development phase that must be given appropriate attention.

The park agency efforts are not over after a contractor is selected. Construction insurance coverage is important to the agency as well as the builder. Construction progress and quality control must be overseen and maintained. The contractor must be supervised as well as be provided with necessary assistance and approval for such things as material substitutions, work order changes, tests, and partial payments.

Final acceptance of the project from the contractor marks the end of the development phase for the park area or facility.

GLOSSARY OF TERMS

Advertisement
The public solicitation for proposals, usually appearing in the classified advertisements section of local newspapers or official gazette; a precontract document. See also Notice to Bidders.

Bid Basis
The manner in which all bidders must submit costs for proposed construction job; always stipulated in the instruction to bidders and usually indicated in the advertisement or notice to bidders.

Cost-Plus-Fixed-Fee. An infrequently used bid basis that pays the winning contractor a set fee for the job in addition to the actual costs of construction.

Cost-Plus-Percentage. A very infrequently used bid basis that pays the winning contractor the actual construction costs plus an additional percent of these costs.

Lump-Sum. A commonly used bid basis for construction that is not easily separated into identifiable work units.

Unit-Price. The most common bid basis for construction when the types of work unit required cannot be determined before the work is completed.

Bid Form
A standard form, prepared by the park agency or consultant, used by all bidders for a construction project that stipulates all bid item and alternative quantities and provides a uniform submission.

Bond
A guarantee that certain obligations will be met.

Bid Bond. A pledge usually backed by a cashier's check for a set amount, that a bidder will accept the contract if it is awarded to him.

Contract Bond or Surety. A guarantee, made by a surety company, that the contractors will complete the work as indicated in the contract.

Payment Bond or Surety. A guarantee, made by a surety company, that the contractor will pay for all his labor, materials, fees, licenses, and other expenses directly related to the job.

Performance Bond or Surety. A guarantee, made by a surety company that the contractor will complete the contract as required.

Competitive Bid Contract

A contract awarded to a contractor who has submitted a secret bid in competition for the job with others; required by law for public works.

Construction Drawings

Graphic illustrations of the physical characteristics of the areas and facilities to be constructed; part of the construction contract documents.

Contract Agreement

The legal covenant signed by the contractor and the park agency that comments both to all the contract documents.

Contract Documents

The contract, specifications, and drawings prepared for the project.

General Conditions

The general specifications for construction of projects; these establish the responsibilities of all parties involved; usually standarized for all public works contracts by the owner-agency. Sometimes duplicated as the general conditions of both the contract and specifications.

Instructions to Bidders

Detailed directions about bid submission and contract awarding procedures and project information given to bidders; a precontract document.

Notice of Award

An official written notification to the successful bidder of a public works contract that he was awarded the contract.

Notice to Bidders

A public notice from the park agency that it is accepting bids for a contract, usually posted in a common location in a public building and submitted to commercial trade periodicals, official government serial reports, and other publications; a precontract document. See also Advertisement.

Notice to Proceed

An official written notification to the contractor authorizing him to begin construction.

Proposal

Written offer by a bidder to complete the project established in the contract documents; the proposal form is usually standarized for public works.

Public Works
All construction projects funded by government support, that is, all public park agency construction.

Specifications
Written directions of required workmanship and quality of materials necessary to complete the construction project; part of the construction contract documents.

   Descriptive Specifications. Most commonly used type of construction specification; describes composition and quality of materials, construction process, and standards in detail.

   General Specifications. See General Conditions.

   Performance Specifications. Written descriptions of the required achievements of certain bid items; frequently used for contracts acquiring machinery, vehicles, or other manufactured equipment.

   Reference Specifications. Standard specifications for materials or workmanship that have been developed by a governmental agency, professional or technical associations, or manufacturing or research institute.

   Technical Specifications. Written descriptions of the special procedures and materials of the particular project under contract, usually listed in chronological order of the construction.

BIBLIOGRAPHY

Abbett, Robert W. *Engineering Contracts and Specifications,* Fourth Edition. Wiley, New York, 1963.

Clough, Richard H. *Construction Contracting,* Second Edition. Wiley-Interscience, New York, 1969.

Cohen, Henry A. *Public Construction Contracts and the Law,* F. W. Dodge Corp., New York, 1961.

Dunham, Clarence W. and Robert D. Young. *Contracts, Specifications, and Law for Engineers.* McGraw-Hill, New York, 1958.

Lewis, Jack R. *Construction Specifications.* Prentice-Hall, Inc., Englewood Cliffs, N.J., 1975.

Mead, Daniel W. and Joseph R. Akerman. *Contracts, Specifications and Engineering Relations,* Third Edition. McGraw-Hill, New York, 1956.

Rosen, Harold J. *Construction Specification Writing.* Wiley-Interscience, New York, 1974.

Rutledge, Albert J. *Anatomy of a Park.* McGraw-Hill, New York, 1971.

5
actualization

The construction of physical facilities in a park is the culminating implementation step of physical planning for the park. This provides the setting, or stage, for the recreational activities. Previously, this development was considered to be the extent of the park department's obligation to park users. Today, however, most park agencies recognize that their real responsibility is to provide opportunities for quality recreational experiences, not just the facilities. This responsibility requires that the various plans and controls necessary to provide the proposed recreation experiences be carefully prepared, coordinated, implemented, evaluated, and revised as needed. This is actualization of the park planning process.

ACTUALIZATION OVERVIEW

The actualization phase of park planning is not chronologically distinct from the predesign, design, and development phases of the process. These previously discussed phases are procedurally ordered because of the logical progression of the physical planning and implementation steps required to provide a physical facility. Actualization—*making sure that all experience determinants, nonphysical as well as physical, are appropriate for the proposed recreation activity*—is incorporated throughout the entire park planning process, before and concurrent with the

83

physical planning phases and continuing after completion of facility development. This shown in the chart, Figure 5-1.

It is this phase of park planning that represents the contribution and achievements of the various nondesign park and recreation specialists in principal authoritative roles, underscoring their additional assisting efforts in preparation of the physical plans. It is as experience actualizers that these specialists are truly park planners.

Actualization requires merging of the complementary park management processes of planning, control, and evaluation. Plans, control documents, and evaluation instruments are the tools and media of this process.

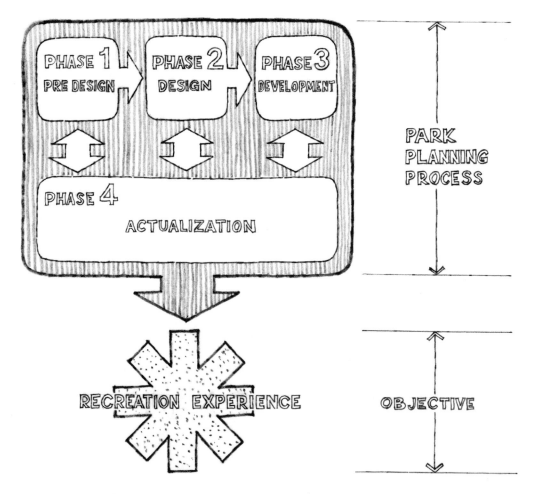

Figure 5.1

Predesign, design, and development are chronologically sequential in the park planning process. Actualization is necessarily coincidential as well as subsequent to these phases to successfully provide the intended recreation experiences.

PLANS

A plan is a predetermined course of action over a specified period of time representing a projected response to an anticipated environment in order to accomplish a specific set of adaptive objectives.* A plan has three characteristics:

1.   It must involve the future while simultaneously considering past and present experience.

2.   It must involve actions.

3.   It must involve decisions to take future actions at the time the plan is authorized.†

While each plan has specific objectives with a special emphasis, all should be directed toward the common purpose of assuring the means (i.e., human and physical resources and ancillary support services) to provide a recreational experience of a predetermined quality.

The number and intricacy of these plans are directly related to the complexity of the recreation experience delivery systems. In addition to physical plans, program, functional, and fiscal plans (see Chapter 1) are commonly prepared to assure goal actualization. Examples of these plans are discussed later in this chapter.

CONTROLS

Control documents complement plans by describing acceptable standards or parameters for development, operation, maintenance, and use of activity resources. A control document may define or establish standards for the quality of performance, service, or development; protect park assets from wastage, misuse, abuse, or loss; set limits of responsibility and authority; direct planning concerns; and facilitate evaluation of results.‡

The ultimate controls for park planning are the goals and objectives of the specific park as well as those for the entire system "controlled" by the park department.

One of the values of a good control document is the ability to establish effective end results within a frequently repetitive pattern. A good control document provides guidance without demanding unquestioning compliance and permits imaginative decision making applied to recurring problems or situations affecting the recreational experiences to be provided. Examples of park control documents include policies, procedures, rules and regulations, performance standards, agency specifications,

* Robert G. Murdick, "Nature of Planning and Plans," *Advanced Management Journal,* 30:4, October, 1965, p. 38.
† Albert Davis, "Planning—Elements and Problems," *Advanced Management Journal,* 32:3, July, 1967, p. 39.
‡ William T. Jerone III, *Executive Control: The Catalyst,* Wiley, New York, 1961, pp. 29–34.

audits, inventories, job descriptions, operations manuals, reservations and permits, budgets, and certification requirements. Sometimes many of these, such as personnel standards, are handled by other departments instead of the park agency.

Preparation and utilization of these control documents are essential to the experiential purpose of park planning. While not plans, they are fundamental elements of the actualization phase of park planning. Without these controls, the entire park planning process would be truncated short of success.

EVALUATION INSTRUMENTS

It is necessary to have some means of appraising the efforts to meet the goals and objectives of the park department. This is part of the overall management process, of course, but there is also salient purpose for evaluating the various components of the park planning process. Planning, control, and evaluation are interwoven processes. Evaluation is based on control and affects plans. It provides the means for looping back through the park planning process and insuring that the process is dynamic and continuous. An evaluation instrument may be quite simple or very elaborate. It may be applied unconsciously, by paper and pencil forms, or even statistically documented through a complex computer analysis. To be effective, any evaluation must (1) be based on a well-prepared control, (2) identify and appraise significant measurable qualities or characteristics of the effort or situation, and (3) provide a foundation for improvements.

Use of an evaluation instrument is important because it implements the three essential steps of proper park plan or program effectiveness determination: (1) comparison of measurable elements or attributes critical for success to established criteria, (2) evaluation of identifiable deviations from these standards or expectations, and (3) recognition of remedial or new measures to achieve improved results.

The techniques of evaluation are as varied as the needs to appraise a situation—checklist evaluations, supervisory evaluations, peer evaluations, self-evaluations, program participant evaluations, cost/benefit analyses, environmental impact or deterioration monitoring, inspections, cost effectiveness accounting, efficiency studies, and survey sampling are just a few examples.

Actualization is inherent in park planning since it affects all the roles of a park agency. Park planners are involved in the preparation of innumerable plans and the supportive controls and evaluation means for these plans to be successful.

KEY PARK PLANNING
ACTUALIZATION COMPONENTS

It is necessary to coordinate all the quality determinants of a recreational experience. There are four primary factors to be considered in the actualization process: the activity, the participants, the physical resources, and the human resources.

ACTIVITY FACTORS

There are several important plans, controls, and evaluations directly related to the activity that affect the subsequent physical planning for the activity facility or area. *Program planning* should be based on the activity analysis and should be well along prior to physical planning because of the special program needs that must be included in the design. Determination of the experience opportunities offered for each activity is the initial element of program planning (see Chapter 2, The Predesign Phase). These program plans are complemented by program manuals, guides, schedules, performance standards and other controls. Various program effectiveness evaluation techniques are used to identify weaknesses and implement improvements.

PARTICIPANT FACTORS

The participant is the benefiting recipient of the recreational experience being planned, thus there are several factors concerning these individuals that are important to actualize the quality desired for their experiences.

There are pre-experience plans such as public relations and information programs as well as controls (fees and charges, reservations, and permits) that are frequently braced by skill competency requirements verified by mandating tests (i.e., evaluation).

Concurrent with the recreational occasion are several participant-directed factors that must be anticipated and provided for: some participants benefit from *supervision services*, especially children or other special populations; *safety, emergency, health, and sanitary programs,* including lifeguard, first aid, search and rescue procedures, sanitation manuals and inspections, and other provisions for the protection of public welfare are also included. Regular inspections should insure compliance with all applicable codes and regulations. Chapter 11 discusses these welfare concerns in detail.

PHYSICAL RESOURCE FACTORS

Physical resources include the natural resources that comprise the parksite, the activity facility or area (man-made resources), and the utilities and attendant mechanical retinue to sustain the activity.

NATURAL RESOURCES.   Natural resource-directed actualization concerns are related to either self-replenishing resources and site characteristics or nonrenewable resources and site qualities.

Management plans, controls, and impact evaluations are essential to the self-replenishing natural park environment. Examples of these include water supply protection and management plans, pollution controls, fish and wildlife management plans, forestland management plans, natural hazards inventory and control program, vector control program, environmental impact monitoring programs, and others.

Nonrenewable natural site qualities may require stringent controls and protection programs to insure continuance of essential activity requisites. Because of the possible irreparable consequences, many federal and state controls have been established to help planners identify and study alternative effects on these resources. Environmental impact statements (EIS's), required of most federal projects as well as by many states, document these situations. Other actualization procedures affecting nonrenewable resources include preparation of soil erosion and sedimentation control plans, scenic and aesthetic protection plans, and extraction controls and landscape restoration plans for surface and subsurface mining.

Each of these must be based on the fundamental goals and objectives originally established for the park and must support the experiential requirements of the activity analysis.

ACTIVITY AREAS AND FACILITIES.   The development and maintenance of activity areas must be carefully coordinated to insure that all efforts are complementary to the proposed experience. The physical plans and controls necessary (e.g., agency specifications, general development plan, construction details and specifications, and competitive bid procedures) have been explained in Chapters 3 and 4. The functional plans and controls include maintenance zoning, maintenance manuals and specifications, schedules, and special contractual services procedures.

UTILITIES AND MECHANICAL EQUIPMENT.   Many activity developments require special utilities (swimming pool filtration and disinfection plants, ice skating rink refrigeration plants, ski lifts, and snowmaking facilities are some examples) in addition to the basic sanitary utilities such as water treatment and wastewater treatment and disposal plants. These utilities must be designed and installed according to carefully prepared specifications and operated and serviced according to detailed manuals.

In addition to these utilities, machinery are also used in the maintenance and operation of activity facilities. Maintenance equipment includes trucks, tractors, mowers, trimmers, scrubbers, vacuums, clippers, compactors, spreaders, and pavers. Operations equipment includes cash registers, typewriters, copiers, calculators, recorders, public address systems, tele-phones, radios, and other service equipment. To be used effectively and safely, operations and service manuals, inspection forms, and amortization/use records may be prepared and used for these.

HUMAN RESOURCE FACTORS

There are two factors relative to recreation service personnel that are commonly recognized: employee performance (preparation, control, and evaluation) and employee remuneration and benefits. The latter aspect, which is composed of wage and salary schedules, promotion criteria, collective bargaining programs, workman's compensation, medical insurance, occupational safety and health programs, and other personnel management programs, does affect employee job satisfaction and incentive to work. But this aspect is considered to be only secondary in contributing to actualization of planned recreation experiences. It is common for a large portion of the personnel working in park agencies to be part-time employees, consultants, one-time program specialists, and volunteers. The majority of these individuals are not affected by the agency salary and employee benefits package.

The most important human resource factor to experience actualization is personnel performance preparation, control, and evaluation. Recreation services provided by people in a variety of positions—supervisors, activity leaders, custodians, maintenance men, receptionists, reservation clerks, lifeguards, guides, program specialists, accountants, rangers, wardens, greens-keepers, instructors, and other specialists—have a direct affect upon the quality of the recreational experience offered to park users. *The preparation, control, and evaluation of human resources are just as essential as the comparable efforts established for the physical resources of a park.*

Preparation plans and programs for park personnel are extremely varied. College programs are available from the associate degree level to the doctorate. Vocational schools offer speciality training and correspondence courses are available in a variety of topics. Park departments provide orientations, workshops, and short courses as part of in-service employee, seasonal, and volunteer training programs. Implicit in all these opportunities should be the understanding that personnel preparation is a joint responsibility of the individual and the agency.

Control is achieved by job descriptions, personnel manuals, and performance standards. These are effectuated by in-spections, observations, rating sessions, and other techniques for performance evaluations.

It is beyond the scope of this book to develop the full personnel development process. This has been the function of many excellent previous books and such an attempt here would be only an abridged duplication of their fuller efforts. What is important to be emphasized here is the significance human resources and services have upon the ultimate product of the park planning process—the recreation experience.

SUMMARY

The actualization phase of park planning is essential to interlink all the experience determinants, nonphysical as well as physical, into a complementary unit. This process must precede, coincide, and follow the physical planning phases (design and development) of the park planning effort. Actualization combines planning, control and evaluation of activity attributes, participants, physical resources, and human resources to assure successful attainment of the recreational experience by the participant as established in the activity analysis.

GLOSSARY OF TERMS

Actualization
A continuous process of assuring that all experience determinants are appropriate for the proposed recreational activity.

Control Documents
Written guidelines to standardize routine, repetitive materials or services; protect park assets, set limits of responsibilities and authority; direct planning; facilitate evaluation of efforts.

Evaluation Instrument
A device used to appraise measurable efforts to meet established objectives set by definitive standards or a similar control.

Plan
A predetermined course of action over a specified future period of time in order to meet set objectives.

Program
The coordinated effort of recreational service agencies to organize, administer, guide, lead, direct, or offer resources for all those spontaneous, organized, routine, special, recurring, or intermittent activities that can or may occur at a park*.

BIBLIOGRAPHY

Davis, Albert. "*Planning—Elements and Problems,*" *Advanced Management Journal,* 32:3, July, 1967, pp. 39–44.

Hjelte, George and Jay S. Shivers. *Public Administration of Recreational Services.* Lea & Febiger, Philadelphia, 1972.

* Definition of program paraphrased from an extensive explanation of program in George Hjelte and Jay S. Shivers, *Public Administration of Recreational Services,* Lea & Febiger, Philadelphia, 1972, p. 437.

Jerome, William T. *Executive Control: The Catalyst.* Wiley, New York, 1961.

Maintenance Standards and Cost Analysis. Dallas Park and Recreation Department, Park Maintenance and Development Division, Dallas, Texas (mimeo), n.d., ca. 1975.

Meyer, Harold D., Charles K. Brightbill, and H. Douglas Sessoms. *Community Recreation, A Guide to Its Organization,* Fourth Edition. Prentice-Hall, Inc., Englewood Cliffs, N.J., 1969.

Murdick, Robert G. "Nature of Planning and Plans," *Advanced Management Journal,* 30:4, October, 1965, pp. 36–46.

Murphy, James F., John G. Williams, E. William Niepoth, and Paul D. Brown. *Leisure Service Delivery System: A Modern Perspective.* Lea & Febiger, Philadelphia, 1973.

U.S. Department of the Interior, National Park Service. *Activity Standards.* U.S. Government Printing Office, Washington, D.C., 1972.

U.S. Department of the Interior, National Park Service. *Management Policies.* Washington, D.C., April, 1975.

part two
support
provisions

Physical planning of park support provisions—circulation, lighting, water systems, wastewater systems, solid waste, health, safety, and emergency provisions—are understandably the domain of those experts who have the special training and competencies required. Many members of these special professions are required to be licensed by the state to protect the health, safety, and welfare of the public.

Because of this need for special training, these members of the park planning team may be unaware of important considerations and needs of the other aspects of recreation experience planning. Conversely, other members of the planning effort may have been reluctant to question the seemingly uncompromising requirements made upon the rest of the planning efforts by the "unalterable" plans of these specialists.

Part Two is offered as an opportunity to all members of the park planning team—designers and nondesigners alike—to appreciate the basic planning considerations for these various support facilities and systems, so that all may understand better how their contributions must be interwoven with the contributions of other specialists and so that the total planning effort is truly an interdisciplinary collaboration, not just a compilation of separate professions.

6
circulation

The circulation systems of a park form the infrastructure or framework that links all the activity and support areas together. There can be many types of circulation systems and subsystems in a park: (1) vehicular roads and parking lots, (2) pedestrian walks, paths, and trails, (3) equestrian trails, (4) bicycles or ORV (off road vehicle) routes, and so on.

This chapter discusses only vehicular and pedestrian circulation because they are universally used in urban and rural parks.

VEHICULAR CIRCULATION

Park roads and parking areas are the most significant of the circulation systems. They have the largest impact on the use and service of activity centers. Vehicular routes require more site design and engineering talent than other circulation systems. They are also inherently the most dangerous intrusion into a recreational setting.

FUNCTION AND PLANNING CONSIDERATIONS

The function of park roads is to provide corridors for the controlled movement of automobiles and other vehicles. Park roads are necessary to channel this traffic flow for proper access

95

and vehicle storage, to protect the natural resources of the park, to serve as edges between use areas, and to protect the park user.

ACCESS AND PARKING.   Park roads are essential elements of large parks. Roads provide access for the activity centers and developments and link activity areas. Because of the special natural resource requirements of certain activities, several development centers utilized by the same recreationists are often located considerable distance apart. Park roads provide the connection, or linkage, between them.

PROTECTION OF RESOURCES.   Well-planned park roads can protect the actual natural conditions that attracts the park visitor. Park roads, unlike commercial routes, should not be imposed on the land to conform to optimum freight-carrying vehicle requirements. Traveling park roads should be part of the recreational experience of the park. Outstanding natural park elements should be valued highly and protected when automobile routes are planned.

PROTECTION OF PARK USERS.   Separation of vehicular traffic from pedestrian traffic—trails, paths, and walks—is important. Roadways and parking lots are preactivity support facilities and should be located outside the nucleus of the activity area or where pedestrian crossings are minimized.

   Park roads should be constructed for the motorist's safety as well. Sharp curves, blind intersections (i.e., those with visual obstructions), extremely steep grades, congestion, improper pavement materials, and insufficient width are unsafe park road situations that should be avoided.

VEHICULAR CIRCULATION SUBSYSTEMS

Park road subsystems may be classified simply by use—either public-use roads or service roads.

   Public use roads are open to park users. These roads are classified as either primary or secondary park roads.

   Primary roads are usually two way, wider, and carry more traffic than secondary roads. They may be major park entrances, through roads, access routes to high use activity areas, or they may act as collector routes for several secondary park roads.

   Secondary roads may be one way or two way, often narrow, and carry light traffic. They may service a single activity, special-use area, or provide necessary internal circulation within such an area. Examples of secondary park roads include campground loop roads, picnic area roads, interpretive roads, and short roadways to individual parking lots.

   Nonpublic service roads are essential, but often unnoticed by park users. These roads are supplementary to the public park roads. They provide access for maintenance and operational activities of the park staff when public roads are not available. Because these roads carry only staff vehicles, pavement construction and geometric considerations are less demanding. Service roads are often low-grade controlled access extensions of public roads used to provide suitable access for emergency or service vehicles at swimming areas, shelters, comfort stations, fire lanes, watchtowers or utility structures (e.g., pumphouses, control gates, transformers, or treatment plants) as well as circulation to and within maintenance complexes. Figure 6.1 shows the infrastructure of a park public use and service road system.

ROUTE CONFIGURATION.   Public use park roads can be classified into various kinds of route configurations. These are determined by the relationship of the road to the entire park, to the individual activity areas, and the type of traffic. The configuration of the vehicular path through a park can have a major influence on user control, access, safety, and convenience. The impact on the park is often greater if an improper traffic

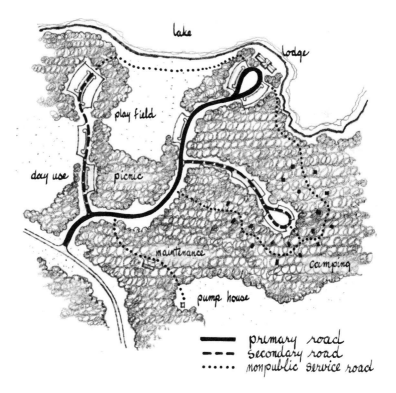

Figure 6.1

Park vehicular circulation routes include primary and secondary public use roads as well as nonpublic service roads.

plan is used for a primary park road because of the larger number of vehicles traveling the road at greater speeds.

There are four major park road configurations: spinal, peripheral, terminating, and loop. Often a well-designed, complex road system will combine several of these or their variations.

A primary spinal road provides access through the park for nonpark traffic as well as park users. It always offers more than one entrance to the park. Often a spinal road is not exclusively administered by the park agency. Development, maintenance, and law enforcement may be functions of other governmental agencies. Park activity areas may be located on either side of the primary spinal road. These areas are serviced by adjacent parking or secondary feeder roads. This road plan may divide the park into separate activity areas and encourage conflicting transient users. Park users must use this public route to drive from one park area to another (see Figure 6.2). Variations of the spinal road configuration are called *meandering* and *ring* systems. Both have multiple park entrances with through traffic, and both separate activity areas with a primary vehicular circulation corridor. Figures 6.3 and 6.4 are examples of these road plans.

A peripheral road also may have multiple park entrances and through traffic but does not have the added disadvantage of separating most activity areas with a primary road (see Figure 6.5).

The following configurations are similar because each usually has only one park entrance. This eliminates nonrecreational

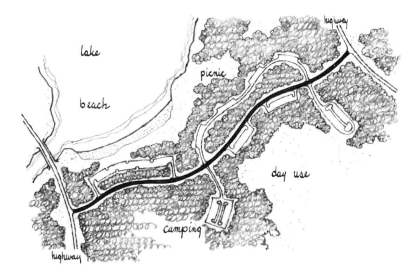

Figure 6.2

A primary spinal road may cause conflicts between park traffic and nonpark through traffic as well as separating activity areas.

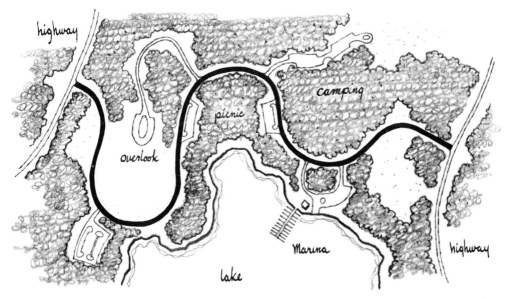

Figure 6.3

A meandering road is often just a variation of the spinal road and has similar problems in a park.

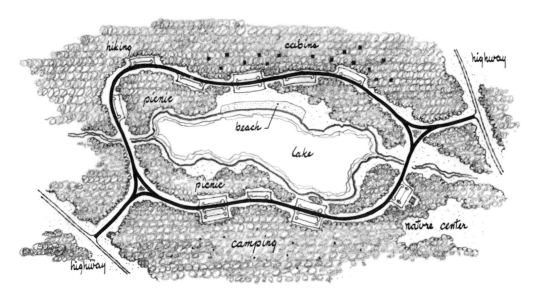

Figure 6.4

A ring road, a modification of spinal road, is frequently used to encircle a major natural element of the park such as a lake, mountain, or other unique areas.

99

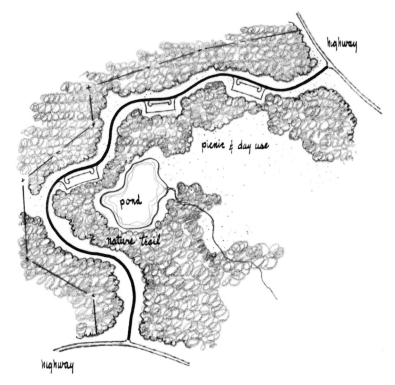

highway

picnic & day use

pond

nature trail

highway

Figure 6.5

A peripheral road is located near park boundaries with all the activity areas on the same side.

through traffic use of the park roads. These schemes are used in parks or park areas where access control is important or in parks small enough that a single entrance is adequate.

The terminating road (cul-de-sac, dead end) is often used as a primary park entrance road from an outside public road at small parks or as a secondary feeder road to activity areas having centralized parking. It is a two-way road ending at the parking. Figure 6.6 shows a terminating road used in a park.

A loop road will begin as a two-way entrance but may become one-way at the start of the loop(s). Secondary loop roads are often used in activity areas that have dispersed small parking lots such as campgrounds and family picnic grounds. Interpretive roads are often one-way loops commencing from an interpretive center. Figure 6.7 shows a series of campground loop roads.

An open-loop or J-pattern is a variation of the loop that often is used as a two-way, single entrance, peripheral system to provide maximum access control with good vehicular/activity relationships. Figure 6.8 illustrates an application of the open loop. Secondary roads may branch from a single-entrance park road with fewer traffic problems than if they were connected to a multiple-entrance park road.

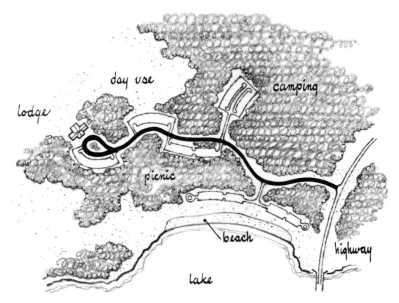

Figure 6.6

A terminating road provides the only entrance into an activity area or park.

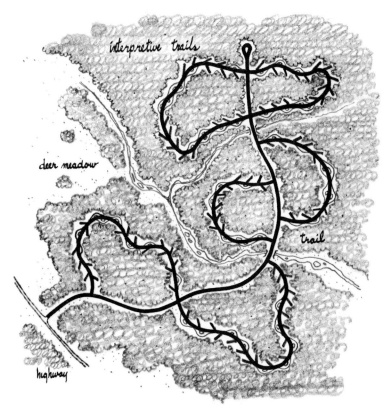

Figure 6.7

Loop roads are often used for internal circulation in special park areas such as campgrounds.

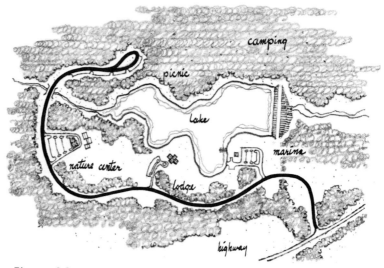

Figure 6.8

An open loop road, or partial ring, combines many of the characteristics of both ring and terminating roads.

ROADWAYS

The wearing surface of park roads is known as the roadway. It must be suited to the use of the road, the volume of traffic carried, and must be compatible to the adjacent activity areas. The use of the road, development norm, and budget determine what type of roadway is used. Primary park roads are often heavy duty; secondary and service roads may not be as improved. Eight generic roadway classes are described below: cleared, cleared and grubbed, scarified, unbonded aggregate, asphalt surface treatment, penetration, asphaltic concrete, and portland cement concrete. While many federal and state roadway specifications are available for each of these roadway classes, this general discussion illustrates their major distinctions and applications.

Cleared roadways have not had any roadbed work done. No changes in the existing grade have been made. Road alignment is usually determined by avoiding impassable barriers such as mature trees, large boulders, or waterways. Only minimal brush-and-limb clearing is done to provide a passable right-of-way for vehicles. Indigenous herbaceous vegetation is usually permitted to cover the roadway to help prevent erosion rutting, ditching, or washouts. It may or may not be periodically mowed. These roads are often usable only during dry seasons.

This roadway is used for very low cost, low-maintenance access to back-country management stations that require regular but infrequent visits (e.g., resource data monitoring stations, control points, automatic beacons, etc.).

A cleared roadway is predominantly used as a service road. With agency approval, some outdoorsmen have established and utilized cleared roads for back-country resource-based activities such as fishing, rock climbing, and rapid water canoeing. Only four-wheel drive, high-axle, or all-terrain vehicles are suited for cleared roadways.

Cleared and grubbed roadways are similar to cleared roadways except that more care has been taken to determine alignment. Smaller trees in the proposed roadway are cut down and their roots grubbed clear. Small boulders are pushed aside and the cavities are rough filled. Small streams are forded or bridged with simple structures. Cleared and grubbed roads are straighter because many of these barriers are removed but often the road still follows existing slopes.

These roads often provide access along park property boundaries, fence lines, utility right-of-ways to service structures, and for other management areas that are periodically but infrequently visited and have a more direct corridor requirement.

Cleared and grubbed roadways are frequently used by hikers, trail bicyclists, snowmobilers, and other off-road vehicle riders, equestrians, snowshoers, cross-country skiers, and other recreationists seeking access. Multiple use of such roadways is acceptable if each use is compatible to the primary function of the road and other secondary uses and does not cause undue deterioration to the wearing surface.

Scarified roadways are often constructed in areas having subsoils or parent materials physically suitable for the wearing surface of a road. After the road has been cleared of all vegetation, roots, and other debris, all the organic soil is removed. Steep road slopes are minimized by cut or fill (of nonorganic matter) using local material immediately available. The wearing surface is formed by scarifying the subsoil (clay, gravel or loose rock).

The quality of the scarified wearing surface depends on the characteristics of local materials. Many "dirt roads" are very good routes for low-volume, lightweight traffic, but many have the disadvantages of being impassable during rainy periods, may be quite dusty during dry periods, and—if the wearing surface is composed of sharp hard stone—can be very hard on tires.

Roads of this type can be used by most conventional passenger cars and recreational vehicles on a limited sustained daily basis, weather permitting. But if access to an area or facility must be available without fail, this type of road should not be considered. Scarified roads are adequate for service access for routine management operations. Because it is the simplest roadway usable by conventional vehicles, it often provides access to rustic or semiprimitive recreation activity areas by the public.

The following roadways are classified as improved, all-weather surfaces with especially prepared load-bearing pavements. All are usable by conventional vehicles.

Unbonded aggregate roadways have wearing surfaces several inches thick made of compacted gravel, granulated slag, crushed stone, river stone, or rock. The roadway should be constructed on a well-prepared nonorganic base. It provides an acceptable, economical, all-weather road for low-speed, low-volume, lightweight traffic on a sustained daily basis. If the aggregate used is a soft stone such as limestone, traffic may cause a dust problem during dry periods. Sprinkling with water, salt, oil, or another wetting agent may reduce the amount of dust if it is a nuisance to travelers.

Unbonded aggregate is an acceptable service road surface for maintenance roads to treatment plants, water pumps, storage tanks, fire towers, and other operational facilities requiring all-weather access.

It is an acceptable roadway for secondary two-way public-use park roads for campground loops, family picnic areas, interpretative or scenic roads, as well as one-way roads, if the use is to be all-weather, low speed, low volume, and lightweight. The activity areas serviced by these roadways are usually rustic, with low development norms.

Asphalt surface treatment roadways have a heavy petroleum oil-soil wearing surface made by applying a slow-curing liquid asphalt to a nonorganic earthen base. The oil reduces water absorption and provides a firm dustless surface. Often a blotter covering of hard, sharp, fine aggregate such as sand, pea gravel, or stone chips is spread over the oil. The wearing surface is usually less than one inch thick. A surface treatment is not a pavement in itself.

A surface treatment roadway is a low-cost, all-weather, dustless road that is skid resistant if clean. However, it may bleed the tar-like oil on very hot days. This will coat tires and splash cars if the cover aggregate is too light or thinly covering the asphalt.

It is sometimes used as an alternate roadway for loose aggregate roadway park situations.

Penetration macadam roadways are made by spraying liquid asphalt to penetrate between mineral aggregates placed in three layers. Each layer of stone (which is progressively smaller from the bottom layer to the top) is sprayed with liquid asphalt. The asphalt is then covered with intermediate-size aggregates. This pavement is very stable because of the mechanical interlock of the large aggregate and the binding coats of asphalt. A penetration wearing surface treatment may be used on top of the macadam. Penetration macadam roadways are good all-weather, skid-resistant, dustless roads for medium to heavily trafficked park roads. These roadways are sometimes called "built up" roadways because they are often built up in layers. These may be applied over a period of several years if there is not major surface deterioration. They are suitable for any park road that does not carry heavy traffic.

Asphaltic concrete roadways (plant mixtures) are made from carefully prepared and heated asphalt, coarse aggregate, fine aggregate, and mineral dust mixes that are transported from the mixing plant and laid while still hot. Hot mix pavements are usually constructed in layers over a firm subbase. The base course may be composed of crushed stone, slag, gravel and sand, or it may be asphalt bound. A full-depth asphalt pavement has asphalt mixtures for all courses above the subgrade. A one-inch hot-mix wearing course is laid over the load-bearing courses to provide a smooth driving surface. Asphaltic concrete roadways are ideal for heavy primary park roads.

Portland cement concrete roadways are made from a mixture of portland cement, aggregate, and water. The pavement may be reinforced with steel rods. The thickness of the concrete slab depends on the bearing strength of the subgrade and the estimated traffic load. Concrete roads may be set in rigid, removable forms, or may be placed over the subbase by slipforming the pavement. Concrete roads are rigid and will not conform to any foundation settling whereas flexible asphalt roads will conform to this movement.

This type of road is most often reserved only for those park situations requiring a rigid pavement or an extremely heavy-duty (reinforced) load-bearing surface,

Table 6.1 is a summary chart of park roadway use.

SIGNIFICANT PARK ROAD-DESIGN CONSIDERATIONS

Park designers and engineers specify park road characteristics according to criteria established by agency construction standards or professional judgment based on situational conditions. The following park road design considerations are useful when a park professional without design training consults with his project designer.

ROAD WIDTH.   Park roads are composed of the roadway (traffic lanes) and adjacent shoulders. The width of the *roadway* depends on a combination of factors: traffic volume, safety, type of terrain, engineering requirements, design speed, type of vehicles using the road, function of the road, and, of course, administrative guidelines of the agency. Roadways that are too narrow can be mildly distracting to outright dangerous to the users. The pavement edge may weaken and crack or, under heavy stress, break down if vehicle wheels are constantly forced to travel on this outer edge. This situation can increase park user dissatisfaction and maintenance expenditures significantly. A roadway that is too wide for its intended use is not only wasteful and expensive but can also diminish the park experience because the incongruity of the road development and the recreationists' anticipated experience norm for the activity.

Table 6.1
Roadway types for park-designated road functions

Park Road System 1. Amount of Use 2. Function of Road 3. (Vehicle Required)	Roadways							
	Cleared	Cleared and Grubbed	Scarified	Unbonded Aggregate	Asphalt Surface Treatment	Penetration Macadam	Asphaltic Concrete	Portland Cement Concrete
Service Roads 1. Periodic, infrequent (less than monthly) 2. Inspection 3. (4WD, ORV)	*							
1. Periodic, infrequent (monthly) 2. Inspection, maintenance 3. (pickup, light truck, conventional auto)		*	*					
1. Regular, frequent (weekly) 2. Maintenance 3. (Most trucks and autos)			*	*	*			
1. Daily 2. Maintenance 3. (Any truck or auto)				*	*	*	*	*
Public Roads *Secondary* 1. Very infrequent (2–3 trips/month) 2. Access to backcountry activities 3. (4WD, land ORV's)	*	*						
1. Infrequent or very light traffic (less than 100/day) 2. Access to rustic use areas 3. (Pickup, high-axle auto)			*	*				
1. Regular light-medium traffic (up to 1000/day) 2. Access to moderately developed use areas. Scenic drives 3. (Rec. vehicles, conventional autos)					*	*	*	
Primary 1. Daily/medium to heavy traffic (more than 1000/day) 2. Access to major day-use areas 3. (Conventional autos)					*	*	*	*

Primary park roads should have a 20- to 22-foot (rarely 24 foot)-wide roadway and 3- to 5-foot shoulders. Two-way secondary park roads should have a 18- to 20-foot-wide roadway and 2- to 3-foot shoulders. One-way secondary park roads should have a roadway not less than 12 feet wide and 2-foot-wide shoulders.

Nonpublic roads should have the minimum width necessary to carry the appropriate vehicles to serve the road's purpose.

Shoulders provide structural support and drainage for the roadway, as well as emergency space for disabled vehicles. Shoulders along park roads should not be used for parallel parking. In a cut situation with high banks or a fill situation with a deep drop, shoulders also provide a psychological safety buffer between the roadway and the road edge. Sometimes the shoulder at a fill is often constructed wider than the shoulder at a cut for this reason.

Shoulder pavement depends on the road classification, use, adjacent activities, and the immediate landscape. Road shoulders are the transition from the roadway surface to the adjacent landscape. Where appropriate, a stablized turf shoulder kept short is quite adequate and visually merges with the herbaceous vegetation next to the road.

In sparsely vegetative areas, a shoulder of compacted crushed aggregate common to the park landscape is more suitable. In appropriate situations such as in arid regions, the coarse-grained, inorganic soils present may be scarified into shoulders.

Along very busy primary park roads it may be necessary to provide improved shoulder surfacing such as compacted aggregate, surface treatment, or macadam. The shoulders should be functional without being obvious.

ROAD GRADIENT.   The design steepness of a park road, known as gradient or profile, is determined by the type of vehicles using the road, the roadway pavement material and construction techniques, design speed, and the existing land forms. The conventional automobile normally can negotiate steeper gradients than can camper vans, buses, or towed vehicle units (such as vehicles with boats or camper trailers). Many main-tenance vehicles (such as refuse and dump trucks) also must be considered when the road gradient is established. Those road pavements with an unbonded base and wearing course are not as satisfactory on steep grades as the macadam, asphaltic concrete, or portland cement concrete pavements. Slow park speed limits often prevent a heavy vehicle from getting an accelerated run for a steep grade. The land forms traversed by a park road connecting activity areas often determine the gradient, within established design limits. For cross-surface drainage, 0.5 percent should be considered as a minimum grade.

The gradient of a primary park road used by heavily loaded trucks (such as supply trucks, tractor-trailers, and delivery trucks servicing park restaurants, lodges, or other supply consuming developments) should ideally not exceed 3 percent. This is also true for primary or secondary roads serving large boat marinas and large recreational vehicle campgrounds.

Park roads used by conventional automobiles, pickups, light trucks, and small travel camper or boat trailers should normally have a 6 to 7 percent desirable maximum grade, but grades up to 10 percent are acceptable for short distances to better fit the road to the existing landscape and avoid excessive cut or fill.

Whenever the gradient of a road changes more than 0.5 percent, a transitional vertical curve is recommended. At hilltops these are called crest curves; in valleys they are called sag curves. Aesthetically, by reducing the number of vertical curves and avoiding the use of short length curves, designers eliminate extreme changes in gradient that appear visually abrupt and disjointed. Short humps or dips in a park road profile are also undesirable.

ROAD ALIGNMENT AND INTERSECTIONS.   Park roads linking external public access roads to activity areas or linking activity areas within the park should be as direct as possible without disrupting intermediate uses. Road circulation patterns must be efficient but also must conform to the natural patterns of the landform and vegetation. A carefully designed circumventing park road around a steep hill or mature tree stand, while not as direct as a straight road, is often a better park road. The road location is often controlled by factors beyond change—for example, the best use area for specific activities, unique areas, lakes and other water bodies, swamps, areas subject to landslide, bridge sites, and land ownership. Linking (or avoiding) these critical positions is done with either tangent or circular road alignments. Tangents are straight and totally predictable—often desirable for clear orientation. They are quite suited to flat terrain or where the predominate man-made patterns are angular. A circular alignment may be more interesting because it brings more of the landscape into view, provides a changing visual panorama to the driver and encourages driver alertness. Usually park designers combine these elements into short tangent-long curve alignments or continuous curvilinear alignments, using given topography and other controls to establish basic direction.

The smallest curve and road intersections should never have a turning radius of less than 55 feet. Those roads used by tractor trailers and towed vehicle units such as camper or boat trailers should not have curves with radii of less than 80 feet.

When a two-way road is reduced into a one-way loop the traffic should flow to the right to prevent crossing lanes. This intersection should be at an acute angle to the right of the original alignment. Intersections of secondary roads to primary roads should be as near as possible to a right angle, permitting adequate visual clearance in both traffic directions.

VISUAL CLEARANCE.   The visual clearance zone along a park road is the area within which all visual obstructions should be eliminated so that drivers as well as nonmotoring park users are visually aware of the potential conflict between traffic and the pedestrian. The visual clearance zone is determined by the road alignment, profile, use and speed limit, type of activity area adjacent to the road, and land forms and density of vegetation stands near the road. Intersections of circulation routes are especially critical—where hiking and equestrian trails must cross roads at the same level or at the junction of two or more roads— as are areas bordering parking lots where people often leave their cars carelessly or intent on quickly beginning an activity. Here especially children are excited and may be less aware of the visually obstructed dangers present with moving traffic.

Visual clearance is measured two dimensionally in relation to the traffic lane of a road. One of these dimensions, *sight distance,* is the length of roadway ahead visible to the driver. Stopping sight distance is the total distance a vehicle travels while the driver perceives the hazard, reacts, and stops the vehicle.

Park roads are normally designed as low speed (25 to 30 mph) routes. (This does not include parkways.) As a general guideline, it has been recommended that the sight distance for park roads be at least 175 feet. At road intersection and crossings 300 feet is recommended.*

The second dimension of visual clearance is the direct *line of sight* between each motorist or between motorist and recreationist (or animal) approaching the road. This distance is determined by the relationship of the motorist's sight distance and the nonmotorist's hazard perception and reaction distance. The latter is inconsistent—a hiker or horseback rider may be more alert to this potential conflict zone than a child playing ball or someone who is otherwise intently engrossed in an activity. Therefore visual clearance for roads through or adjacent to unregimented, high activity areas—picnic areas, turf sports fields or playgrounds for example—must be greater than for controlled activity/traffic encounters such as trail crossings. Where visual obstruction cannot be realistically eliminated (e.g., a rock wall, buildings, or dense vegetation adjacent to a road curve, overhead structures, or other obstructions blocking motorists' line of sight at sag or crest curves in the road gradient), or where motorized circulation is unavoidable in unregimented pedestrian movement (such as parking lots and campgrounds), traffic speeds must be greatly reduced to minimize stopping distance.

DRAINAGE.   Proper facilities for drainage are essential to good park roads. The function of proper drainage is to remove surface water from the road pavement and shoulders and to intercept

* George E. Fogg, *Park Planning Guidelines,* National Recreation and Park Association, 1975, p. 44.

and remove subsurface water that might weaken the roadway subbase. Where surface runoff flows perpendicular to the road, culverts or bridges are used to control cross drainage.

One inch of rainfall per hour is analogous to almost seven and one half gallons of water falling on every acre of parkland each second. This water either evaporates, percolates into the ground, or flows over the surface as runoff. The runoff, dependent on the permeability of the surface and subsurface, is expressed as the *runoff coefficient*. The larger the runoff coefficient, the more impervious the surface. Table 6.2 shows the wide range of runoff coefficients for surfaces commonly found in parks.

Park roads are usually crowned: the center of the roadway is slightly higher than the edge of the pavement to direct the flow of surface runoff. Portland cement concrete roadways have a cross slope of ⅛ inch for each foot in width of the half road from the crown. Asphalt roadways have a ¼ inch per foot crown. Unbonded aggregate or scarified roadway are usually constructed with a ½ inch per foot minimum crown. Sometimes the entire roadway is pitched in one direction for drainage.

In urban parks, the park road often has a curb and gutter to channel the runoff into storm drains. The minimum slope for gutters should not be less than 0.5 percent.

In many resource-oriented parks the runoff water drains from the roadway crown over the pavement and shoulder into a drainage ditch or along runoff dikes constructed on the outside edge of the shoulder to spillways into drainage structures; no curb is used.

Drainage ditches are usually constructed parallel to the road to channel the surface runoff and divert water from the roadbed subbase. If runoff conditions permit, gently side-sloping turf swales are used for ditches of 1 to 3 percent gradient. Where ditches are steeper than 3 percent, or where soils are highly erodible, ditches are paved with concrete, asphalt, mortared stone blocks, or asphalt surface treatment.

Culverts are used to carry runoff water under a roadbed. Small

Table 6.2
Runoff coefficients for common park surfaces[a]

Surface Material	Coefficient Factor
Portland cement or asphaltic concrete pavement	0.70–0.95
Penetration macadam	0.60–0.80
Unbonded aggregate (gravel, crushed stone, etc.)	0.20–0.70[b]
Unpaved (sacrified, cleared and grubbed)	0.20–0.75[c]
Natural turf and wooded parkland	0.10–0.35[d]

[a] Adapted from Hickerson, *Route Surveys and Design,* (p. 270) and Parker and MacGuire, *Simplified Site Engineering for Architects and Builders,* (p. 178).
[b] Depending on the compaction and size of the aggregate.
[c] Depending on the local materials used for the roadbed.
[d] Depending on surface slope, vegetation cover and permeability if subsoil.

culverts are located carefully calculated distances apart to divert drainage ditch runoff from the upslope side of a road to prevent a water volume buildup sufficient to weaken the roadbed. The spacing of these culverts is based on land use, estimated runoff volume, and size of the culvert. Storm water in parks is channeled into drainage ditches and streams or into subsurface storm sewers. Large culverts carry many of the park streams under roadbeds. Culverts can withstand higher water velocities than a bridge and are less of a distracting visual element in the park. There are five general types of culverts: corrugated flexible iron or steel pipe, precast concrete pipe, vitrified clay pipe, concrete masonry box culverts, and stone or concrete arches.

AUTOMOBILE BARRIERS

Park roads and parking lots are support areas specifically intended for automobiles. It is sometimes necessary to physically contain the vehicles with barriers: either for the safety of the motorist, for the protection of natural elements and conditions of the park setting, or to exclude the vehicles from recreational activity areas such as walks and trails, turf sports fields, picnic areas, and campgrounds.

These barriers are often subtly placed along roads and parking lots by park designers so the controls are very unobtrusive. This is done in situations where more evident barriers would be incongruous or where automobilists might resent obvious obstructions. Examples of such unobtrusive control are carefully planned living barriers (individual or groups of trees and shrubbery, hedgerows, and thickets), steep embankments rising from the roadway shoulder of parking lot, and even impassable swales or ditches that may serve a dual purpose of channeling surface drainage and controlling access.

There are some park situations that require evident auto-mobile containment. Barriers used include individual and connected structures and obstructions. These barriers are selected by the park designer to provide the structural strength necessary to contain cars, be an attractive part of the modified landscape, consistent with park architectural and natural materials, and should be economical to construct and maintain. Examples of individual barriers often used in parks include local well-implemented boulders and wooden, reinforced concrete or metal posts and bollards. Connected linear barriers often used in parks include elevated wooden, flexible steel or reinforced concrete railings on appropriate posts as well as masonry walls and fences. These elevated barriers, usually at least 16 to 18 inches high, are used when it is desirable to accentuate vehicle control. Some are only bumper height, others are visible above the hood of automobiles as well.

Tire stops only 6 to 8 inches high are not as emphatic as elevated barriers. These can be made of a variety of materials including indigenous stone, wood, masonry, concrete, and asphalt. These may be used singly or as a monolithic curb.

All connected barriers can be continuous or discontinuous. It is important to consider accessibility and pedestrian passage where elevated barriers are used. Continuous tire-stop barriers (curbing) may function as surface drainage runoff gutters if properly designed. This curbing should be occasionally broken or ramped to provide access to recreationists using wheelchairs.

AUTOMOBILE PARKING

The use of private family transportation has been a boom to recreation but a bane to parks. Each parked automobile displaces almost 200 square feet of parkland, even without including the area lost for driving aisles between parking bays. An activity area attracting 150 vehicles needs approximately one acre of land for parking. But proper treatment of the design aspects of this problem can minimize these effects. Well-designed parks have adequate, convenient, safe and appropriate vehicle parking provisions.

PLANNING CONSIDERATIONS

There are several important factors that determine the type, size, location, and surfacing of parking lots in recreation areas. Usually a combination of several of these factors must be considered when planning for parking lots.

ACTIVITY AREA SERVICED.   Some activities, such as picnicking and auto camping, incorporate the vehicle into the experience norm as a storage facility, sleeping or dining facility, or as a energy source for recreational equipment. Other activities, because of the length of time of the activity period or the number of participants (including spectators who are actually vicarious participants), require large lots not necessarily designed for numerous daily turnovers. Examples of these activities might be competitive team sports or spectator events such as baseball, football, ski jumping, or other competitions. The proximity of the activity facility to the parking lot, that is, the walking distance, is also a factor.

TYPE OF ROAD.   The speed limit, traffic volume, and wearing surface of the park road adjoining the parking lot are important for parking lot design. A secondary, low-speed, low-volume, unpaved road does not impose as many safety and construction controls on parking lot design as does a primary paved road carrying a high volume of cars.

COMMON DANGER ZONES.   A park road has inherent danger zones along its complete periphery, including the edge of pavement and shoulders. At any point of intersection—road junction or crossing—the inherent danger zone is enlarged.

An automobile also has inherent danger zones. When a car is visualized simply as a moving people container, it may be understood that the locations where people leave this protective auto shell are danger zones. These danger zones are the sides, where doors open away from the shell and people get out as well as the back where people either exit (as from a station wagon) or unload recreational equipment from trunks or near doors.

To be minimized is the overlap of these two danger zones—those of the roadway periphery and intersections and those of each automobile.

TOWED VEHICLES.   Camping trailers, boat trailers, and other towed vehicles have special parking concerns. Most camping vehicles other than self-propelled campers have eliminated the left side (driving side) entrance, putting the exit danger zone to the right or rear of the rig. The length of the two vehicles (automobile and towed rig) requires extralong parking spaces. Some drivers with rental rigs or with limited tow experience may have a difficult time backing both units. Parking facilities planned for these vehicles must consider these distinctions.

CONTROL.   Placement of parking lots has a great influence on activity area use. Proximity, accessibility, safety, convenience, and size of the parking facilities are factors that can help control the satisfaction with and appropriate use of an area. Improper control of these parking lots can help overtax portions of a park and diminish the quality of the recreational experience.

TYPES OF PARKING LOTS

The plan, or physical layout, of a parking lot can be classified according to the lot's relationship to the adjoining road and the entrance and placement of the parked vehicles.

PULLOVER.   A parking lot used primarily for short-term parking is the pullover. The parking area is an enlarged or widened section of the roadway or shoulder outside of the usual traffic lane. The automobile enters the pullover simply by veering off the roadway and stopping parallel to the road. Pullovers should always be located to the right and facing the direction of the adjacent traffic lane, never located so that cars must cross over approaching traffic lanes. Pullovers are suitable for short stops next to information booths, interpretative signs, or a minor scenic vista *where people do not get out of the car.* Pullovers are not recommended for primary park roads or other high-speed, high-volume routes because the parked vehicle side is in the road peripheral danger zone. Three pullover parking spaces is the maximum number that should be placed together (see Figure 6.9).

In parking situations where people will get out of the car it is

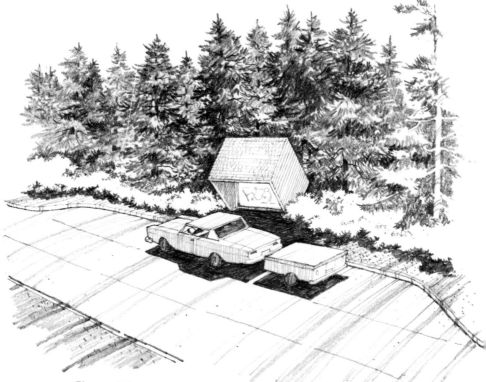

Figure 6.9

Pullover parking areas are appropriate for short stops next to information exhibits where people do not get out of the car.

best that the side of the car not be parallel to the road. The following types of parking lots are used for those situations.

HEAD-IN.   When moderate- to long-term parking is necessary adjacent to a low-volume secondary park road, a head-in parking lot is often appropriate. The parking area is similar to the pullover because it is also an enlarged section of the roadway or shoulder outside the traffic lanes. The automobile enters the head-in parking lot by turning off the traffic lane and stopping with its rear facing the road. When leaving this parking lot, the car backs into the traffic lane and pulls forward to drive away. A head-in lot (Figure 6.10) is safer than the pullover for recreationists leaving the car because the car doors are further from the traffic lanes. It should not be used on primary or other high-speed, high-volume roads because the trunk is next to the road and leaving the lot requires backing into the roadway.

No more than six to eight parking spaces should be used for each head-in lot. These lots should be placed so that parking automobiles do not cross over traffic lanes. Head-in lots servicing both traffic directions should not be located immediately across from each other. This increases the problem of the rear-end danger zone for both traffic lanes at the same time. Adjacent head-in lots should be at least 75 feet apart. (Note: a car traveling 25 mph, a normal speed on park roads, moves approximately 37 feet per second.)

SPUR.   A common one or two space variation of the head-in is the parking spur. This is usually used for long-term parking where it is important to have safe access to the vehicles' trunk or rear end. The spur is usually a single parking space positioned at an obtuse angle from the direction of the traffic. It should be used only on low-speed, low-volume secondary park roads. The automobile enters the spur by stopping on the road and backing into the parking area. This places the trunk in the back of the spur, away from the road. To leave the spur, the automobile simply pulls forward in the direction of traffic. Spurs are ideal parking facilities for family campsites where each activity unit has its own off-road parking separate from others (Figure 6.11). The trunk is used for storage. Skilled trailer campers back their rig into a deep spur and unhitch. The trailer is suitably parked and the towing vehicle is available for side trips. Spurs are best used as back-in spaces. Parking vehicles should not cross over traffic lanes.

Figure 6.10

Head-in parking lots are suitable for small parking needs on secondary roads where traffic is light and slow.

Figure 6.11

Spurs provide ideal parking for family campsites where each campsite has its own off-road parking separate from others.

PULL-THROUGH.   An adaptation of the pullover parking space is the pull-through. This type of parking space is used for moderate- to long-term parking. Each space is a single lane that turns away from the road at an acute angle, parallels it a sufficient distance to permit parking, and then rejoins the road pointing in the direction of traffic. The parking lane is separated from the road by an area which may include shrubbery, trees, earth mounds, or other physical buffers. A parking vehicle simply veers into the pull-through and stops. To leave, the driver pulls forward into the traffic lane. This type of parking has the advantage of eliminating the necessity of stopping or backing onto or off the road. Because of this it is excellent for camper trailers and day-use marinas. It requires more space because the entrance and exit lanes are separate. Figures 6.12 and 6.13 show two types of pull-through parking situations.

BUFFERED HEAD-IN.   By separating the head-in parking lot from the road and connecting this lot to the road with entrance/exit lanes, a buffered head-in lot is created. This separation of parking lot and road eliminates the potential vehicle rear- end- traffic danger as illustrated in Figure 6.14. It is also possible to provide parking on both sides of the parking lot without causing the problem of dual cross traffic lane head-in parking discussed earlier. Traffic through a buffered head-in lot is best if it is only one way. Buffered head-in parking lots are acceptable on primary as well as secondary park roads. These lots usually have less than 30 spaces.

DESTINATION.   Large parking lots that are at the end of one or more secondary roads leading only to it are destination lots. There may be many bays of parking spaces with multiple circulation aisles on a destination lot. The lot is sometimes visually softened with planting medians and grade changes between sections or bays. Destination lots similar to the one in Figure 6.15 are used where large numbers of vehicles must be parked for a single activity area such as a large swimming beach,

Figure 6.12

A pull-through eliminates the problem of backing a trailer into a parking space for many drivers.

Figure 6.13

Pull-through parking bays provide very convenient day-use parking at boat launching areas.

spectator facilities, skill or sports fields or amphitheaters, or when used as a multiple-activity centralized parking lot.

PARKING LOT LOCATION CONSIDERATIONS

There are two common types of parking schemes for parks and recreation areas. A centralized scheme is used if several activity areas can be served by the same parking lot. A dispersed scheme is used when it is better to provide separate parking for each activity area. Large parks will often use a combination of both centralized and disposed parking.

CENTRALIZED PARKING.   A centralized parking scheme does not imply that the parking be physically in the center of the park. In fact, this may be the worst location for a centralized parking area for many recreation areas because of automobile/ pedestrian conflicts and interactivity use patterns as well as possible resource limitations that would restrict parking in the middle of the park. A centralized parking scheme does provide one designated parking area for the park convenient to several or even all of the activity areas. It is most often used where the need for parking is greatest, such as spectator parking at competitive sports fields and intensive-use facilities such as swimming pools, skating rinks, and alpine ski slopes.

Usually a centralized scheme is more economical than a dispersed approach. It is cheaper to build and easier to maintain, control, and police. Another advantage to the park visitor is the relative ease of finding a parking space during a busy day without having to drive from parking area to parking area.

Some centralized parking schemes, if not carefully planned, may be ill fitted to the landscape. Large destination parking lots without adequate landscape treatment such as bay separation, planting, and earth forms can be visually unattractive. Massive amounts of exposed surfaced parking absorbs heat from the sun and hot automobiles. Runoff drainage from large impervious parking lots can be inadvertently concentrated into erosion-causing volumes of surface water. Latecomers and secondary facility users may have to walk—and possibly carry heavy recreation equipment—across a large parking lot.

DISPERSED PARKING.   To provide parking as close as possible to several separated activity areas, a system of smaller lots dispersed through the park is best. There are some activity areas

Figure 6.14

A buffered head-in parking lot separates the road traffic from the parking lot, making access to the auto trunks safer.

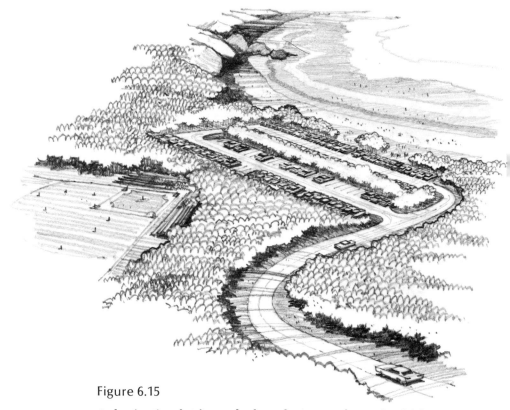

Figure 6.15

A destination lot is used where large numbers of vehicles must be parked for high capacity activity areas.

that often utilize an internal dispersed parking scheme to prevent or reduce concentrated use on areas that would occur if all the parking were centralized, reduce long carrying distances for users, provide ready access to parked vehicles as part of the activity and spread out traffic. This is especially helpful in large family picnic and camping areas.

Besides providing an obvious convenience for recreationists using these small group-sized activity unit areas, a dispersed parking scheme separates the paving areas. Because the lots are smaller, they are easier to design into the existing landscape and may be less of an eyesore than a single centralized parking complex of a similar capacity. Surface runoff water is not as large for each of the lots and is less of an erosion problem.

A dispersed parking system of small lots is more expensive to build and maintain than a centralized destination parking lot. The separate construction phases of clearing, grading, and surfacing is spread out over many sites. More roadway must be constructed to connect these smaller dispersed parking lots. This may increase possibilities for automobile/pedestrian conflicts. Availability of parking is not as readily apparent in a dispersed parking system as a centralized system.

PARKING LOT SURFACE TYPES

The wearing surface of a parking lot must be durable and suited to the volume of use, and seasonal use patterns.

PERVIOUS SURFACING.   Parking lots that have very light use, such as those in sparsely visited use areas, overflow parking, or in areas where it is important to reduce runoff, permit rain to percolate into the ground, or minimize visual intrusion into the natural scene, are often constructed with a pervious surface.

Turf surfacing.   If an adequate base exists, turf may be used as the parking surface for infrequently used parking lots. Turf should not be used if the lot is needed during those periods when grass is vulnerable to damage—wet seasons when the soil is soft, the grass wet and slippery and traction poor, or drought periods when the turf would suffer from crushing and leaf reduction, soil compaction and wear. Turf maintenance may be a limiting factor if barriers are used to keep cars out of activity areas.

Stabilized turf surfacing.   When a grass-covered parking area is desired for a moderately used facility, an inadequate base may be improved with a bed of compacted crushed stone that is choked and topped with a thin layer of fertile soil. This is seeded (or often is "invaded" with native herbaceous plants). This stabilized turf is more tolerant to use during wet seasons than the natural turf areas.

Open-jointed paving.   A combination of stabilized turf and paving blocks on a prepared base can be used as a refinement of a turf parking area. There are a number of techniques to do this: hollow-core masonry blocks placed side by side and filled with topsoil; precast concrete beams separated by topsoil, similar to corduroy pavement; unmortared solid cast block or stone; precast concrete paving waffles filled with topsoil. The surface texture, pattern, and porosity will vary according to the design.

Unbonded aggregate surfacing.   A wearing surface of crushed stone, rock, chert, slag, gravel, or river rock is good for parking areas that have long-term use with little turnover, servicing all day use areas such as launching access boat trailer parking lots, trailhead parking lots, and group picnic areas. It is also an economical parking surface for camping spurs and other long-term or moderate-use facilities. Dust is not as much of a problem on a soft-stone aggregate parking area as it is on a roadway because of less traffic volume and slower speeds.

The permeability of this surface depends on its construction. The more it is compacted and the tighter it is choked with fine powderlike particles, the more water repellent it becomes.

IMPERVIOUS SURFACING.   The bonded wearing surfaces are most impervious to water and are best for year-round, all-weather parking. Because rain and snow melt are contained on top of the surface, puddling and runoff considerations require very careful site design. Large lots as well as those with complex or steep gradients may require elaborate subsurface drainage structures.

Penetration macadam.   This wearing course, basically an *in situ*-prepared asphaltic concrete, is the same built-up pavement used for light- to moderate-volume park roads.

Paving block.   There are numerous types of paving blocks—stone, brick, tile, asphalt, wood. Usually the paving blocks cover an impervious base separated by a setting bed and grout of cement or asphalt. Construction is usually costly. (Expensive automobiles are often shown in advertisements on paving block parking areas as part of a luxurious setting).

Asphaltic concrete.   This is the most commonly used year-round, all-weather parking surface. It is prepared under controlled conditions and delivered and layed while hot just as hot plant-mix asphaltic concrete roadways are. The thickness of the wearing coarse depends on the subgrade material and base. The parking area may be formed with an asphalt curbing if necessary.

Portland cement concrete.   This type of parking surface is usually reserved for those parks that have a unique parking problem requiring pavement of an extremely heavy-duty load-bearing surface.

SIGNIFICANT PARKING LOT DESIGN CONSIDERATIONS

PARKING ANGLES.   The angle of each parking stall is affected by the type of activity area the parking lot services. Most commonly used in recreation areas is the perpendicular (90 degree) stall. It is easily handled by most drivers and permits selection of stalls on either side of a double-bay lot with either a one-way or two-way aisle. Perpendicular stalls may be used in parking lots with only one entrance, that is, the aisle may be dead end. Other common head-in parking angles (60 degrees, 45 degrees or 30 degrees) are not functional in dead-end aisles.

The more acute the head-in parking angle, the easier it is for a driver to maneuver into place. For this reason angled parking is often used for short-term parking for registering or seeking information at contact stations.

Back-in parking situations such as camping spurs are usually 45-degree angles for the convenience of campers backing a trailer or camping rig.

In large, multiple-bay parking lots the parking angle should be the same for all stalls throughout the lot.

PARKING STALL SIZE.   The width of each parking stall should not be arbitrary. Many activities require wide stalls because bulky items must be loaded and unloaded from the car: picnic baskets, portable grills, charcoal, coolers, personal flotation devices (PFDs), sleeping bags, tents, paddles, bats, ball equipment, and the like. For those activity areas where these are used, a 10-foot stall should be standard. Those parking lots that service spectators may be reduced to 9½ feet. This will permit more stalls for spectators without inconveniencing them as much as if they had to squeeze bulky items out. (But consider seasonal use of the lot. Winter clothing is bulkier than light summer wear.) Parking stalls reserved and designated for persons with a physical disability should have a minimum width of 12 feet to allow movement of people using wheelchairs or walking aids.

The depth of a parking stall will also vary, depending on the parking angle, use of tire stops, and the activity area served by the parking spaces.

A destination 90 degree parking bay with either a front curb or tire stops set within two feet of the front edge of the stall requires a minimum depth of 20 feet if located at activity areas where people would be apt to load and unload trunks and wagon rear doors. A similar head-in parking lot on the side of a traveled park road would be better with 25-feet deep stalls from edge of roadway pavement to front end of stall to move the parked vehicles farther from the traffic lanes.

Back-in parking spurs are usually a minimum of 30 feet deep but may be 50 to 65 feet deep for trailer units.

Pull-through parking stalls such as camping loops or parallel auto-boat trailer stalls at boat launching areas are necessarily deeper to provide space for the vehicle and the travel unit. This depth is at least 50 feet.

DRIVING AISLE.   The driving aisle between double parking bays is an important factor in planning a parking lot. The surfacing material should be all-weather and often more durable than the parking bay surfacing. Often a large destination parking lot will be constructed of asphalt driving aisles and loose aggregate or stabilized turf parking bays to reduce the visual impact of the pavement surface.

The width of this aisle depends on the parking angle as well as whether or not the aisle is two directional. For 90 degree parking the two-way aisle should be 24 feet wide. In a 60-degree parking lot an aisle of 18 feet is acceptable because aisle traffic is one way and parked vehicles can maneuver back into the aisle in a shorter space because of the angle. One way pull-through lots require two aisles at least 18 feet wide.

SLOPE.   The slope of the parking bays' surface can vary depending on the surfacing material, depth of the stall, and local conditions. It is better to drain the parking surface runoff away from the activity area if the topography permits. Unless a curb and gutter or subsurface storm drainage is provided to intercept storm water, the parking stall should slope toward the traffic aisle or roadway. A steep wet surface, especially stabilized turf, is often difficult to hold traction when starting a parked vehicle. Therefore it is better to be able to start downgrade from the parking bay. The amount of slope can be very slight for impervious surfacing such as asphalt or concrete. Under excellent construction controls these surfaces may drain at 0.5 percent slope. Because it is not always possible to control construction grades however, a minimum slope of 2 percent is recommended. Porous surfacing such as loose aggregate or stabilized turf should be steeper. As a guideline, it is recommended that parking stalls not slope more than 10 percent.

The back portion of a camping parking spur or loop should not exceed 2 percent to insure safe and adequate leveling of trailers and campers.

TIRESTOPS, CURBS, BARRIERS, MEDIANS

Tirestops are used when a physical barrier is needed to hold a vehicle from rolling off the parking space. They are not barriers to prevent entry into an activity area—vehicles may be driven over them without damage to the car— but they do provide a subtle control to prevent drivers from leaving the pavement. Tirestops may be constructed of solid wood ties, concrete, metal, or a synthetic material such as high-impact plastic. Tirestops are usually not more than 8 inches high and are installed in sections six to eight feet long. Use of tirestops instead of curbing eliminates the continuous curb riser, which may be a barrier to some individuals and equipment. Tirestops should always be mounted securely on the parking surface at least two feet from the front edge of the pavement. This will provide space for the overhang of the vehicle in front of the wheels and reduces turf maintenance next to the parking lot.

Curbs intercept and channel runoff better than tirestops. They should not exceed 8 inches in height. Adequate space free from trees, shrubbery, or other obstacles should be provided behind the curb to allow the vehicle to overhang the curb in front of the wheels. Walks should not be located immediately next to the curb or vehicles will infringe into the pedestrian route with bumpers, grills, hot engines, and oil stains.

Barriers that hold the vehicle without permitting the front overhang to protrude past them include walls, rails, fences, posts, bollards, hedgerows, and boulders. These barriers are used when it is important to prevent vehicular trespass.

Medians separate adjacent bays in multiple-aisle parking lots or divided traffic lanes. They supply space to provide plant materials that visually relieve a stark paved area, for shade trees to cool the pavement and vehicles, for significant grade changes between tiered parking bays, and to provide pedestrian routes through large parking areas. The latter is very important in large destination lots to minimize traffic-pedestrian conflicts during heavy use periods.

Medians should be wide enough to maintain economically as well as offer the amenities above. Medians between tiered bays should have a slope no greater than 3:1 if turf cover and soils are stable. Steeper medians between bays are acceptable if soils permit and low maintenance, erosion-preventing ground cover is used instead of grass.

PEDESTRIAN CIRCULATION

PLANNING CONSIDERATIONS

The concern for pedestrian needs should be as evident in planning as the concern for vehicular traffic. In road and parking lot design, it is important to know what type of vehicle—heavy truck, automobile, camper rig, or ORV—will use the facility. It is just as important to plan for specific pedestrian needs when developing a system of walkways in a park.

USE.   Pedestrian routes may be utilitarian linkages between activity areas and other support facilities. Walks connecting parking lots, recreation buildings, shelters, comfort stations, or playing courts are primarily used by people walking between these facilities; the use of the walk is incidental to the use of the facility. Other pedestrian routes may actually be part of the activity area. Nature walks, hiking trails, and jogging paths are examples of pedestrian ways that are directly activity related.

PROTECTION OF RESOURCE.   Walks and trails channelize foot traffic along a selected corridor. This protects fragile vegetation from trampling, susceptible soils from wear and compaction, and limits user impact to a specific management zone. The absence of a defined pedestrian route sometimes deters use of an area. This may actually be a desirable planning decision to protect wildlife habitats or sensitive unique natural resources.

PROTECTION OF USER.   Pedestrian routes can often direct walkers through potentially hazardous zones in parks. Walks separate pedestrians from vehicular routes and possible danger. Well-designed trails offer access to scenic vistas, overlooks and other attractions to hikers of varying degrees of strength and hiking competencies. For example, some trails are planned to accommodate strollers or afternoon hikers in loafers or sandals. Others are well-developed for the backpacking hiker with boots, stamina, and experience. Not all pedestrian routes should be planned for a common (participant) denominator.

TYPES OF PEDESTRIAN WAYS

Each park has a pedestrian circulation system similar to its vehicular circulation system. The three major components of the walking system are walks, trails and paths. These are distinguishable by their design, surfacing, type and amount of use, expected maintenance, and the footwear most commonly used by the walker/hiker.

Walks are usually utilitarian support routes servicing parking lots (see Figures 6.10 and 6.14), restrooms, community buildings, and other intensive development. Walks are most common in urban parks where street shoes are practical. Use is possibly heavy; surfacing is durable and impervious. Walks are obviously "designed" with well-defined edges, direction, and patterns. The land forms are often modified to accept this engineered pedestrian structure. Walkways are usually suitable for paraplegic use. Park walks are expected to be clean, free from leaves or other litter, and are often trimmed to keep grass from growing over the edge.

Trails are activity-directed facilities for hiking. Trail use is a major part of the resource-based park experience. Trails are constructed of indigenous materials (usually pervious). This often necessitates the use of hiking boots for comfort and protection. Trails are designed to conform to the land characteristics. A wide variance of development criteria are applied to fit the natural circumstances. Trail width is flexible; surfacing often blends into the adjacent land without a distinct edge. Heavy use has a direct deteriorating impact on the trail. Leaves and other natural litter are acceptable on trails.

Paths are the park compromise between walks and trails. Paths are planned for either utility or activity. Their design is informal and not completely resource controlled; surfacing may be pervious or impervious; street shoes are suitable footwear. Paraplegics and others with mobility disabilities can use many paths. Path maintenance is related to the surrounding area maintenance standards and expectations.

Many "trails" and "walks" are so named by long use of these generally descriptive terms in their non-genetic sense. Many "nature trails" are really paths. Some are actually walks.

SURFACING.   The proper walking surface is important to pedestrian comfort and satisfaction. There is no "ideal" surface that can be used anywhere. Each walkway must be carefully studied before a surface material can be chosen. This decision should be based on these factors:

□ *Use.*   Why will people travel the route? How will they be dressed? Will they be carrying or moving heavy apparatus or equipment? When will they come?

□ *Season.*   Will heavy or frequent spring rain cause problems? Would summer temperatures make the surface too hot to walk on with barefeet? What effect would winter snow removal or frost have upon the surface?

☐ *Inherent Material Characteristics.* Is the material permeable? Erosion resistant? Durable and scuff free? Odorless and mildew free? Susceptible to windblow? Rigid, pliant, or aggregate?

☐ *Congruence.* Does the surfacing fit the development level and visual character of the surrounding area?

☐ *Cost.* What are the comparative costs of alternative materials including initial construction and regular maintenance at an established level?

☐ *Multiple Use.* Will this pedestrian corridor ever have to be used by other travel modes on a periodic basis (maintenance, fire patrol, ORV, equestrian, etc.) that would affect the surfacing selection?

☐ *Degree of Refinement.* What is the maximum grade acceptable for this walkway? Will there be curbing? Cut and fill? Retaining walls? Bridges? Gates? Culverts? Water breaks? Will this walkway be accessible to people with disabilities?

Table 6.3 shows the variety of materials that have been successfully used for walks, trails, or paths.

Table 6.3
Surfacing materials for park pedestrian ways

Type of Materials	Type of Pedestrian Way Where Commonly Used		
	Walks	Paths	Trails
Pervious Walking Surfaces			
Indigenous earth		*	*
Clay		*	*
Grass		*	*
Unbonded organic aggregate (wood chips, bark, pine needles, corduroy, marine shells)		*	*
Unbonded inorganic aggregate		*	*
Natural aggregate (gravel, sand, shale, crushed stone)			
By-product aggregate (cinders, slag)		*	
Recycled (pulverized tire bodies, plastic particles, shingle grit)		*	
Impervious Walking Surfaces			
Tooled or manufactured units (cobbles, brick, flagstone, tile, block)	*	*	
Bonded aggregate—monolithic surfacing (concrete, asphalt, penetration)	*	*	
Structures			
(puncheons; pile supported, flotation, and suspension boardwalks)	*	*	

SIGNIFICANT DESIGN CONSIDERATIONS

Walks, trails, and paths have different uses and settings. These variations require a large latitude of development levels. These considerations are sometimes overlooked when pedestrian walkways are planned.

WIDTH.   Municipal codes often specify a standard public sidewalk width. This "official" width may be from three to five feet. Park walks may be 18 inches or over 50 feet wide. The width is determined by park designers based upon an estimate of use, safety, and function. One rule of thumb is to allocate 2 feet of width per person. Using this guide, a minimum of 4 feet is needed where two people walk side by side. This width is affected by the actual or perceived edge or side of the walkway. A walk through an open area with turf on both sides does not seem as narrow as a similar walk immediately next to a wall, shrubbery, or other visual constraints.

Many urban park departments use several walk widths within the same park. The widest walks are major pedestrain routes as well as collector routes for several activity areas. These walks are used as a visual unifying design element that ties the separate facilities together. Often these wide walks are used as service roads for park maintenance, operations, and emergency vehicles. When this is done, the walk width and bearing strength must be designed for these pieces of equipment. Steps and railings may limit such multiple use of walks. Smaller walks and paths are used for low pedestrian traffic such as secondary access ways into activity areas, walks to comfort stations or other services. A more detailed discussion on emergency circulation routes is provided in Chapter 11.

Backcountry trails may be only 18 inches wide. Intensively used day trails may be 6 to 10 feet wide. The width will vary with the land character, surfacing used, construction techniques, and amount of use.

SLOPE.   This must be considered two ways. The first is the *gradient* of the walkway along the length. This is important for the safety and comfort of the user, retention of the surfacing materials and protection of the adjacent natural resources. Park walks or paths are best designed at a gradient of less than 5 percent. Under very limiting natural conditions, steeper grades up to 10 percent may be used for short distances. It is important to remember that steep grades are physically demanding and may prevent use by paraplegics and people with walking disabilities or heart conditions. Steep asphalt walks may wash- board or subside with use during the summer. Unbonded surfacing materials are recommended only on gradients of less than 5 percent.

The cross slope of a walkway is sometimes called the *pitch* or wash. All walkways should slope to the outside to permit runoff.

Walks less than six feet wide are usually elevated on one side to carry the runoff in one direction. Wider walks may be crowned to split the runoff. If unique local conditions warrant, park designers may swale the walk and use it as an open drain to channel rain water away from problem areas. An adequate pitch for concrete is ⅛ to ¼ inch per foot. Asphalt should be pitched ¼ to ½ inch per foot; earthern or grass trails ½ to ¾ inch per foot.

Cross slopes for pervious walking surfaces such as wood chips, gravel, or other loose aggregate should not exceed ¼ inch per foot. Adequate subsurface drainage should be provided for these materials.

DRAINAGE.   When trail lengths run down the fall line of a slope (i.e., straight down the hill) it is often necessary to use water breaks or bars in addition to cross pitch to direct runoff and reduce trail erosion. Use of side gutters should be limited to only those situations when it is absolutely necessary. These should be as short as possible. Long gutters collect large volumes of runoff and increase erosion problems unless the water is properly disposed. Small amounts of runoff from trails disposed over large areas by water breaks or cross pitch cause less problems. Where small springs or seepage discharge above a trail, it is recommended adequate cross trail subsurface channels, pipe, or culverts be provided at the point of natural runoff to keep the surface dry and stable. These must be large enough to prevent blockage from silt, leaves, and other litter.

CLEARANCE.   It is important to consider the spatial requirement of walks, trails, and paths as well as the surface needs. People walk on a trail but through space. Overhead and lateral obstructions and obstacles such as tree limbs and branches, bushes, tree trunks, and rock walls can nullify the benefits of the best walking surface. Normally any extended canopy should be above the overhead extended reach of hikers. A canopy or ceiling less than this (usually eight feet in height) is too low for long distances. An occasional limb or other overhead obstacle should not be removed however, if it still permits natural and comfortable use of the trail. This consideration is directly related to the experience expectations and development level. What would be expected and acceptable along a backcountry trail might be undesirable along a large high-use walk or path.

Lateral clearance on walks, trails, and paths is based on the same development factors. A narrow tandem or single file foot trail 18 inches wide may require a cleared corridor at least three feet wide for backpacking. A five-foot-wide walk usually needs a cleared swath six feet wide. The occasional tree trunk or bush on one side of a walk or path does not cause problems but a long walking distance with close vegetation or other obstacles on both sides is tight.

SUMMARY

The vehicular and pedestrian circulation systems of a park are the interconnecting links that tie the activity areas together. proper circulation planning must consider protection of the users and protection of the natural environment as well as functional access and parking. Park roads may be either public use or service roads. The public use route configuration within a park is an important factor that affects access, safety, traffic distribution, and control. The construction of the roadway should be based on the use, development norm, and budget. Other significant park road designs considerations include road width, shoulders, gradients, alignment, intersections, visual, drainage, and control barriers.

Parking for automobiles in parks must be adequate, convenient, safe, and appropriate to the parking needs.

Pedestrian ways may be either walks, paths, or trails. Each type has basic planning concerns and design considerations. A large variety of materials have been used on pedestrian ways. Proper selection should be based on amount of use, season, inherent material characteristics, congruence, cost, possible multiple use, and development norm.

GLOSSARY OF TERMS

Centralized Parking
A scheme of automobile parking in a park that has a designated parking area convenient to several or all of the activity areas.

Dispersed Parking
A scheme of automobile parking in a park that has one or more small lots as close as possible to each of the separated activity areas.

Nonpublic Service Roads
Supplementary roads that provide access for maintenance and operational activities of the park staff.

Paths
Park pedestrian ways that are a compromise between walks and trails; may be for either utility or activity.

Primary Roads
The major park public use entrance, access, or collector roads; usually two way with the heaviest traffic volume in the park.

Public Use Roads
Park roads that are open to park users.

Roadway
The wearing surface of the road that makes up the traffic lane(s).

Secondary Roads
The low-traffic-volume park roads that connect individual

activity areas to the primary park road; may be used as an internal road within an activity area.

Trails
Activity-directed park pedestrian ways constructed of indigenous materials and conforming to existing land forms; may require hiking boots.

Walks
Utilitarian park pedestrian ways servicing parking lots, restrooms, community buildings, and so on; landforms may be modified to accept walks; street shoes always appropriate.

BIBLIOGRAPHY

Asbaugh, Byron L. *Trail Planning and Layout.* National Audubon Society, New York, 1965.

Asphalt for Off-Street Paving and Play Areas-Manual Series No. 9 (MS-9). The Asphalt Institute, March, College Park, Md., 1964.

Asphalt Surface Treatments and Asphalt Penetration Macadam. The Asphalt Institute, College Park, Md., March, 1964.

Bayliss, Dudley C. *Planning Our National Park Roads and Our National Parkways.* National Park Service, Washington, D.C., 1957.

Clay Pipe Engineering Manual. Clay Products Association, Barrington, Ill., 1962.

Fogg, George E. *Park Planning Guidelines.* National Recreation and Park Association, Arlington, Va., 1975.

Hickerson, Thomas F. *Route Surveys and Design,* Fourth Edition. McGraw-Hill, New York, 1959.

Highway Research Board. *Parking Turnouts and Rest Areas.* Bureau of Public Roads, Washington, D.C., 1952.

National Park Service, Park Road Standards Committee. *Park Road Standards.* United States Government Printing Office, Washington, D.C., May, 1968.

The Park Practice Program-Design. National Recreation and Park Association and the National Park Service, Washington, D.C., (Periodically supplemented)

Parker, Harry and John W. MacGuire. *Simplified Site Engineering for Architects and Builders.* Wiley, New York, 1954.

United States Army Corps of Engineers. *Recreational Facilities Design.* U.S. Army Engineer District, Fort Worth, Tx., June, 1973.

Vogel, Charles. *Trails Manual.* Published by the author, San Mateo, Calif., 1968.

Vollmer Associates. *Parking for Recreation: A Primer on the*

Techniques of Parking Vehicles at Public Recration Facilities. American Institute of Park Executives, Wheeling, W. Va., 1965.

Wilcox, Arthur T., Editor. *Park Automobile Barriers.* Park Management Series Bulletin 1, American Institute of Park Executives, Michigan State College, Agricultural Experiment Station, East Lansing, Mich., 1954.

7
lighting

The provision of an appropriate level and quality of illumination in a park is a basic support consideration. The bulk of our daily activities, during work or recreation, are predominately experienced visually and only secondarily by our other senses of touch, hearing, taste, or smell. In a park, lighting is important during the day as well as at night. Both natural lighting and artificial lighting are planning elements in this situation. Natural lighting is kaleidoscopic in character and effects. Most people prefer some natural lighting even when in a building, but use artificial lighting for most tasks because it can be controlled so well. The amount of mix, or the combination of natural and artificial lighting in a park, depends on the time of day, required consistency of illumination, the activity or function, development norm, and economics.

There are five major functions of park lighting. Very often, provision of proper illumination in a specific situation serves several of these functions.

Activity lighting provides the necessary illumination to do a specific task or performance. The activity may be a daily chore of personal hygiene such as washing hands or combing hair, a work assignment such as typing a letter or lubricating a machine, or a recreational event such as playing (or watching) a ball game or picnicking. Each activity has optimum lighting conditions. Figures 7.1, 7.2, and 7.7 show recreation and work situations requiring activity lighting.

133

Figure 7.1

Hard surface court areas such as tennis are usually illuminated with a general lighting system. Here, direct lighting is supply by low-level luminaires using fluorescent lamps. Wiring is underground; lighting is controlled by a coin-operated manual switch.

Safety lighting provides necessary illumination during normal situations to protect human well-being and reduce chances of accident or harm to people. Illumination of walks, halls, steps and ramps, and road crossings are examples of lighting for safety (Figure 7.3).

Security lighting provides a degree of protection to property, equipment, and goods. The possessions may be public (park buildings, machinery, apparatus, or areas) or personal (users' automobiles, equipment, or money). Security lighting discourages vandalism and crime by implementing detection and aiding park patrols. Figure 7.4 shows one security lighting application.

Emergency lighting is needed when normal lighting provisions fail and people need temporary supplementary illumination to evacuate or carry out essential tasks. Exit, evacuation, and escape route lighting in stadiums, fieldhouses, auditoriums, and other public assembly buildings are auxiliary emergency lighting systems that are separate from normal energy supplies. A typical installation is shown in Figure 7.5.

Aesthetic lighting is used to enhance the beauty or attractiveness of a visual element. Lights may be used to illuminate fountains, statues, waterfalls or building facades. The lighting itself may be aesthetic: chandeliers, gaslights, globe luminaires, and many other fixtures provide inherent charm or beauty to a setting. (Notice Figures 7.2, 7.3, and 7.7.)

GENERAL PLANNING CONSIDERATIONS FOR PARK LIGHTING

It is important to understand the basic factors of good illumination, the approaches to planning lighting schemes, and to know the various components to an artificial lighting system

Figure 7.2

Direct supplementary light is provided for the work counter at this indoor skating rink by these suspended luminaires.

Figure 7.3

Park walks are illuminated for safety in this illustration by using attractive pedestrian-scaled general diffuse luminaires containing incandescent lamps. In the background are taller directional units that reflect the functional light onto the cars.

before participating in park illumination planning. The development norm determined in each activity analysis (see Chapter 2), complexities of the essential support elements of the park, and the development and annual operating budgets affect lighting plans. A competent lighting specialist may be the planning team leader for this segment of planning if the lighting requirements are complicated. All contributory members of the planning process at this stage need a basic understanding of park lighting considerations.

FACTORS OF GOOD ILLUMINATION

There are no universal lighting characteristics that, if obtained in *all* situations, would provide "good illumination." There are two basic factors that must be carefully considered to determine how each lighting application can be best suited to its function. These factors—illumination quantity and quality—must be specifically coupled to the lighting function, its environment, and use experience norms.

QUANTITY OF ILLUMINATION.   The amount of light needed is directly related to the activity, experiential mood, and the surrounding environment. Some activities are fast moving, require small equipment, or otherwise require high visual acuity. Examples of these activities include most indoor and outdoor court and field sports (e.g., tennis, basketball, football, baseball) as well as close work such as clerical work, typing, machinery repair, and equipment maintenance. The quantity of natural light can range from 100,000 footcandles in strong, direct sunlight to 0.5 footcandles in the moonlight. Strolling or jogging through the park is one visual experience at noon, a completely different experience at midnight. While we can only plan the timing of an event outdoors to coincide with the appropriate amount of natural light, we have been able to regulate the quantity of artificial light to meet most functional and experiential levels.

Figure 7.4

A photoelectrically controlled dusk-to-dawn luminaire equipped with a long-life mercury vapor lamp provides bright security illumination for this park garage and equipment.

Figure 7.5

Emergency lighting is needed in public assembly facilities. These units automatically illuminate exits and evacuation routes when normal lighting systems fail.

This is especially noticeable for social recreation—certain dance styles are appropriate at relatively bright conditions, others are suited to relatively dim lighting; meals are eaten in very high light levels or candlelight, for example.

The most salient quantitative measure of illumination is at the task or performance center, as viewed by the most important observer(s). (These observers may be the activity participants, the officials, inspectors, or coaches, or the spectators, present or via television.) It is more important to know the amount of light where it is needed rather than the amount of light being produced by a lamp. This is because the lamps are usually mounted long distances from the use area and their light may be partially diminished before reaching the area.

This functional illumination level is measured in footcandles (or metric lux). One footcandle equals one lumen per square foot; a lumen being a unit of light emanating from a source, such as a lamp.

Table 7.1 lists the recommended minimum illumination levels for selected park areas and facilities. These recommendations are for normal operating situations. Higher initial levels should be installed if dust particle content of the air in these areas is sufficient to decrease functional illumination, luminaire cover lens or exposed lamps are not cleaned regularly, or if lamp lumen output is permitted to deteriorate with age before relamping.

Table 7.1
Recommended minimum levels of illumination for selected park areas and facilities[a]

Area or Facility	Recommended Minimum Illumination	
	Footcandles[b]	Dekalux[c]
Circulation Routes		
Building halls or corridors	20	22
Elevators or stairs	20	22
Building entranceways, active	5	5.4
Park roads		
Primary	0.4	0.4
Secondary	0.2	0 0.2
Park walks	0.5–1	0.5–1
Steps, ramps	1	1
Parking lots	1	1
Eating Areas		
Picnic pavilion	30–50	32–54
Quick service dining room	50–100	54–110
Emergency Lighting Facilities[d]		
Floors of means of egress (passageways, hills, corridors, stairways, ramps, landing, exit doors)	1	1
Exit signs	5	5.4
Maintenance and Operations Areas		
Offices, general to business machine operation	70–150	75–160
Kitchen, general	70	75
In food preparation and cleaning areas	150	160
Shops		
Rough woodworking and painting	50	54
Fine woodworking, finishing; mechanical bench	100	110
Utility room, janitor's closet	15–20	15–20
Vehicle and equipment repair	100	110
Sanitary Facilities		
Laundry room	30	32
Locker room	20	22
Shower room	20	22
Toilet and washroom, general	30	32
In areas used for grooming, shaving, make-up	50	54

Table 7.1   (Continued)

Area or Facility	Recommended Minimum Illumination	
	Footcandles[b]	Dekalux[c]

Security Lighting

  The amount of illumination necessary for security will depend on the location and relationship to surroundings. Usually provisions for safety exceed those necessary for security. After normal use periods, certain areas (building entrances, storage yards, parking lots, etc.) may be illuminated with security lights controlled photoelectronically or by timers. If the areas are surrounded by dark surroundings, the following *minimum* levels are recommended if the lighting is part of a complete security system, including patrols.

Building entrances, interiors	5	5.4
Outdoor areas	1	1

Recreation Areas (Nonsports)

Amphitheaters, spectator bleachers and stadiums; seating areas (before and after performance event)	5	5.4
Cabins, cottages, dormitories		
General	10	11
Reading areas	30	32
Study, handicraft	70–150	75–160
Camp stove, self-service	200	220
Community center		
Lounges, small meeting rooms, reading areas, table games	30	32
Craft rooms (depends on visual task)	50–150	54–160
Dance hall	5	5–4
General recreation rooms	50	54
Exhibit halls, museums		
General	30	32
Supplementary—special exhibits	100	110
Playgrounds	5	5.4
Visitor center	30–50	32–54

Sports Areas (Outdoor)

  The amount of illumination necessary for sports activities will depend on the experience and development norms, plus the additional visual requirements of spectators. The following recommendations are for the comfort and enjoyment of amateur players without spectators. Where these activities occur indoors or are provided as free-operated facilities, participants usually expect much higher illumination levels.

CATEGORY I. OUTDOOR SPORTS AREAS REQUIRING RELATIVELY UNIFORM MULTIDIMENSIONAL ILLUMINATION DISTRIBUTION OVER ENTIRE PLAYING AREA

Hard-Surface Court Areas

Basketball courts[e] (Recreational)	10	11
Roller skating rink	10	11
Tennis court		
(Tournament)	30	32
(Club)	20	22
(Recreational)	10	11

140

Table 7.1   (Continued)

Area or Facility	Recommended Minimum Illumination	
	Footcandles[b]	Dekalux[c]
Volleyball court (recreational)	10	11
Recreational Turf Areas		
Badminton court (recreational)	10	11
Croquet court	5	5.4
Golf, practice putting green	10	11
Lawn bowling green (recreational)	5	5.4
Volleyball court (recreational)	10	11
Turf Fields		
Field hockey (recreational)	20	22
Football field (recreational)	10	11
Soccer field (recreational)	10	11
Water		
Swimming pools (recreational)	10	11
Winter		
Ice hockey rink (recreational)	10	11
Ice skating rink	5	5.4
Ski slope	1	1.1
Sledding run	1	1.1
CATEGORY II. OUTDOOR SPORTS AREAS REQUIRING UNIDIRECTIONAL OR EMPHASIS ILLUMINATION FOR SPECIAL PORTIONS OF THE PLAYING AREA		
Hard-Surface Court Areas		
Shuffleboard courts (emphasis on back courts)		
(Tournament)	10	11
(Recreational)	5	5.4
Recreational Turf Areas		
Horseshoe courts (emphasis on pits)		
(Tournament)	10	11
(Recreational)	5	5.4
Quoits (emphasis on back courts)	5	5.4
Special Individual and Dual Sports Areas		
Archery range		
(Recreational) Shooting line	5	5.4
Target	5	5.4
(Tournament) Shooting line	10	11
Target	10	11
Handball court (unidirectional to frontwall)		
(Recreational)	10	11
Golf course		
Tee	5	5.4
Fairway	1–3	1–3.2
Green	5	5.4
Golf driving range		
Tee	10	11
At 200 yards	5	5.4

141

Table 7.1   *(Continued)*

Area or Facility	Recommended Minimum Illumination	
	Footcandles[b]	Dekalux[c]
Rifle range		
Firing point	10	11
Range	5	5.4
Targets	50	54
Skeet range		
Firing points	5	5.4
Targets (at 60 feet)	30	32
Trap range		
Firing points	5	5.4
Targets (at 100 feet)	30	32
Turf Fields		
Baseball field—90 foot baseline		
(Municipal) Infield	20	22
Outfield	15	16
(Recreational) Infield	15	16
Outfield	10	11
Baseball field—60-foot baseline		
Infield	30	32
Outfield	20	22
Softball field		
(Industrial) Infield	20	22
Outfield	15	16
(Recreational) Infield	10	11
Outfield	7	7.5
Softball field—slow pitch		
(Tournament) Infield	20	22
Outfield	15	16
(Recreational) Infield	10	11
Outfield	7	7.5

[a] Based on illumination level recommendations of these or equivalent areas indicated by John E. Kaufman (Editor), *IES Lighting Handbook,* Illuminating Engineering Society, New York, 1972; *Current Recommended Practice for Sports Lighting,* Illuminating Engineering Society, New York, 1968; and the Life Safety Code of the *National Fire Codes*, National Fire Protection Association, Boston, 1972.

[b] One footcandle = one lumen per square foot.

[c] One dekalux = 10 lux = 1.076 footcandles.

[d] From *National Fire Code*, Section 101, "Life Safety Code," pp. 48 and 52.

[e] Many sports areas have been classified into *recreational, club,* or *tournament* levels by the Illuminating Engineering Society. These classes determine the minimum quantity of illumination required. Only those classes most commonly found in park settings have been listed here and are shown in parentheses.

QUALITY OF ILLUMINATION.   The amount of illumination must be complemented by good lighting quality. Essential quality considerations include glare control, uniformity of light distributed over the use area, the direction of the light, and color rendition. These considerations apply to both natural and artificial lighting.

Glare is a problem when visual discomfort or distraction results from excessive brightness contrast in an individual's field of vision. Severe glare may even be momentarily blinding. It may be caused by either natural or artificial lighting and may be either direct—by looking into a light source—or indirect—by looking at reflections from glossy surfaces. There are a number of glare control techniques for park lighting. Basically these are all ways to control brightness contrast. Natural glare can be controlled for outdoor activities by proper solar orientation with regard to critical lines of sight. Architectural controls such as overhangs, shades, blinds, louvers, polarized windows, and refractors help reduce natural glare indoors. Often simple common-sense interior design and room arrangement avoid low windows behind focal points such as basketball forecourts or in other areas where glossy floors or pool surfaces could cause glare. Careful positioning of artificial light sources outside the normal field of view for the activity or task area is one way of preventing glare. This includes determining proper mounting heights and luminare location. Beam spread can be controlled by proper shield reflectors and louvers. Glare may be reduced by using indirect lighting in some situations.

Uniformity of illumination is generally not absolutely constant nor feasible in large task or activity areas. There are a few situations where disproportionate illumination levels may even be desirable.

For most general lighting situations, where the visual task may be located anywhere in an area—either in a room such as a visitor center, office, shop, or meeting room, or outside in such areas as picnic areas, patios, walks, parking lots, and marinas— the maximum and minimum levels should not vary from the average more than plus or minus 16 percent.

Certain activities (such as the Category I Sports Areas listed in Table 7.1) have significant high- to low-level variation problems. This is especially true of aerial sports where a ball may travel through several zones of varying amounts of brightness. This can visually make the ball appear to alternately accelerate and slow down as it travels through the air. In these activity areas, acceptable uniformity of horizontal illumination occurs when the ratio of maximum to minimum illumination does not exceed 3:1 within a specified area.*

* *Current Recommended Practice for Sports Lighting*, Illuminating Engineering Society, New York, 1968, p. 12.

Uniformity may not always be desirable. For example, use of spot lights in performing arts productions is representative of recreational lighting situations that require uneven illumination distribution for emphasis. Most applications of lighting for aesthetics are based on visually highlighting an object (e.g., waterfall, fountain, statue, or facade) from its surroundings.

Direction of light is a quality consideration that is very important for some activities. Many sports areas are predominately unidirectional (see Category II Sports Areas in Table 7.1). These areas are best illuminated with higher levels of light from one direction. These areas usually have important vertical visual elements—targets, walls, or players as examples—which are viewed usually from one position or angle. Lateral illumination on these elements are more important than on the horizontal surface of the activity area. This is also true for many security lighting situations where trespassers can be either highlighted or silhouetted with proper lateral illumination. Other activity areas are best illuminated from several directions to reduce harsh shadows and provide modeling of participants and other elements such as balls, goals, and other apparatus or equipment. Multidimensional lighting can diffuse and soften shadows. This is important in most general indoor lighting situations well as many sports areas (see Category I Sports Areas in Table 7.1). Many sports lighting systems companies provide sophisticated flood-light-aiming diagrams designed especially to match luminaire locations, heights, beam spreads, and angles to provide high lighting quality and level.

Color rendition is important for certain visual tasks such as personal grooming, social and business relations, and photo reproduction. The lighting for mirrors in restrooms, for offices, meeting rooms, visitor contact stations, dining rooms, and other areas where people view each other at close distances should be as natural as possible. People may be critical of color rendition that does not show "true" color in areas where judging of fashions, flowers, artwork, food, produce, or animals are common, where colored sports equipment may be used or exhibited, or in locations where skin tones should be complimentary.

Use of color-altering lighting may enhance visual elements in a park or may create special effects or moods. This is a common lighting technique in restaurants, ballrooms, theater productions, museums, and merchandising. If done subtly and tastefully, use of color control in park lighting can be an effective experiential control technique.

The combined elements of good illumination, the quantity of light, and lighting quality—glare control, uniformity of distribution, direction, and color rendition—have an effect on park user enjoyment and comfort. These lighting characteristics are different for each lighting situation. Proper control of these factors can instill positive, pleasant reactions by facility users or it may provoke negative, uncomfortable reactions. Both responses have appropriate use occasions in parks.

LIGHTING SYSTEMS

Artificial lighting systems, indoor or outdoor, can be classified as general, localized general, or local lighting. Selecting a lighting system is based on the type of visual task to be performed, the surrounding area around the activity center, and spatial flexibility necessary for relocating visual tasks.

GENERAL LIGHTING

A lighting system that provides a generally uniform level of illumination over the entire activity area may be classified a general lighting system. The luminaires are arranged in a balanced pattern to evenly distribute light in the field, court, area, plaza, or room. There is no special consideration for special locations or things within the area illuminated by the system. The use definers and apparatus—benches, goals, nets, desks, tables, or chairs—are arranged within the boundaries (or walls) of the area according to game rules or other functional considerations with no constraints because of lighting. Figure 7.1 is a good example of a general lighting system. General lighting systems are used outside as well as indoors. Luminaires in general lighting may provide direct lighting (e.g., floodlights, area luminaires with reflectors, and luminous ceilings), indirect lighting (very common for indoor sports courts), or general diffuse where light is eminated in all directions from a luminaire [e.g., postmounted or pendant globes or cubes enclosing the lamp(s)].

LOCALIZED GENERAL LIGHTING

In activity areas that must be carefully designed in coordination with the lighting level and quality factors, a localized general lighting system is used. Sports areas that require emphasis on illumination for special portions of the playing area (e.g., baseball, infield; archery, targets; golf, greens—see Figure 7.7) as well as indoor areas that have especially located lighting over counters, workbenches, craft tables, or other visual task centers may use localized general lighting. The luminaires supply some of the general lighting needs of the entire area or room as well as that of the specific task centers by providing direct or general diffuse lighting for the principal portion with some spillover into the rest of the area.

Figure 7.6

Dramatic effects can be achieved with controlled local direct lighting such as in this application of concealed spotlights and floodlighting. Notice the downlights along this walk used to safely direct pedestrians without distracting from the primary attraction. The aesthetic lighting may be controlled by a semiautomatic timer.

LOCAL LIGHTING

There are some lighting situations where it is necessary or desirable to provide light only for a small visual task center or focal of attention. This may be done by closely positioned direct lighting or by distant spotlights. Often local lighting is installed as portable units such as table or desk lamps, movable spotlights, or weighted base pole lamps. Permanent local lighting may provide illumination for mirrors, work counters, exhibits or displays, wash the wall with patterns of light, and illuminate a flag, statue, or special park signs. Usually local lighting alone is too stark; it usually supplements a general lighting system. Figures 7.2 and 7.6 show use of local lighting in parks.

Lighting a park requires several lighting systems. While all may be connected to the same power line, each activity areas has its own system of lights.

ARTIFICIAL LIGHTING COMPONENTS

The basic parts of artificial lighting are the lamps, luminaires, mounts, controls, and wiring. Each component makes a contribution to good illumination.

LAMPS

The source of artificial light is the lamp. There are many kinds of lamps today. Technology is continually improving light output, lamp life, efficacy (lumens per watt), color rendition, optical controls, and lumen depreciation (dimming with age). Because of these continuing changes, specific lamp characteristics are not detailed here. Current information should be obtained from lamp manufacturers or lighting industry periodicals before selecting a specific lamp for a park lighting system.

INCANDESCENT FILAMENT LAMP.   The first electric lamps used glowing (incandescent) filaments. Today's incandescent lamps, including the quartz-iodine lamp, have several characteristics that make them useful for park lighting. They have low initial installation costs, good optical control (e.g., they provide instant light when turned on, have no restart delay after a power breakage, and may be easily dimmed to any desired brightness below their lumen rating), have very good natural color rendition, can be used over a wide temperature range, and are available in a wide variety of special colors and shapes. There is a large selection of luminaires that use incandescent lamps—from floodlights to decorative chandeliers—for any of the park lighting functions. Incandescent lamps maintain a very high percent of their lumen rating over the lamp life, not becoming significantly dimmer as they get older.

Compared to the other types of electric lamps however, incandescent lamps have shorter lamp life and lower lamp efficacy. They are also more susceptible to vibration and shock failures.

Most common uses of incandescent lamps in parks are for activity lighting where maximum control is important (coin-operated tennis courts or theatrical spot lights where timing is important, for example), where color rendition is important (supplementary local lighting for personal grooming or for emphasizing natural colors in exhibits), and where there is need for good activity lighting only a few times a year, for emergency lighting that must be provided instantly when other lighting systems fail, and for aesthetic purposes where the lamp and its fixture are decorative elements of the park design.

FLUORESCENT LAMPS.   A tube-shaped lamp that produces light by passing electricity through a gas instead of a filament is the fluorescent lamp. These lamps, which are now used more than incandescent lamps in the United States, have a number of properties that make them useful for park lighting. Fluorescent lamps require less energy to operate than incandescent lamps, provide more lumens per watt, have a much longer lamp life, are not as apt to be a glare source (the two to eight foot long tubes glow instead of producing a single point source of bright light), and have a balanced color rendition.

The following additional characteristics may limit use of fluorescent lamps for certain uses. They have low brightness and poor light projection over long distances, initial installation cost is higher than incandescent lamps, and they are sensitive to humidity, surrounding temperatures, and wind.

Fluorescent lamps are excellent for park applications where low mounting heights are possible, low brightness and uniform light distribution is needed, and high annual use occurs. They are used indoors extensively for (1) public recreational activity areas (visitor centers, craft and table game rooms, locker rooms, meeting rooms, restrooms, bowling alleys, and others or (2) for park work centers (offices, shops, conference rooms, and garages, for example) and outdoors (1) for low-level activity areas (tennis, shuffleboard, and horseshoe courts, group picnic pavilions, and others), (2) for safety lighting in halls, stairways, walks, steps, ramps, and parking lots, (3) for emergency lighting in some instances instead of incandescent lamps, and (4) for aesthetic lighting, especially to evenly illuminate a large wall or other flat partition. The color of fluorescent lamps depends on the composition of the phosphor coating inside the tube. Lamps may be selected that produce warm or cool white. Special fluorescent lamps are available that are suitable for plant growth without natural sunlight.

MERCURY VAPOR LAMPS.   The first of the high-intensity discharge (HID) lamps to be developed was the mercury vapor lamp. Light is produced by passing electricity through mercury vapor held at high pressure inside an inner bulb. The outer bulb is usually phosphor coated to partially correct the unbalanced light that is predominately in the blue-green portion of the color spectrum.

Mercury vapor lamps have several desirable characteristics for park lighting: the longest lamp life of any lamp in general use today, high lamp efficacy, good light projection over long distances, and practical resistance from vibration and shock failures.

These lamps, like all gaseous-discharge lamps, require a ballast. There is a slow development of brightness when the lamp is first turned on, requiring almost five minutes before it is at full emission. It takes almost twice that long to come back to full brightness after a power interruption.

Mercury vapor lamps are used whenever high-mounted luminaires are needed for very heavy annual use or where high labor costs make it quite expensive to relamp frequently. Mercury vapor lamps have been used in automatic dusk-to-dawn lights for more than eight years before needing replacement.

Park use of mercury vapor lamps include (1) activity lighting for indoor and outdoor sports lighting, (2) safety lighting along walks, roads, and parking lots, (3) security lighting of supply yards, building entrances and facilities, and (4) limited aesthetic applications that need heavy-use, high-mounted floodlights.

METAL HALIDE LAMPS.   A modification of the mercury high-intensity discharge lamps was the addition of metal halides. This improved light output, color rendition, and lamp efficacy. Compared to mercury vapor lamps, metal halide lamps are generally brighter, cheaper to use, and provides truer skin and warm color tones. Presently metal halide lamps have less than the normal life of mercury vapor lamps, however this is expected to improve as technical improvements are made. The initial start up time is a little less than mercury vapor but may take up to 15 minutes to come back to full brightness after a power interruption.

Metal halide lamps are used instead of mercury vapor lamps in many activity installations such as sports fields because fewer luminaires are required to achieve the desired light level. They are not as practical as mercury vapor lamps for long-burning situations such as safety and security lighting however, because of their relatively short lamp life.

HIGH-PRESSURE SODIUM.   The third high-intensity discharge lamp uses a ceramic arc tube containing sodium under high pressure. This lamp has a very high lumen per watt ratio (over twice that of mercury vapor) and excellent maintenance of lumen output with practically negligible dimming over use. The lamp life is comparable to metal halide. High-pressure sodium lamps emit a distinctive yellow or gold light that complements most warm colors and skin tones but darkens blues and greens. This lamp does not attract insects. The initial start up and restart delays are the shortest of all the HID lamps, with full initial brightness after approximately three minutes. After a brief power interruption, hot high-pressure sodium lamps can come back up to full brightness after only one minute.

These lamps have park applications for general activity lighting indoors and outside—in gymnasiums, pools, sports fields, offices, and garages, for safety lighting in areas where the yellow color indicates special design features, and for some special aesthetic effects.

LOW-PRESSURE SODIUM LAMPS.   A comparatively new lamp is the low-pressure sodium lamp, which has an inner U-shaped discharge tube where the sodium metal vaporizes in neon and argon gas. An outer vacuum jacket tube protects this tube and provides thermal insulation from surrounding temperatures. The lamp is similar to a fluorescent tube, approximately one to four feet long, depending on wattage, and also produces a line source of light. It produces more lumens per watt than high pressure sodium lamps with a comparable lamp life. The lamp maintains almost constant brightness over the entire life. Its color is similar to high-pressure sodium, is noninsect-attracting, and projects well over long distances (especially in mist or fog). The ballast is not as complicated as those necessary for HID lamps. Low-pressure sodium lamps come to full brightness approximately 10 minutes after initial start. Restart after a brief power interruption is immediate. A special luminaire is needed.

Low-pressure sodium lamps are useful in parks for general outdoor activity, safety, and security lighting.

NEON LAMPS.   Thin glass tubes filled with neon gas with electricity passing through them glow red. Addition of other elements produces other colors. Neon lamps have limited use in parks other than for aesthestics because of their low brightness and monochromatic color production. They are used extensively for advertising and have exceptional light projection properties for long distances, especially in foggy conditions. Because of this characteristic, neon beacons are used for navigation.

GAS LAMPS.   Gaslights emit light from one or more glowing (incandescent) mantles attached to a gas-supplied orfice. A single upright mantle is comparable to a 40-watt incandescent lamp. Inverted mantles under slightly higher gas pressure will provide brighter light. Mantles shielded from wind or mechanical disturbance have an indefinite life. Single and multiple mantle gaslights have been used for safety lighting in front of recreation buildings as well as commercial buildings. Gaslights are often selected for their aesthetic effects even though their lumen rating is quite low.

Open-flame gaslights has no mantles and are used primarily for aesthestic effects rather to supply functional light. Examples of open-flame gaslights inclue fishtail burners and gas or luau torches.

LUMINAIRES

The lighting fixture that is designed to position, protect, and supply power to the lamps, distribute the light, and provide necessary controls to protect the surroundings is the luminaire. In addition to the lamp socket or holders, the luminaire housing may include an integral jacket for thermal, moisture, acoustic, and vibration control. A cover is often included to further protect the lamp or for a decorative appearance. Luminaires may also have reflectors, refractors, polarizers, diffusers, or shields to control light distribution.

These various luminaire components are used when lighting situations warrant. Outdoor housings are usually more substantial than indoor fixtures because additional protection is necessary. Covers are available in a wide variety of materials, shapes, colors and light-transmitting properties. Light distribution controls that are incorporated in luminaires may be grouped into reflectors (which redirect the light by bouncing it in a predetermined pattern), refractors and polarizers (which bend the light as it passes through a medium such as a prism), diffusers (which scatter the light in all directions), and shields, such as baffles and louvers (which block light from certain angles).

Luminaires are selected on the basis of functional, technical, safety, economic, and aesthetic reasons. The priorities of these elements will affect the ultimate selection.

TYPES OF LUMINAIRES.   There are numerous luminaires available from manufacturers. While some fixtures are designed especially for one type of lamp, others accept several different lamps. Luminaires may be grouped into several categories based on two light controls—direction and distribution.

Indoor luminaires have been classified as *direct lighting units* if 90 to 100 percent of the light is emitted toward the activity area. This is usually the case for suspended or ceiling luminaires. Up to 10 percent of the light may be directed to the ceiling to softly illuminate it. The light distribution provided by *semidirect units* is mostly down (60 to 90 percent) from overhead luminaires. The upward portion of light from these units provide more general lighting in the room. *General diffuse lighting units* provide light almost equally in all directions. Light utilization is not ideal for small task centers, but this type of luminaire is very good for general lighting in light rooms with light-reflective surfaces. Indoor units that direct 60 to 90 percent of their light upward, or away from the task area, are *semiindirect units.* These units provide slightly more footcandles on a task area than a completely reflected light of equal output. *Indirect lighting units,* which release 90 to 100 percent of their lightoutput away from the activity (or visual task) area are able to illuminate large areas by using light-colored highly reflective ceilings to bounce the light onto the area. This is an excellent way to reduce glare, especially for fast-moving aerial activities such as indoor tennis, volleyball, or other sports where the participant may frequently look up during play.

Outdoor luminaires may also be broadly grouped on the basis of light direction and distribution.

General outdoor lighting units provide practically equidirectional lighting from the luminaire. These units usually have the lamp or lamps enclosed in a decorative enclosure—cube, sphere, globe, cylinder, or other shape—which, while it may be frosted, colored, or in some manner be a light diffuser, does not block or reflect the light in a significant way. These general luminaires may be posttop mounted, pendent, or laterally supported. These are often used as decorative pedestrian-scaled units along walks, near entrances, and in plazas. Figure 7.3 shows an example of a general outdoor lighting application along a park walk.

Most outdoor luminaires are *directional.* Some units, such as street lights and downlights used along steps and walks, direct their light toward the desired area by incorporating reflective canopies, shields, and refractive lens. This effectively utilizes the light in the activity area and does not waste light illuminating tree branches or open sky. The tall parking-lot luminaires in the background of Figure 7.3 direct the light downward to the cars instead of emanating it everywhere.

A large number of outdoor directional luminaires might be classified as light *projectors.* Examples of these units include searchlights, spotlights, and floodlights. The National Electrical Manufacturers Association (NEMA) has designated several floodlight types based on beam spread. Selection of the proper NEMA floodlight designation is important to insure the most efficient lighting with good uniformity, minimum glare, and lighting light "spillage" outside the activity area. Most sports-lighting is done with floodlights.

It is important that a competent lighting specialist design the lighting installation. In addition to beam spread, factors such as luminaire mounting heights, locations, and aiming are important sports lighting considerations. *Current Recommended Practice for Sports Lighting,* published by the Illuminating Engineering Society (IES), provides basic lighting directions for sports events. Most lighting manufacturers can provide specific data for their equipment. While early floodlights were designed only for function, now these directional units are available in attractive styles which do not detract from a park setting when not in use. Figure 7.7 shows an example of a floodlight park situation.

SUPPORT MOUNTINGS

Luminaires must be supported in the most appropriate location to provide the needed light. Indoor permanent lighting fixtures

Figure 7.7

High-mounted floodlights provide extra illumination on the infield as well as adequate overall lighting for the entire ballfield in this localized-general activitiy lighting installation controlled by manual switches.

are usually mounted or suspended from the ceiling or anchored to wall brackets. Outdoors they are mounted atop or from posts (sometimes called standards) by crossarms, attached to exterior walls, suspended from cables, recessed into retaining walls, bollards, or other architectural elements, set in lighting wells below the surface, or even submerged under water. These luminaire support mounts may be wood, masonry, metal, or other durable, weather-resistant material.

Selections of the support devise depends on the required mounting height, weight of the luminaire(s) to be supported, the lighting function, aesthetics, and development norm. Early elevated lighting installations depended on creosoted poles. This is still a very popular basic standard. In addition to these spartan poles, numerous lighting standards are available today that are appropriate to any park development norm and are complementary to any architectural design and material. These should be selected to carry out the total park motif.

WIRING

The electricity that energize the park luminaires is provided by a network of wires. All major wiring should be designed by a competent electrical engineer and installed by a qualified electrician. Underground wiring, while more expensive to install initially, is recommended wherever possible to reduce possibility of vandalism, accidental injury, or death caused by contact with aerial wires, storm damage, and unsightliness from overhead wires. (It is recognized that there are some situations were overhead wiring in a park may be unavoidable. There the lines should be sited in the safest, most serviceable, and unobtrusive corridors.) It is often possible to bury electric cable in utility corridors adjacent to public or service roads. Accurate as-built plans should be kept on site and consulted before any excavation is done.

CONTROLS

There are numerous electric controls that can be used in park lighting. Switches or other devices can start, stop, alter (increase or decrease) power supply, oscillate, or otherwise regulate lighting. Fuses or circuit breakers protect the units from damage or from possibly becoming a dangerous hazard by disconnecting the electricity. Transformers change voltage as necessary. Most of these controls are essential components to the power network of a park and must be specified by a competent electrical engineer.

Park planners should advise the designer about appropriate control requirements—especially switch types and locations—for park lighting to insure the most appropriate utilization, access, protection, and management. Switches may be manual, automatic, or semiautomatic. Manual switches are commonly used for most activity lighting, including recreational activities (such as sports fields) and work areas (such as decks or shops). Some lighted facilities are operated by coin operated controls to restrict power usage to actual use periods. Some agencies use coin-operated use revenue to offset operating costs; others use these devices only as a use control. Timers, which may be quite simple clock controls or very sophisticated programmable regulators, are used to light some activity areas as well as having a large number of possible safety and security applications. Photosensors have wide use for dusk-to-dawn safety lighting installations in park walks, roadways, parking lots, and security use.

The location of lighting switches will depend on the necessity for ready access, convenience for people authorized to use them, probability of vandalism, costs, security, liability, and security. Some manual switches may be mounted on an outside wall or standard for outside lighting, or inside the activity room for recreation rooms, craft rooms, meeting rooms, and so on. Usually these controls are not secured because other provisions—locked gates or doors, for example—control access and use. Other switches are located in control panels mounted in restricted access areas such as a supervisor's office or facility manager's room. Automatic and semiautomatic controls should be located where they would not be subject to tampering.

Each lighting system should be thoroughly studied by members of the planning team to determine the type of lighting controls necessary and where the controls should be located.

SUMMARY

Park lighting is a basic support element that should have careful consideration by park planners. In complex installations, it is recommended that a competent lighting specialist direct this portion of the planning. Park lighting is more than just sports lighting; there are five major park lighting functions: activity, safety, security, emergency, and aesthetics.

The primary planning considerations for good lighting are the provision of the appropriate quantity of illumination with careful attention to all the lighting quality factors. These quality factors include glare control, uniformity of illumination levels, direction of the lighting, and color rendition.

Visual requirements, surroundings, and design constraints determine which lighting system is needed. There are three basic systems: general lighting, localized general lighting, and local lighting. Each system incorporates these lighting components: lamps, luminaires, support mountings, wiring, and controls. There are many different variations for each of these items. Each must be selected to provide the correct application for the lighting situations.

GLOSSARY OF TERMS

Activity Lighting
A function of a lighting system that provides the necessary illumination for a person to do a specific task or performance.

Aesthetic Lighting
A function of a lighting system that enhances the beauty or attractiveness of a visual element.

Beam Spread
The directed light distribution angles of a luminaire.

Emergency Lighting
The function of a lighting system that provides temporary supplementary illumination for evacuation or performance of essential tasks when normal lighting provisions fail.

Footcandle
A measurement of illumination distributed over an area; used to gauge the quantity of light provided.

General Lighting
A lighting system that provides a generally uniform level of illumination over the entire activity area.

Illumination Quality
A factor of good lighting that determines how a lighting application can be best suited to its function(s). Quality considerations include glare control, uniformity, direction, and color rendition.

Illumination Quantity
A factor of good lighting, measured in footcandles, based on the lighting functions, its environment, and use experience norms; a recognized standard level of illumination.

Lamp
A device that emits artificial light.

Lamp Efficacy
A measure of lamp efficiency to produce light when energized by a given amount of power, expressed in lumens per watt.

Local Lighting
A lighting system that provides illumination only for a small visual task area or focal of attention.

Localized General Lighting
A lighting system that provides basically uniform overall lighting for the entire use area in addition to supplementary lighting for special portions of the area or specific task centers within the total.

Lumen
A measure of brightness coming from a light source such as a lamp.

Luminaire
The device, or fixture, that positions, protects, and supplies power to lamps; distributes the light and protects the immediate surroundings from undesirable emissions.

Safety Lighting
A function of a lighting system that provides sufficient illumination to protect people from accidents or assault.

Security Lighting
A function of a lighting system that provides protection to property, equipment, and goods by discouraging crime and aiding detection of offenders.

Watt
A measure of power; amount of electric energy used by electric lamps.

BIBLIOGRAPHY

Bond, John. *Lighting Design in Building.* Peter Peregrinus, Ltd., Stevenage, England, 1973.

Committee on Sports and Recreational Areas. *Current Recommended Practice for Sports Lighting.* Illuminating Engineering Society, New York, 1968.

Committee on Sports and Recreational Areas. "Tennis Court Lighting—A Revision to the IES Sports Lighting Practice," *Journal of IES,* 4:4, July, 1975, pp. 292–295.

Hopkinson, R. G. and J. D. Kay. *The Lighting of Buildings.* Frederick A. Praeger, Inc., New York, 1969.

Kaufman, John E. (Editor) *IES Lighting Handbook,* Fifth Edition. Illuminating Engineering Society, New York, 1972.

National Fire Codes. "NFPA Code 101—Life Safety Code"; "NFPA Code 70—National Electrical Code," National Fire Protection Association, Boston, 1972.

8
water
system

The provision of an adequate and safe supply of water in a park or recreation area is essential for public consumption and use, fire protection, removal of sewage, and park maintenance and operations. Park visitors need water for drinking, cooking, washing, bathing, and laundering. Adequate fire protection is needed for recreation buildings, for fire-use areas such as campgrounds, and for the park maintenance shops, garages, vehicles, and other support facilities. In parks with flush sanitary facilities, most of the water is used for sewage removal (see Chapter 9, Wastewater). In addition, water is used for park irrigation and sprinkling, cleaning, and employee use.

The water system in a park is considered a "public water system" if it has at least 15 service connections or regularly serves an average of at least 25 individuals daily at least three months out of the year, unless the park obtains all its water from, but is not owned or operated by, an external public water system.* All public water systems are required to meet the National Drinking Water Standards.

A park may have some or all of the following water system parts: a collection facility, transmission lines, a treatment plant, storage structure(s), a distribution network, and service fixtures.

* U.S. Environmental Protection Agency, Interim Primary Drinking Water Standards, *Federal Register,* 40:51, 141.2 (f), March 14, 1975, p. 11994.

PLANNING CONSIDERATIONS FOR A PARK WATER SYSTEM

Where feasible, it is recommended that water be obtained from an approved external public water system. This approach will greatly reduce development and operation budgets by providing park users and staff with properly treated water without the costs of developing collection facilities, a treatment plant, and their continuing operational expenses. If water main capacity is sufficient, parks connected to public water service may also be able to eliminate storage structures and require only installation and maintenance of a park water distribution network and the service fixtures.

There are many park areas, however, that are not located near an existing public water system. Most county, state, and national parklands must develop and operate an independent water system for the park or even several small systems in isolated sections of a single large park. These situations require a sanitary survey of the water source(s) and a careful study of the projected water needs. A competent environmental engineer should coordinate this portion of the park planning process. Other contributors will include local health department officers, fire rating experts, geologists, soil scientists, hydraulic engineers, maintenance personnel (e.g., turf specialists and plumbers), and site designers.

The following general discussions of the major functional units of a park water system—collection, transmission, treatment, and distribution—provides a basic understanding of this vital support element to park planners. Water service fixtures are discussed in a separate section about park user considerations.

WATER SOURCES AND COLLECTION

Water supply sources are predominately located in subsurface groundwater-bearing formations or surface waters. Ground-water collection developments are many times more numerous than surface water facilities; the groundwater systems usually have smaller capacities, however. Selection of a park water source is based on the availability, location, quantity, and quality of the raw water, the economies of processing and transporting it, and the projected use demand.

SURFACE WATER.   Still-water bodies such as lakes and reservoirs have a more uniform year-round water quality and are usually cheaper to process than rivers and streams. The major problems of surface water sources are pollution and eutrophication. The Water Pollution Control Act of 1972 is the basis for a nationwide water quality program. Rivers and lakes are classified according to water uses (including the park-related uses of public water supply, water contact recreation, and fish propagation and wildlife) and monitored to insure that physical, chemical, biological, and temperature characteristics remain within established criteria. State water quality agencies can provide evaluations and recommendations about surface waters considered for new public water sources.

Because the purest surface water is usually available in remote, sparsely inhabited areas at or near the point of rainfall or snowmelt, large parks are able to construct upstream water reservoirs in stream valleys before the water has flowed a considerable distance and received pollutants from adjacent agricultural, residential, or industrial sources. Treatment of these reservoirs is easy and economical but lengthy transmission lines must carry the water to the use areas. Downstream or multiple purpose reservoirs are more subject to pollution and eutrophication; water treatment for these sources is more costly but transmission requirements are usually minimal.

RECREATIONAL USE OF WATER SUPPLY RESERVOIRS. It is not possible to state that recreational use of water supply reservoirs is irreparably harmful or, on the other hand, that it should always be permitted without fear of water quality degradation. That decision depends on many interrelated factors: water quality of the impoundment, amount of water treatment provided, area and volume of the reservoir, soil types and erodibility of the shoreline, kinds of recreational use permitted (water contact, surface water activities, or water-enhanced land activities), recreational-use capacity and behavior controls, season of use, sanitary provisions, statutory controls, and other water-quality protection measures. These and other factors will change from reservoir to reservoir and even change at the same reservoir over a period of time—planners should check first with the appropriate water quality agencies.

SURFACE WATER INTAKES. A water intake structure is the equivalent to a groundwater well or spring; that is, it is the mechanism by which raw water is drawn from the water source. The location of the intake is as important as the location of a well. Proper screening of intakes will minimize operating problems.

River intakes should be located in deep water or along a shore with consideration for currents, sandbars, ice and debris, boating patterns, and upstream from sewage and industrial discharge points.

Lake and reservoir intake locations are determined by surface and subsurface currents, shoreline pollution, sediment deposits, and water stratification patterns. Towers with multiple inlet ports are used in lakes and reservoirs with fluctuating water levels. Additionally, thermal stratification of the impoundment in the summer may create three distinct zones: the epilimnion (warm surface layer), the hypolimnion (cooler bottom layer), and the thermocline (a thin zone of rapid temperature change between these layers). In the winter the water temperature from surface to bottom is more uniform; in spring and fall there is a period of vertical circulation. The water quality at various levels changes throughout the year, so multiple inlet ports are used to withdraw water at the depth providing the best overall water quality.

GROUNDWATER. Subsurface water is usually purer, more readily available, and cheaper to obtain and treat than surface water (depending on well depth.) It is available for use at or very near the point of supply, which eliminates the costs of transmission pipes. It is not necessary to construct large dams for reservoirs because the subsurface water-bearing strata are natural reservoirs. Groundwater is relatively inexpensive to provide at several separated activity centers in a large park, rather than a single, large surface water supply. The usual problems of groundwater are bacterial contamination, hardness, and the presence of dissolved minerals and salts (especially iron and manganese).

The geology of the park is an important factor in groundwater utilization. Igneous formations are not usually good sources of water; sedimentary formations are quite good. Deposits of unconsolidated rock such as sand or gravel usually provide abundant volumes of water and sandstones; shales and some limestones have good accumulations. Joints, seams, crevices, and faults in metamorphic formations also may yield ample groundwater. Groundwater pollution may be a problem where excessive faulting occurs, such as in limestone areas.State and federal water resources departments within the respective Geological Survey offices are essential information sources for groundwater studies and investigations.

Bacterial, chemical, physical, and microscopic analysis of water samples must be done by appropriate public health laboratories. The results of the laboratory analysis should indicate the type and amount of treatment required.

WELLS AND SPRINGS. The two most-frequently used means of obtaining water from subsurface water-bearing strata are wells and springs. They are the groundwater supply counterpart to surface water intakes.

Wells are generally classified as shallow wells or deep wells. Shallow wells are not usually recommended for parks because the water table is more apt to be contaminated with pathogenic organisms and the yield may be affected by seasonal fluctuations of the groundwater. Deep wells (more than 25 feet deep) are usually drilled and may be 4 to 12 inches in diameter or more. They are less apt to be contaminated and are more dependable than shallow wells or springs. It is recommended that the American Water Works Associations's *Standard for Deep Wells, AWWA A100-66* be used as a basis for deep-well construction.

Springs may be classified as gravity or artesian. Gravity springs occur when the aquifer laterally comes to the surface because of a significant drop in surface grade below the water table or when impervious obstructions to the groundwater causes an overflow at the surface. Artesian springs occur when faults in impermeable strata permit underlying water under pressure to escape to the surface. Artesian springs are usually more free from pathogenic contamination than gravity springs. Springs may be mere trickles; others may gush over a million gallons of water a day. Flows from springs often are more subject to drought than are wells. Proper construction to protect the water quality is important. Either wells or springs, if the water quality and quantity are acceptable, can be an excellent source of park water.*

PUMPS.   For major park water supplies, automatic pumping stations should be located as close to the water intake, well, or spring house as possible to transmit the raw water to treatment facilities. Auxiliary pumps operated by portable generators should be provided to insure an uninterrupted supply of water during temporary maintenance and repair on the primary pumps, or to meet emergency water requirements, such as a major fire.

For secondary water supplies, such as a small remote activity center with no high gallons per minute (gpm) demands, a single small pump is sufficient. Low-volume, pure groundwater can frequently be provided by a hand pump.

WATER TRANSMISSION

Many parks have the water collection facilities—either from upstream reservoirs or isolated wells—located a considerable distance from the treatment plant and distribution network. In these cases, water conduits, or transmission lines, transport the water the required distance. Transmission lines may link the collection facility to the water works by gravity or pumping.

WATER QUALITY AND TREATMENT

Potable water must not only be bacteriologically safe; it should be attractive and palatable as well. The presence of patho-genic contaminants, unpleasant odor or taste, high turbidity (cloudiness), murky color, and purgative effects are common criticisms by the public.

As a protection, all public water systems must meet stringent Environmental Protection Agency Drinking Water Standards according to the federal Safe Drinking Water Act of 1974 (P.L. 93-523). These standards establish maximum physical, chemical, biological, and radiological contaminant levels and specify sampling, analysis, and reporting requirements for public water supplies.

WATER TREATMENT PROCESSES.   It is possible to have groundwater supplies that require no treatment. Deep-well

* See *Manual of Individual Water Supply Systems,* EPA 430-9-73-003, U.S. Environmental Protection Agency, 1973.

water is normally uncontaminated or may require only removal of dissolved gases and minerals such as irons and manganese by aeration, oxidation, and filtration. Some groundwater requires softening as well. Chlorine normally is used to provide residual protection in the water distribution system and disinfect the water if necessary.

Surface water requires much more treatment than groundwater. Plain sedimentation of the water to remove silt and other heavy matter is often considered the first step. This settling process, without a chemical additive, may occur naturally in the reservoir or lake, or presettling basins may be constructed (particularly if the water source is a river or stream) to prepare the raw water for treatment. Chlorine is added after presedimentation to disinfect the water. Then a coagulant such as alum causes most of the suspended particles and microorganisms to stick together as a mass or floc, which agglomerates and settles out. Other additives, such as soda ash, hydrated lime, quicklime, or sulfuric acid may be used to obtain the proper chemical reactions. Some river treatment plants must use two consecutive chemical coagulation and sedimentation processes to achieve the desired level of treatment.

After this clarification the water is filtered to remove the remaining suspended materials and floc. Activated carbon may be helpful in taste and odor control. Final filtration may be through slow sand, gravity, rapid sand, or pressure filters. The type of filter to be used is based on the amount of water to be treated, the possibility of future expansion, and the operating budget. The rapid-sand filter, which can be used for all size plants, requires very skilled competent supervision and operation. The other types of filters are often used in smaller plants, where adaptable.

After filtration, essentially all of the bacteria and suspended solids have been removed. Final chlorination is used to kill any remaining bacteria and complete the water treatment. It is now ready to be pumped to storage or through the distribution network for use in the park.

Wastes from water treatment include sludge from the settling basins and tanks and filter backwash. These wastes must be disposed of according to federal and state water quality and pollution control regulations.

Park water treatment plants may be constructed on site or may be installed as a predesigned and prefabricated packaged unit. Advantages to modular prefabricated package plants include the ease of installation and ability to enlarge the capacity simply by adding more modular units. These plants can process from 10,000 gallons to one million gallons per day.

The treatment plants should be located outside major park activity areas because in these areas it may be subject to vandalism or other problems. The plant also should be outside

possible flood, erosion, or other problem areas. All structures—
inlet towers, wells, spring houses, pumping stations, valve or gate
housing, basins and tanks, and processing buildings—should be
well secured with appropriate means including locks, fences, and
other security devices. Necessary vehicular access routes should
be all-weather roads of sufficient strength to carry heavy service,
maintenance, and delivery trucks.

DISTRIBUTION PUMPING

High-lift pumps move the potable water from the treatment
plant to either the service storage structures or into the distribution network. The capacity of the pumps, measured in
gallons per minute (gpm) must be balanced with the capacity of
the treatment facilities and the water demand, while minimum of
500 gpm is necessary to service a standard Class B fire hydrant,
which is quite adequate for park fire protection. Pump capacity
is also an important factor in determining water storage
requirements for fire fighting. It is essential that the head
characteristics of the pump be such that proper pressures can be
provided throughout the system. Centrifugal pumps are normally
used for large installations.

The pumps should be housed in a shelter to protect them from
mechanical and fire damage. Separate power service should be
provided to the pumphouse, without a direct line to other
buildings. If possible the structure should be at least 60 to 75 feet
from the nearest building for fire protection. Auxillary power
sources are desirable for use during emergencies such as
interruption of normal power, especially if park water service
storage capacity is small.

WATER SERVICE STORAGE

While parks that are provided water from external public water
systems often do not need water storage structures, they are
usually a necessary part of an independent water system. The
service storage structure(s) may be necessary for one or more of
these functions: (1) to help meet peak water demands during
high-use periods, (2) to maintain adequate water pressure to
operate hydrants, flush sanitary fixtures, and other water outlets
throughout the system (3) to provide a reserve supply of water for
fire fighting or during a malfunction of either treatment plant or
distribution pumps, and (4) to reduce operating costs (by
eliminating continuous distribution pumping and permit storage
refill during reduced power rate periods).

The storage capacity is based on these functions. Because not
all functions may be needed at every park, the purpose(s) of
the water storage units should be designated before volume
requirements are set.

PEAK DEMAND.   The maximum flow of water required if all water service fixtures were in use simultaneously is the peak demand. For preliminary planning purposes, a simple method of determining peak demand would be to add the minimum recommended flow rates for every proposed water service fixture. Table 8-1 lists some typical examples.

The emergency fire flow protection requirements usually greatly exceed the normal park peak demand. To reduce expensive peak volume requirements for the water system (which affect treatment plant, distribution pump, storage, and distribution capacities), the normal park peak demand or fire flow requirements, whichever is higher, is used to determine capacities in most park water systems that use potable water for fire control, but in municipalities or large parks where normal activities and domestic water use continue during a fire, the combined peak demand is used. The water storage facilities must supply the peak park demand minus the capacity of the distribution pumps.

Table 8.1

Minimum recommended flow rates and pressures for selected park water service fixtures[a]

FIXTURE, SERVICE SIZE	FLOW RATE (at point of discharge) (gpm)	FLOW PRESSURE (psi)
Lavatory, ordinary basin faucet, $\frac{3}{8}$-inch supply	3	8
Lavatory, self-closing basin faucet, $\frac{3}{8}$-inch supply	$2\frac{1}{2}$	8
Sink, faucet $\frac{1}{2}$-inch supply	3	8
Laundry, $\frac{1}{2}$-inch tub cock	4	8
Shower, $\frac{1}{2}$-inch supply	4	8
Toilet, tank type, $\frac{3}{8}$-inch supply	3	8
Toilet, flush valve type, 1-inch supply	15–35	25
Urinal, flush valve, $\frac{3}{4}$-inch supply	15	15
Drinking fountain, $\frac{3}{8}$-inch supply	$\frac{3}{4}$	15
Wall hydrant, $\frac{1}{2}$-inch sill cock	5	10
Hose bib, $\frac{1}{2}$-inch supply	5	10
Standpipe, Class I, 4-inch supply	500	Not less than 20
Standpipe, Class II, 2-inch supply	100	20–80
Fire hydrant, Class B, 4-inch supply	500	Not less than 20

[a] Adapted from recommended flow rates and pressures from *The BOCA Basic Plumbing Code, 3rd Edition* and the *National Fire Code*: NFPA Standard No. 14—"Standpipe and Hose Systems," NFPA Standard No. 24—"Outside Protection" and NFPA Standard No. 25—"Water Supply Systems for Rural Fire Protection."

GRAVITY WATER PRESSURE.   Elevated tanks or reservoirs above all points of the distribution network can provide necessary water pressure so each water service fixture will operate most efficiently. This pressure is based on the head, or vertical distance from the water elevation in the tank or reservoir to the fixture. While most park water fixtures require low pressure [less than 15 pounds per square inch (psi)] the pressure loss of the distribution lines may be substantial. For example, almost one psi is lost every 100 feet of fairly smoth six-inch water line carrying 500 gpm; pressure losses in smaller lines can be even more significant. Parks with flush sanitary fixtures need to provide 20 psi at each fixture. The pressure at fire hydrants must be at least 75 psi for effective fire fighting using hoses direct from the hydrant.

Table 8.2 shows head and equivalent water pressure for selected vertical distances. Elevated tanks over 150 high or located within 1500 feet of a landing area must have appropriate warning lights for aircraft.

AUXILIARY AND FIRE RESERVE.   The auxiliary and fire reserve capacity needed for a park is not a set gallons-in-storage standard. The amount of water required depends on the maximum daily water usage, location of the storage tanks, accessibility to surface water suitable for fire control, and economics.

FIRE RESERVE.   A water supply used for fire fighting in a park is usually considered to be adequate if it can deliver a fire flow of 500 gpm for a minimum of two hours. This requires that 60,000 gallons of water be available for fire control even though many fires, if discovered early, can be controlled within half an hour.

Table 8.2
Water pressure of a column of water per foot head

Feet Head	Water Pressure (psi)
1	.43
2	.87
3	1.30
4	1.74
5	2.17
6	2.60
7	3.04
8	3.47
9	3.91
10	4.34
20	8.68
25	10.85
50	21.70
100	43.40

This amount of water is quite often several times the maximum daily usage and is economically unfeasible for many small park potable water storage systems. For fire control, therefore, it is often best to prepare contingency plans for use of water in nearby swimming pools, ponds, lakes, reservoirs, streams, or other suitable surface water bodies instead of storing such an excessive amount as part of the potable water system. The capacity of swimming pools, for example, may range from 200,00 to 500,00 gallons—well in excess of the two-hour fire flow requirement.

Fire pumpers are capable of drawing water from screened intake lines from surface water impoundments and discharging it into separate nonpotable fire control distribution pipe lines. Auxilliary pumps are necessary for every incremental vertical lift of 23 feet.*

POTABLE RESERVE.   The minimum storage capacity for potable water has been set at between one to two times the maximum daily flow rates, depending on the type of activities provided, wastewater requirements of the park, ability of the park to partially or even completely suspend programs in the event of water supply failure, and the possible economy of daylight use of stored water that is refilled at night during cheaper power rate periods.

TYPES AND LOCATIONS OF STORAGE STRUCTURES.   Potable water storage structures are either elevated tanks, standpipes or underground basins, or reservoirs. Generally a standpipe (Figure 8-1) is a tank whose height exceeds its diameter; a reservoir (Figure 8-2) has a diameter greater than its height. These structures may be constructed of steel, wood, concrete, or masonry.

If water is stored in ground level or subsurface tanks, they must be located above flood-prone elevations, above and at least 50 feet away from any sewage system, and at least 50 feet away from adjacent buildings (for fire safety). These storage structures usually require booster pumping. If the storage structures are elevated to provide gravity pressure for the water distribution, it is good to locate them as close to the service facilities as possible to minimize pressure loss caused by lengthy pipelines. Other factors to be considered when locating water storage structures in recreation areas—especially possibly incongruous elevated tanks or standpipes—are the settings (which may be very natural or obviously man-made), the visual and experiential relationships of the visible storage structure and the activity, possible multiple use of the structure for recreation, as well as the inherent hazards of a challenging structure for adventurous climbers.

---

* William C. Arble, Fire Protection Specialist for Pennsylvania Technical Assistance Program, personal communication, April 5, 1975.

Figure 8.1

Water standpipes may be incorporated into park use as elevated activity facilities such as this interpretive observatory.

RECREATIONAL USE OF WATER STORAGE STRUCTURES.
Many park agencies have recognized the coincident recreational asset a water storage structure provided. Elevated tanks and standpipes have been incorporated into parks as activity centers—scenic overviews, observatories, and local historical and environmental education orientation stations—as shown in Figure 8-1. Ground-level reservoirs with reinforced bearing roofs support a wide variety of recreational facilities in the same manner that parking garages and other building roofs are used for such things as hard surface courts, skating rinks, measured jogging paths, dance patios, performing arts stages, playgrounds, and other facilities. Figure 8-2 shows efficient recreational use of a large area-consuming storage reservoir.

DISTRIBUTION NETWORK
The park water distribution system is composed of a network of pipes, necessary control valves and, if required, fire hydrants. The purposes of the system are to transport potable water from

the park's treatment plant or storage structure (or from a corporation stop tapped into an external public water main if the park does not supply its own water) to service connections for individual outdoor water service fixtures and park buildings with plumbing, to protect the water from contamination while in transport, and, if required, provide water for fire fighting. In some parks it is best to develop a dual distribution system—small pipelines for potable water and large dry pipelines for fire control, using the surface water reservoirs discussed earlier.

NETWORK PATTERN.   The physical arrangement of the piping is determined by the location and proximity of service connections and the importance of continuous, uninterrupted flow during system repairs and emergencies.

A simple dendritic scheme (Figure 8.3) is often used for limited park water distribuiton from an external main: a park distribution main from the supply main branches into secondary

Figure 8.2

This playground is actually the roof of the water reservoir for the park. Park planners can incorporate the water storage structure into a cluster of activity facilities such as this recreation pavilion. Water treatment and pumping facilities are conveniently located in a wing of the building.

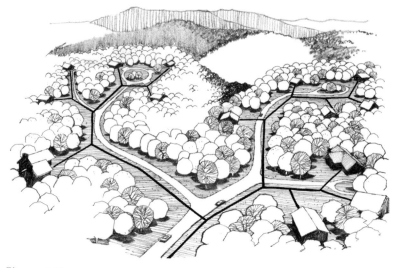

Figure 8.3

A branched water-distribution system is an economical scheme for widely dispersed park water facilities.

feeder lines that supply the service lines to the outside drinking fountains and faucets as well as park buildings. This branching pattern is the most economical for widely dispersed facilities. It is also used for simple distribution networks in parks with their own water supply. If not used sufficiently, however, the water in dead-end lines may become stagnant. This is why water frequently should be drawn from remote facilities linked to a branch network. There may also be problems with fire flow on smaller networks with dead-end mains. Fire hydrants should not be located on the end of four-inch or smaller mains.

For park developments that are clustered or have greater needs for continuous service during periods of repair or emergency, a looped pattern is recommended. The mains are interconncected so that the network can deliver water to any service connection from more than one direction. Hydraulically, this greatly reduces the frictional head loss in the mains and helps maintain necessary pressure for emergency needs. Figure 8-4 shows a looped distribution pattern for a high-density recreation development.

The design of a park water distribution system can be quite complicated and should be done by a qualified engineer.

DISTRIBUTION COMPONENTS.   Pipes, valves, and hydrants are the basic parts of the park water distribution network. The pipes make up the water conveyance structure; the valves control the pressure, flow, and direction of the water; hydrants provide high pressure and flow outlets for fire fighting.

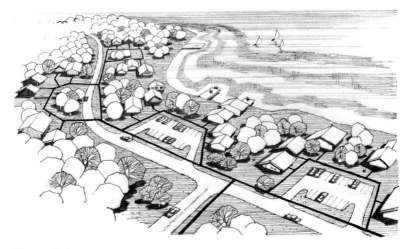

Figure 8.4

A looped water-distribution system provides continuous service from more than one direction should an emergency or repair require shutdown at any point in the branch lines.

The *pipelines* are graduated from the largest to the smallest lines—the supply main to the arterial (feeder) mains to the distribution mains (secondary feeders), which are tapped by service lines. Park mains are made of ductile iron, cast iron, concrete, asbestos cement, plastic, or steel. Service lines are usually copper or plastic.

The size of water mains is based on the required flow (demand) and pressure. Pipe material and length of the run can also cause sufficient head loss to require a larger size. In parks where fire protection is not a function of the water distribution system, branch patterns should not use six-inch mains over 2400 feet long, four-inch mains over 1200 feet or two-inch lines longer than 300 feet. If lines are connected at both ends, two-inch lines should be no longer than 600 feet and four-inch lines not more than 2000 feet*. If the system is used for fire protection, no main should be smaller than six-inches. The maximum recommended length for a six-inch main is 2000 feet for a 500 gpm fire flow and only 500 feet for a 1000 gpm fire flow. An eight-inch line will carry two times as much water as a six-inch line for the same head loss.†

Park service line sizes are based on the accumulative flow requirements of the water fixtures on the building or on the connection. They should never be less than three-quarter-inch

* Joseph A. Salvato, "The Design of Small Water Systems," *Public Works*, 91:5, May, 1960, p. 129.
† Salvato. *ibid.*

Table 8.3
Estimated fire flow required for selected park buildings[a]

Park Building Examples	Estimated Fire Flow (gpm)
One-story wood frame construction, ca. 2000 sq ft floor area, no adjacent buildings	
Day Lodge, Museum, Dining Hall, Outdoor Education Center, Craft Building, Pavilion	1,200
Two-story masonry and wood construction, ca. 3000 sq ft floor area, no adjacent buildings	
Dormitory, Overnight Lodge, Conference Center, Exhibit Hall	1,000
One-story woodframe construction with wood shingle roofing, ca. 150 sq ft floor space, adjacent buildings, less than 30 feet apart	
Rental Cabins	1,000
One-story wood frame or ordinary construction, ca. 150 sq ft floor space, adjacent buildings more than 50 feet away	
Small Contact Station, Visitor Center Bathhouse, Comfort Station, Utility House, Refuse Transfer Stations	500

[a] Based on calculations using formulas and tables in *Guide for Determination of Required Fire Flow,* Second Edition, Insurance Services Office, 1974.

and are usually not more than two inches unless the building has fire standpipes installed.

Fire hydrant connections should not be less than six inches in diameter.*

Water pressure in the mains should not be less than 20 psi for lines without fire hydrants or 75 psi for lines with fire hydrants nor more than 125 psi. (However, pumpers can perform adequately at 20 psi.) It is necessary to provide the flow pressure recommended for each water fixture and hydrant at the entrance to each unit, after any head loss along the distribution line.

Park water distribution systems not used for fire protection should have a flow capacity based on the accumulative peak demand water rquirements of all the areas and buildings of each service main. (For preliminary planning purposes, it may be assumed water flow equals sewage flow. See Tables 9.4 and 9.5.) Table 8.1 lists the recommended pressure and flow for selected park water service fixtures.

Water systems used for fire control should have a flow capacity of not less than 500 gpm and larger if the estimated fire flow for any Class A fire hazard (extinguishable by water) is greater than this. Table 8.3 shows the estimated fire flow for selected park buildings.

Distribution control valves are used to shut off water in mains and service connections (gate valves and butterfly valves), to

* National Fire Protection Association, *National Fire Codes,* NFPA Standard No. 24, "Outside Protection," § 4101.

permit flow in only one direction (check valves), and to decrease high water pressure in lateral service lines to acceptable levels for small fixtures (pressure-reducing valves).

Hydrants provide high pressure-and-flow discharge for fire fighting, pavement cleaning, natural ice rink flooding, portable snow-making, and other uses. Hydrants used for fire fighting should have a flow capacity of at least 500 gpm. Smaller hydrants are suitable for maintenance and other high-volume water needs.

Fire hydrants should be located at strategic points in fire hazard activity areas such as picnic areas and campgrounds where fires are a normal part of the recreational activity. The maximum recommended distance between hydrants in these areas is 450 feet, for a hydrant service area of slightly more than $3\frac{1}{2}$ acres. For building protection, every exterior wall of the structure should be capable of being serviced by hose not over 250 feet long. Some park buildings can adequately be protected by one hydrant, other buildings may require additional service. For average conditions hydrants should be placed about 50 feet from the building protected.* At marinas where piers or docks extend from shore, hydrants should be located so that hose lines less than 250 feet long can reach each boat slip.†

Fire hydrants should be located so that they are readily accessible to public or park fire vehicles (i.e. approximately two feet from the shoulder of any all-weather public use road or adjacent to a similar service road) at the same grade as the access route. Pump outlets should face the vehicle lane; hydrants should be free from any obstructing trees, pole, or fence; and set at a convenient height for the fire fighters.

DISTRIBUTION CROSS-CONNECTIONS AND RELATION TO OTHER BURIED UTILITIES.   There should be no cross connection between potable water lines and nonpotable water lines such as sewers or impure recycled water.

Water pipe should be laid below frost line if possible. Some engineers recommend water lines be laid above and 10 feet away from sewers. Both may be laid in the same trench if the water line is at least 18 inches above the sewer and offset on a shelf of undisturbed soil.

USER CONSIDERATIONS FOR PARK WATER FIXTURES

Of all the water needs in a park, public consumption use and removal of sewage are most conspicuous to the park user. Water distribution connections supply a large number of various water service fixtures. Basically, these may be categorized as either

* National Fire Protection Association, ibid., NFPA Standard No. 24, "Outside Protection," § 4202.
† National Fire Protection Association ibid., NFPA Standard No. 303, "Marinas and Boatyards," p. 31.

sanitary fixtures or supply fixtures. *Sanitary fixtures* are used briefly for personal care and then discharge a very large portion of the water supplied to it as wastewater into the sewer system. Chapter 9 discusses park wastewater systems. Examples of sanitary fixtures include toilets, urinals, drinking fountains, shower heads, lavatories, sinks, and faucets. *Supply fixtures* provide water for consumption or other use with none discharged into the sanitary sewers. Examples of supply fixtures include hydrants, sprinklers, hose bibbs, pool inlets, and street washers. It is possible for some fixtures, such as drinking fountains and faucets to be either sanitary or supply fixtures, depending on the presence or absence of a sewer connection.

DRINKING FOUNTAINS

Convenience, location, capacity, and sanitation are important considerations of park drinking fountain planning. Each fixture

Table 8.4
Recommended minimum number of drinking fountains in selected outdoor recreational activity areas or facilities

Activity Area or Facility	Drinking Fountains	Comments
Amphitheater	One for each 500 spectators One for performers	If facility is used for rehearsals and for performances with intermissions

Athletic fields
  Baseball fields
  Football fields
  Soccer fields
  Softball fields
  Tracks
	One for each 100 participants
	One for each 500 spectators
		If facility is used regularly for events attracting large numbers of spectators, located near seating area(s)

Boating sites
  Docks
  Launching ramps
  Marinas
	One for each 20 slips, or
	One for each four ramps, or
	One for each 50 parking spaces	

Campgrounds	One for each 40 sites, or One for each six acres, or One for each section	
Golf course	One for each nine holes, or One for each 2000 yards	Located adjacent to tee

Hard surface courts
  Basketball
  Handball
  Racquetball
  Squash
  Tennis
	One for each eight courts	

Horseback riding areas
  Arenas
  Stables
	One for each 100 riders	

must be where it is convenient for the most people it serves. There should be sufficient opportunities to use a fountain without a long wait. Each fountain should be equipped to provide clean, potable water in an inviting and sanitary manner in a convenient fashion for everyone. Table 8.4 lists recommended minimum drinking fountain provisions in selected outdoor recreational activity areas or facilities.

There are numerous acceptable drinking fountain designs. Many styles are available as proprietary manufactured units or appliances, with features such as antifreeze plumbing, vandal-resistant pedestals or casings, hand or foot values, coolers, or hot water taps. It is possible to custom design drinking fountains to reflect the park motif or theme, and to use similar construction materials in all the park elements. Figures 8.5–8.6 show examples of how these fixtures have been incorporated into the experience setting of a park. Properly prepared agency specifications for drinking fountains, based upon the American National Standards Institute, Inc. *ANSI Standard A112.11.1-1973,*

Table 8.4   (Continued)

Activity Area or Facility	Drinking Fountains	Comments
Picnic areas		
Small group units	One for each six acres, or One for each 100 tables	Service radius for each fountain is approximately 300 feet maximum
Large group unit	One for each 150 picnickers	Located outside sanitary facilities
Playground	One for each 100 children	Located within 150 feet of playground
Sanitary facilities (separate building)	One at each building	Located outside the toilet rooms
Scenic and interest stops Historic sites Outdoor education and natural science exhibits Overlooks	One for each 30 parking spaces	
Swimming facilities		
Beaches	One for each 350 lineal feet of shoreline, or One for each 500 bathers	Located within 250 feet of shoreline
Pools	One inside enclosure, or One for each 500 bathers One outside enclosure	Located at shallow end of pool If spectator facilities are available
Winter activity areas Downhill skiing Ice skating areas Sledding/toboggan runs	One for each 100 participants	Sheltered and winterized

Figure 8.5

Drinking fountains can reflect the experiential motif of the park, as demonstrated by this nautical fountain at a marina.

will permit economical competitive bidding on acceptable manufactured units or will provide the criteria for special designs.

HOT WATER NEEDS

All recreational buildings that have special rooms for public visit or use (e.g., visitor information or orientation centers, outdoor

Figure 8.6

The National Park Service has effectively used drinking fountains to complement the park setting, such as this "town pump" fountain in a historical park.

education, historical, or cultural centers, museums, performing centers, camp dormitories, or cabins, crafts and organization rooms, etc.) should have sanitary facilities for these indoor areas with hot as well as cold water connections to the lavatories. Showers in bathhouses, fieldhouses, gymnasiums, camp wash houses, and other recreational facilities must be adequately equipped with sufficient hot water. Rapid recharge water heaters must be sized to the capacity and use of each facility.

Swimming pool heaters are separate units because of the volume and the separation of the pool water from the water distribution/wastewater disposal system of the park.

WATER SERVICE FOR PARK EMPLOYEES

When planning the water system for a park, the water needs of park employees should be incorporated into the basic plan. Roving field and mobile employees are able to use the facilities provided in the various activity areas of the park or carry portable water containers for use at a project site. There are other permanent work stations, however, that must be provided with basic sanitary fixtures—toilets, lavatories, and separate drinking fountains or coolers located outside the toilet room. Some of these permanent work stations include park offices, shops, garages, fire towers, water treatment plants, sewage treatment plants, and ranger stations. (Table 9.3 shows the recommended sanitary fixture standards for these situations.)

SUMMARY

A park water system is essential for public consumption and use, fire protection, removal of sewage, and park maintenance and operations. Because so much water is discharged into the sewer system, it is important that water supply, treatment, and distribution be planned at the same time as wastewater collection, treatment, and disposal.

It is recommended that, if possible, a park be connected to an approved external public water system. This feature will eliminate the development costs and annual operational expenses of the water supply facility and treatment plant.

The water system of a park should be planned with the direction of a competent sanitary engineer. The guidelines offered here are for preliminary planning purposes only and to familiarize other members of the park planning team with these essential support facilities.

GLOSSARY OF TERMS

Flow
Quantity of water through a pipe, measured in gallons per minute (mpg).

Head
Vertical distance (usually in feet) from the water elevation in a storage tank or reservoir to the water service fixture.

Head Loss
Reduction in water pressure, measured in pounds per square inch (psi), or in feet of water.

Hydrant, Fire
A water outlet providing very high-pressure-and-flow discharge for fire fighting.

Peak Demand
The maximum flow of water required if all water service fixtures were in use simultaneously.

Reservoir, Storage
A storage structure for treated water.

Reservoir, Supply
An impoundment of surface water that is the source of raw water for the water system.

Sanitary Fixtures
Water service fixtures that are connected to the sewer and wastewater system.

Standpipe (outlet)
A water outlet, usually smaller than a hydrant, that provides high-pressure-and-flow discharge; frequently installed to service separate floors of a multiple-story building for fire fighting.

Standpipe, Storage
A cylindrical storage structure for treated water.

Supply Fixture
Water service fixtures that are not connected to the sewer and wastewater system.

Water Service Fixture
An apparatus or appliance that uses water to function and is permanently attached with plumbing to the water system.

BIBLIOGRAPHY

BOCA Basic Fire Prevention Code, Third Edition. Building Officials and Code Administration International, Inc., Chicago, 1975.

BOCA Basic Plumbing Code, Third Edition. Building Officials and Code Administration International, Inc., Chicago, 1975.

Fair, Gordon M., John C. Geyer, and Daniel A. Okun. *Elements of Water Supply and Wastewater Disposal,* Second Edition. Wiley, New York, 1971.

Grading Schedule for Municipal Fire Protection. Insurance Services Office, Public Protection Grading Department, 160 Water St., New York, New York, 1974.

Guide for Determination of Required Fire Flow, Second Edition. Insurance Services Office, Public Protection Grading Department, 160 Water St., New Your, New York, 1974.

Hammer, Mark J. *Water and Waste-Water Technology.* Wiley, New York, 1975.

National Fire Codes

"NFPA Standard No. 14—Standpipe and Hose Systems"
"NFPA Standard No. 22—Water Tanks for Private Fire Protection"
"NFPA Standard No. 24—Outside Protection"
"NFPA Standard No. 25—Water Supply Systems for Rural Fire Protection"
"NFPA Standard No. 224—Homes and Camps in Forest Areas"
"NFPA Standard No. 303—Marinas and Boatyards"
National Fire Protection Association, Boston, 1972.

Salvato, Joseph A., Jr. "The Design of Small Water Systems," *Public Works,* 91:5, May, 1960, pp. 109-133.

Salvato, Joseph A., Jr. *Environmental Engineering and Sanitation,* Second Edition. Wiley, New York 1972.

U.S. Council on Environmental Quality, *Recreation on Water Supply Reservoirs—A Handbook for Increased Use.* U.S. Government Printing Office, Washington, D.C., 1975.

U.S. Department of Health, Education and Welfare. *Environmental Health Practice in Recreational Areas.* DHEW Publication No. (HSM) 72-10009, U.S. Government Printing Office, Washington, D.C., 1972.

U.S. Department of Health, Education and Welfare. *Manual for Evaluating Public Drinking Water Supplies.* Public Health Service Publication No. 1820, U.S. Government Printing Office, Washington, D.C., 1969.

U.S. Environmental Protection Agency. "Interim Primary Drinking Water Standards," *Federal Register,* 40:51, March 14, 1975, pp. 11990-11998.

U.S. Environmental Protection Agency. *Manual of Individual Water Supply Systems,* EPA 430-9-73-003. U.S. Government Printing Office, Washington, D.C., 1973.

9
wastewater

Proper control of human and domestic wastes in recreational areas is an essential factor of park planning. A well-planned and operated park sewage system is necessary to protect the health and convenience of the users, preserve the national resources of the park—the surface waterways, fish and wildlife, groundwater, and vegetation—from harmful pollution, and control park-generated points of pollution from adversely affecting water quality below the park.

Parks often have several special sewage management problems: seasonal operation and shutdown, wide fluctuations in peakload wastewater production because of varying park use patterns, widely distributed and occasionally remote activity areas, and high effluent discharge standards for park surface waters (streams and lakes) used for fishing, boating, swimming, and other recreational activities.

A park sewerage plan includes the collection, treatment, and disposal of human wastes as well as wastewater from lavatories, drinking fountains, showers, toilets, kitchen or campground sinks, trailer sanitary discharge stations, and laundries. Park sewerage systems are based on the availability of water, support facilities provided, experience/development norms, amount of use at service areas, climatic, soil and geologic conditions, applicable health and water quality standards, as well as economy of development and operations. Because of these factors, a complete sewerage system (including all the wastewater accomodations and facilities, sewers, and treatment plant) is usually the most expensive capital investment in a park. In addition, proper operation and maintenance of the system require skilled, technically trained personnel. To reduce development and operations budgets while conforming to local, state, and federal health and water quality codes, it is recommended that, where feasible, a park should tie into approved external sewer systems and treatment plants.

There are certain basic considerations that should be understood by park planners to help them provide necessary data to qualified environmental or sanitary engineers who will prepare the park sewage plan.

USER CONSIDERATIONS OF PARK WASTEWATER PLANNING

The appropriate location, convenience, adequacy and cleanliness of park restrooms are concerns most often noted by park users. The successful planning, design, and maintenance of a park wastewater system should be based upon these considerations. Poorly planned, improperly designed, or inadequately maintained sanitary facilities are usually most subject to frequent complaints by users and resultant poor public relations than any other park accomodation as well as being the cause for numerous problems for maintenance employees.

DISTANCE TO SANITARY FACILITIES AND MINIMUM NUMBER OF SANITARY FIXTURES

An adequate number of toilets, lavatories, sinks, and other necessary plumbing fixtures should be available at park and recreational areas. There are three basic user groups for which sanitary accomodations are planned: activity participants, spectators, and park employees.

Sanitary facilities are the accommodations—a room or separate building—solely used for human defecation, urination, and washing. These facilities are furnished with toilets and lavatories, often with urinals as well, if the facility is for the exclusive use of men. Drinking fountains should never be included in the same room as these sanitary fixtures. Sanitary facilities are commonly called restrooms, the ladies' room, men's room, toilet rooms, comfort station, or relief station.

Participant sanitary facilities may be limited to restroom functions at activity areas such as playgrounds, picnic areas, sports fields and courts, and other day-use areas (e.g., skating, skiing, visitor centers, and outdoor education centers), or these facilities may be combined with showers, lockers, and dressing rooms for overnight activity areas or activity areas that require on-site bathing and clothes changing. Examples include campgrounds, pools or beaches, sports arenas, gymnasiums, and athletic clubs.

Spectator accommodations are usually separate from the participant facilities, especially when participant accommodations are combined with showers, lockers, and dressing rooms.

Sanitary provisions for employees may be met as additions to public accommodations or as separate facilities. Field staff usually have access to participant facilities in day-use areas but separate provisions should be made for employees who are assigned to a restricted work center such as park offices, registration contact stations, garages, shops, water or sewage treatment stations, fire towers, or supply depots.

The minimum number of sanitary fixtures for each activity area or work station should be based on the design load (number of people who have convenient access to the service facilities), the length of the activity period, and the relationship of the occupancy time of the sanitary facility to an acceptable waiting time. Another important planning factor is the walking distance from the farthest activity unit—picnic table, campsite, or sports field, for example—to the sanitary facilities.

The estimated design load can be determined by totaling the people at one time (PAOT) for each activity unit (from the activity analysis—see Chapter 2) within the projected "service zone" for the sanitary facilities. This flexible distance should be based on user convenience and economics, as well as the visual and functional characteristics of the landscape. Intensive recreational use areas in urban parks may be adequately served by one centralized facility that also houses equipment storage, lighting controls, maintenance, or other functions needing shelter. A common service distance guide for intensive recreational use areas is the equivalent length of the playing fields for either baseball, football, or soccer. This service radius, which may vary from 300 feet to almost 400 feet, is not finite, and should be logically interpreted by planners for each situation. In resource-based activity areas such as primitive to intermediate experience/development level campgrounds, users often accept distances up to almost one tenth of a mile.

Age of the recreationists, arrival sequence of the activity area, and the length of stay are important factors to consider when determining the number of sanitary fixtures in a service facility and its location. Young children have frequent need to use the toilet that must be nearby; playgrounds and other childrens' program areas should have convenient facilities. Visitor information centers that are the first activity area used by traveling recreationists have a heavy demand on their sanitary facilities. Activities that require several hours (picnicking, boating, golf, organized sports, watching concerts, etc.) will usually require more accommodations than shorter activities.

Unless inflexible time constraints are imposed on the sanitary facilities—possibly at intermissions or rest periods during sports or performing arts events where large numbers of spectators attend—there is usually no waiting inconvenience for park users. A study in one state park system during Sundays and holidays determined that the average time to use toilets was less than three minutes, the average time for men to use urinals was just over one minute, and approximately one minute was needed to use the lavatory.*

Tables 9.1, 9.2, and 9.3 show the minimum number of fixtures for sanitary facilities for recreation participants, spectators, and park employees. It is important that all these groups be considered when studying park wastewater needs.

DESIGN OF SANITARY FACILITIES

Architects, as part of the park planning team, design a sanitary facility by studying the functional use and efficient maintenance requirements of the room or building. Important design factors include access and circulation, lighting, ventilation, weather protection, security, and selection of equipment, fixtures, and materials.

ACCESS AND CIRCULATION.   Sanitary facilities should be directly accessible from the activity areas they are servicing. Usually the sanitary facilities servicing outdoor recreation areas are separate comfort stations, bathhouses, or restroom buildings with direct outside entrances. It is possible to locate these facilities to service outdoor areas, such as playgrounds, sports fields and courts, or outside program areas as well as servicing the inside of a building (recreation center, administrative offices, game or craft rooms, etc.) Outside users should not have to enter the activity building to find an inside entrance to the restrooms. Two entrances—one to the outside and one to the building interior—have been successfully used for these situations to provide sanitary facilities to both program areas without expensive duplication of fixtures, construction, and space. It is important that each door can be well secured to control access.

Circulation within the room should be direct and convenient, progressing from the entrance to the toilet or urinal to lavatory to towel container or hand-drying apparatus to rubbish container without backtracking or crossing through the pattern. This efficient circulation pattern is very important during heavy use periods such as program intermission or conclusions.

---

* Brij M. Garg and Sat P. Goel, *Engineering Report: Sanitary Fixture Requirements for Pennsylvania State Park Facilities,* Department of Environmental Resources, Commonwealth of Pennsylvania, Harrisburg, Pa., 1973, pp. 5–6.

Table 9.1

Recommended minimum number of sanitary fixtures for park facilities predominately used by activity participants[a]

Type of Activity Area	Type of Sanitary Fixture			
	Toilets		Urinals	Lavatories
	Men	Women		
DAY USE				
Category I				
Childrens' playgrounds, program areas, play rooms	One for every 40 boys One for every 35 girls		One for every 30 boys	One for every 50 children using sanitary facility
Category II				
Volleyball, basketball, horseshoes, badminton, tennis, archery, skating, baseball, softball, football, soccer, field hockey, target shooting, bowling, picnicking, etc.	Base of two for up to 250 men Three for 250–500 men Four for 500 men One additional for every 500 more men	Base of two for up to 50 women Three for 50–100 women Four for 100–250 women Two additional for every 250 more women	Base of two for up to 250 men One additional for every 250 more men	Base of two for up to 250 individuals using each sanitary facility Three for 250–500 individual each One additional for every 500 more individuals each
Category III				
Swimming pools Beaches	Base of two for up to 150 men One additional for every 75 more men	Base of two for up to 100 women One additional for every 50 more women	Base of two for up to 150 men One additional for every 75 more men	Base of two for up to 200 individuals using each sanitary facility One additional for every 100 more individuals each

184

	Men	Women		
Category IV Visitor information centers, museums, exhibit buildings, restaurants, shops, community recreation building	Base of two for each sanitary facility for up to 70 PAOT Three each for 70–110 PAOT Four each for 110–160 PAOT Five each for 160–225 PAOT Six each for 225–300 PAOT		Urinals may be provided in men's sanitary facilities in lieu of toilets but for not more than one third of the recommended number of toilets	Base of two for up to 70 individuals using each sanitary facility One additional for every 45 more individuals each
OVERNIGHT USE Category V Non-self-contained campsites	Base of two for up to 30 campsites One additional for every 15 more campsites	Base of three for up to 30 campsites One additional for every 10 more campsites	Base of two for up to 30 campsites One additional for every 15 more campsites	Base of two for each sanitary facility for up to 30 campsites One additional each for every 10 more campsites
Category VI Organized camps (dormitory or group cabin)	One for every 10 men	One for every 8 women	One for every 25 men Over 150 men, one additional unit for every 50 men	Base of two for each sanitary facility for up to 20 individuals One additional for every 10 more individuals each
Category VII Family cabins	One for each dwelling unit		n.a.	One for each dwelling unit

[a] These recommendations are based on interpretations from U.S. Department of Health, Education and Welfare, *Environmental Health Practice in Recreational Areas*, DHEW Publication No. (HSM) 72-10009, U.S. Government Printing Office Washington, D. C. 1968; *The BOCA Basic Plumbing Code—1975*, Building Officials and Code Administrators International, Inc. Chicago, Ill., 1975; Brij M. Garg and Sat. P. Goel, *Engineering Report-Sanitary Fixture Requirements for Pennsylvania State Park Facilities*, Pennsylvania Department of Environmental Resources, Harrisburg, Pa. 1973; and *Camp Standards with Interpretations for the Accreditation of Organized Camps*, American Camping Association, Martinsville, Ind., 1972.

Table 9.2
Recommended minimum number of sanitary fixtures for recreational facilities with separate accommodations for spectators[a]

Examples of Recreational Facilities	Type of Sanitary Fixture		
	Toilets	Urinals	Lavatories
Amphitheaters, stadiums, bleachers, and grandstands, fieldhouses, fairs, festivals, auditoriums, performing arts centers, and theaters	Base of one for each sanitary facility up to 100 PAOT Base of two each for each sanitary facility up to 101–200 PAOT Base of three each for each sanitary facility up to 201–400 PAOT One additional for each 500 more men and One additional for each 300 more women	Base of one for up to 200 PAOT Base of two for 201–400 PAOT Base of three for 401–600 PAOT One additional for each 300 more men	Base of one for each sanitary facility up to 200 PAOT Base of two for 201–400 PAOT Base of three for 401–750 PAOT One additional each for each 500 more PAOT

[a] Based on the minimum number of plumbing fixtures for buildings of assembly—other than places of worship—from *The BOCA Basic Building Code—1975,* Building Officials & Code Administrators International, Inc., Chicago, Ill., 1975, p. 87.

LIGHTING.   Well-illuminated sanitary facilities can encourage cleanliness, reduce vandalism, and reduce labor costs for maintenance and repairs. Natural lighting can supplement or replace lamps during the day if clearstory windows or skylights are sufficient and well placed. During overcast days and nights when the facility is open, moisture and vandal-resistant lighting fixtures should provide 30 footcandles of illumination. Light interior colors also reflect light and make the room appear spacious.

VENTILATION.   All sanitary facilities should have natural flow-through air circulation or mechanical ventilators to reduce condensation, control odors, and maintain a comfortable temperature. All open windows should be covered with insect screens. Complete air change and circulation from floor level to ceiling is desirable, with no stale air pockets.

WEATHER PROTECTION.   All sanitary fixtures should be protected from the weather to prevent storm water from entering the sanitary wastewater disposal system, eliminate maintenance that may be caused by wind or rain deposition (leaf litter, dust, etc.) and protect the water and sewer lines from freezing. Sanitary facilities that are used in the winter should be heated or the plumbing should be designed to prevent ice accumulation and damage.

MATERIALS.   Use of proper construction materials in public sanitary facilities can reduce maintenance costs, encourage cleanliness, and reduce vandalism.

Floors should be nonslip, impervious to moisture, readily

Table 9.3
Recommended minimum number of sanitary fixtures for park employees[a]

Type of Work Area	Type of Sanitary Fixture	
	Toilets[b] per Employees	Lavatories per Employees
Category I Administrative offices and registration contact station, visitor center (If employees use the same sanitary facilities available for the public, increase the facilities the appropriate number.)	One for up to 15 employees Two for 16–35 employees Three for 36–55 employees Four for 56–80 employees Five for 81–110 employees	One for up to 15 employees Two for 16–35 employees Three for 36–60 employees Four for 61–90 employees Five for 91–125 employees
Category II Garages, shops, supply centers, water or sewage treatment stations, watch towers or other nonpublic areas where employees are assigned for at least a half day	One for up to 10 employees Two for 11–25 employees Three for 26–50 employees Four for 51–75 employees Five for 76–100 employees	One for each 10 employees
Category III Mobile crews—maintenance, park police, or rangers, and the like	No additional fixtures necessary so long as these employees have transportation immediately available to nearby sanitary facilities	
Category IV Field construction	Temporary facilities should be provided at the construction site	
	One for every 30 individuals	One for every 30 individuals

[a] Categories I–III are based on U.S. Department of Labor Occupational Safety and Health Standards, 1910-141 Sanitation, *Federal Register*, 39:125, June 27, 1974, p. 23674.
Category IV is based on minimum number of plumbing fixtures for temporary working facilities from *The BOCA Basic Building Code-1975*, Building Officials and Code Administrators International, Inc., Chicago, Ill., 1975, p. 90.
[b] The number of facilities to be provided for each sex shall be based on the number of employees of that sex for whom the facilities are furnished. Where sanitary facilities will be occupied by no more than one person at a time, can be locked from the inside, and contain at least one toilet, separate facilities for each sex need not be provided. Where facilities will not be used by women, urinals may be provided instead of toilets, except that the number of toilets in such cases should not be reduced to less than two thirds the minimum recommended.

cleanable, and slope to a floor drain. A rounded molding covering the junction of the floor and nonmasonry walls is often desirable.

Walls and partitions should be smooth, impervious, and readily cleanable. An entrance screen provides privacy to users. Either outside baffle walls, interior panels, or tandem doors are effective screens. Partitions should separate each toilet. If the men's urinals and lavatories are adjacent, a separating partition is recommended.

Doors at outside entrances should be heavy duty (such as metal doors) with no windows or louvers, mounted on tamperproof hinges, and equipped with flush dead-bolt locks for security. If toilet stall doors are used, they should open both ways and be equipped with an inside latch.

Windows are used only to admit light and possibly for ventilation. They should be above eyelevel from the outside. Windows should be well constructed with unbreakable transparent or translucent materials and protected glass reinforced to reduce shattering. Insect screens should cover all openings.

Service galleries are desirable to conceal plumbing valves, tanks, drains, and cleanouts; electrical lines, panels, and circuit breakers, as well as other connections that may be subject to service maintenance, repairs or possible damage from public abuse.

Sanitary fixtures, including toilets, urinals, and lavatories should meet American National Standards Institute Standard A112.19.2-1973. Self-closing faucets eliminate water waste. A key-operated water outlet or wall-recessed hydrant is useful for maintenance. Sturdy toilet tissue dispensers should hold a large supply of tissue (or an extra roll of paper if it is a roll holder) in a protected container to prevent abuse. If paper hand towels are used, a rubbish container should be located next to the towel dispenser. Unbreakable mirrors and soap dispensers are often required by state or local health codes.

FUNCTIONAL CONSIDERATIONS OF PARK WASTEWATER PLANNING

There is a direct relationship to the availability and use of potable water and the wastewater system of a park. Because of this relationship, it is desirable to plan the functional roles and requirements of both systems at the same time.

RELATIONSHIP OF WASTEWATER SYSTEM TO POTABLE WATER SYSTEM

Approximately 60 to 80 percent of the water distributed to park fixtures and appliances is not consumed by park visitors but is discharged as wastewater into the sewer or other liquid waste disposal system. For every 100,000 gallons of water distributed throughout a park, as much as 80,000 gallons may be discharged as wastewater. Much of this water is used primarily as a transportation medium for other wastes and does not need to conform to potable water quality standards.

Those water fixtures or appliances that do provide water for consumption or cleaning must be supplied with potable water. These include drinking fountains, picnic and campground hydrants, lavatories, sinks, showers, swimming pool inlets, laundry and dishwashing machines, and maintenance hose bibbs or spigots used for cleaning or washing facilities and areas where personal contact is likely (e.g., picnic tables, counters, benches, partitions). Large amounts of the water from many of these units are not consumed but are adulterated by a small amount of contamination and are discharged as wastewater. Table 9.4 shows the relationship of water inflow and wastewater for many park water service facilities.

Table 9.4
Percent of wastewater generated by selected park water fixtures or appliances

Fixture or Appliance	Normal Water Usage[a]	Est. Percent Wastewater
Drinking fountain		
Continuous flowing	75 gph	99
Valve controlled, 25 sec avg use	$\frac{1}{2}$ gal/use	80
Dishwashing machine, domestic type	6 gal/load	100
Hose bibb, $\frac{3}{4}$ in. maintenance	Up to 300 gpm	none
Hydrant, $1\frac{1}{2}$ in. fire	Up to 2400 gpm	none
Kitchen sink		
Domestic type	$7\frac{1}{2}$ gpm	60
Domestic type, with garbage grinder	$7\frac{1}{2}$ gpm	75
Laundry machine, domestic	30–50 gal/load	100
Lavatory (wash basin)	$1\frac{1}{2}$ gal/use	98
Shower head	25–30 gal/use	99
Toilet or urinal		
With flush tank	4–6 gal/use	100
With 5 sec flush valve @ 25 psi	$2\frac{1}{2}$–3 gal/use	100
Water spigot, picnic or campground	1–3 gal/use[b]	10

[a] Adapted from Metcalf and Eddy, Inc., *Wastewater Engineering: Collection, Treatment,* Disposal, McGraw-Hill, New York, 1972, p. 31.
[b] Estimated.

EFFECTS OF WATER USE ON THE WASTEWATER SYSTEM

GRAY WATER. Wastewater that is just slightly contaminated, such as spent water from drinking fountains, supply spigots, showers, or wash basins, may be called "gray water." Disposal may be directly into the ground after simple biological stabilization by percolation and aeration through shallow leaching pits, french drains, absorption fields, or sand bed filters if permitted by local regulating agencies. These economical devices for low volume gray water treatment are quite adequate for low-volume wastewater processing if the soil permeability is suitable, seasonal ground water is sufficiently below the bed and overloading does not occur.

In arid locations where water supplies are limited or areas where potable water treatment is expensive, it may be useful to recycle this water for nonpotable uses after simple stabilization and disinfection. Under these conditions, the costs of separate storage and distribution for this recycled water may be economically compensated by substituting it for the limited or costly potable water to flush toilets and sanitary holding tanks, pressure clean park vehicles and equipment, irrigate special landscaping, as well as for auxiliary fire control.

BLACK WATER.   Wastewater that is highly contaminated with human excreta or other significant putrefiable matter (such as food wastes) may be called "black water." It may contain pathogenic bacteria, viruses, and intestinal parasites. Examples of park water fixtures and appliances that generate black water include toilets and urinals, kitchens or campground sinks (especially those with garbage grinders), trailer sanitary discharge stations or individual hookups, dishwashers and laundry machines. Black water treatment requires a combination of physical and biological processes to remove the organic matter and harmful organisms. This treatment may be done by one of a variety of wastewater treatment processes. Only after complete and often costly treatment and disinfection is this liquid waste ready for disposal or reuse. The type and amount of treatment is based on volume, economic, environmental, and technical considerations. A qualified sanitary engineer should be consulted to identify and evaluate these factors and make a professional recommendation for the proper wastewater treatment.

It is important to check local and state health and water quality regulations early during the planning for park wastewater control. Acceptable practices are not uniform from state to state.

TYPES OF WASTEWATER SYSTEMS

There are a number of ways of classifying waste disposal systems. One method is to distinguish between portable and fixed sanitary facilities. While portable accomodations are occasionally needed in park and recreation areas—at special events, construction sites, or during temporary failure of the permanent facilities, for example—most are fixed. Of these permanent facilities, it is easiest to plan for sewage disposal at processing sites some distance from the sanitary facility where the wastes are transported by gravity-flow water in a system of sewers or for disposal at, in, or below the sanitary facility without sewers.

WATER-CARRIAGE SEWAGE DISPOSAL SYSTEMS

Where feasible and appropriate to the established development norm of the park, a water-carriage system of sewers and a treatment plant is the most desirable way to handle wastewater from flush toilets, lavatories, fountains, showers, and other sanitary fixtures and appliances. It is recommended that, whenever possible, park facilities should be linked by a sewer system to an outside approved sewage treatment plant. Where such a sewage system is not available, appropriate collection and disposal means must be established for the park. The degree of treatment necessary is based on health and water quality standards for the effluent discharge points. A park may use a combination of water-carriage and non-water-carriage disposal means to serve high density activity areas, low-density activity sites, or remote-employee assignment stations. A qualified sanitary engineer should prepare the overall sanitary plan for the park with input from other members of the park planning team, the activity analysis for all the proposed activities in the park, and PAOT projections for at least the next 10 years.

COLLECTION.   Sanitary sewers carry wastewaters normally by gravity flow to sewage treatment plants. Sewer connections to comfort stations, bathhouses, laundries, lodges, cabins, park restaurants, or other small wastewater-generating buildings are usually six inches in diameter, buried below frost line to prevent freezing and are sloped away from the structure at a minimum 2 percent grade. Several structures are linked by the sewer branches and submains to the trunk sewer, which carries the collective wastewater discharges to the treatment plant. Service manholes should be placed at all changes in sewer grade or alignment, at all intersections other than the building lateral, and every 300 feet along the line*. Whenever possible, it is desirable to run sanitary sewers within the park road corridor or within other utility right-of-ways to minimize impact on the landscape and provide ready accessibility for maintenance if necessary. Figure 9.1 illustrates a multiple support corridor network for a park.

TREATMENT.   Water-carriage sewage treatment involves a combination of physical and biological processes. A common, low-volume disposal system for unsewered park areas is the

* Some municipalities may permit manholes at distances greater than 300 feet, depending upon sewer size.

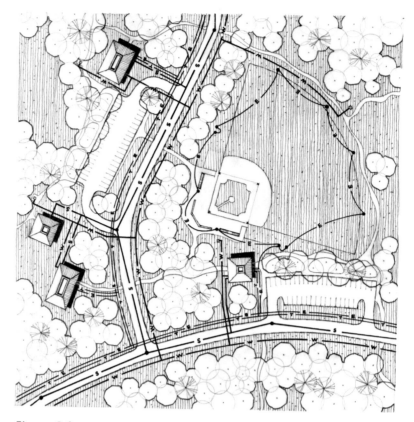

Figure 9.1

Portion of a park plan that illustrates the use of road and utility corridors to provide convenient access for service with minimum impact.

septic tank and subsurface disposal field. Large-volume treatment plants may be custom-designed and constructed on-site or they may be one or more prefabricated manufactured units or "package treatment plants" that are delivered intact. Large-volume plants should be designed for a per capita flow of not less than 100 gallons per day†. Table 9.5 shows how this daily flow is possible in a park.

Primary treatment is used to remove settleable organic wastes, which is 30 to 50 percent of the suspended solids, and the scum that floats on the surface. A septic tank is one example of several devices that provides primary treatment. *Secondary treatment* is a biological process of removing the organic materials still in the wastewater after primary settling—conventionally by aeration in open basins (activated sludge systems) or by passing through a fixed-growth biological media (trickling filter systems), followed

† Joseph A. Salvato, Jr. *Environmental Engineering and Sanitation, Second Edition,* Wiley-Interscience. New York, 1972, p. 358.

Table 9.5
Quantities of wastewater generated by various recreation areas and facilities

Area or Facility	Unit	Wastewater (GPD/Unit)
Amphitheater[a]	Seat	2
Bowling alley, no food service[b]	Lane	75–160
Camp, day, central bath[b]	Capita	35
Camp, day (no meals served)[d]	Person	15
Camp, summer	Capita	50
Campground (developed)[c]	Person	25
Campground—trailer village[c]	Person	35
Cottage, summer[b,d]	Capita	50
Dance Halls[b]	Capita	2
Dormitory, bunkhouse[c]	Person	50
Fish-cleaning station[c]	Station	7500
Hotel[c]	Capita	75
Hotels, with private bath (2 people per room)[d]	Person	60
Laundromat[c]	Washing machine	500
Laundry (coin operated)[b]	Machine	300
Lodge or cabins[c]	Person	50
Motel, luxury (1.5 people per room)[b]	Capita	70
Motel, average (1.5 people per room)[b]	Capita	60
Offices[b]	Employee	20
Picnic parks[b]	Capita	5
Restaurants, average[b]	Seat	80
Cafeteria[c]	Table seat	150
Cocktail lounge[c]	Seat	20
Coffee shop[c]	Counter seat	250
Dining room[c]	Table seat	150
Mess hall[c]	Person	15
Rest areas, roadside[b]	Capita	5
Service stations, vehicular[b]	Bay	1000
Gas station[c]	Station	2000–5000
Swimming pool and bathhouse[d]	Person	10
Swimming pool, bathhouse, and snackbar	Capita	15
Theater, drive-in[b]	Stall	5
Theater, movie[b]	Seat	5
Visitor center	Visitor	5

[a] Based on sewage flow for assembly halls—Homer W. Parker, *Wastewater Systems Engineering*, Prentice-Hall, Englewood Cliffs, N.J., 1975, p. 12.
[b] From Homer W. Parker, op. cit.
[c] From Metcalf & Eddy, Inc., *Wastewater Engineering—Collection, Treatment Disposal*, "Design Unit Sewage Flows for Recreation Facilities—Yellowstone National Park," McGraw-Hill, New York, 1972, p. 34.
[d] From U.S. Department of Health, Education and Welfare, *Environmental Health Practice in Recreational Areas*, DHEW Publication No. (HSM) 72-10009, U.S.G.P.O., Washington, D. C., 1968.

Figure 9.2

In low-volume parks with suitable soils, primary treatment of organic wastes can be accomplished with a septic tank. A subsurface disposal bed permits leaching of the effluent.

by final settling. The effluent is usually disinfected with chlorine prior to discharge. The combined primary and secondary treatment plus disinfection processes is often termed *complete treatment. Tertiary treatment* may remove nitrates, reduces phosphates, and normally includes a final polishing of the effluent by filtration. The effluent is usually disinfected after this advanced treatment.

It is beyond the scope of this text to explain all the various wastewater treatment processes that may be used in park and recreation areas. The following descriptions only outline some of the basic processes.

SEPTIC TANK AND SUBSURFACE DISPOSAL FIELD.   A septic tank is an underground waterproof valut where solids settle, the organic matter decomposes anaerobically, and scum and sludge are stored (Figure 9.2). The influent is collected by gravity-flow sewers from the park sanitary facilities and discharged into the septic tank that should detain the liquid waste about a day before it flows to a subsurface leaching system. The recommended minimum size for a septic tank is 750 gallons.* It may be as large as 10,000 gallons. A septic tank can give adequate service for years if properly maintained. It should be inspected annually and cleaned every three to five years. The basic design guide for septic tank systems is *The Manual of Septic Tank Practice.*

The septic fluid from the tank runs to a distribution box where it is sent to the absorption field drain tile or perforated pipe set in gravel beds. It is important to locate the absorption field in an area free of seasonal flooding, exposed to the sun, and cleared of

* Salvato, *op. cit.,* p. 281.; check local regulations for minimum requirements.

shrubbery or trees. No component of the system should be closer than 50 feet from any water source. Percolation tests should be made to select suitable soils with capability to handle the effluent.

Primary treatment of sewage is not adequate for most large-volume processing plants, and secondary treatment has become required practice for new installations.

TRICKLING FILTERS.   A stationary biological bed of crushed stone five to seven feet deep called a trickling filter (Figure 9.3) is actually a controlled environment for biological slime or gelatinous film over which wastewater from a primary sedimentation tank is dosed. The liquid is then sent through a secondary settling tank for sludge removal. Finally disinfection for odor control and bacterial reduction is often required before the effluent is discharged.

Typical problems of trickling filter plants are effluent quality and odors caused by organic loading and cold weather operations. During the summer, filter flies may be a problem.

ACTIVATED SLUDGE.   Basically this process uses biologically active growths mixed with the degradable wastewater. The fluid is aerated by stirring and bubbling air through it in aeration tanks (Figure 9.4). A heavy mass of floc (the activated sludge) settles out and is recycled to the aeration tanks as the effluent passes through secondary settling basins and is disinfected before disposal.

The activated sludge system is very versatile but requires more capable operators than the other processes. It does not have cold weather problems like the trickling filter.

A modified form of the activated sludge process is the

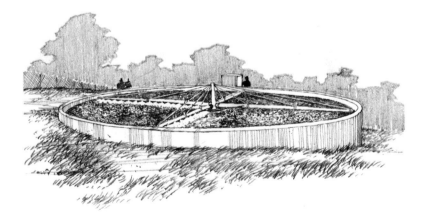

Figure 9.3

Trickling filters such as this are frequently used in secondary treatment of wastewater in parks.

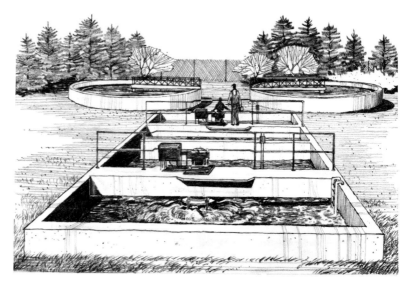

Figure 9.4

Activated sludge aeration tanks are part of another form of secondary treatment of park wastewater. The effluent then passes through the settling basins shown behind the tanks.

oxidation ditch (Figure 9.5). It uses no primary settling tank. Raw sewage is discharged into an elongated oval-shaped ditch where it is mixed with the active organisms. The liquid is circulated around the ditch at a minimum velocity of one foot per second to prevent settling. The biochemically stabilized liquid passes through a secondary settling tank where the sludge is returned to the oxidation ditch. The effluent may then be disinfected as in the other processes.

The oxidation ditch is well suited for the fluctuating peak loads in recreation areas as well as the seasonal variance of sewage. Concentric ditches can operate with these variations without loss of efficiency.

PACKAGE TREATMENT PLANTS.   Prefabricated manufactured treatment facilities are now available. These are factory-assembled units that offer extended aeration, contact stabilization (both variations of the activated sludge process) trickling filter, physical/chemical, or other package treatment operations. Figure 9.6 shows one type of unit.

Even though the package plants are manufactured products, they should be acquired only with the guidance of a qualified sanitary engineer. Package plants require very careful operation. They may have peak loading, sewage strength, and quality problems. Biological systems will not ordinarily produce a really good effluent *if it is not carrying at least half its design loading.**

---

* Homer W. Parker, *Wastewater Systems Engineering,* Prentice-Hall, Inc., Englewood Cliffs, N.J., 1975, p. 214.

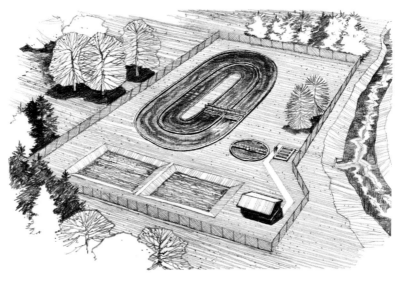

Figure 9.5

A park wastewater treatment plant using an oxidation ditch. Notice the secondary settling basin and disinfection facility to the right of the oxidation ditch.

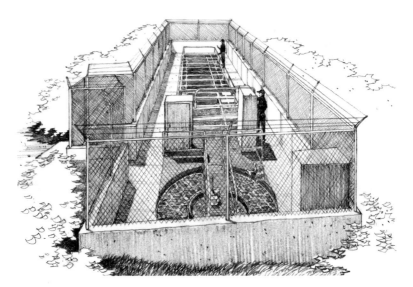

Figure 9.6

Prefabricated package treatment plants are compact and may be installed for a variety of site requirements. Here the units have been partially recessed underground. All wastewater treatment plants should be fenced to protect the public and prevent unauthorized entry.

197

However, a package system is superior to a septic tank system even when improperly operating.

Package physical/chemical treatment plants offer the potential for producing a high quality of effluent under the varying loading conditions encountered in many recreational areas. These plants are relatively new but should be considered as an alternative to biological systems where effluent requirements are high and waste loadings are highly variable.*

Other water-carriage wastewater treatment processes exist. Those discussed, however, are the most commonly used or offer the greatest potential for future application in parks and recreation areas.

ALTERNATIVE EFFLUENT DISPOSAL TECHNIQUES.   The conventional disposal of treatment plant effluent is to discharge it into an approved waterway (assuming the effluent meets the water quality standards for the receiving waterway).

It is possible to reuse the treated effluent by installing a separate water distribution and storage system for the reclaimed water. Reclaimed water has been used to irrigate golf courses, roadside rest areas, picnic areas, baseball fields, lawns, woodlands, and other recreational facilities. It has been pumped into abandoned gravel pits and other impoundment areas for recreational lakes for boating and fishing.

NON-WATER-CARRIAGE DISPOSAL SYSTEMS

In large parks where remote, very low density activity centers or work stations cannot be feasibly linked to the sewer network, or where water supplies are not sufficient to operate a water-carriage sewage treatment system, it is still possible to provide adequate, economical, and sanitary means for the disposal of human excreta. There are a large number of non-water-carriage methods available. Basically, these may be categorized as infiltration, decomposition, destruction, or hold and removal devises.

INFILTRATION.   The waste is fermented in a pit, cesspool, or tank, and allowed to infiltrate the soil in this type of dispersal system. It may take place with or without water, but the action is greatly reduced during cold weather. The capacity of the soil to absorb the waste is critical for proper operation. Examples include pit privy or latrines, vault privies, and aqua privies.

DECOMPOSITION.   Usually by an aerobic process, the wastes are decomposed in these units by oxidation, which generates pathogenic organism-killing high temperatures in a very short time. Some units use natural bacteria commonly found in the soil

* David A. Long, Professor of Civil Engineering, Pennsylvania State University, personal communications, February 16, 1976.

as digesters. Others operate on the principle of a minature activated sludge treatment plant by providing aeration. There are many proprietary decomposition toilets manufactured. These are basically compost privies, continuous aeration, or digester units. Some of the manufactured units require electricity or gas to provide aeration, circulation, or heat.

DESTRUCTION.   The incinerating toilet consists of a dry flush toilet over a combusion chamber where the wastes are reduced to a small amount of ashes. Fumes are vented to the atmosphere. These are powered by electricity, natural gas, or bottled liquid propane. They may be permanently installed, used as portable units, or may be mounted on a vehicle. There are several manufacturers of incinerating toilets.

HOLD AND REMOVAL.   These toilets, with either dry flush and conventional holding tanks or low-volume flush with holding or recirculating tanks, may be the most common non-water-carriage system used in the United States. Depending on the device and the size of the holding tank, the stored wastes must be removed regularly (or quite infrequently if the capacity is large) and properly treated. Low-volume flush units use between one quart to three gallons of liquid per flush compared to five to seven gallons per flush for conventional water-carriage toilets. Several manufactured low-volume flush toilets use fluids that do not mix with the wastes and can be separated from the stored liquid wastes in the holding tank and recycled for flushing. Examples of hold and removal devices include pump-out or Pullman vaults, chemical privies, recirculating fluid toilets, and recirculating chemical toilets.

A vacuum system is also available. Less than a quart of water per flush carries the wastes through a vacuum-pressurized pipe (approximately $\frac{1}{2}$ atmosphere) to a metal holding tank. Removal and treatment of the wastes are the same as the other hold and removal toilets.

Many of the manufactured toilets of this type may be permanently installed, serve as portable units, and may be used on vehicles, including planes, buses, campers, and trains.

Table 9.6 lists some of the uses, siting, construction, and maintenance requirements of selected non-water-carriage systems used in parks.

SUMMARY

Proper control of human and domestic wastes in parks is essential to protect the health and conveniences of the users, preserve the natural resources of the park, and prevent park-generated pollution from adversely affecting water quality below the park. Common sewage problems in parks are caused by seasonal operation and shutdown, fluctuating wastewater

Table 9.6
Sanitary excreta disposal methods[a]

Facility	Suitability	Location	Construction	Maintenance
Sanitary earth pit privy	Where soil available and groundwater not encountered. Earth can be mounded up if necessary to bring bottom of pit 2 ft above groundwater or rock.	Downgrade, 100 ft or more from sources of water supply; 100 ft from kitchens; 50 to 150 ft of users; at least 2 ft above groundwater; 50 ft from lake, stream.	Deep pit; insects and animals excluded; surface water drained away; cleanable material; attractive; ventilated pit and building. Pit 3 ft × 4 ft × 6 ft deep serves average family 3 to 5 yr.	Keep clean and flytight; supply toilet paper. Apply residual fly spray to structure and borax, fuel oil, or kerosene to pit. Natural decay and desiccation of feces reduce odors. Keep waste water out. Scrub seat with hot water and detergent.
Masonry vault privy	To protect underground and surface-water supplies.	Downgrade and 50 ft or more from sources of water supply; 100 ft from kitchens; 50 to 150 ft of users.	Watertight concrete vault; flytight building; cleanable material; ventilated vault and building. Capacity of 6 ft^3 per person adequate for 1 yr.	Keep clean, flytight, and attractive. Supply toilet paper. Apply residual spray. Clean pit when contents approach 18 in. of floor. Scavengers can be used.
Septic privy (Lumsden, Roberts, and Stiles: LRS privy.)	Where cleaning of pit is a problem and odors unimportant.	Same as pit privy.	Watertight vault with tee outlet to leaching pit, gravel trench, filter, vault, etc. Provide capacity of 250 gal plus 20 gal for each person over 8 yr.	Add 2 gal water per seat. Keep clean and flytight. Supply toilet paper. Agitate after use. Clean vault when depth of sludge and scum = 12 to 18 in.
Excreta disposal pit	For disposal of pail privy and chemical toilet contents.	Downgrade and 200 ft from sources of water supply; 100 ft from kitchen.	Shored pit with open joint material. Tight top and access door.	Keep flytight and clean. Drain surface water away.

Type			
Chemical toilet (cabinet and tank type)	A temporary facility. To protect water supply, where other method impractical. Temporary camp, vehicle, boat.	May adjoin main dwelling. Tank type same as masonry vault privy.	Same as masonry vault privy. Tank may be heavy gauge metal with protective coating. Provide capacity of 125 to 250 gal per seat.	Use $\frac{1}{4}$ lb lye for each ft^3 of vault, or 25 lb caustic per seat in 15 gal water. Keep clean. Clean vault when $\frac{2}{3}$ to $\frac{3}{4}$ full. Odor control. Empty and recharge as directed.
Incinerator toilet	Where electricity or gas available.	Within the facility.	Enclosed compartment.	Keep clean and supply toilet paper.
Recirculating toilet	Airplanes, boats, fairgrounds, camps.	Within the facility.	Enclosed prefabricated unit.	Keep clean. Empty contents in approved facility and recharge with chemical.
Removable pail privy (bucket latrine)	A temporary facility; to protect water supply, where pit privy impractical.	Same as masonry vault privy.	Same as masonry vault privy. Provide easily cleaned pails.	Provide collection service, excreta disposal pit, and cleaning facilities, including hot water (backflow preventer), long-handled brushes, detergent, drained concrete floor.
Portable box, earth pit, latrine	At temporary camps.	Same as pit privy. Army recommends latrine 100 yd from kitchens.	Earth pit with portable prefabricated box.	Same as earth pit privy. Provide can cover to keep toilet tissue dry.
Bored-hole latrine	In isolated place or when primitive, inexpensive, and sanitary facility is needed	Same as earth pit privy.	Bored hole 14 to 18 in. diameter and 15 to 25 ft deep with bracing if necessary. Seat structure may be oil drum, box, cement or day tile riser with seat, or use squatting plate. Platform around hole.	Same as earth pit privy. Line upper 2 ft of hole; in a caving formation line hope to support earth walls.

Table 9.6 (Continued)

Facility	Suitability	Location	Construction	Maintenance
Saddle-trench latrine	At temporary camp for less than one day.	Same as earth pit privy.	Trench 1 ft wide, $2\frac{1}{2}$ ft deep, and 4 ft long for 25 men.	Frequent inspection. Keep excreta covered. Provide toilet paper with waterproof cover.
Cat hole	On hikes or in field.	Same as earth pit privy.	Hole about 1 ft deep.	Carefully cover hole with earth
Squatting latrine	Where local conditions and customs permit.	Same as pit privy.	Similar to privy or bored-hole latrine. See sketches.	Same as privies and latrines.

Criteria: Confines excreta; excludes insects, rodents, and animals; prevents contamination of water supply; provides convenience and privacy; clean and odor free.

Note. If privy seat is removable and extra seat is provided, it is easier to scrub seats and set aside to dry. A commercial plastic or composition-type seat is recommended in place of improvised crudely made wooden seats. Deodorants that can be used if needed include chlorinated lime, cloroben, iron sulphate, copperas, activated carbon, and pine oil. Keep privy pits dry. Solutions for chemical toilets include lye (potassium hydroxide), caustic soda or potash (sodium hydroxide), chlorinated lime (1 lb in $2\frac{1}{2}$ gal water), copper sulfate (1 lb in $2\frac{1}{2}$ gal water), and a chlorinated benzene.

[a] Joseph A. Salvato, Jr. *Environmental Engineering and Sanitation*, Wiley-Interscience, New York, 1972, pp. 366–367. Reprinted with permission of publisher.

202

loading because of park use patterns, widely distributed and occasionally remote activity areas, and high effluent discharge standards for park surface wastes.

It is recommended that parks connect to approved external sewer systems and treatment facilities because of the high development and operating costs to have a private park system.

Park users are very conscious of park sanitary accommodations, particularly the walking distance to facilities, the type and number of fixtures, and the design and maintenance of the facilities.

Water-borne sewage systems are related to the availability of water, which is used as the transporting medium to carry wastes through a sewer network to a sewage treatment plant.

In areas beyond the sewer system or where water is not available, several alternative non-water-carriage sewage devices may be used to protect the park, the public, the park employees, and the quality of the watershed.

GLOSSARY OF TERMS

Black Water
Wastewater that is highly contaminated with human excreta or other significant putrefiable organic matter that may contain pathogenic organisms.

Gray Water
Wastewater that is just slightly contaminated and is relatively harmless.

Non-Water-Carriage Disposal System
A human excreta disposal device that does not use a network of sewers to transport water-borne wastes to sewage treatment facilities. The system may alter, reduce, destroy, or store the wastes for removal.

Sanitary Facility
Accommodations (a room or separate building) equipped with sanitary fixtures for human defecation, urination, and washing.

Sanitary Fixtures
Toilets, urinals, lavatories, and other sewer-connected fixtures that are provided in sanitary facilities.

Water-Carriage Sewage Disposal System
A means of wastewater collection, treatment, and disposal that uses a network of sewers to transport water-borne wastes to the sewage treatment plant located a distance from the sanitary facility.

BIBLIOGRAPHY

Babbitt, Harold E. and E. Robert Baumann. *Sewerage and Sewage Treatment,* Eighth Edition. Wiley, New York, 1958.

BOCA Basic Plumbing Code, Third Edition. Building Officials & Code Administrators International, Inc., Chicago, 1975.

Butler, Robert M., N. Henry Wooding, and Earl A. Myers. *Spray-Irrigation Disposal of Wastewater,* Special Circular 185. Pennsylvania State University Cooperative Extension Service, University Park, Pa., 1974.

Camp Standards with Interpretations for the Accreditation of Organized Camps. American Camping Association, Martinsville, Ind., 1972.

Fair, Gordon M., John C. Greyer, and Daniel A. Okun. *Elements of Water Supply and Wastewater Disposal,* Second Edition. Wiley, New York, 1971.

Garg, Brij and Sat. P. Goel. *Engineering Report: Sanitary Fixture Requirements for Pennsylvania Park Facilities.* Pennsylvania Department of Environmental Resources, Harrisburg, Pa., 1973.

Goldstein, Steven N. and Walter J. Moberg, Jr. *Wastewater Treatment Systems for Rural Communities.* Commission on Rural Water, Washington, D.C., 1973.

Hammer, Mark J. *Water and Wastewater Technology.* Wiley, New York, 1975.

Metcalf & Eddy, Inc. *Wastewater Engineering: Collection, Treatment, Disposal.* McGraw-Hill, New York, 1972.

Minimum Cost Housing Group. *Stop the Five Gallon Flush! A Study of Alternative Waste Disposal Systems,* Third Edition. School of Architecture, McGill University, Montreal, 1973.

Parker, Homer W. *Wastewater Systems Engineering.* Prentice-Hall, Inc., Englewood Cliffs, N.J., 1975.

Salvato, Joseph A. *Environmental Engineering and Sanitation,* Second Edition. Wiley-Interscience, New York, 1972.

U.S. Department of Health, Education and Welfare. *Environmental Health Practice in Recreational Areas,* DHEW Publication No. (HSM) 72-10009., U.S. Government Printing Office, Washington, D.C., 1968.

U.S. Department of Health, Education and Welfare. *Manual of Septic Tank Practice,* Public Health Service Publications No. 526, U.S. Government Printing Office, Washington, D.C., 1967.

U.S. Department of Labor. Occupational Safety and Health Standards. 1910.141, "Sanitation," *Federal Register,* 39:125, June 27, 1974, p. 23674.

Wilcox, Arthur T. (Editor). *Park Sanitary Facilities.* American Institute of Park Executives and Michigan State University Agricultural Experiment Station and Cooperative Extension Service, East Lansing, Michigan (n.d.).

10
solid
waste

Proper and efficient collection, storage, and disposal of the solid waste generated in a park or recreation area are essential elements of the support services and facilities that must be considered in park planning. Because of the health and sanitary problems inherent in some solid waste left in parks, these problems must be carefully studied along with liquid waste treatment, drinking water, and safety/emergency provisions. The objectives of a park solid waste plan should be to protect the public health, safety, and well-being; insure the most convenient, efficient and economical collection, processing, and disposal of solid waste while contributing minimum degrading effects on the quality and aesthetics of the recreational setting. The beneficiaries are the park users as well as the employees who provide support services for the visitors.

Indicators of solid waste problems include objectionable odors, presence of vectors (insects—flies, bees, ants, roaches, and their larvae—and rats, mice, and other disease-transmitting animals), marauding dogs and cats, nuisance fires, hazardous accumulations of dangerous debris and refuse, and basic unsightliness.

TYPES OF PARK SOLID WASTE

The solid waste generated by park use and maintenance may consist of garbage, nonputrescible rubbish and litter, trash, and

205

other special waste materials. Each type of solid waste has individual characteristics that affect park planning. Each is created by identifiable groups of people, is composed of certain materials, and requires separate collection, storage, and disposal considerations.

GARBAGE

Garbage is composed of food wastes or food preparation residue. This includes, for example, partially eaten hamburgers, candy bars, potato salad, banana peels, and unconsumed stale or flat beverages. Garbage is the messiest, the most obvious and potentially the most pathogenic of all the solid wastes left by park users. Major problem areas are picnic areas, pavilions and group shelters, lodges, campgrounds, food concession, and other food consumption areas. Primary planning concerns are proper sanitation, vector control, and prevention of odors. These factors may make garbage the most important element in solid waste planning. The special facility and handling requirements also make proper control of it the most expensive for the park.

RUBBISH AND LITTER

Rubbish and litter make up the largest quantity of solid waste left by recreationists. For planning purposes, the distinction between rubbish and litter is minor: litter is simply rubbish that is lying scattered about. (Some agencies call all rubbish "litter." This euphemism is used to encourage park visitors to use waste containers—"litter baskets.") Other than this locational difference, they are the same. Combustible rubbish (paper, wrappers, instant film residue, cups, cardboard boxes, packaging and containers) is accumulated at picnic and camp sites, spectator facilities, overlooks, administrative offices, equipment storage rooms and maintenance buildings—generally anywhere people congregate. This is also true for noncombustible rubbish (beverage containers, glass or metal cans, lids, tabs, crockery or broken and worthless metal equipment). Rubbish may be windblown and scattered (i.e., an area may become littered) if the waste materials are not properly contained and collected. It is a bulky, voluminous discard, requiring large amounts of storage. Combustible rubbish may be fuel for prank or vandalism fires. Broken glass and sharp metals are hazardous to both park users and employees.

Usually garbage and rubbish are deposited together as *mixed refuse* and should be treated as garbage that requires the most restrictive waste controls. Occasional food residue in a litter basket or rubbish container, however, does not warrant the expense of installing garbage cans and modifying collection schedules. Common sense judgments must always be used to insure sanitary, convenient, efficient, and economical solid waste control.

TRASH

Trash is composed of a variety of solid waste materials: construction or demolition refuse (scrap lumber, pipe, masonry, and other rubble from new construction sites, razed buildings, or other structures); ashes from picnic or camp grills, fire rings, fireplaces, furnaces, and incinerators; and vegetable/animal residue. Most trash is very bulky and heavy. It is usually neither deposited in waste containers nor collected periodically like garbage and rubbish. Trash should be collected and disposed of as soon as the accumulation becomes unattractive or a nuisance. If the trash is a construction by-product of a public works project or work done by park personnel, removal should be required of the contractor or project superintendent as part of the general specifications. Economically, it is best to reduce haul distance by locating a deposition site as close as possible. Structural debris, rubble, and ashes can often be buried or used for fill material if covered with sufficient topsoil.

Vegetable residue (leaves, tree litter, branches, limbs, brush, and yard trimmings) from new project area clearing and grubbing operations or tree and turf maintenance is heavy and bulky. Small materials may be chipped or shredded and used as a mulch or ground cover or composted and used as a planting medium. Large materials may be cut and used for rustic structures or for firewood. The recyclable or reusable qualities of this type of solid waste minimizes disposal problems.

Animal residue, including manure, bedding, stall litter, as well as dead animals, create sanitary problems similar to garbage. Dead animals should be disposed of immediately by burial or other suitable means. Other animal wastes may be processed and used as an organic agricultural type fertilizer. Care must be taken to minimize odor and vector problems during storage. Dispersal areas must be outside regular public use zones. Predominate wind direction, water erosion, runoff, and sedimentation are also disposal site selection factors.

SPECIAL WASTE

Special waste is usually made of maintenance refuse, sewage treatment residue, or junked vehicles and applicances. The most common of these is maintenance refuse, including paint, chemicals, petroleum-based products, pesticides, and fertilizer wastes. This refuse is produced through routine or special maintenance, special projects, and in garages and workshops. It should not be mixed with other wastes for disposal because the materials may be toxic, highly combustible or explosive, or otherwise potentially detrimental to park personnel, park visitors, or the environment.

Sewage treatment residue (solids from sewage treatment plants or septic-tank sludge) is a periodic but infrequent solid waste in parks with these sanitary systems. Because of the inherent

Table 10.1
Park solid waste materials by type, composition, source, and park consideration[a]

Type of Waste	Composition	Usual Park Source	Park Considerations
Garbage	Edible wastes or food discards	Picnics, camping meals, food concession and other food consumption areas	Insect and vector control, odors, sanitation
Rubbish and Litter			
Combustible	Paper, boxes, packaging, containers	Picnics, camping, spectator gatherings, administrative offices, equipment storage and maintenance parts buildings	Bulky, may be windblown and scattered if not properly handled. Subject to prank and vandalous fires.
Noncombustible	Tin cans, glass, crockery, metal equipment	Picnics, camping meals, spectator gatherings	Bulky, may be heavy, may be dangerous if broken
Trash			
Construction/demolition wastes	Scrap lumber, pipe, masonry, other rubble or construction debris	New construction or razed buildings and other structures	Very bulky, heavy, unsightly; may be used in the park for fill to reduce hauling costs
Ashes	Residue from fires	Picnic, camp grills, fire rings fireplaces, furnaces, and park incinerators	Inert, heavy, may be unsightly in public use areas; may be used in the park for fill
Organic residue—vegetable	Leaves, tree litter branches and limbs, brush yard trimmings	High maintenance cleanup, clearing for new development	Very bulky, heavy—small material may be chipped or shredded and used as mulch and surface cover or may be composted; large material may be cut and used for rustic construction or firewood

208

Type	Source	Origin	Remarks
Organic residue—animal	Animal manure, dead animals	Stables, demonstration farms, zoos	Sanitation, bulky, heavy, insect and vector control; manure may be composted or dried and used in the park as a plant nutrient in areas where use would not be offensive; dead animals must be buried or removed by approved contractors immediately
Special Waste Maintenance refuse	Paint, chemical, petroleum, pesticide, and fertilizer wastes	Routine or special maintenance work, special projects, garages, workshops	Materials may be toxic, highly combustible or explosive, or otherwise potentially detrimental to personnel or environment; should not be mixed with other wastes for disposal
Sewage treatment residue	Solids from sewage treatment plants, septic tank sludge	Sewage treatment system	Sanitation, bulky, heavy; Disposal on approved sites only
Junked vehicles and appliances	Stripped vehicle bodies, discarded stoves, refrigerators, lawn mowers, apparatus	Sometimes dumped illegally on park property; may be "stored for parts" by park personnel	Very bulky, heavy, unsightly; may be dangerous to children

[a] Adapted from Joseph A. Salvato Jr., *Environmental Engineering and Sanitation*, Second Edition, Wiley, New York, 1972, p. 389.

pathogenic characteristics of these residues, special storage facilities and collection equipment are usually necessary. These waste provisions should be independent from the garbage/rubbish waste provisions of the park.

Junked vehicles and appliances are occasionally dumped illegally in isolated sections of parkland, especially if the area is adjacent to a low-traffic road. These items may include stripped auto or truck bodies, discarded stoves, refrigerators, television sets, lawn mowers, and other apparatus. These illegal, covert dumps are often matched by park-owned scrap heaps—broken or inoperative park-owned equipment "stored for replacement parts" for other serviceable equipment. These equipment junk yards and illegally abandoned vehicle/applicance dumps are unsightly, generate additional accumulations, and harbor pests. The junk is usually very bulky, heavy, and may become "attractive nuisances" to children who could be seriously injured or entrapped inside while playing. These discarded materials should not be permitted in the park; when an item is abandoned, either by the park agency or illegally, it should be secured and disposed of as soon as possible.

Table 10.1 summarizes the major types of park solid waste materials.

PARK SOLID WASTE MANAGEMENT PLANNING

There are three operational functions that must be planned and specified for solid waste control in a park. These functions affect the physical arrangement, use, and development of activity areas and support facilities: collection, storage, and disposal of solid wastes. *Collection* of solid waste from activity areas may be done frequently or infrequently, regularly or as occasionally as required, by park employees or a service contractor. *Storage* may be limited to the precollection waste containers or may include intermediate transfer storage facilities for economical hauling. *Disposal* may be on site or off site; waste materials may be contained, reduced, destroyed, or reused.

Each park situation will direct the optimum methods for each of these operational functions. There are some basic requirements; individual circumstances may limit the necessity for all the functions being done by the park agency; options within each function should be carefully considered.

FACTORS AFFECTING PHYSICAL PLANNING FOR SOLID WASTE FACILITIES

The principal facilities for solid waste control in a park are the precollection waste containers, the circulation route for collection, transfer storage facility if needed, and disposal area or facility. Other considerations include necessary equipment and personnel training.

Before park solid waste facilities can be planned these factors must be established:

Each activity area in the park will usually produce a certain type (or types) of waste. Areas where food preparation or consumption is a common occasion will generate garbage; spectator areas produce mixed refuse; practice or competition areas, overlooks, docks, and trails predominately collect rubbish and litter.

The amount of waste produced will vary from area to area. Generally this amount is determined by the collective character of the individual visitors, the length of their stay, the activities engaged in, and the enforced rules of the park. Table 10.2 shows the different waste generation rates for selected recreation activity areas.

Frequency and method of waste collection can affect the capacity of site and transfer storage containers. So can the site

Table 10.2
Waste generation rates for recreation sites[a]

Recreation site	Average rate of waste generation (90 percent confidence interval)
Campgrounds (lb/camper day)	1.26 ± 0.08
Campgrounds (lb/visitor day)	0.92 ± 0.06
Family picnic area (lb/picnicker)	0.93 ± 0.16
Group picnic area (lb/picnicker)	1.16 ± 0.26
Organization camps (lb/occupant day)	1.81 ± 0.39
Job Corps Civilian Conservation Corps Camps	
Kitchen waste (lb/corpsman day)	2.44 ± 0.63
Administrative and dormitory waste (lb/corpsman day)	0.70 ± 0.66
Resort areas	
Rented cabins (with kitchens) (lb/occupant day)	1.46 ± 0.31
Lodge rooms (without kitchens) (lb/occupant day)	0.59 ± 0.64
Restaurants (lb/meal served)	0.71 ± 0.40
Overnight lodges in winter sports areas (wastes from all facilities) (lb/visitor day)	187 ± 0.26
Day lodge in winter sports areas (lb/visitor day)	2.92 ± 0.61
Recreation residences (lb/occupant day)	2.13 ± 0.54
Observation sites (lb/incoming axle)	0.05 ± 0.03
Visitor centers (lb/visitor)	0.02 ± 0.008
Swimming beaches (lb/swimmer)	0.04 ± 0.01
Concession stands (lb/patron)	0.14 (1 site)
Administrative residences (lb/occupant day)	1.37 ± 0.35

[a] Charles S. Spooner, *Solid Waste Management in Recreation Forest Areas*, U. S. Environmental Protection Agency, Solid Waste Management Office, USGPO, Washington, D. C., 1971, p. 2.

container distribution and container/visitor ratio. Collection schedules should reflect seasonal and weekly park use patterns. Investment in larger or more waste containers may be more economical if an area generates more waste than can be stored between collections if it does not adversely affect the recreational experience of the park users. The following example illustrates the impact of some of these variables.

When solid waste containers in camping areas are spaced between two or three campsites, they require more frequent collection than when each site has its own container. Frequent collection, particularly in remote areas, adds to the total travel distance involved in collection and disposal. Supplying more containers reduces the needed collection frequency and the route miles traveled.

Using the average waste generation rate for one camper, 1.26 lb per camp day, and an average density (as collected) of 170 lb per cu yd, a [32 gallon] solid waste container will accommodate the wastes of 16 camper days. When five persons per campsite is assumed, one can, spaced between every three sites, will hold wastes accumulated in 1.1 days. This situation will require collection daily. If containers are spaced between each two sites, they will hold the wastes that accumulate every 1.7 days, and collection every 2 days will be adequate. A solid waste container at every site, however, will hold the wastes accumulated in 3.4 days and will require collection only twice a week.*

Development and maintenance norms determine physical planning for solid waste facilities the same as for circulation and parking, lighting, and other support facilities.

Vector control is a major factor in solid waste equipment selection and facility development. Insects, rodents, and other scavengers are attracted to poorly developed or maintained solid waste (predominately garbage) facilities. These creatures are a health hazard to the public and are usually one of the principal legal bases for state and federal solid waste regulations.

SOLID WASTE FACILITIES

WASTE CONTAINERS.   Of all the solid waste facilities, the precollection waste containers should be most apparent to park visitors. This is not to say they should be blantantly or incongruously visible in the park landscape. But the success of the entire solid waste control plan is heavily dependent on the acceptance and use of waste containers by the public. These containers should be convenient, attractive, and functional, with adequate capacity and appropriate for the type of waste

* Charles S. Spooner, *Solid Waste Management in Recreational Forest Areas,* U.S. Environmental Protection Agency, 1971, p. 25.

deposited. Public waste containers are necessary for garbage, rubbish, and mixed refuse.

GARBAGE AND MIXED REFUSE CONTAINERS.   These should conform to established health practices. Most important is vector control, cleanliness, and capacity. Other important concerns include protection from the weather, scavenger control, and convenience for park visitors and maintenance personnel. Garbage containers should be constructed of durable, rust-resistant, nonabsorbent material such as heavy-duty galvanized metal or plastic. They should be rodent proof with close-fitting lids to prevent access by flies and other insects. Lids should fit over the container to shed rain and keep the refuse dry. Self-closing lids are preferable—detachable lids may be inadvertently left off, exposing the refuse to rain, insects, and animals. There are devices to keep detachable lids secure. Figures 10.1–10.3 illustrate several acceptable garbage containers.

Plastic liners are useful to keep the containers clean and improve collection efficiency. Bags may be tied and removed

Figure 10.1

In natural areas where large scavengers may be present, mailbox drop lids can protect garbage containers and reduce spillage.

Figure 10.2

**Liners keep containers clean and improve collection efficiency.
Lever holds lid securely.**

without lifting the container. Several bags may be picked up
before the maintenance man loads them on the collection
vehicle, thus reducing steps and time. These plastic liners must
be strong. It has been found that bags of about 2.00 mil thick
give reliable service; thinner bags often tear and spill waste.*

Individually serviced containers should be large enough to
adequately hold the expected garbage generated between
collections but not so large that servicing them is difficult.
Garbage is heavy; the maximum capacity of the container should
be limited to a standard 32-gallon size, which holds 0.15 cubic
yards or about twenty-five pounds of garbage. Use of free or
cheaply obtained used 55-gallon metal barrels for garbage
containers is false economy and a hardship on maintenance
operators. If filled, the garbage in one of these tall barrels may
weigh almost 44 pounds. The weight of the refuse and height of
the barrel can greatly reduce collection efficiency.

Individual containers should be elevated above the ground,
either on a concrete slab or preferably mounted on a wooden or
metal rack. There are almost as many designs for racks and stands

* Harry R. Little, *Design Criteria for Solid Waste Management in Recreational
Areas,* Report SW-91ts, U.S. Environmental Protection Agency, 1972, p. 15.

Figure 10.3

Swing-gate containers for mixed refuse are convenient and may be more attractive than common garbage cans.

as there are recreational areas, but if they are to work properly, they should hold the container upright and stationary, keep the cover with the container, and provide surroundings that are easily kept clean and free from litter.* Some stands may damage plastic containers.

If scavengers such as bears, raccoons, or stray dogs and cats are a problem, the containers and stands should be of durable construction and effectively anchored to prevent them from being knocked over and the refuse spilled.

Bulk containers, usually with 1 to 10 cubic yards capacity, are often used in large recreation areas and in cities where municipal or private refuse collection contractors have the containers and self-loading vehicles. These have greatly reduced labor costs and freed maintenance personnel for other tasks. Figure 10.4 illustrates one type of bulk container being serviced by a self-loading packer truck. Bulk containers have been successful in park areas of concentrated heavy use generating large amounts of refuse.

* Ibid., p. 10.

Figure 10.4

Bulk containers have reduced labor costs in campgrounds and other recreation areas that generate large amounts of waste.

Service roads to these containers need to be constructed of heavy duty all-weather pavement for the packer trucks; adequate manuvering area must be provided at the container. These service requirements have often caused planners and administrators to locate these bulk containers at the edge of parking lots or other exposed locations as postdevelopment solutions. When solid waste storage and collection are part of the integral park planning process, these bulk containers and their service space requirements can be appropriately incorporated into the physical design.

The location of either individual-sized or bulk containers should be based on convenience of the user and efficiency of collection. Individual containers should be in the activity area or as close to it as possible along a user circulation route where it is apparent and convenient. Garbage containers should not be more than 150 feet from the point of expected generation.

RUBBISH CONTAINERS.   These containers need not conform to all the restrictive conditions necessary for garbage containers. Important considerations are cleanliness, capacity, protection from the weather, and convenience for park visitors and maintenance personnel. Most indoor wastebaskets and litter containers (in administrative offices, contact stations, visitor centers, cabins, lodges, restrooms, and interpretive centers) are for rubbish. Indoors a cover or lid is not necessary for weather protection but may be provided for aesthetic reasons. Park areas where large amounts of food waste is not common, such as swimming pools, overlooks, trails, docks, historic sites, and playgrounds may be adequately served by rubbish containers. Rubbish is lighter than garbage but may be more space consuming because of the empty beverage cans, cups, boxes, and other packaging. Because of this, capacity and collection frequency is more important than vector control. Rubbish containers may have perforated, woven wire, or slat sides. Covers or lids are preferred to prevent the refuse from becoming rain soaked and heavy or windblown and littered. Figures 10.5–10.6 show some types of acceptable rubbish baskets.

In an effort to reduce littering and encourage a habit of using refuse containers, some parks have installed animal and clown heads as rubbish container lids. Wastes are deposited through the swing lid "mouth." A more elaborate effort has been made by the Maryland-National Capitol Parks and Planning Com-

Figure 10.5

Rubbish containers such as this may be more open than garbage containers.

Figure 10.6

Refuse containers are part of the furniture of a park. It is important that they are well placed for convenience and are visually compatible to the total designed environment.

mission, which installed a child-scaled brick house complete with a litter-hungry animal figure. Through a recorded message the figure encourages children to feed him soft litter such as candy wrappers and paper. A small vacuum is used to suck the light materials from the childrens' hands. Figure 10.7 shows the M-NCPPC litter eater.

CIRCULATION ROUTES FOR COLLECTION.   The object of refuse collection in a park is to remove the solid wastes from the activity areas and transport it to a central transfer station or directly to the disposal facility. Access routes to the precollection refuse containers are part of the service road system of the park. For a detailed discussion of these vehicular circulation routes, see Chapter 6, Circulation.

   Collection vehicles may be multifunctional pickups and stake-body trucks, dump trucks, tractor-drawn wagons, or specially designed refuse packer trucks. All but the last may be used for other jobs after collection has been completed. A large park may use several types of vehicles—a small, light unit to service scattered or remote units or those not on heavy-duty pavements, a larger vehicle to service concentrated units, those adjacent to good roadways, and to service bulk containers. Care must be used to prevent spillage during collection and transportation when vehicles other than specially designed refuse trucks are used.

TRANSFER STATIONS.   Many parks use transfer stations to convey bags of refuse collected from individual refuse containers to a large bulk container. The transfer station may be located in a maintenance and storage area, or adjacent to a sewage treatment plant or some other support center away from public activity areas. This procedure is commonly used in parks where the internal collection is done by park employees with common park vehicles, and bulk hauling and disposal requiring special equipment is done under a private contract. Transfer stations should be studied as part of the total physical/management plan and incorporated into the development plans prior to construction. Transfer stations must be accessible by both park

Figure 10.7

Children may be trained early to deposit litter if their attention is gained.

collection vehicles and heavy duty haulers. Transfer must be simple and quick. Storage containers must meet all vector control and health standards established for garbage containers. Capacity of the containers should be based on amount of solid waste generated in the park and the frequency of transfer and haul. The station should have access to a fire hydrant and be well screened from public areas and protected from wildlife, scavengers, and vandalism. Figure 10.8 illustrates one possible layout for a park solid waste transfer station.

DISPOSAL FACILITIES.   The type of solid waste often determines the method of disposal. Inorganic trash (construction and demolition wastes) and ash are suitable landfill materials and may be used as roadfill or other park construction if well compacted and settled. Vegetable residue is highly recyclable in many economical forms. Stable litter and animal manure may be composted or used as a natural fertilizer by the park. (Some agencies permit organic gardeners and farmers to take all the organic residue they want. Thus the agency gets rid of one type of solid waste with a minimum of labor expenses.) Special waste are disposed of separate from other refuse and are usually handled on an individual needs basis.

The predominant disposal problems for parks are garbage, rubbish and litter, and mixed refuse. In the past, large parks have operated small open dumps for this refuse. These have generally been quite unsatisfactory, often providing food and refuge for rats, snakes and over vermin, feral dogs and cats, and bears. Park

Figure 10.8

Park solid-waste transfer stations may be needed in large parks. The park collection vehicles empty into large trailers that are hauled to regional disposal plants.

dumps have caused odor and smoke nuisances and have been fire hazards and possibly a source of ground water pollution. These should be eliminated.

Solid waste management is regulated by each state. Most states have established strict disposal controls and regulations for solid waste disposal sites and their operation.

It is strongly recommended that park systems contract for solid waste disposal with established state-approved permittees. The two common acceptable waste disposal methods are incineration and sanitary landfill. Each requires specially prepared areas or facilities, trained operators and constant environmental monitoring. The park that can meet these requirements and can successfully operate its own solid waste disposal plant is the exception; for most parks, this support function should be another separate agency's role.

SUMMARY

Planning for appropriate solid waste management, including facilities and services, should be done as an integral step of the park planning process. There are three operational functions of solid waste management: collection, storage, and disposal. The principal refuse-related support facilities include suitable waste containers, collection service routes, transfer stations, and disposal plants. Planning decisions are based on the type and amount of waste generated for each activity area, the frequency and method of collection, development, and maintenance norms.

Storage may be in precollection waste containers or in bulk storage at transfer stations. Collection may be done by park employees or as a service contract. It is strongly recommended that park systems utilize external, state-approved disposal services.

GLOSSARY OF TERMS

Park Solid Waste
Garbage, rubbish and litter, trash, and other refuse generated or left in the park that must be collected, stored, and disposed of by park management.

Park Solid Waste Facilities
All waste containers, collection circulation routes, transfer stations, and disposal areas or plants required for adequate solid waste management for the park.

Vector
An animal or insect that transmits infectuous diseases from one person or animal to another by biting the skin or by depositing infective material on the skin, on food, or on another object.

BIBLIOGRAPHY

American Public Works Association, Committee on Solid Wastes. *Refuse Collection Practice,* Third Edition. Public Administration Service, Chicago, 1966.

American Public Works Association, Institute for Solid Wastes. *Municipal Refuse Disposal,* Third Edition. Public Administration Service, Chicago, 1970.

National Research Council, Committee on Solid Waste Management. *Policies for Solid Waste Management, Public Health Service Publication No. 2018.* U.S. Department of Health, Education and Welfare, Washington, D.C., 1970.

Mantell, Charles Letnam. *Solid Waste: Origin, Collection, Processing, and Disposal.* Wiley, New York, 1975.

Hagerty, D. Joseph, Joseph L. Pavoni, and John E. Heer, Jr. *Solid Waste Management.* Van Nostrand Reinhold, New York, 1973.

Salvato, Joseph A. Jr. *Environmental Engineering and Sanitation.* Wiley, New York, 1972.

Little, Harry R. *Design Criteria for Solid Waste Management in Recreational Areas.* U.S. Environmental Protection Agency, Washington, D.C., 1972.

Spooner, Charles S. *Solid Waste Management in Recreational Forest Areas.* U.S. Environmental Protection Agency, Washington, D.C., 1971.

U.S. Department of Health, Education and Welfare. *Environmental Health Practice in Recreational Areas,* DHEW Publication No. (HSM) 72-10009., U.S. Government Printing Office, Washington, D.C., 1968.

Weaver, Leo, "Refuse and Litter Control in Recreation Areas," *Public Works,* 98(4), April, 1967, pp. 126–218, 160.

11
health, safety, and emergency provisions

Park planners must be concerned with three public welfare potentialities: (1) health problems that may originate in the park and be transmitted elsewhere by infested carriers or affected individuals (e.g., typhoid, dysentery, infectious hepatitis, pinworm or ringworm infections, food poisoning, skin rash, and similar ailments), (2) health or safety problems originating in the park that require immediate emergency aid (e.g., severe food poisoning, traumatic exposure, or accidental injuries from falls, burns, collisions, firearm discharge, near drowning or asphyxiation, vicious animal attacks, and property destruction), and (3) health or safety problems originating elsewhere but that require emergency aid in the park (e.g., heart attack, appendicitis, respiratory arrest, physical overexertion, and other forms of physiological collapse).

The first and second of these potentialities can be eliminated, or at least minimized, by appropriate preventative predevelopment planning augmented by supportive continuous postdevelopment health and safety programs. Emergencies, by definition, are inherently unexpected and require immediate *post facto* action. The probability of needing emergency services in certain activity areas is so apparent, however, that the physical development of these areas must facilitate a well-prepared contingency plan for provisions of these emergency needs.

The first consideration of health, safety, and emergency provisions for an activity area should be done during the initial activity analysis in the predesign phase of the park planning process (see Chapter 2). This analysis will help identify inherent hazards in the activity and the environment as well as physiological profiles of typical participants. Careful attention should be given to these public welfare factors; negligence in planning here could possibly mean unnecessary discomfort or suffering to individuals, perhaps even a preventable fatality. Issues of legal liability and possible high damage judgements against the park agency and responsible staff are additional significant causes for careful planning.

The level of park development, type of activity, number of participants, user preparation, previous experience and present expectations, and local environmental conditions have an impact on the health, safety, and emergency plans for a park. Each park requires a unique plan based on its needs. In some resource-oriented parks, visitors expect and receive outing experiences unpampered and unlinked to any modern protection or emergency system other than what they themselves provide. More intensely developed parks may require the same health, safety, and emergency elements expected and provided in any community.

Planning for the public welfare in a park is a constant process, beginning with the first activity analysis, continuing through design, development, and actualization of the participants' recreational experiences. Principal members of the park planning team for this aspect of the process should be trained health and safety specialists. Large land management agencies that provide recreation, such as the National Park Service and the U.S. Forest Service, have staff specialists with these competencies.

Smaller agencies utilize the resources of local or state health departments, health offices, professional fire and emergency aid specialists, state departments of commerce, labor, or industry, the U.S. Public Health Service, U.S. Occupational Safety and Health Administration, the National Safety Council, and the American Red Cross.

Not every situation described in this chapter is found in all parks; not every health, safety, and emergency provision is necessary for all parks. These are presented only as a guide of some of the basic elements that must be considered, if appropriate. These elements can be grouped into three categories: park nonemergency endemic health considerations, potentially serious park safety hazards, and park emergency provisions.

PARK NONEMERGENCY ENDEMIC
HEALTH CONSIDERATIONS

Park environments, including support developments, often contain conditions or organisms that may commonly harbor a disease or infectious agent. Such endemic, or prevalent, health considerations may transmit communicable diseases or infections directly or indirectly by contaminated materials (e.g., sewage, solid waste, water, food and milk) or vectors (usually arthropods, rodents, or other vertebrates).

While these diseases and ailments may be very serious, the length of the incubation period following exposure may be sufficiently long enough that the infected individual(s) has left the park. Emergency assistance, while perhaps necessary following the onset or outbreak of the disease, is not specific to the park even though the park may be the origin of the health problem.

Because control of communicable disease is a fundamental responsibility of government, careful control of the public humanistic support facilities providing food, milk, and drinking water as well as sanitary wastewater and solid waste disposal has been legislated at many levels. It is essential that park planners are familiar with the governing health codes and regulations for the park.

WATER-BORNE DISEASES AND AILMENTS

Several types of disease agents are found in contaminated or polluted water. The most common problems are associated with either impure park drinking water supplies or water from contaminated natural springs, streams, or lakes that are used by campers, hikers, and others as a supplementary water source. Ingested pathogens in this drinking water may cause considerable discomfort and perhaps ultimately death. Symptoms include abdominal pain, diarrhea, vomiting, nausea, and possibly fever. Incubation periods for water-borne diseases such as typhoid fever, bacillary dysentery, cholera, gastroenteritis, and infectious hepatitis may be as short as a few hours or as long as two weeks to a month, making identification of the disease source very difficult.* This makes it essential that *all sources of drinking water in parks be approved and regularly certified by the proper public health agency.*

The Safe Drinking Water Act of 1974 (P.L. 93-523) required the U.S. Environmental Protection Agency to prepare national drinking water standards. Each state has enforcement re-

---

* Joseph A. Salvato, Jr. *Environmental Engineering and Sanitation*, Second Edition, Wiley, New York, Fig. 1.2, 1972, facing pp. 16–17.

sponsibilities. Most park drinking water systems are subject to the regulations. Chapter 8 covers park water system planning.

Those convenient springs, streams, lakes or other waters that may be casually used by thirsty recreationists should be regularly tested as well, at all access points. Signs for unsafe water should be prominently posted (see Figure 11.1).

In addition to diseases transmitted by drinking water, there are a number of ailments that are related to water areas such as pools, swimming beaches, and boating waters used for water skiing. These may be caused by parasitic worms, fungi, algae, and other pathogenic organisms. While these ailments are not as serious as the diseases mentioned in the last paragraph, considerable discomfort may result from infections. Symptoms include possible skin rashes and itching, pain, diarrhea, and nausea. Examples of these ailments include swimmer's itch,

Figure 11.1

Readily accessible streams or other natural water bodies are tempting to thirsty park users. These waters should be regularly tested and posted if unsafe. Hikers should be encouraged to bring potable water in canteens and sources of safe water should be noted on trail maps and signs.

swimmer's ear, septic sore throat, intestinal roundworms, and ringworms.

Public swimming pools and beaches must conform to established state standards and must operate under special permits. Properly designed, constructed, and operated artificial pools meeting public health department (or some other appropriate state agency) criteria usually provide the healthiest of these swimming experiences. The success of a pool depends on the training and care of the pool manager who oversees the clarification and disinfection of the water, controls the pH level, makes necessary water quality tests, keeps detailed records, and supervises the attendants, lifeguards, and water purification plant operator. If possible, it is advantageous to incorporate the pool manager into the planning process for a new pool at the initial stages of planning rather than hiring or assigning him to the pool after construction. The training and experience of a competent pool manager makes him a major member of the planning team throughout all planning stages.

Beaches and water ski areas are much harder to control. The chemical, bacterial, and physical characteristics of potentially harmful pollutants, water circulation and volume, quality and quantity of the water, and presence of aquatic weeds or debris that harbor parasite-infested snails (the host for the swimmer's itch-causing larvae) are major considerations for these water bodies. Plans for the control of endemic conditions should be established prior to design and development of natural waters for swimming and waterskiing.

As part of the health and safety plans for swimming areas, the physical development plans and specifications as well as the appropriate state review inspections and permits should be supplemented with a carefully prepared operations manual for the facility. As an actualization document, the manual would provide the basis for proper testing and control of the water quality as well as the additional personnel, maintenance, and public use policies which are not within the scope of this chapter.

FOOD- AND MILK-BORNE DISEASES

Food poisoning is usually caused by disregard or ignorance of fundamental sanitary principles by planners, designers, builders, or operators of food dispensing or serving facilities, or by the consumers themselves. Food poisoning in parks may occur from eating previously contaminated food that was brought into the park, or from eating food contaminated by flies and other insects or food handling by unclean individuals, or by improper storage and protection while in the park. Certain plants growing in the park are also poisonous and should not be eaten. Examples of food poisoning including staphyloccus intoxication, salmonellosis, clostridium perfringens, and streptococcus infections. Symptoms include nausea, vomiting, abdominal pains, and diarrhea, occurring just a few hours after eating (depending on the disease contracted).*

Park agencies have a responsibility to protect park users by providing adequate sanitary conditions and maintaining sufficient sanitary standards for food and milk storage, preparation, handling, and consumption. This includes picnic and campground facilities such as grills, fireplaces, tables, garbage containers, scrub basins, water faucets, and their surrounding environment. Water for washing and park wastewater facilities are discussed in Chapter 8 and 9. Sanitary storage, collection, and disposal of garbage from these areas is discussed in Chapter 10.

As part of their health provision, some park agencies have regulated the type of food and beverage containers permitted, as well as enforcing other antilitter and sanitation regulations.

A park food service sanitation program should include all eating and drinking establishments, including fixed establishments and mobile units, that is, all kitchens, mess halls, commissaries, cafeterias, refreshment stands, vending machines, and restaurants in the park, whether operated by the park agency or by a private concessioner. *It should conform with state and local health codes* and include physical plans, specifications for equipment approved by the National Sanitation Foundation, food and facility permit inspection procedures and schedule, operations manuals for cleaning, sanitation, and storage of all equipment, job descriptions of all personnel, and a personnel training manual. Each state health department has specific regulations for the physical development and operations of public food establishments. These have been based on a national model prepared by the Food and Drug Administration of the U.S. Department of Health, Education and Welfare.†

PROBLEM INSECTS AND ANIMALS

Parks are often inhabited by a great variety of wildlife. Even urban parks, with a high level of development, nursery-stocked exotic plant materials, carefully groomed turf fields, lawns and little "natural areas" may offer harborage for those animals tolerant of man's presence. These parks are often populated with tree or ground squirrels, rabbits, chipmunks, mice, gophers, perhaps even raccoons. Bees and wasps may construct hives or nests in park areas. Flies, mosquitoes, chiggers, and other insects may be prevalent here as well. Natural parks provide forage and

* Ibid.
† This model ordinance was previously published in the *Food Service Sanitation Manual* (1962). This has been revised in "Food Service Sanitation-Proposed Uniform Requirements for State and Local Regulatory Agencies," U.S. Department of Health, Education and Welfare, Food and Drug Administration, *Federal Register,* 39:191, October 1, 1974, pp. 35438–35449.

habitat for additional wildlife. Some of these may adapt to the presence of man to the point of supplementing natural diets with the offerings or garbage provided by park visitors. In addition to the animals mentioned above, skunks, opossum, bears, deer, and other wild animals can become health and safety problems in parklands. Feral dogs and cats, abandoned by thoughtless owners, may maraud and scavenge singly or in packs through any park.

Park planners must evaluate the significance of these wildlife populations in each park. The presence of many of these animals can be a valuable part of the recreational experience. Only an exceptional problem may make some animals' presence undesirable. Other animals may be a constant threat to park users' health, safety, or comfort.

As part of the site analysis in the design phase of the planning process, a wildlife survey should identify insect and animal populations, habitation, and forage. This should be the basis for park vector and pest management plans. Management and control plans should deal with two wildlife concerns: (1) health and safety problems and (2) pest and nuisance problems.

COMMON VECTORS AND DANGEROUS WILDLIFE.   Any insect or animal that transmits disease-producing agents is a *vector*. Transmission may be by biting, depositing infestations in saliva or feces, or from filth or organisms carried on the feet, fur or body of the vector. Special control of vectors in parks is essential to minimize the spread of communicable diseases such as typhus, amebic dysentery, choriomeningitis, leptospirosis, poliomylitis, and salmonella infection.[*]

The most common vectors found in parks are rats, mice, flies and cockroaches. These are attracted by convenient access to garbage and other filth generated by park users (Figure 11-2). Proper solid waste storage, collection and disposal, along with a careful sanitation plan for storage and protection of food and water supplies are essential for vector control. All structures should be designed, constructed, and maintained in a rat-proof manner. All fly- and roach-breeding places should be eliminated by designing and maintaining all food preparation, storage, and consumption areas—including all park food service establishments, picnic areas, and campsites—and all refuse containers and sanitary waste facilities as clean and sanitary as possible. See Chapter 10, Solid Waste.

Good design, good maintenance, and proper sanitary control measures are the primary means of vector control. Secondary measures include insecticides, pesticides, poisoned baits, and traps.

Bees and wasps, while not normally carriers of infectious organisms, may present a serious threat to park users if hives

[*] Joseph A. Salvato, Jr., op. cit.

Figure 11.2

Improper sanitary control, poor maintenance, and carelessness with park wildlife are invitations to communicable disease problems in parks.

or nests are located near activity areas. Bee and wasp stings are very painful, potentially disabling, and have even been fatal. Vegetation that attract bees, such as lindens, clover, and crownvetch should not be planted in large amounts near use areas. Hives and nests should be relocated or destroyed by trained specialists.

Feral dogs and cats are often vicious to small children who think the animals are pets. Wild dog packs may hurt deer or farm animals such as sheep, goats, cattle, or hogs that are often found in park farm zoos. Rabies must always be suspected. Skunks and raccoons have also been attracted to campgrounds and picnic areas in search of edible wastes. In addition to their notorious defense mechanism, skunks may also be rabid. This is true for raccoons as well.

The distribution and use of pesticides are regulated by the Federal Insecticide, Fungicide, and Rodenticide Act of 1947 as amended by the Federal Environmental Pesticide Control Act of 1972. Many state and local ordinances have adopted these national controls. Stringent certification standards are required for trained applicators of many hazardous pesticides. Only certified applicators may use restricted pesticides.

POTENTIAL INSECT AND ANIMAL PESTS.   There are a number of insects and animals that are not normally health or safety hazards but do cause discomfort, inconvenience, or a nuisance. The eradication or control practices for these pests should be based on the development norm for the affected activity area, agency policies, and budget. One situation may warrant a careful and effective control; another situation may require only suitable notification of area users that these pests are prevalent.

INSECT PESTS.   Mosquitoes, ticks, fleas, chiggers, and biting flies (i.e., sandflies, blackflies, greenflies) may be transmitters of insect-borne diseases. The potential for malaria, encephalitis, and Rocky Mountain spotted fever does exist. Typically, however, these insects are more of a nuisance and annoyance than a hazard in the United States today.

Where control programs are desirable, a predevelopment entomological survey should locate existing and potential mosquito breeding places. Water management and proper surface drainage is a key to mosquito control. All stagnant pools may be filled as one means of control (if permitted by wetlands legislation). Ponds are often stocked with surface feeding fish that feed on the larvae.

Weeds, high grass, and heavy brush harbor mosquitoes and chiggers. Park maintenance plans should distinguish priority zones in and adjacent to activity areas where users are in close contact with the ground—grass beaches, picnic areas, athletic fields, campgrounds, and amphitheaters for example—where these insects would unduly detract from the recreational experience. Limited relief is possible by fogging areas with insect repellents just prior to use.

It is virtually impossible to eliminate ticks. Heavy-use areas that are tick infested should be identified and closed during tick season. Back-country areas used for hiking as well as other areas that cannot be feasibly closed should be posted at all trailheads or permit offices during tick season.

Biting fly control requires large area treatment. Usually park planners must cooperate with county or regional agencies to have an effective control program.

ANIMAL PESTS.   Frequently animal populations become unbalanced because of synthetically favorable conditions in parks. These animals soon become nuisances and pests. Raccoons and squirrels may become quite adept at raiding waste containers; chipmunks and ground squirrels gain access to cabins, tents, and other structures in search of carelessly stored food; rabbits destroy neighbors' crops and gardens; woodchucks and gophers burrow playfields and leave open holes for horses

and people to trip in. Usually complete elimination of these
animals is not desirable, but proper controls must be maintained
to insure that problems do not develop.

A wildlife habitat and forage inventory is an important portion
of the predevelopment site analysis. The complexity of such a
study will depend on the parksite, projected uses, and significance of the wildlife to the recreational experiences. The
predevelopment study will provide only benchmark data on the
park wildlife. Regular monitoring over time is needed for
rational park wildlife management, judgments, and decisions.

The concept of park wildlife sanctuaries is appropriate if
compatible with the primary uses of the park, but blanket
protection of all wildlife in a park without regard for the consequences can be detrimental to both the balance of nature and
the principal recreation objectives of the park.

NOXIOUS VEGETATION

There are a large number of plants that are potential problems in
parks. One definition of a weed is a plant that is out of place.
Under that definition, all these problem plants are weeds. Some
may have needles or thorns, others may produce unpleasant
odors or messy fruit, and others may have destructive, quick-
growing root systems. Located in an unobtrusive area of the
park, outside development areas, most of these plants are not
health hazards. Two groups of plants, however, are regular park
health hazards to large groups of park users every year: (1) skin
irritants and (2) respiratory debilitants.

SKIN-IRRITANT PLANTS.   Three plants that commonly produce
a skin rash, blisters, and severe itching are *poison ivy, poison
oak,* and *poison sumac.* The poison is contained in the leaves,
flowers, fruit, bark, and roots of these plants. It is potent even in
dried leaves in the fall. Its effects on people are noticeable after
direct or often indirect contact—picking up baseballs, footballs,
golf balls, or tennis balls that have bounced or rolled through
these plants, touching the outside of gloves or work clothes
worn while pulling up the plants, or petting a dog or cat that
brushed against the plant. Reactions to the poisonous substance
vary between individuals. Few people seem to have a natural
immunity, however, and many have been hospitalized with
severe outbreaks.

Two control measures are recommended: physical or chemical
eradication. Small clumps of young plants may be carefully
grubbed out by the roots. The entire plant must be removed to
be effective. The debris should be removed, never burned—the
smoke will carry the poison long distances and may be inhaled
and damage the throat and lungs. Grubbing out the plants can
be time consuming and costly.

Application of chemical brush killers is effective for large patches and old plants. Extreme care must be taken to limit chemical contamination. Before selecting and using chemicals, check with the appropriate herbicide control agency.

RESPIRATORY DEBILITATING PLANTS.   Millions of people in the United States suffer from hay fever and the more serious ailment, asthma. The pollen season occurs during middle to late summer and into fall each year, paralleling usual peak use periods in parks, vacations, and summer school recess. While many pollens cause hay fever sneezing, itchy watering of the eyes, sinus irritation, and other discomforts, the most significant is ragweed pollen. A park control program is warranted only if the effort is compatible with controls for the surrounding area: an urban park in a residential neighborhood cannot be a ragweed nursery but a small rural park may be surrounded by ragweed infested lands with no governmental weed control enforcement. A large national park may be able to provide ragweed-control zones as part of the overall maintenance and resource management plans. Careful scheduling and control of mowing and spraying of mapped ragweed-infested areas prior to pollen development, in cooperation with adjacent land owners and governmental agencies, revegetation of treated areas with low pollen-producing grasses, and a seasonal pollen-count program effectiveness study in affected use areas are useful control techniques. Wind direction and velocity are important factors.

Noxious weed control, like mosquito control, requires large area treatment. Parks planners must cooperate with county or regional agencies for an effective control plan.

POTENTIALLY SERIOUS PARK SAFETY HAZARDS

Park planners must always consider the potential inherent safety problems in park and recreation areas. Because of the wide diversity of experience levels sought by recreationists (see Recreation Experience Norms, Tables 2.1 and 2.2, in Chapter 2), it is very difficult to provide equitable safety controls that satisfy the entire public. Some park visitors seek recreational activity that is relatively free from restrictions, controls, and close supervision. Other visitors, vying for a share of the same or adjacent land, require a rather structured environment to maintain the integrity of the activity and sound safety practices.*

There are actually two distinct groups that must be considered in park safety planning. The first group is the visitors who utilize the parkland and facilities as part of their recreational experiences. The other group is the support personnel who work in the park in various service capacities for the park agency. The

---

* *Recreational Safety Newsletter,* January, 1976, p. 2.

park safety program must be directed to both groups to be successful. The National Park Service park safety standards are included in Appendix 11.

A simple definition of an *accident* is an unplanned event involving personal injury and/or property damage resulting from preventable unsafe acts, equipment, or conditions.* Notice that an accident may result in injury to an individual or damage to private or public goods. Accidents are preventable and are caused by either unsafe acts or by hazards.

An *unsafe act* is personal action that directly caused or permitted an accident. The person who committed the unsafe act may or may not have been involved in the accident. A *hazard* is a physical or environmental condition that may cause or attribute to an accident. Three predominent types of hazards may cause park-related accidents: (1) unsafe equipment, including personal sports and recreation equipment, service machinery, tools, and vehicles, (2) unsafe development (facilities) that may include activity areas such as swimming pools, shooting ranges, playgrounds, campgrounds, and support areas such as shops and garages, and (3) unsafe environmental conditions, including cliffs, dead trees, rapids, lightning, and severe weather.

UNSAFE ACTS.   A complete safety program must attempt to eliminate or minimize each of these causes through hazard control and behavioral modification (education and policy enforcement). Because so many accidents occur because of an unsafe act—through negligence, ignorance, or irresponsibility—some park agencies have established proof-of-competency policies that require would-be users of recreational facilities to show proof of an approved course of instruction including safety practices prior to issuing a permit or granting admission to a designated use area such as a sailing, powerboating or water-skiing lake, rock climbing or repelling area, a spelunking cave, target range, or whitewater canoe stream. Many states require applicants for hunting licenses to pass a hunter's safety course before issuing the permits.

The National Safety Council prepares a variety of publications and aids including the *Safety Education Data Sheets,* a *Recreational Safety Newsletter,* and special accident prevention manuals that provide safety recommendations to recreational participants and employees.

UNSAFE EQUIPMENT

Another high portion of recreational accidents occur due to unsafe equipment. Some agencies have established regu-

* Based on definitions by Alton L. Thygerson in *Safety-Principles, Instruction, and Readings,* Prentice-Hall, Englewood-Cliffs, N.J., 1972, p. 1 and Charles M. Binford, Cecil S. Fleming, and Z. A. Prust, *Loss Control in the OSHA Era,* McGraw-Hill, New York, 1975, p. 147.

lar inspection regulations for boats, snowmobiles, bicycles, trailbikes, campers, and similar equipment. The U.S. Consumer Product Safety Commission has established the National Electronic Injury Surveillance System (NEISS) for product-related injuries. "Sports and recreation equipment" is a major category of this monthly report of injuries associated with equipment.

Thorough guidelines for safety education, safety inspections, and safe practices policy enforcement are available from appropriate state and federal agencies and special-interest organizations for each activity. To obtain organization names, officers, mailing addresses and services for a specific activity, consult *The Encyclopedia of Associations,* or Appendix 12, Information Sources for Specific Activities.

Product standards for many of the sports and recreation equipment, park apparatus and equipment, and occupational safety are available from sources such as the American National Standards Institute Inc. (ANSI), Underwriters Laboratories, Inc. (UL), and the American Insurance Association (AIA).

The Occupational Safety and Health Administration (OSHA) in the U.S. Department of Labor has established standards for private industry. In 1974, President Ford made these standards applicable to all federal employees. Many states have established comparable guidelines.

These readily available sources of detailed information can assist park planners with the unsafe acts and equipment aspects of park safety planning. Full item-by-item explanations for each specific act or product is beyond the scope of this limited discussion.

UNSAFE ENVIRONMENTAL CONDITIONS

Many types of accidents can be caused by natural elements. Park visitors may be struck by objects, fall, drown, suffer from exposure, be burned, electrocuted, poisoned, or attacked by wildlife. Most of these incidents, fortunately, occur quite infrequently however, because of limited hazard exposure by the typical recreationists. Falls, drownings, and being struck by objects are the predominant park accidents caused by natural conditions, and many of these are actually caused by unsafe acts by people who don't know how to react in unfamiliar situations.

Park planners should incorporate the knowledge and skills of a competent safety specialist in all phases of park planning to insure satisfactory hazard control. Failure to provide safety devices has been found to result from negligence.* As part of the site analysis, all natural safety hazards should be inventoried and appraised based on the severity of the hazard, impact on proposed land use and activity patterns, control requirements,

---

* Betty van der Smissen, *Legal Liability of Cities and Schools for Injuries in Recreation and Parks,* W. H. Anderson Co., Cincinnati, 1968, § 4.10, pp. 203–204.

and budget. Imminent hazards must be rated more significant than probable hazards; dangerous conditions in a major heavy-use activity area are more important than similar conditions in backcountry areas because of more accident opportunities or because of the environmental modification and development expectations by the public. Hazard control may require complete removal, access restrictions, or simply visitor awareness.

After development, follow-up inventory appraisals should be conducted regularly. The safety program, as part of the total park plan, should be a dynamic process; no part of the plan should ever be final.

TYPICAL NATURAL HAZARDS.   Park visitors are attracted to natural edges and borders such as the water's edge at lakes and streams or the edge of a cliff. These edges are potential hazard zones. Often they are unstable and may collapse when walked on. Other fall hazards include rock slide areas, open shafts and caves, and other areas where people may climb.

VEGETATION.   Trees are subject to mechanical failure because of damage or decay. All defective or faulty trees in proposed use areas or travel corridors should be inventoried and rated on these factors: probability of tree failure, probability of accident on failure (including striking permanent buildings, vehicles, or other property as well as individuals), the damage potential of the possible failure (a small limb causes less damage than an entire tree), and possible loss value.*

WATER.   Water areas may be hazardous if they are deep, full of rapids, or too cold. Water-related accidents include drownings, being swept over falls or onto rocks, and exposure to cold water. Ice areas are subject to constant change and require careful safety appraisal frequently.

FIRE.   Grass and forest areas are subject to periods of high fire susceptibility. Wildfire pose threats to people, buildings, and wildlife. Fire safety plans for large natural areas should include a fire danger and fire weather monitoring system.

WILDLIFE.   The presence of wildlife can be a rewarding and memorable part of a recreational experience; it may also be a very dangerous hazard. Park visitors have been bitten, trampled, gored, clawed, butted, or stung by seemingly "docile" wild animals. Few park visitors are experienced wildlife experts and do not know how to recognize animal warnings. Wildlife management plans should incorporate considerations for human as well as wildlife safety protection and well being.

* Lee A. Paine, *Accident Hazard and Evaluation and Control Decisions on Forested Recreation Sites,* U.S.D.A. Forest Service Research Paper PSW-68, Berkeley, Calif., 1971 and *Administrative Goals and Safety Standards for Hazard Control on Forested Recreational Sites,* U.S.D.A. Forest Service Research Paper PSW-88, Berkeley, Calif., 1973.

Figure 11.3

**Site selection, development, and periodical inspections are
essential elements of a park safety program. Failure to check
natural hazards and poor site planning, coupled with unsafe acts
by park visitors, can make an activity area such as this a
dangerous liability.**

PARK DEVELOPMENT HAZARDS.   Most park accidents are not
caused by "natural elements" in the park. In the national parks,
for example, most mishaps to the public occur within the
developed portions of the park system and, as elsewhere, the
leading cause of injuries and fatalities is the automobile.*
Following automobile-caused accidents, drowning and falls are
the major categories of park deaths and injuries. The preventive
measures taken in the predesign, design, and development
phases of park planning can greatly reduce the likelihood of
serious accidents caused by physical hazards. These measures
must be supplemented in the actualization phase to prevent
reduction of safety provision effectiveness due to disregard or
improper maintenance. (Figure 11.3) The most common park

* Jack Hope, "Safety in the Parks," *National Parks and Conservation,* 46:11,
November, 1972, p. 11.

hazards in developed areas are probably (1) *structural in-adequacies* such as weak railings, slippery or unstable surfacing, faulty hardware, and weak or damaged weight-bearing structures, (2) *poor visibility* caused by daytime visual obstructions or insufficient artificial lighting at night (see a detailed discussion of safety lighting in Chapter 7), (3) *inadequate barriers or control restrictions* at inherently hazardous situations—for example, no guard fence or wall atop a high precipice or overlook, an unfenced pool, accessible high voltage transmission lines, unsecured electric transformers, gas valves, and flammable liquid storage facilities, (4) *circulation obstacles* such as low clearance or narrow passageways, unnecessary steps, poorly marked or locked building exits, and equipment storage located in emergency circulation routes, and (5) *insufficient fire prevention*—for example, no control of smoking or other ignition sources in fire-susceptible locations, improper installation of electric wiring, omissions of lightning arresters, dangerous storage of flammable and combustible materials, and disregard for fire-resistive construction.

Park administrative, maintenance, and operations areas may contain as many hazards as the public use areas. Employee accident rates in parks and recreation areas have been recognized by the National Safety Council as being three times greater than the national all-industry average.* Park employees suffer from falls, being struck by objects, burns, asphyxiation, and machinery-caused injuries. While accidents are possible anywhere, these work areas should especially be planned in strict adherence with safety guidelines: kitchens, garages, repair shops, woodworking shops, paint shops, machine shops, welding shops, chlorination rooms, boiler or furnace rooms, warehouses, and unloading docks. There are numerous sources of detailed standards and recommendations applicable to these occupational situations. Specific codes and regulations are available from local or state health and safety agencies and should be consulted. *Accident Prevention Manual for Industrial Operations* (1823 pp.) and the 10-volume *National Fire Codes* (9500 pp.) are excellent references for park safety, containing much more applicable information than their titles suggest.

PARK EMERGENCY PROVISIONS

Every park and recreation area should have a well-prepared park emergency plan. The plan must be specifically related to each park—activities provided, size of the park, number of people using the park, proximity to public hospitals, fire stations, police and other emergency services, and probability of natural disaster

* National Safety Council, *Public Employee Safety Guide for Parks and Recreation,* Chicago, 1974, p. 5.

(flood, hurricane, tornado, cyclone, or earthquake) that would require special consideration.

The first objective of a park emergency plan should be the safety and protection of park visitors and employees, including immediate assistance to injured individuals and removal of others from danger. Next, protection of all property must be considered. Finally, the preservation or restoration of park services and operations must be included in the emergency plan.

TYPES OF PARK EMERGENCIES

The emergency plan must be responsive to a variety of situations. It is just as bad to overreact or take improper steps than it is to not be prepared in an emergency. The type of park emergency is determined by four factors: (1) the impact on people, (2) the impact on property, (3) the need for immediate, interim assistance and (4) the impact on program. The following examples illustrate the possibilities.

☐ An individual collapses or requests emergency transportation to a hospital in a large assembly area such as a stadium or amphitheater. No first aid is required beyond making the person comfortable until (s)he is transported to the hospital. No other individuals are in danger, no property damage occured, and the program is uninterrupted.

☐ A child is injured on a piece of broken play apparatus and requires immediate first aid. The apparatus area must be closed off, thus ending activities for a portion of the playground.

☐ A community center alarm is sounded but the cause is unknown. All occupants must be evacuated and all facilities secured. The building is inspected to determine the cause of the alarm.

☐ A storage tank explosion has ignited several fires in the maintenance center and injured two employees. The injured require immediate first aid. The buildings must be evacuated. Interim fire fighting is necessary to contain the blaze until the city fire equipment and personnel arrive.

COMPONENTS OF A PARK EMERGENCY PLAN

Preparation of a park emergency plan requires consideration during several phases of the park planning process. The predesign activity analysis helps identify possible emergency situations. The design directive, including the agency specifications, directs the physical development of a park to have emergency access, safety routes, first aid, and fire-fighting provisions. Following development, personnel training, facility inspections, and careful emergency procedures must be implemented as part of the plan.

There are two principal components to the park emergency plan: the physical provisions for an emergency in the park and an established strategy for emergency procedures. These components must be coordinated. This requires that the plan be a collaboration between the safety specialist, park designer, administrator, line supervisor, and the community emergency service agencies.

PHYSICAL EMERGENCY CONSIDERATIONS.   Park designers must include emergency support in the physical development of a park. Four considerations are essential to park emergency support provisions: emergency communications, emergency circulation (including access routes for emergency vehicles and personnel evacuation routes), and two interim assistance provisions—first aid and fire fighting.

EMERGENCY COMMUNICATIONS PROVISIONS.   Information means are essential in emergency situations for one or more of these reasons: to help locate emergency support services or apparatus, to alert others who may possibly be endangered, and to summon assistance.

Signs or other graphic devices that identify exits, alarms, telephones, first-aid or medical aid stations, building fire extinguishers or standpipes, and other emergency provisions should be prominent, understandable and well illuminated. Because these signs provide information that may be vital to the well-being of individuals or property, they should be readily distinguished from general informational or regulatory signs.

It is recommended that park agencies adopt the national uniform safety color code* and exit marking standards.† Two colors—red and green—should be used to mark emergency provisions. Red should be used to identify fire protection equipment and apparatus (alarm boxes, fire exit signs, extinguishers, fire hose locations, etc.). Green should be used to designate the location of first aid equipment. Other colors (i.e., orange, yellow, blue, purple, black, and white) are used to denote specific physical hazards and provide safety warnings or instructions.

Alarms provide nonverbal signals to alert people of an emergency situation. Alarms may be activated automatically by heat or smoke sensors or by electric impulse or they may be activated manually by an individual. Automatic alarms have the advantage of being effective without depending on the presence

---

* American National Standards Institute, "ANSI Z53.1-1967: Safety Color Code for Marking Physical Hazards."
† National Fire Protection Association, "NFPA 101-1970: Life Safety Code."

of people. While still subject to false alarms, automatic systems reduce the incidences of mischievous signals by thoughtless individuals.

Local alarm systems are used to alert building or area occupants of an emergency situation. An employee should be trained to direct the evaluation of the premises; others should immediately turn off all equipment and lock predesignated storage cabinets; still others should be prepared to investigate the cause of the alarm and take appropriate action. Local alarms do not notify park or community fire or emergency service departments.

Remote alarm systems immediately signal distant fire departments, ranger stations, police departments, or others of an emergency. Usually a basic response unit will investigate the alarm and summon backup units if the situation warrants. Remote alarms have the advantage of immediate contact with emergency departments without human delay.

Local alarms are essential for park structures or areas of public occupancy where immediate, orderly evacuation could save many people from danger. Remote alarms are essential for vital park structures and utilities that may be unmanned during long periods of the day. Combination alarms are often installed in community centers, information or exhibit centers, gymnasiums, and other program facilities that may be closed and unoccupied at times.

Vocal emergency communications can be provided by a public address system, a private telephone system, the public telephone, or by radio. A *public address system* is frequently required by local or state building codes for public buildings of assembly where large numbers of spectators gather (i.e., fieldhouses, performing arts theaters, amphitheaters, stadiums, meeting halls) or where emergency announcements must be heard over noisy activities (e.g., beaches, pools, skating rinks, bowling alleys, gymnasiums, dance halls, cafeterias). *Telephone systems* may be private internal systems for large parks, linking key areas and personnel or they may be part of the regular system serving the community. *Radios* have the convenience of mobility. Emergency vehicles with radio transceivers can be dispatched immediately instead of waiting until they return to the garage or base station. Portable walkie talkies can be used for traffic control, search and rescue, and other emergencies.

Private internal agency systems such as radios and private direct telephone lines should be controlled by trained personnel only.

The means to summon emergency assistance (alarms or verbal systems) should be accessible to the public in all major park program structures and areas. These should not be kept in locked rooms or compartments. Clear directions and emergency numbers should be prominently posted by the alarm or telephone.

EMERGENCY CIRCULATION PROVISIONS.   There are two aspects to consider when mapping the emergency circulation patterns of a park: park visitor and employee evacuation routes and access corridors for emergency vehicles—ambulances, firetrucks, tow trucks, and other specially equipped units.

Evacuation routes are designated ways to leave a structure or area of immediate danger. They are not exit ways out of the entire park (but may be so in small parks or recreation areas). Evacuation routes must be provided in all park buildings as well as other program areas and facilities where large crowds assemble.

EVACUATION ROUTES FOR PARK ACTIVITY FACILITIES OTHER THAN BUILDINGS.   Any park program or support facility having an anticipated occupancy of at least one person per 100 square feet should have designated emergency evacuation routes. Examples of these units include open-air amphitheaters, stadiums, pavilions, festival grounds, plazas, skating rinks, swimming pools, and beaches. The evacuation routes for each facility should provide a continuous and unobstructed way of exit travel from any point to a place of safety.* These routes should be constructed of a smooth, nonslip material, equal to the recommendations for park walks in Chapter 6.

The width of each route is based on the capacity of the facility or area portion it serves, the total number of routes, and the necessity for steps or ramps. It is recommended that evacuation routes never be less than 44 inches in width. A level walk of this size has an emergency capacity of 200 people. Each additional 22 inches will serve 100 more individuals. Points of exit from large spectator facilities may be as wide as 10 feet or more. Evacuation ramps and steps 44 inches wide serve 120 people going down, 90 people going up.

For each program unit, a minimum of two evacuation routes should be provided, remote from each other to insure an alternate way to leave if one route should become unusable. Occupants of these facilities should not be more than 100 feet from an evacuation route at any point in the structure or area.

Ramps instead of steps are preferred for evacuation routes because they provide less opportunity for individuals to trip or stumble. Ramps should not exceed a gradient of 1 to $1\frac{3}{16}$ inch per foot. Change of direction on ramps should be made only at level landings; slope should not vary between landings.

Gates should be as wide as the evacuation passageway and should swing open in the direction of exiting pedestrian traffic.

Turnstiles, if used to control admissions, should provide at least 22 inches clear width. If the turnstile is incapable of turning in

* This corresponds closely with the definition of a "means of egress" for buildings in the "Life Safety Code: NFPA Code 101," National Fire Protection Association, 1972, p. 16.

the direction of exit, an adjacent outward swinging evacuation gate within a distance of 20 feet is necessary. Figure 11.4 illustrates a typical situation.

The evacuation route must be kept free from obstructions such as benches and waste containers. Overhead clearance should be at least 6 feet, 8 inches. The route should be illuminated with a minimum of one footcandle if the facility is used at night. (See Chapter 7 for more information about safety and emergency lighting.) Park walks serving as emergency evacuation routes should be reasonably straight and direct to large open places of refuge such as a parking lot or field.

EVACUATION ROUTES FOR PARK BUILDINGS.   Because the primary necessity for building evacuation is to escape fire, architectural evacuation routes are planned for that emergency. Building evacuation provisions, technically designated as "means

Figure 11.4

Where one-way turnstiles are necessary for control, such as in this indoor pool, emergency evacuation exits should be prominently located. These doors, equipped with simple push bars, open outward and have no external hardware to prevent improper entrance.

of egress," are well defined in local and state building codes and in "NFPA Code 101: Life Safety Code" of the *National Fire Codes* and should be consulted by park planners and architects before building plans are prepared. These regulations contain standards for the three basic components of a building evacuation system: the *exit access* (usually corridors, passageways, hallways, and other internal circulation routes), the *exit* (a protected way of travel to the outside such as smokeproof towers, enclosed staircases and ramps, and horizontal exits), and the *exit discharge* (door to the outside or other refuge).

The basic considerations of exit width, egress capacity, minimum distance to exits, fire-rating requirements for exit enclosures and all fire doors, and control hardware must conform or exceed the regulations established in these building codes.

Most public use park buildings built today may be classified "low fire hazard" signifying that the only probable danger requiring the use of emergency exits will be from panic, fumes, or smoke, or fire from some external source. Many maintenance and operations buildings (i.e., garages, warehouses, paint shops, machine shops), however, have "high hazard" contents that are liable to burn with extreme rapidity or from which poisonous fumes or explosions are to be feared in the event of fire. Very stringent evacuation provisions should be established and vigorously maintained to insure adequate emergency escape routes for all park building occupants—recreationists and park employees alike.

EMERGENCY AID ACCESS PROVISIONS.   Park evacuation routes provide safe and rapid movement *from* a facility; park emergency aid access routes provide convenient and rapid movement *to* a facility for those responding to an emergency situation. The three most frequent assistance requests in a park may be for an ambulance, for a law-enforcement officer, and for fire-fighting equipment. Direct vehicular access to fire hydrants and one or more facility entrances is necessary to save essential time in the removal of possibly critically injured or ill individuals, to stop potentially dangerous disturbances, assist in rescue operation, and to control and extinguish fires.

Ambulances, ranger or police cars, vans, and other emergency vehicles that have a comparatively small turning radius (less than 55 feet) a wheel base of under 150 inches, and a width of under 8 feet can use all the necessary park service routes described in Chapter 6. These routes may include structurally sound pedestrian walks if they are wide enough as shown in Figure 11.5. If possible, emergency evacuation routes and aid access routes should be separate to reduce conflict and increase efficiency. If it is necessary that a walk provide both emergency access and evacuation, the combined necessary widths should be added to determine the total walk breadth.

Figure 11.5

Combination park vehicular service roads/pedestrian walks are usually appropriate emergency aid access routes to nature centers, auditoriums, and other places of assembly. Use of these routes must be preplanned as part of an accepted emergency procedure by all assisting agencies and staff.

No impassible obstacles and obstructions should be permitted in emergency access routes, including other parked vehicles. These routes should be free of steps and sharp turns, with a suggested overhead clearance of 8 feet and a usual side clearance of 4 feet or more on each side. The route should be maintained in an accessible condition during any season the facility is used.

In some parks, a separate emergency access route—which is normally kept closed by locked gates—is provided. Keys are given to all emergency agencies servicing the park. This has significantly reduced response time and avoided possible conflict with slow, heavy park traffic during peak use periods.

Special considerations must be made for large fire-fighting engines and other heavy-duty emergency vehicles. Each building of occupancy and all vital support facilities should be accessible to these pieces of emergency apparatus. These vehicles require heavy duty, all-weather, easily maneuverable roads to all fire hydrants or within moderate hose distance to insure sufficient pump efficiency to extinguish fires.

Local fire marshals, insurance carriers, and fire company officials should be involved in the planning of park buildings and water systems. Each emergency agency servicing the park should be familiarized with all access routes, procedures, and park emergency facilities.

INTERIM PARK FIRE PROTECTION.   A well-conceived park fire protection plan includes provisions for both professional fire-fighting services and supplementary interim fire control. Fire hydrants, building standpipes, communications, water supply, and emergency access routes are essential elements of park fire protection. Another important element of this plan is a system of portable fire extinguishers to control fires in the early stages of development. All fires should be immediately reported to the appropriate individual, office, or agency and arrangements made to evacuate people to safety before fire confinement or control is attempted.

Proper fire training of all park employees is important. Underwriters' Laboratories, Inc. note that fire extinguishers are only 40 percent effective when used by an inexperienced operator. This means that any fire extinguisher in the hands of a trained operator has $2\frac{1}{2}$ times the fire-fighting capacity it has when used by a novice.*

CAUSES OF PARK FIRES.   Almost all fires in parks are caused by the same hazards that are found in any community. There is a popular misconception that park accidents, fires, and other emergencies are caused by extraordinary natural phenomena. Actually these situations are usually the results of common mistakes, oversights, and equipment failures. Table 11.1 identifies common park fire causes. Almost all of these factors are human actions or devices that are only incidentally in a park.

SELECTION OF PORTABLE FIRE EXTINGUISHERS.   Different types of fires have been classified according to the system indicated in Table 11.1.† The selection of fire extinguishers should be based on the class of fire most apt to occur, the type of building construction, occupancy content, hazard rating, ambient temperature conditions at the extinguishers' storage location, service area of each extinguisher, strength, agility, and training of possible operators, extinguisher recharge, test and maintenance service availability, and other standards prescribed by local fire codes.

Portable fire extinguishers are rated by letter and number. The letter identifies the type of fire the extinguisher is effective

* National Safety Council, *Accident Preventive Manual for Industrial Operations,* Seventh Edition, 1974, p. 1360.
† The fourth type of fire, Class D (fires of combustible metals) does not typically occur in park settings.

Table 11.1
Fire causes classification and possible park occurence sites

Fire Cause	Fire Classification[a]	Possible Park Fire Occurrence Site
Smoking and matches	Class A Class B	*May ignite combustible material anywhere.* Outside, may start grass, brush or forest fires. Inside, particularly hazardous in areas of public assembly or near storage of combustibles and flammable liquids.
Electricity	Class C	Most are the result of improper wiring, mechanical failure of insulation materials, or disabled engines. Electrical fires may occur in support centers, (i.e., machine shops, garages, utility houses, transformer stations, etc.), in vehicles, in use areas (i.e., camp laundries, cabins, craft centers), or anywhere that makeshift wiring is permitted.
Heating appliances	Class A	May occur when boiler furnaces, hot ducts, and flues are not well constructed and maintained. Use of portable heating units requires particular care.
Sparks and embers	Class A Class B	Outside fires (including those in fire rings, firebox stoves, fireplaces, and fire pits), especially in campgrounds and picnic areas, may be very hazardous during high-fire-risk periods. Sparks may also be discharged from faulty equipment or vehicles. Other spark sources include chimneys, incinerators, and interior fireplace hearths.
Spontaneous combustion	Class A Class B	Usually the result of improper maintenance or poor storage practices. Frequently occurs in solid waste containers and storage facilities containing combination of combustibles and discarded flammable substance containers.
Flammable liquids and gases	Class B	*Very hazardous outside as well as inside.* These items include gasoline, kerosene, grease, cooking oils, cleaning fluids and solvents, liquid propane, butane, acetylene, paints, and other chemicals. Use areas include both public use and support centers: campgrounds, cabins kitchens, laundries, garages, shops, warehouses, vehicles, and restaurants. These areas require ventilation to exhaust flammable vapors and gases.

Table 11.1   (Continued)

Fire Cause	Fire Classification[a]	Possible Park Fire Occurrence Site
Lightning and static sparks	Class A Class B Class C	Not a major problem if proper lightning rods, arresters, grounds, and surge capacitors are installed on buildings, other structures, and equipment that act as a conductor for natural electric discharges.

[a] Fire classifications are based on fire descriptions adopted by the National Fire Protection Association *National Fire Codes*, NFPA Code 10-1972:
  Class A fires are fires in ordinary combustible materials such as wood, cloth, paper, rubber, and many plastics.
  Class B fires are fires in flammable liquids, gases, and greases.
  Class C fires are fires that involve energized electrical equipment where the electrical nonconductivity of the extinguishing media is of importance. (When electrical equipment is deenergized, extinguishers from Class A or B fires may be used safely.)

against and the number signifies its fire-quenching potential (the higher the number, the greater fire dousing capability). Local fire regulations should always be consulted prior to selection.

FIRE EXTINGUISHER SIZE AND PLACEMENT IN PARK BUILD-INGS.   The number of fire extinguishers needed to protect a structure is determined by the severity of the hazard, anticipated rate of spread, fire intensity, and accessibility. The size and placement of extinguishers should be determined by a competent fire safety specialist. As minimum standards, the criteria established in the *National Fire Codes** should be followed.

Class A fire extinguishers should be conspicuously located and readily accessible in hallways or corridors near exits or enclosed stairways, and next to a fire alarm as shown in Figure 11.6. It is recommended that no point in an building of occupancy be more than 75 feet from a fire extinguisher.†

Most public use park buildings of less than 6000 square feet (i.e., visitor centers, nature centers, exhibits, park offices, meeting rooms, community buildings, natatoriums, roller rinks, small gymnasiums) are considered light hazards and should be equipped with no less than two fire extinguishers of 2A rating or greater on each floor, located near remote exits, but not more than 75 feet apart. Where extra hazards are present, buildings of this size require at least two 6A extinguishers per floor comparably located.

Class B fire extinguishers should supplement these Class A units and be installed in all rooms where flammable liquids are used or stored (kitchens, custodial storerooms, garages, paint

* National Fire Protection Association, *National Fire Codes*, "NFPA Code 10-1972: Installation of Portable Fire Extinguishers," Chapter 4.
† Ibid.

Figure 11.6

A Class A fire extinguisher is mounted near the exit of this exhibit center. The fire alarm, emergency lights, and illuminated exit sign are complementary emergency provisions.

shops, and all park vehicles). Light hazard areas require a extinguisher rated 5B within 30 feet of all points or one rated 10B within 50 feet of all points in the area. Extra hazards may increase the minimum extinguisher size to as great as a 40B rating.

Extinguishers with Class C ratings should be installed where energized electrical equipment must be protected, such as auto repair or machine shops, garages, utility houses, near an electric kiln, scoreboard, and amateur radio broadcast center. Since the fire itself is either a Class A or a Class B type, the extinguisher should be sized and located according to Class A or B criteria. Whenever possible, electricity should be turned off before approaching a Class C fire.

Multipurpose fire extinguishers with combined ratings (e.g., 2A : 6B : C, etc.) are available for buildings where several types of fire hazards are present. Always obtain the advice of the local fire officials and the park agency fire insurance carrier before installing any extinguisher.

PARK FIRST AID AND EMERGENCY DISPATCH PROVISIONS.
Park emergency treatment for injuries or incapacitating ailments
is a basic support service, the same as the provisions of fire
protection, safety facilities, drinking water, wastewater, and solid
waste disposal. Like these other support elements, the amount
and type of emergency treatment is based on agency policy, user
experience norms and expectations, level of development, and
other considerations.

There are two principal components to a park emergency
treatment service: (1) first aid, and, if necessary, (2) transportation to appropriate medical facilities that have competent
physicians.

PARK FIRST AID.   The first aid responsibilities and roles required of park departments have not been well defined in the
past. There are two legal liability facets of first aid in such
situations—the duty to administer first aid and the responsibility
for administering first aid appropriately and properly.* There are
two typical types of park first aid recipients. Each must be
considered in the preparation of park emergency treatment
plans:

☐ *The ambulatory victim:* An individual who has
sustained an injury or other physical ailment that
requires prompt attention but that has not prevented the
person from leaving the scene of the accident and, either
unaided or with untrained assistance, go to a stationary
first aid station. Many of these individuals return
immediately to their interrupted activities (recreation or
work) after treatment. This is the most common type of
park first aid recipient. Treatment is usually for small cuts,
abrasions, removal of splinters or barbs, sunburn, or skin
rash.

☐ *The nonambulatory victim:* An individual who has
sustained major trauma that prevents independent
movement, or whose condition requires that the person
be kept immobile, or when there is occasion to suspect
that unskilled transport may cause further injury or
suffering. *In situ* first aid is limited to reducing suffering
and immobilizing the victim in preparation for
appropriate, skilled transport to an emergency medical
facility for subsequent treatment by a physician.
Examples of potential incapacitating traumas include
fractures, deep wounds, paralysis, spine injury,
unconsciousness, strokes, heart attack, severe
hemorrhaging, or dislocations.

STATIONARY FIRST AID PROVISIONS.   Convenient and
prominently identified first aid provisions to care for ambulatory

---

* Betty van der Smissen, op. cit., § 4.13, pp. 205–206.

injuries should be located in every major public park program facility (e.g., swimming pool, skating rink, gymnasium, recreation center, outdoor education center, firearms range, sports complex). The first aid supplies should never be spread through out the facility but should be kept together, under the control of designated trained personnel.

Separate first aid provisions for employees should be kept readily available at all major work centers, such as the park maintenance and repair center, and at remote daily stations (e.g., ranger stations or camp contact stations, water or wastewater treatment plants, or other isolated, manned work facilities). Careful control of the centralized employee first aid station by a competent first aider is important to prevent improper self-administration by employees and depletion of supplies and to insure completion of safety, insurance, and workman's compensation paperwork.

First aid facilities can be as basic as desk or cabinet first aid kits in the office of a program leader or supervisor who is trained to render first aid, or it may be as elaborate as an industrial-type infirmary or emergency clinic with a full-time staff of physicians, registered nurses, and technicians. It is recommended that, as a minimum, a separate room be available for administering first aid for the privacy of the injured individuals. The federal General Services Administration requires a 16-unit first aid kit for every 25 employees in installations on which fewer than 100 workers are employed per shift and a separate, staffed first aid station with a minimum of 100 square feet of floor space for installations in which 100 to 300 persons are employed.*

PORTABLE FIRST AID PROVISIONS. Two types of portable first aid kits supplement park stationary first aid accommodations. These units are used primarily to treat the nonambulatory victims but are also used for minor ailments in remote locations. Mobile 10-unit or larger first aid kits ("auto," "truck," or "travel" kits) should be kept in all park vehicles used by field supervisors, park foremen, superintendents, rangers or park police, and search and rescue teams. All these personnel should be trained to offer proper assistance.

A personal first aid kit is logical required equipment for recreationists using backcountry areas where self-reliance is necessary. It is the policy of many park departments to require all organized groups that have been granted exclusive use of an area or facility by reservation (e.g., group camps, picnics, trail rides, or hikes) to provide their own first aid provisions, including qualified first aiders.

EMERGENCY DISPATCH PROVISIONS. Casualties should not be placed hurriedly in the first available vehicle and rushed pell-

* General Service Administration, *Accident and Fire Prevention-Construction and Alteration Work,* GSA Handbook PBS P5900.3, Appendix B, 1974.

mell to a hospital. On the contrary, they should be held at the scene of the accident until adequate emergency care has been rendered by qualified personnel and they have been made ready for transport.* The provision of transportation for these individuals is an essential part of the park emergency provisions. These are usually ambulances with special life-saving devices. It is suggested that parks make arrangements with community or private ambulance services that meet the federal medical requirements for ambulances† and personnel standards of the Ambulance Association of America.

Emergency dispatch instructions should be prominently posted at every first aid station, included in every first aid kit, and displayed at every emergency communications facility.

In park settings there are situations that require moving an injured person from the scene of the accident and conveying that individual some distance *prior* to placing him in an ambulance. Careful provisions should be made for these possible occasions.

It may be necessary to move the injured person if (s)he is in imminent danger because of fire, flooding water, escaping gases, or other danger. These problem situations are unpredictable and must be solved extemporaneously. There are other park accident situations where it is impossible for an ambulance to directly approach the injured party for evacuation. Many of these situations are predictable and must be considered in the park emergency plan. There is no liability in transporting cases provided proper precautions are taken.‡

Examples of these occasions include accidents on ski slopes, where the National Ski Patrol must use casualty sleds and snowmobiles to bring injured to a designated receiving area because ambulances are limited to cleared roadways and parking lots, water accidents at beaches or as a result of a boating or waterskiing accident, where lifeguards, Coast Guard, or other water safety patrol must use floats and stretchers to bring the injured to an ambulance zone, or when search-and-rescue teams have to bring out casualties from rugged back country.

The probability of accidents occuring in these and similar park settings that are inaccessible to an ambulance is sufficient to require preparation of appropriate emergency physical and procedural plans for these contingencies.

SUMMARY

Park plans must reflect the necessity to protect the welfare of recreationists and park support personnel at all phases of the

---

* George J. Curry, *Immediate Care and Transport of the Injured,* Charles C Thomas, Pub., Springfield, Ill., 1965, p. 27.
† U.S. Department of Health, Education and Welfare, Public Health Service, Division of Emergency Health Services, *Medical Requirements for Ambulance Design and Equipment,* PHS Publication No. 1071-C-3, 1970, p. 7.
‡ Betty van der Smissen, op. cit., § 4.14, p. 208.

planning process. It cannot be an oversight, nor should it be left to a single member of the planning teams ("the health and safety expert") to incorporate all these essential considerations.

Park health and safety plans are preventative—that is, they assess probable problems and initiate preventative or corrective actions, including physical and procedural adaptations, in an effort to eliminate or at least minimize problems. Health concerns in park and recreation areas include water, food and milk-borne diseases caused by pollution or contamination, vectors and other infectuous wildlife, and noxious vegetation. Park safety hazards may be unsafe acts, equipment, or environmental conditions. The greatest portion of accidents occur in developed program or support areas, not in the natural park setting.

It is no reflection on health and safety provision effectiveness to insure adequate emergency services in parks. Instead, contingency support facilities, procedures, and personnel training for emergency situations are essential elements of a park plan. The basic park emergency support considerations include special communication, evacuation and emergency aid access routes, fire protection, first aid, and emergency dispatch of sick or injured.

GLOSSARY OF TERMS

Accident
An unplanned event involving personal injury or ailment or property damage resulting from preventable unsafe acts, equipment, or conditions.

Emergency Aid Access Route
A designated service roadway that provides a convenient and rapid approach to a facility for support vehicles responding to an emergency situation.

Evacuation Route
A preplanned way to leave a structure or area during occasions of imminent or possible danger.

First aid
Assistance rendered to a casualty to help reduce suffering and immobilize the victim in preparation for transport to a medical facility for subsequent treatment by a physician OR prompt care to minor injuries to relieve pain and prevent additional disability that could require medical treatment.

Hazard
A physical or environmental condition that may cause or attribute to an accident or illness.

Interim Fire Protection
Supplementary fire control prior to the arrival of community or departmental fire-fighting apparatus and personnel.

Noxious Vegetation
Plants that are inherently injurious to health.

Vector
Any insect or animal that transmits disease-producing agents.

BIBLIOGRAPHY

Accident and Fire Prevention—Construction and Alternation Works, GSA Handbook PBS P 5900.3. General Services Administration, Washington, D.C., February 16, 1962 (with subsequent dated revision inserts).

Accident and Fire Prevention—General, GSA Handbook PBS P 5900.2. General Services Administration, Washington, D.C., 1960 (with subsequent dated revision inserts).

Binford, Charles M., Cecil S. Fleming, and Z. A. Prust. *Loss Control in the OSHA Era.* McGraw-Hill, New York, 1975.

Building Firesafety Criteria, GSA Handbook PSB P 5920.9. General Services Administration, Washington, D.C., April 27, 1972.

Curry, George J. (Compiler and Editor) *Immediate Care and Transport of the Injured.* Charles C. Thomas, Pub., Springfield, Ill., 1965.

Encyclopedia of Associations. Gale Research Co., Detroit, 1975.

Hope, Jack. "Safety in the Parks," *National Parks and Conservation Magazine,* 46:11, November, 1972, pp. 10–14.

Kazarian, Edward A. *Food Service Facilities Planning.* ANI Publishing Co., Westport, Conn., 1975.

Karen, Herman. *Environmental Health and Safety.* Pergamon Press, New York, 1974.

Matwes, George J. and Helen Matwes. *Loss Control: A Safety Guidebook for Trades and Services.* Van Nostrand Reinhold, New York, 1973.

National Fire Protection Association. *National Fire Codes:* "NFPA Code No. 10-1972: Standard for the Installation of Portable Fire Extinguishers," "NFPA Code No. 100-1972: Life Safety Code," "NFPA Code No. 295-1972: Recommendations for Wildfire Control and Environmental Improvement," National Fire Protection Association, Boston, 1972.

National Safety Council. *Accident Prevention Manual for Industrial Operations.* National Safety Council, Chicago, 1974.

National Safety Council. *Public Employee Safety Guide: Parks and Recreation.* National Safety Council, Chicago, 1974.

National Research Council, National Academy of Sciences, Committee on Emergency Medical Services. *Medical Requirements for Ambulance Design and Equipment,* PHS Pub. No. 1071-C-3. U.S. Department of Health, Education and Welfare, Public Health Service, Division of Emergency Health Services, Rockville, Md., 1970.

National Research Council, National Academy of Sciences, Committee on Emergency Medical Services. *Training of Ambulance Personnel and Others Responsible for Emergency Care of the Sick and Injured at the Scene and During Transport*, PHS Pub. No. 1071-C-4. U.S. Department of Health, Education and Welfare, Public Health Service, Division of Emergency Health Services, Rockville, Md., 1970.

Paine, Lee A. *Accident Hazard Evaluation and Control Decisions on Forested Recreation Sites*. USDA Forest Service Research Paper PSW-68. Berkeley, Calif., 1971.

Paine, Lee A. *Administrative Goals and Safety Standards for Hazard Control on Forested Recreation Sites*. USDA Forest Service Research Paper PSW-88. Berkeley, Calif., 1973.

"Recreational Safety in Park Management," *Recreational Safety Newsletter,* January, 1976 pp. 2–3.

Salvato, Joseph A., Jr. *Environmental Engineering and Sanitation*. Wiley-Interscience, New York, 1972.

Thygerson, Alton L. *Safety: Principles, Instructions and Readings*. Prentice-Hall Inc., Englewood Cliffs, N.J., 1972.

U.S. Consumer Product Safety Commission. *NEISS News* (National Electronic Injury Surveillance Systems). Issued monthly.

U.S. Department of Health, Education and Welfare, Food and Drug Administration. "Food Service Sanitation-Proposed Uniform Requirements," *Federal Register,* 39:191, October 1, 1974, pp. 35437–35449.

U.S. Department of Health, Education and Welfare, Public Health Service. *Environmental Health Practice in Recreational Areas*. DHEW Publication No. (HSM) 72-10009, U.S. Government Printing Office, Washington, D.C., 1972.

U.S. Department of Health, Education and Welfare, Public Health Service. *The Vending of Food and Beverages—A Sanitation Ordinance and Code*. PHS Publication No. 546, U.S. Government Printing Office, Washington, D.C., 1971.

U.S. Department of Interior, National Park Service. *Safety Management: Guidelines, Requirements, and Responsibilities*. U.S. Government Printing Office, Washington, D.C., 1973.

U.S. Department of Labor, Occupational Safety and Health Administration. "Occupational Safety and Health Standards," *Federal Register,* 39:125, June 27, 1974.

U.S. Environmental Protection Agency. "Interim Primary Drinking Water Standards," *Federal Register,* 40:51, March 14, 1975, pp. 11990–11998.

van der Smissen, Betty. *Legal Liability of Cities and Schools for Injuries in Recreation and Parks*. W. H. Anderson Co., Cincinnati, 1968.

appendix 1
natural resource descriptors used to identify special environmental characteristics important to outdoor recreation activities

NATURAL RESOURCE DESCRIPTORS USED TO IDENTIFY SPECIAL ENVIRONMENTAL CHARACTERISTICS IMPORTANT TO OUTDOOR RECREATION ACTIVITIES*

Primary Natural Resource Descriptor Group	Environmental Features

Land descriptors	1. Physiographic features
	  (a) Gradient
	  (b) Area
	  (c) Proximity to surface water
	  (d) Susceptibility to flooding
	  (e) Aspect
	2. Pedologic features
	  (a) Depth to bedrock
	  (b) Stoniness/rockiness of surface
	  (c) Fertility
	  (d) Erodibility
	  (e) Susceptibility to compaction
	  (f) Subsurface texture
	3. Hydrologic features
	  (a) Depth to ground water
	  (b) Soil permeability
	  (c) Surface wetness
	4. Utilization features
	  (a) Capability to support building and road foundations
	  (b) Capability to supply potable water

Surface water descriptors	1. Biologic features
	  (a) Aquatic (floating) flora
	  (b) Terrestrial (rooted) flora
	  (c) Aquatic fauna
	  (d) Bacteriological indicators
	2. Chemical features
	  (a) Dissolved oxygen
	  (b) pH
	  (c) Salinity
	  (d) Nutrients
	  (e) Mineral elements
	3. Utilization features
	  (a) Pollutants (chemical, biological, radioactive, visual, thermal)
	  (b) Artificial restrictions or controls on free flow
	  (c) Incompatible uses
	  (d) Access areas capable of supplying required support
	4. Physiographic features (flow water)
	  (a) Low-flow river width

Primary Natural Resource Descriptor Group	Environmental Features
	(b) Low-flow current velocity
	(c) Low-flow channel depth
	(d) Turbidity
	(e) Turbulence
	(f) Presence of debris and obstructions
	(g) River bed gradient adjacent to shore
	(h) User perception stimuli (water color, odor, taste, temperature)
	5. Physiographic features (still water)
	(a) Lake water surface area
	(b) Water elevation fluctuation
	(c) Depth
	(d) Location and strength of water movements (current, tide, etc.)
	(e) Shoreline length and configuration
	(f) Depth of thermocline
	(g) Lake bed gradient adjacent to shore
	(h) Presence of debris and obstructions
	(i) User perception stimuli (water color, odor, taste, temperature)
	(j) Turbidity
Vegetation descriptors	1. Woody vegetation
	(a) Composition, overstory, and understory
	(b) Stand density
	(c) Crown density
	(d) Height of predominant branching
	(e) Regeneration indicators
	(f) Insect and disease infestation
	2. Herbaceous vegetation
	(a) Composition
	(b) Density
	(c) Height
	3. Utilization features
	(a) Tolerance to trampling, thinning, clearing
	(b) Susceptibility to fire, insects, disease, pollutant injury

(Continued)

Primary Natural Resource Descriptor Group	Environmental Features
	(c) Capability to supply wildlife cover, habitat, forage (d) Capability to provide weather mitigation for users (shelter, shade, fuel, etc.) (e) Season attractions (flowers, foliage, fruit)

Meteorological descriptors	1. Precipitation
	   (a) Rainy days within activity season
	   (b) Mean monthly snowfall during winter activity season
	   (c) Mean monthly snow-cover depth
	2. Wind
	   (a) Mean monthly wind velocity
	   (b) Monthly prevailing wind orientation
	   (c) Probability to severe wind storms
	3. Temperature
	   (a) Mean daily high and low temperatures during activity season
	   (b) Period of subfreezing temperatures
	   (c) Frequency and extent of temperature extremes
	4. Light
	   (a) Mean daily length of daylight during activity season
	   (b) Mean daily cloud cover during activity season

Wildlife descriptors	1. Fauna
	   (a) Seasonal natural game populations
	   (b) Seasonal natural nongame populations
	   (c) Migratory patterns
	2. Management practices
	   (a) Hunting regulations
	   (b) Habitat and cover establishment or improvement.
	   (c) Stocking

* Source: Betty van der Smissen and Monty L. Christiansen, *Standards Related to Water-Oriented and Water-Enhanced Recreation in Pennsylvania Watersheds*, Project A-033-Pa. Office of Water Research and Technology, U.S. Department of the Interior. Project report in press as research publication of the Institute of Land and Water Resources of the Pennsylvania State University, University Park, Pa.

appendix 2

sample activity analysis for a facility-oriented activity

*Example One: Public Neighborhood Tennis in Midwestern United States
*Example Two: Private Tennis Center in Eastern United States

SAMPLE ACTIVITY ANALYSIS FOR A FACILITY-ORIENTED ACTIVITY
EXAMPLE ONE: PUBLIC NEIGHBORHOOD TENNIS IN MIDWESTERN UNITED STATES

	ACTIVITY FACTORS
Recreational tennis, singles and doubles play.	*Brief description of activity*
Introductory, entry- and novice-level play with basic instruction and casual competition available through limited programmed participation; ample unstructured play opportunities.	*Activity experience opportunities to be provided*
Commonly accepted tennis rules apply; no dress restrictions; no fees or reservations; courts close at dark; play is limited to one hour if others are waiting for a court.	*Established rules and regulations*
Four tennis rackets are available for checkout from the park program leader when on duty; balls must be supplied by players.	*Special participant equipment needs*
10–20 minutes/match with a maximum one hour courtesy limit if others are waiting.	*Length of activity period*
Majority of participants are anticipated to be at the second (modified basic) experience level.	*Proposed experience norm*
It is estimated that three quarters of the players will be neighborhood children and teenagers learning the sport and developing skills during summer free time and after school in the spring and fall. Most of the adults are expected to be neighborhood housewives or married couples playing at a novice to advance-novice level in early morning or early evening.	*User profile*
A maximum of four players/court is permitted during unprogrammed use; 20 youngsters are instructed at each class.	*Participation Rate per Activity Period*
Daily use is expected to be strongest in early morning, midmorning through early afternoon and late afternoon to dusk. The first and last periods reflect the coolest periods of summer days as well as pre- and postwork periods for adults. Programmed participation will be in the midmorning to past noon.	*Daily Participation Patterns*

Participation is predominantly warm season, from May through October. Programmed participation is provided Monday through Friday in July and August. Weekend participation is heaviest in May, June, September, and October.

Seasonal, Monthly, Weekly Park Participation

RESOURCE AND FACILITY FACTORS

Special area and facility requirements

One battery of two regulation-size tennis courts is to be provided; the courts should be oriented to minimize sun interference during summer early morning and late afternoon play; overhead clearance of at least 20 feet is desirable; full backcourt and half side court fencing should be provided; no fencing between courts, no complementary activity provisions.

A modified basic development norm is recommended. Courts should be color-coated all-weather surfacing. Facilities should be well constructed and support services well trained to cope with energetic but uncoordinated youngsters just learning the game.

Development norms

Court location should be above seasonal flood plain, recharge areas, wetlands, or areas with shallow water tables; sufficiently away from water bodies, cliffs, or other dangerous natural areas that balls hit over the fence are not problems to retrieve; and free from trees that would cast daytime shadows and increase court litter with leaves and twigs. Principal climatic factors are rainy or windy days and temperatures/humidity extremes.

Special environment requirements

SUPPORT FACTORS: SERVICES

Maintenance

Courts will be swept with a push broom by the players if "bird bath" puddles or too much dirt and litter prevent play. Waste containers checked daily. Surfacing will be recoated and lined every two to three seasons.

Instruction in entry-level skills will be provided on a group basis to youngsters. No private lessons will be scheduled. A challenge board for adult competition will be available but no seeded tournament will be scheduled.

Programming

A person trained in emergency care should be available during programmed instruction.

Safety and security

(Continued)

No operations support services necessary. *Operations*

No refreshments and supplies support services necessary.

SUPPORT FACTORS: FACILITIES

Automotive parking for support personnel only: spaces for program leader, maintenance worker, and refuse pickup. *Refreshments and supplies*

Participants will walk or ride bicycles to park. One 12-unit bike rack should be adequate. *Circulation and parking*

No power or lighting provisions necessary. *Power and lighting*

A first aid kit during programmed months is needed. Courts should be accessible to ambulances. A public telephone should be reasonably accessible. *Fire, safety, and emergency*

No shelter necessary; one small bench for waiting players for each court is suggested. *Shelter and park furniture*

No separate drinking water for the tennis area; players may use centralized park water fountain. *Water*

No separate comfort station for the tennis area; players may use centralized park facilities. A medium-sized waste container is adequate for the entire battery. *Sanitation*

No security facilities necessary. *Security*

A small storage box for program materials, equipment, and first aid kit is necessary during programmed months—may be centrally located for entire park. *Support equipment*
Storage and work areas

No refreshments and supplies facilities necessary. *Refreshments and supplies*

SAMPLE ACTIVITY ANALYSIS FOR A FACILITY-ORIENTED ACTIVITY
EXAMPLE TWO: PRIVATE TENNIS CENTER IN EASTERN UNITED STATES

	ACTIVITY FACTORS
Registered amateur and semiprofessional tennis; singles and doubles play.	*Brief description of activity*
All programmed experiences: basic-level play; skills development; casual and registered competition; ample social and attentive spectator opportunities.	*Activity experience opportunities to be provided*
USTA rules always apply; tennis attire required; all courts must be reserved.	*Established Rules and Regulations*
Reservation periods are one hour.	*Length of Activity Period*
Participants expect a refined experience norm regardless of their skill competencies.	*Proposed Experience Norm*
	PARTICIPANT FACTORS
A diverse but dedicated clientle of users— by membership only—youth and adults enrolled in a wide variety of beginners and special skills development programs; executives, professionals, career people, and wives.	*User profile*
A maximum of 4 players per court is permitted during reserved play; 10 members to an instructional group.	*Participation rate per activity period*
Instructional groups are predominately held in late morning and midafternoon; reservations are required for all other play on a 24-hour basis with prime times occuring 6–9 A.M.; 11–2 P.M.; 5–9 P.M.	
Participation is year round; special outdoor clinics and round-robin club tournaments are held monthly in summer; indoor special events are complementary to the social season and holidays.	*Daily participation patterns*
Batteries of 12 indoor and 16 outdoor courts to be provided; lighting for club and tournament play for all courts; wind and visual screening on all backcourt fencing; all outdoor courts to have full sidecourt fencing, sprinkler systems to be installed where appropriate; portable umpire chairs and bleachers for tournaments and exhibitions; separation screening, serving machines, practice walls, video recorders, etc. used in instruction and development programs; men's and women's lockers, showers, saunas; food and beverage preparation facilities; lounge and dining area; pro shop.	*Seasonal, monthly, weekly peak participation*

(Continued)

RESOURCE AND FACILITY FACTORS

A refined development norm to be maintained. Entire facility to be "well appointed." Indoor court surfacing to be cushioned synthetic; outdoor courts to be pervious cushioned. Indoor units to be air conditioned.

Special area and facility requirements

Facility should be above 20-year flood plain, on area capable of supporting building and road foundations.

Development norm

All courts groomed daily appropriate to surfacing; all auxiliary and support facilities cleaned and serviced according to high standards of maintenance quality.

Special environmental requirements

SUPPORT FACTORS: SERVICES

Landscape maintenance contracted.

Maintenance

Trained tennis instructors under the direction of a resident pro. Lessons provided on group or private basis. A fall club schedule of clinics, various tournaments, and social events complementary to tennis provided year round. Programmed involvement emphasized. A program director coordinates all scheduled events.

Programming

A person trained in emergency care should be available at all times. No special security personnel needed.

Safety and security

Club director and secretary handles reservations, memberships, correspondence. Special personnel contracted for needed functions.

Operations

Meal and beverage service provided on limited menu basis by small kitchen, bar, and dining staff. Pro shop handled by trained tennis supply manager. Special parties catered by outside contracts.

Refreshment and supplies

Separate automotive parking for support personnel and members; separate service entrance.

Circulation and parking

SUPPORT FACTORS: FACILITIES

Building to be adequately climate-controlled for year-round use. Lighting for proper tennis play, auxiliary and social activities, internal and external safety, security, emergency and aesthetic effects.

Power and lighting

A first aid kit should be provided for indoor and outdoor activity areas. A medical file of all member's physicians, emergency services, and fire department should be provided. An adequate fire sprinkler and alarm system should be installed: extinguishers in kitchen and storage areas. Telephone and public address facilities should be provided.	*Fire, safety, and emergency*
Outdoor canopies and umbrellas over small seating groups and tables will be available to waiting players and casual viewers. Portable bleachers will be provided for exhibitions. Indoor lounges, dining area, and observation area will be furnished appropriate to the development norm.	*Shelter and furniture*
Several drinking fountains are to be immediately adjacent to courts. Decorative water display to be considered on a landscape feature.	*Water*
Modern sanitation facilities to be connected to public system. Solid waste containers domestic scaled.	*Sanitation*
Club to be well screened and enclosed for privacy and security. Security lighting provided. Passkeys for members and guest registration required.	*Security*
Adequate storage room for custodial equipment and supplies, food and beverage, and supply equipment and stock; separate office for operations and program personnel; winter storage area for outdoor equipment and furniture.	*Support equipment Storage and work area*
A refreshment preparation area for limited menu dining and full bar is required. Large events to be catered.	*Refreshment and supplies*

sample activity analysis for a resource-oriented activity

*Example: Beach Swimming in Northeast United States

SAMPLE ACTIVITY ANALYSIS FOR A RESOURCE-ORIENTED ACTIVITY
EXAMPLE: BEACH SWIMMING IN NORTHEAST UNITED STATES[a]

ACTIVITY FACTORS

A situational unstructured water-oriented experience which includes swimming, wading and sunning. (Diving is not considered an essential component of beach swimming for this example)

Brief description of activity

Unprogrammed recreational swimming. No instruction or competition.

Activity experience opportunities to be provided

Beach open only during supervised periods. Scuba equipment, rafts, or other flotation devices not permitted unless by special permission of beach supervisor. No food consumption on beach. Beach play subject to approval. User fees according to agency regulations.

Established rules and regulations

Swimmers furnish own bathing suits and towels; may furnish or rent beach chairs and umbrellas.

Special Participant equipment needs

The average length of time a person or party will stay at the beach varies widely. For planning purposes, the length of the beach activity is estimated as four hours.

Length of activity period

Majority of participants expect a secondary modern experience norm, with sense of security and control apparent. Provisions for user comfort and convenience expected.

Proposed experience norm

PARTICIPANT FACTORS

User profile

Beach swimming is a social and physical form of recreation. It is estimated that the majority of the users will be family groups with a wide range of swimming competencies. Some unmarried teenage and young adult groups may also use the beach. Few individuals will participate alone.

Swimming, wading, and sunning are unstructured activities without regulation sport field boundaries. Thus no regulation number of players is established. The participation rate depends on the physical size of the beach to swimming water, the capacity of the support services and facilities (number of lifeguards, rest room facilities, parking, etc.), and the psychological effects of crowding.

Participation rate per activity period

(Continued)

Most casual swimmers and sunbathers will come to beach following picnic or noon meal. Heaviest use is expected in the midafternoon. Beach will be open with supervision from 10 A.M.–8 P.M. The late morning and early evening swimmers are more physically active and are in the water more than the afternoon users.

Daily participation patterns

Beach is open from Memorial Day to Labor Day. Peak seasonal use is July and August. Heaviest afternoon use is during weekends.

Seasonal, monthly, weekly peak participation

RESOURCE AND FACILITY FACTORS

Maximum water depth in the designated swimming area is five feet. Beach area may be sand or turf. Area should be designed so that sun glare and reflection does not screen swimmers from lifeguard stations at any time. No power or utility lines should cross the beach or swimming area. All public use areas and public support facilities should be barrier free.

Special area and facility requirements

A secondary modern development norm is proposed. Adequate facilities for user comfort and convenience are to be provided. Water should be unfiltered, unrecycled, and solar heated.

Development norm

The following environmental requirements have been established for this beach swimming area:

Special environmental requirements

(1) Land
   (a) The sun bathing beach area must be immediately adjacent to the designated swimming water area.
   (b) The soil must be of sufficient depth over the underlying bedrock to prevent erosion.
   (c) The groundwater table should be sufficiently deep to prevent marshlike conditions in and around the beach area.
   (d) The slope, or gradient, above water level as well as below water level should not exceed an established minimum.
   (e) The size of the beach area should be from one-tenth (0.1) to three-tenths (0.3) of an acre per estimated 100 swimmers.
   (f) The surface soil should have a desirable texture, limited erosion hazard rating, should be well drained, and capable of bearing

support facilities such as buildings, roads, and septic tank drainage fields.

(g)   Vegetative cover for two areas should be considered:

Beach area: shoreline vegetative cover should be herbaceous within a set distance of the shoreline.

Support areas: support areas should have a woody vegetative composition of deciduous or evergreen types.

(h)   All natural hazards associated with the flora and fauna in the support areas, that is, poisonous snakes and poison ivy, should be of a minimal nature.

(i)   The swimming beach may be in the floodplain, but the support facilities should lie above the 20-year floodplain.

(2)   Water

(a)   Water turbidity must be clear to a minimum depth of five feet.

(b)   The swimming area must be free of nonremovable debris and obstructions above and below the water line.

(c)   Algae must not be present during the activity season.

(d)   The bacteriological index of the water during the swimming season must not exceed established local, state, or federal health standards.

(e)   The dissolved oxygen level in the water must not be less than established local, state, or federal health standards during the activity season.

(f)   The strength of water currents or undertows in the swimming area must be minimal.

(g)   Low-water lake area must not be less than 20 acres.

(h)   Lake water-level fluctuation must be minimal during the activity season;

(i)   Lake must be deeper than five feet.

(j)   Any thermoclines present in the lake must be deeper than five feet.

(Continued)

(k) The following surface water conditions should be considered:
Low-flow current velocity during the activity season should not be so strong that inexperienced swimmers would be swept away.
Water temperature during the activity season should be in a range comfortable to the swimmer.
Aquatic flora and fauna should not be nuisances.
Water pH should not irritate the eyes or skin.
Water color should be pleasing to the eye.
Odor should not be objectionable, if present at all.
Visual surface turbulence should be minimal to prevent loss of visual contact by lifeguards with underwater swimmers.

SUPPORT FACTORS: SERVICES

Maintenance level should be appropriate for a secondary modern development norm. Special consideration must be given to beach cleaning and water quality. All public support facilities must be cleaned and serviced regularly.

Maintenance

No program services necessary.

Programming

Sufficient lifeguards holding current Water Safety Instructor certificates must be provided; a first-aid specialist must be available at all times the beach is open.

Safety and security

If water treatment and sanitary treatment facilities warrant, a certified water quality and treatment plant operator must be provided; user fee collector/accounting attendant should be on duty.

Operations

Refreshment sales and beach equipment rental personnel appropriate to expected experience norm and crowds. May be provided by concessionaire.

Refreshment and supplies

SUPPORT FACTORS: FACILITIES

Separate automotive parking for support personnel; sufficient public parking to accommodate 70 percent maximum beach design load with overflow parking to accommodate remainder; separate service road and entry to support facilities.

Circulation and parking

No activity lighting for night use; safety and security lighting where necessary. Power outlets for appropriate maintenance and operations requirements but no public use outlets.	*Power and lighting*
No shelter for inclement weather. Benches and tables to be provided in a designated eating area. Beach chairs and umbrellas available from concession rental.	*Shelter and furniture*
Drinking fountains to be provided near rest rooms, refreshment sales, dining area, and upper perimeter of beach. Hot showers in dressing stockades.	*Water*
Flush liquid waste system connected to plant, which treats effluent to potable water quality. Large solid-waste containers to be well distributed and serviced.	*Sanitation*
Security control by entry fee control station and mobile security officer(s). Security dusk to dawn lighting at buildings. Coin-operated lockers for swimmers.	*Security*
Adequate storage for custodial equipment and supplies refreshment supplies and rental stock; separate offices for safety and operations personnel.	*Support equipment Storage and work area*
Space for refreshment and rental concession to be provided (to be equipped and serviced by concessionaire)	*Refreshment and supplies*
A swimmer's comfort index chart should be posted showing air and water temperature, wind velocity, weather forecast, etc.	*Other*

[a] Based on activity analysis prepared by William W. Davis in "An Evaluation of the Utilization of the Whipple Dam State Park for Selected Activities Which Would be Complimentary to the Stone Valley Recreation Area," unpublished M.S. thesis, The Pennsylvania State University, University Park, Pennsylvania, 1975.

appendix 3

example of agency park equipment specification

EXAMPLE OF AGENCY PARK EQUIPMENT SPECIFICATION

ITEM: Park Bench, Type D
PERFORMANCE SPECIFICATION:
This standard agencywide park bench must be able to seat four (4) people comfortably. It must be permanently mounted, not portable. Since elderly park visitors may use these benches for lengthy periods of time, the benches should have a backrest. It should be of heavy-duty materials because it will have to stand up under various levels of abuse. The bench should be constructed so that damaged or broken parts can be easily replaced. All materials and parts of the bench must be water repellent and rust resistant. The bench should be attractive without being "showy." The surface must be easily cleanable. The finish must be able to be refinished or recoated without special equipment.

KNOWN BENCH MANUFACTURERS:

J. E. Burke Co.	New Brunswick, New Jersey
American Play-World, Inc.	Hastings, Nebraska
Form, Inc.	South Lyon, Michigan
Game Time, Inc.	Litchfield, Michigan
Miracle Equipment Co.	Grinnell, Iowa
Jamison, Inc.	Los Angeles, California
Playground Corporation of America	Long Island City, New York
General Playground Equipment, Inc.	Kokomo, Indiana
Belson Manufacturing Co., Inc.	North Aurora, Illinois
Mexico Forge	Reedsville, Pennsylvania
Landscape Forms	Kalamazoo, Michigan
Random Industries	Farmington, Connecticut
Kay Park-Recreation Corp.	Janesville, Iowa
Meade Manufacturing, Inc.	Meade, Kansas

MATERIALS SPECIFICATION FOR PARK BENCH, TYPE D

1.0 *Bench Frame*
    1.1   Material
        Park bench frame shall be factory assembled from heavy-duty steel pipe.
    1.2   Size
        The frame pipe shall be at least $2\frac{3}{8}$ inches O.D. Legs shall be of sufficient length to set at least 12 inches in concrete footings.
    1.3   Manufacture
        Each bearing frame member shall be electronically welded at every point of juncture of two or more pieces. All open and exposed ends of pipe shall be capped and welded. Required bolt holes shall be predrilled by manufacturer.

(Continued)

    1.4 Preservative
        All pipe frame units shall be hot-dip galvanized after fabrication.

    1.5 Units
        Park bench shall have not less than two (2) legs.

2.0 *Seat and Backrest*

    2.1 Material
        Park bench seat and backrest shall be splinter-free construction heartwood grade redwood or No. 1 common Douglas fir, cypress, or yellow pine.

    2.2 Size
        The seat and backrest shall be 2 inches × 4 inches (nominal) and at least 6 feet long.

    2.3 Manufacture
        All wood members shall be chamfered at all edges. Required bolt holes shall be centered and predrilled on each slot between 12 inches and 18 inches from each end by manufacturer.

    2.4 Preservative
        Redwood and cypress, if used, shall be soaked a minimum of one hour in a nonswelling, paintable water repellent such as Seal-Treat, Wood Lox, Woodlife, Penta-Seal, or approved equal. Douglas fir or yellow pine, if used, shall be pressure sealed at 30 pounds atmosphere for a minimum of one hour in a nonswelling, paintable water repellent equal to the above. No painting is required of manufacturer.

    2.5 Units
        Each seat shall consist of three inch × 4 inch (nominal) × 6 foot minimum slats. Each backrest shall consist of three 2 inch × 4 inch (nominal) by 6 foot minimum slats.

3.0 *Hardware*

    3.1 Material
        All hardware shall be either hot-dipped galvanized steel or aluminum.

    3.2 Size
        Bolts shall be at least $\frac{3}{8} \times 4\frac{1}{2}$ inch with appropriate lock nuts and washers.

MANUFACTURERS HAVING PARK BENCHES ACCEPTABLE TO AGENCY STANDARD FOR PARK BENCH, TYPE D

Manufacturer	*Product Model(s)*
Playground Corporation of America	SB-6W
General Playground Equipment, Inc.	425N & 425M
American Play-World, Inc.	6-261 & 6-281
J. E. Burke, Co.	P6-AMW
Game Time, Inc.	4046 &4066

Kay Park-Rec Corp.   6PPBG
Woodform by Landscape Forms   LFB437SC
Belson Manufacturing Co., Inc.   PB-100W

DATE OF SPECIFICATION REVIEW: September 19, 1973

REVISED: _____
          _____
          _____
          _____

example of agency park construction specification

EXAMPLE OF AGENCY PARK CONSTRUCTION SPECIFICATION

ITEM: Park Walks, Type 3 (PW-3)

1.0   *Scope*

The work included in this specification consists of furnishing all materials, labor, tools, and equipment to construct all park walks specified as *Nittany Valley Park Department Park Walk, Type 3* on the plans, drawings, or specifications prepared for the above agency.

2.0   *Materials*

    2.1   General

All materials shall conform to the applicable provisions of the latest edition of the State Department of Highways (SDH) Specifications Form 408, 1967 edition or later.

    2.2   Base

Base course of walk shall be SDH Number 4 stone, bound with fine crushed stone.

    2.3   Primer

The prime coat shall conform to SDH MC30 or MC70.

    2.4   Wearing Surface

The bituminous wearing surface shall conform to mix FJ-1A of SHD Form 408 Sec. 422.

3.0   *Methods*

    3.1   General

        3.11   All construction methods shall conform to the applicable provisions of the latest edition of the State Department of Highways Specifications Form 408, 1967 edition or later.

        3.12   All rolling shall be done with a power roller weighing at least ten (10) tons. Use a hand or power tamper to obtain proper compaction of all areas inaccessible to the roller.

        3.13   All nonabutting walks shall have edges that are sharp and true of line.

        3.14   Finished grades shall be true and even, conforming with drawings, free from humps or depressions. All walk surfacing must drain freely.

        3.15   All adjacent appurtenances shall be protected from paving materials.

        3.16   Paving shall be properly curved.

        3.17   Contractor shall provide all necessary temporary barriers, warning lights, and other safety controls. He shall remove them as soon as they are not needed.

    3.2   Subgrade

        3.21   Excavation or fill to proper subgrade shall clear the construction site of organic soils.

(Continued)

3.22.   Subgrade shall be compacted to 95 percent of proctor density.

3.3   Base Course

3.31.   Place base course to a depth of six (6) inches after compaction. Role base course thoroughly until material does not move under roller.

3.32.   Do not apply base course on wet or frozen ground.

3.4.   Wearing Surface Course

3.41.   Place wearing course two (2) inches thick after compaction.

3.42.   Wearing surface shall be rolled true to required grades, shall be free from roller marks, and conform to Paragraph III A4 of these specifications.

appendix 4
natural resource analysis criteria for lake beach swimming for a park planning project in northeast united states

NATURAL RESOURCE ANALYSIS CRITERIA FOR LAKE BEACH SWIMMING FOR A PARK PLANNING PROJECT IN NORTHEAST UNITED STATES*

I. Specific Resource Requirements for Beach Swimming
    The following essential conditions must be present (or absent) for beach swimming to take place.
    A. Land Indicators
        1. Proximity to water surface
            The designated beach area must be adjacent to the surface water.
        2. Depth to bedrock
            The bedrock must be more than three inches (3″) below the land surface within the designated beach area.
        3. Depth to ground water
            The ground water must be more than two feet (2′) below the land surface at a distance 50 feet from the water's edge.
    B. Surface Water Indicators
        1. Turbidity
            A secchi disk must be visible at a water depth of five feet (5′).
        2. Presence of debris and obstructions
            The designated swimming area must be free of any emerged or submerged nonremovable obstructions or debris.
        3. Presence of algae
            The swimming area must have no readily visible presence of algae during the activity season.
        4. Bacteriological index
            During the activity season not more than 100 coliforms/100 milliliters must be present as an arithmetic average value; not more than 1000/100 milliliters in more than one sample.
        5. Chemical indices
            (a) Dissolved oxygen
                 During the activity season, not less than 5.0 milligrams D.O./l. must be present.
        6. Strength of current
            Water flow must not exceed two miles per hour in swimming area.
    C. Surface Water Indicators
        1. Low-flow channel depth in main channel of stream
            Water depth must be greater than five feet (5′)
    D. Surface Water Indicators (Flat Water)
        1. Low-water lake area
            Total lake area must not be less than twenty acres (20 Ac.) surface water.

2. Water level fluctuation
   Elevation of water level must not fluctuate more than five feet (5').
3. Minimum depth
   The water depth of the lake must be more than five feet
4. Depth of thermocline
   The thermocline must not be less than five feet (5') below the water surface.

II. General Resource Requirements for Beach Swimming
The following conditions have a range of acceptable levels for beach swimming with defined thresholds at each end of the range. Conditions past these thresholds are not desirable for the activity.

A. Land Indicators
   1. Gradient
      The designated beach area should slope from 2 to 10 percent (2–10%) for a distance of at least 50 feet from the water's edge.
   2. Area
      The designated beach area should be from one to three acres per 1000 projected swimmers.

B. Surface Water Indicators
   1. Low-flow current velocity
      The current should be from one and one-half to three cubic feet per second for water circulation.
   2. Water temperature
      During the activity season, the water temperature should be from 68 to 85 degrees at a depth of four feet.
   3. Submerged gradient adjacent to beach
      The underwater gradient should be from 5 to 10 percent (5–10%).
   4. Aquatic fauna
      The swimming area should not sustain any aquatic fauna that could adversely affect a swimmer's health or safety.
   5. Chemical index
      The water acidity should range between pH 6.0 to 8.0.

III. Ranked Resource Requirements for Beach Swimming
The following conditions do not determine whether or not beach swimming is feasible, but are determinants of the quality of the experience. Beach swimming may be possible under any conditions of these factors, but enjoyment would be enhanced under certain indicated conditions; lessened under other indicated conditions.

(Continued)

A. Land Indicators
  1. Susceptibility to flooding
     The swimming beach may be in floodplain; the support facilities should be above the 50-year floodplain.
  2. Surface soil texture
     Desirable—sandy, loamy, or clay surface texture
     Acceptable—gravel
     Undesirable—stony, cobbly
  3. Erosion hazard
     Desirable—Soils of S.C.S. Erosion Hazard Class 1 (none to slight)
     Acceptable—Soils of S.C.S. Erosion Hazard Class 2 (moderate)
     Undesirable—Soils of S.C.S. Erosion Hazard Class B (high)
  4. Drainage
     Desirable—Soils of S.C.S. Drainage Classes 3 and 4 (moderately to well drained)
     Acceptable—Soils of S.C.S. Drainage Class 5 (somewhat acceptably drained)
     Undesirable—Soils of S.C.S. Drainage Classes 1, 2, 6 (either very poorly or excessively drained)
  5. Utilization capacity
     a. Capacity to support building and road foundations
        Desirable—Soils of S.C.S. "slight limitations" rating
        Acceptable—Soils of S.C.S. "moderate limitations" rating
        Undesirable—Soils of S.C.S. "severe limitations" rating
     b. Permeability of soil B horizon
        Desirable—Soils having a percolation rate of greater than two inches per hour
        Acceptable—Soils having a percolation rate of one to two inches per hour
        Undesirable—Soils having a percolation rate of less than one inch per hour
B. Surface Water Indicators
  1. Low-flow river width
     Desirable—greater than 100 feet
     Acceptable—50 to 99 feet
     Undesirable—less than 50 feet
  2. Water color
     Desirable—clear to greenish-blue tint
     Acceptable—greenish tint
     Undesirable—brownish tint

        3. Odor

Desirable—odorless

Acceptable—grassy to slightly fish odor (slightly objectionable)

Undesirable—very fishy to septic odor (objectionable)

        4. Visual surface turbulence for water five feet deep

Desirable—calm to rippling water surface

Acceptable—strong rippling to light boiling water surface

Undesirable—strong boiling to torrential water surface

        5. Biologic features (rooted aquatic flora)

Desirable—less than one-third coverage

Acceptable—one-third to one-half coverage

Undesirable—more than one-half coverage

C. Vegetative Water Indicators

        1. Shoreline vegetation composition

Desirable—only herbaceous vegetation within 50 feet of shoreline

Acceptable—mixed herbaceous vegetation with a few shrubs and trees within 50 feet of shoreline

Undesirable—heavily treed within 50 feet of shoreline

        2. Support area woody vegetative composition

Desirable—deciduous vegetation within the support area

Acceptable—evergreen vegetation within the support area

        3. Insect and disease information

Desirable—a vegetative stand showing no signs of infestation

Acceptable—a vegetative stand showing limited signs of infestation

Undesirable—a vegetative stand showing chronic or acute signs of infestation

D. Meteorological Indicators

        1. Probability of rainy days (days with greater than one-half inch of rain/day during the activity season)

Desirable—less than 25 percent probability

Acceptable—between 25 percent and 50 percent probability

Undesirable—more than 50 percent probability

        2. Monthly mean wind velocity

Desirable—calm to moderate winds (less than 1 mph to 18 mph)

Acceptable—fresh breezes (18–24 mph)

Undesirable—strong breezes or greater (25 mph +)

(Continued)

3. Probability of severe wind storms (wind in excess of 55 mph)
   Desirable—less than 25 percent probability
   Acceptable—between 25 percent and 50 percent probability
   Undesirable—greater than 50 percent probability
4. Air temperature (mean daily high temperature)
   Desirable—mean daily high not less than 75°
   Acceptable—mean daily high between 65°–75°
   Undesirable—mean daily high below 65°
5. Monthly extent of cloud cover
   Desirable—mean monthly cloud cover count of 8 or less (clear to scattered clouds covering one-quarter to one-half the sky)
   Acceptable—mean monthly cloud cover count of 9 or 10 (broken clouds to overcast sky, covering more than one-half the sky)

* Source: Betty van der Smissen and Monty L. Christiansen, *Standards Related to Water-Oriented and Water-Enhanced Recreation in Pennsylvania Watersheds,* Project A-033-PA. Office of Water Research and Technology, U.S. Department of the Interior. Project report in press as research publication of the Institute of Land and Water Resources of the Pennsylvania State University, University Park, Pa.

appendix 5
example of standardized general condition for construction

Commonwealth of Pennsylvania
DEPARTMENT OF ENVIRONMENTAL RESOURCES

GENERAL CONDITIONS
FOR
CONSTRUCTION

P. O. Box 1467
Harrisburg, Pennsylvania 17120
1969
Form No. WCE-6

GENERAL
CONTENTS

* Or Board or The Authority.

* Or Board or The Authority.

PREFACE

These General Conditions dated 1969 supersede the General Conditions dated 1963 and shall be a part of the contract documents of all construction contracts being administered by the Bureau of Engineering unless specifically stated otherwise in the Bid Form or the Agreement.

When these General Conditions are used as a part of contracts in which the Commonwealth is acting through the Water and Power Resources Board, the responsibilities, duties, privileges and authority delegated or assigned herein to the Secretary and to the Department shall apply in the same manner to the Chairman and to the Board respectively.

It is understood and agreed that everything herein contained, as well as the Bid Form and the Special Requirements are hereby made a part of these Specifications.

SECTION 1
DEFINITION OF TERMS

1.1 DEFINITIONS

Wherever the words or expressions herein defined, or pronouns used in their stead, occur in these Specifications and the other Contract documents, they shall have the meanings here given:

A *State* or *Commonwealth* shall mean the Commonwealth of Pennsylvania.

B *The Authority* shall mean The General State Authority.

C *Party of the First Part* shall mean the Commonwealth or The General State Authority.

D *Board* shall mean the Water and Power Resources Board of Pennsylvania.

E *Department* shall mean the Department of Forests and Waters of Pennsylvania. Where used in the Specifications and Contract, the word "Department" shall be interpreted to mean "Board" or "The Authority" when applicable.

F *Chairman* shall mean the Chairman of the Water and Power Resources Board.

G *Secretary* shall mean the Secretary, Department of Forests and Waters, unless specifically stated or indicated otherwise. Where used in the Specifications and Contract, the word "Secretary" shall be interpreted to mean "Chairman" when applicable.

H *Bidder* shall mean any individual, firm or corporation submitting a bid for the work contemplated, acting directly or through a duly authorized representative.

I *Engineer* shall mean the Chief Engineer of the Water and Power Resources Board, or a representative duly authorized by the Chairman of the Water and Power Resources Board, or by the Secretary of the Department of Forests and Waters, or by The Authority, acting directly or through his or its properly authorized agents, engineers, assistants, or inspectors, acting within the scope of the particular duties assigned to them or of the authority given them.

J *Contractor* or expressions *Party of the Second Part*, or *Second Party* shall mean the individual, firm, or corporation, which entered into a contract with the Commonwealth or with The Authority for the performance of the work described in the Bid Form, acting directly or through his agents or employees, or the Surety in case of default in the performance of the work.

K *Proposal* or *Bid Form* shall mean the approved prepared form on which the Bidder is to submit, or has submitted, a bid for the work contemplated.

L *Bid* shall mean the written unit or lump sum price figures submitted by the Bidder on the Bid Form.

M *Surety* or *Sureties* shall mean the corporate body or bodies which are bound with and for the Contractor for the satisfactory performance of the work and the prompt payment in full for labor and material as provided in the bonds.

N *Contract* shall mean, collectively, all of the covenants, terms, and stipulations contained in the various portions of the Contract, to wit: Bid Form, Agreement, Bonds, Drawings, Specifications, and Notice to Proceed, also any and all Supplemental Agreements which reasonably could be required to complete the work in a substantial and acceptable manner.

O *Specifications* shall mean the directions, provisions, and requirements contained herein, and any supplements, revisions and special requirements referred to in, or bound with, the Bid Form, together with all written agreements made or to be made, pertaining to the method and manner of performing the work, or to the quantities and qualities of materials to be furnished under the Contract.

P *Bid Guaranty* shall mean the security designated in the Bid Form to be furnished by the Bidder as guaranty of his ability to qualify for award of the Contract and to enter into a contract with the State for the performance of the work and to furnish satisfactory bonds if the work involved in the Bid Form is awarded to him.

Q *Performance Bond* shall mean the approved form of security furnished by the Contractor and his Surety as a guaranty of good faith on the part of the Contractor to execute the work in accordance with the terms of the Specifications and the Contract.

R *Material and Labor Bond* shall mean the approved form of security furnished by the Contractor and his Surety as a guaranty of good faith to pay promptly or cause to be paid promptly in full such sums as may be due for material furnished and/or labor supplied or performed, or for services rendered by Public Utilities, in the prosecution of the work under the Contract.

S *Surety Bond(s)* or *Bond(s)* shall mean the Performance Bond or the Material and Labor Bond or any combination of said bonds.

T   *Notice to Proceed* shall mean a written notice to the Contractor of the date on or before which he is to begin the prosecution of the work.

U   *Works* or *Project* shall mean all of the work to be performed and completed.

V   *Unit* shall mean a specific portion or section of the Works or Project, to be completed under this Contract.

W   *Contract Plans* or *Drawings* shall mean, collectively, all of the drawings, or reproductions of drawings, pertaining to the Contract and made part thereof, and also such supplementary drawings as the Department* may issue from time to time in order to elucidate said Contract Drawings, or for showing details which are not shown thereon, or for the purpose of showing changes in the work as authorized under Section 5.4 of the Specifications titled "Minor Changes and Alterations" and under Section 6.6, "Modification of Specifications and Drawings by Written Agreement."

X   *A.S.T.M.* shall mean the American Society for Testing and Materials. Reference to A.S.T.M. shall refer to the specification or method of test in effect on the date that the project was advertised, except when a specific designation is specified.

Y   *A.A.S.H.O.* shall mean the American Association of State Highway Officials. Reference to A.A.S.H.O. shall refer to the specification or method of test in effect on the date that the project was advertised, except when a specific designation is specified.

Z   *A.C.I.* shall mean the American Concrete Institute. Reference to A.C.I. shall refer to the specification or method of test in effect on the date that the project was advertised, except when a specific designation is specified.

AA   *Highway Department Specifications* shall mean the specifications of the Pennsylvania Department of Highways, Form 408 and/or Form 409, with their supplements, in effect on the date that the project was advertised.

1.2   DIRECTION OR APPROVAL OF ENGINEER OR DEPARTMENT*

Wherever in this contract, the words, *Directed, Required, Permitted, Ordered, Instructed, Designated, Considered Necessary, Prescribed,* or words of like import are used, it shall be understood that the direction, requirement, permission, order, instruction, designation, or prescription, etc., of the Engineer or Department* is intended; and similarly, the words, *Approved, Acceptable, Satisfactory,* or words of like import, shall

* Or Board or The Authority.

mean approved by, or acceptable or satisfactory to, the Engineer or Department*.

1.3 CONTRACTOR'S ADDRESS

The address, given in the Bid Form upon which this Contract is founded, is hereby designated as the place to which notices, letters, and other communications to the Contractor shall be mailed or delivered. The delivery to the above named place of any notice, letter or other communication from the Department*, or its agents, to the Contractor shall be deemed sufficient service thereof upon the Contractor, and the date of said service shall be the date of such delivery. The address may be changed at any time by written notice from the Contractor to the Department*. Nothing herein contained shall be deemed to preclude or render inoperative the service of any notice, letter, or other communication upon the Contractor personally.

SECTION 2
BID REQUIREMENTS AND
CONDITIONS

2.1 GENERAL INFORMATION FOR BIDDERS

Bid Forms will specify the place to which they must be delivered, the date, time, and place of opening of bids, the location and description of the work to be performed, the approximate quantities of work to be performed and materials to be furnished, the date by which the work must be completed, the amount of the bid guaranty, and any special requirements pertaining to the particular works to be constructed which may vary from, or are not contained in, the Specifications. All papers bound with or attached to the Bid Forms are a necessary part thereof and shall not be detached.

2.2 QUALIFICATION OF BIDDERS

Each bidder must present satisfactory evidence that he has been engaged in work of a general character covered by the Bid Form, and that he is fully prepared and has the necessary capital to begin work promptly and to conduct it as required by the Contract. Blank forms are attached to the Bid Form for use in presenting some of the evidence required. The Bidder shall present additional evidence of his experience and fitness within ten (10) days after a request is made, unless the time is extended by the Department*.

All foreign corporations, and individuals or firms doing business under fictitious names, shall register with the Secretary

* Or Board or The Authority.

of the Commonwealth before an award will be made to such corporation, individual, or firm.

2.3 ESTIMATE OF QUANTITIES

The Bidders' attention is called to the fact that the estimate of quantities of work to be done and equipment to be furnished under these Specifications, as shown on the Bid Form, and in the Contract, is approximate and is given only as a basis of calculation upon which the bids will be compared. The Department* does not assume any responsibility that the quantities set forth shall be realized strictly in the work, nor shall the contractor plead misunderstanding or deception because of such estimate of quantities or of the character of the work, location, or other conditions pertaining thereto. The Department* reserves the right to increase or diminish any or all of the above mentioned quantities of work or to omit any of them, as it may deem necessary, and such increase or decrease of the quantities given for any of the items shall not be considered as sufficient grounds for granting an increase in the unit prices bid, except as set forth in Section 6.6 of the Specifications titled "Modifications of Specifications and Drawings by Written Agreement."

2.4 SITE INVESTIGATION

A *General*—The Contractor acknowledges that he has satisfied himself as to: the nature and location of the work; the general and local conditions, including but not restricted to those bearing upon transporting, disposing, handling, and storing of materials; availability of labor, water, electric power, and roads; uncertainties of weather, river stages, tides, or similar physical conditions at the site; the conformation and conditions of the ground; and the character of equipment and facilities needed preliminary to and during the prosecution of the work. The Contractor further acknowledges that he has satisfied himself as to the character, quality, and quantity of surface and subsurface materials or obstacles to be encountered insofar as this information is reasonably ascertainable from an inspection of the site, including all exploratory work done by the Department*, as well as from information presented by the Drawings and Specifications made a part of this contract. Any failure by the Contractor to acquaint himself with the available information will not relieve him from responsibility for estimating properly the difficulty or cost of successfully performing the work. The Department* assumes no responsibility for any conclusions or interpretations made by the Contractor on the basis of the

* Or Board or The Authority.

information made available by the Department*. The Department* also assumes no responsibility for any understanding or representations made by its officers or agents during or prior to the execution of this Contract, unless (1) such understanding or representations are expressly stated in the Contract, and (2) the Contract expressly provides that the responsibility therefore is assumed by the Department*. Representations which are not expressly stated in the Contract and for which liability is not expressly assumed by the Department* in the Contract shall be deemed only for the information of the Contractor.

B   *Topography*—Contours, topography, profiles, and cross sections of the existing ground are shown on the Drawings which accompany these Specifications. These contours, topography, profiles, and cross sections are believed to be reasonably correct but are not guaranteed to be absolutely so and are presented only as approximations.

C   *Subsurface Investigations*—Where subsurface and foundation conditions have been investigated by borings and test pits, boring records for each hole and test pit are included in the Drawings for the information of the Contractor.

Samples from drill holes are available for inspection by the Bidder, who will be advised of the location where the samples are stored on inquiry.

Borings are believed to represent accurately the strata encountered at the locations indicated, but the Department* will not be responsible for deductions, interpretations, or conclusions drawn therefrom. Ground water levels are those observed at the time of the subsurface exploration and may not reflect stable ground water levels at the time of construction.

2.5   BIDS

Bids must be submitted on the forms provided by the Department* for that purpose. They must not be changed in form, and no alteration or interlineation shall be made therein. Should the Bidder decide to explain or to qualify his bid, he should do so in a supplemental statement attached to the Bid Form; but any bid may be rejected which contains explanations or qualifications which change or modify the character of conditions of the Bid Form as printed, or which make it incomparable with other bids as determined by the Department*.

The blank spaces in the Bid Form shall be filled in, where indicated, for each and every item for which a description is given, and the Bidder must state the price (in ink) for which he

* Or Board or The Authority.

proposes to do the work. Unit price figures shall be considered as the price bid. The extensions and the total are only for the information of the Department*, and will not be considered as part of the bid. The Bidder shall sign his Bid Form correctly and enclose it in a sealed envelope which will be furnished by the Department* for the purpose.

If the bid is made by an individual, it shall be signed him; if it is made by a firm or partnership, it shall be signed in the firm or partnership name by a member of the firm or partnership, and the name and address of each member shall be given; if it is made by a corporation, the person signing must be the President or Vice-President of the corporation, attested to by the Secretary or Treaturer of the corporation, otherwise, the signing individual's certificate of authority to execute such documents must accompany the Bid Form and the name of the State under the laws of which the corporation is chartered, and the names, titles and business addresses of the President, Secretary, and Treasurer, must appear therein. Bids will be opened and read publicly at the time and place given in the Bid Form, and Bidders are invited to be present. The withdrawal of a bid at any time before the time set for opening will be permitted.

Telegraphic revisions may be made, but the total amount of the bid shall not be divulged. Such divulgence will disqualify the bid.

Late bids will not be considered, and will be returned unopened.

2.6   BID GUARANTY

Each bid must be accompanied by a monetary deposit in the amount stipulated in the Proposal. The deposit shall be made payable to the "Commonwealth of Pennsylvania," or "The General State Authority," as applicable, and shall be the depositor's check certified by the bank of deposit, or it may be a bank cashier's or trust company treasurer's check or equivalent. When specifically stated in the Bid Form, a bid bond in the same amount, executed by the Bidder and a surety company, may be substituted in lieu of the specified certified check at the Bidder's option. Either the bid bond or the certified check shall be a guaranty that the Bidder will, within ten (10) days after notification of the award or immediately upon receipt of the Contract, if such receipt is more than ten (10) days after notification, execute the Contract and furnish the required Surety Bonds. Said Contract and Bonds shall be on the standard forms prescribed by the Department*. No other forms of bid guaranties will be acceptable. Certified checks or bid bonds will be returned to Bidders to whom the award is not made within seven (7) days after the execution of the Contract or the rejection of all bids. The certified check or Bid Bond of the

* Or Board or The Authority.

Bidder to whom the award is made will be returned to him within seven (7) days after the execution of the Contract by both parties, the furnishing of the required Surety Bonds, and approval of the Contract and Bonds by the Department of Justice.

If any Bidder to whom the award has been made shall fail to execute the Contract or to furnish satisfactory Bonds within the time heretofore specified or extended by the Department*, the award shall thereupon become void, at the option of the Department*, in which case the proceeds of the certified check or bid bond shall become the property of the Commonwealth of Pennsylvania or The General State Authority, as applicable, as liquidated damages, and the Contract may be awarded to the next lowest bidder, and the next lowest responsible bidder shall thereupon assume the Contract as if he were the party to whom the award was first made. Bids otherwise regular which are not accompanied by a certified check or bid bond will be rejected as informal.

2.7   REJECTION OF BIDS

The right is reserved to accept or reject any or all bids, and to waive technical defects, if, in the judgment of the Department*, the best interests of the Commonwealth of Pennsylvania shall require such action.

More than one bid for a project from an individual, firm, corporation, or association under the same or different names shall not be considered.

A joint venture bid will not be acceptable.

Bids in which the bid prices are obviously unbalanced may be rejected.

2.8   ASSIGNMENT OF BIDS

No bidder shall assign his bid, or any of his rights or interests thereunder, without the written consent of the Department*.

2.9   EQUIPMENT SCHEDULE

Contractor shall furnish a list of his available equipment which is pertinent to each project on forms provided by the Department* as a part of the Bid Form.

SECTION 3
AWARD AND EXECUTION OF
CONTRACT

3.1   AWARD OF CONTRACT

When a bid received has been determined by the Department* to be satisfactory, a Contract will be awarded to the lowest

* Or Board or The Authority.

responsible Bidder within forty-five (45) days from the date of opening of bids, subject to the right to reject any or all bids, as herein before stated. This time may be extended with the written consent of the Bidder. The award will be based exclusively on the total results of computations of the estimated quantities and the prices bid, provided the lowest Bidder is qualified as determined by the Department*.

3.2   CANCELLATION OF AWARD

The Department* reserves the right to cancel the award of any contract at any time before its execution or before its approval as to form and legality by the legally designated officials of the Commonwealth or of The Authority.

3.3   EXECUTION OF CONTRACT

The Bidder to whom the award shall have been made must execute the Contract and return it, together with properly executed bonds to the Department*, in Harrisburg, Pennsylvania, within ten (10) days after having been notified to do so by the Department*. If the bidder to whom the Contract shall have been awarded fails, refuses, or neglects to return the Contract and Bonds as herein provided, the amount of the Bid Guaranty shall be forfeited and retained by the Commonwealth or The General State Authority as liquidated damages for such neglect, refusal, or failure. Standard contract forms may be examined by interested parties in the office of the Department*.

No bid shall be considered binding upon the Commonwealth or upon The Authority until the execution of the Contract and its approval as to form and legality by the legally designated officials of the Commonwealth or The Authority.

3.4   PERSONS INTERESTED IN CONTRACT

The Contractor hereby declares that no other person or corporation has any interest hereunder as contractor.

3.5   ASSIGNMENT AND SUBCONTRACTS

The personal services of the Contractor are contemplated under this Contract, hence no more than 40% of the work to be performed can be transferred or sublet. Subcontractors shall be subject to the approval of the Department*, which approval shall be contingent upon the satisfactory performance of the subcontract work. If, in the opinion of the Department*, the subcontract work is unnecessarily or unreasonably delayed, or is not being performed suitably or in accordance with the terms of the Contract, or is not making sufficient progress to complete the work in the required time, or, for any cause whatsoever,

* Or Board or The Authority.

is not being carried on in an acceptable manner, then the Department* may notify the Contractor, in writing, to terminate the employment of such subcontractor. The Contractor shall then comply with such notification within two (2) weeks and shall perform the work either by his own forces or by other approved means.

In any event, the Contractor shall not assign, transfer, sublet, or otherwide dispose of this Contract, or his right, title, or interest in or to the same or any part thereof, without such previous consent in writing of the Department*. If the Contractor shall, without the previous written consent, assign, transfer, convey, sublet, or otherwise dispose of this Contract, or of his right, title, or interest therein to any other person, company, or other corporation or by bankruptcy, voluntary or involuntary, or by assignment under the insolvency laws of any State, this Contract may, at the option of the Department*, be revoked and annulled, and the Department* shall thereupon be relieved and discharged from any and all liability and obligations, growing out of the same, to the Contractor and to his assignee, trustee or transferee; and no right under this Contract, or to any money to become due under this Contract, shall be asserted, excepting as provided herein, against the Department*, in law or equity, by reason of any so-called assignment of this Contract or any part thereof, or of any moneys to become due under this Contract, unless authorized as aforesaid by written consent of the Department*.

3.6   REMOVAL OF EQUIPMENT

The Contractor shall not sell, assign, mortgage, hypothecate, or remove equipment which has been furnished, and which may be necessary for the completion of the Contract without the written consent of the Department*.

3.7   NOTICE TO PROCEED

As soon as practicable after approval of the Contract and Bonds, written notice will be given the Contractor to proceed with the work. If said notice is not given within three (3) months after the date of award and the delay is not caused by the Contractor or weather conditions, the Contract may be declared null and void by either party.

3.8   SURETY BONDS

The Bidder to whom the Contract is awarded will be required to execute a "Performance Bond," covering satisfactory performance of the work contracted, in the penal sum of one hundred per cent (100%) of the amount of the Contract, and in

---

* Or Board or The Authority.

addition, a "material and Labor Bond" covering the prompt payment in full for materials, utility services rendered, and all equipment furnished and/or labor supplied or performed, in the prosecution of the work, also in the penal sum of one hundred per cent (100%) of the amount of the Contract. All bonds must be executed by a corporate surety satisfactory to the Department*. The same Surety must execute all bonds and should the Surety upon such bonds become unsatisfactory to the Department*, the Contractor must promptly furnish such additional security as may be required from time to time to protect the interests of the Department* and of persons, firms, or corporations supplying materials, utility services, equipment, and/or labor in the prosecution of the work contemplated by the Contract. The Surety Bonds shall remain in full force until after the expiration of the remedy guaranty period specified in Section 5.15 herein.

The Bidder shall acquaint himself with and shall abide by all provisions of Act. No. 385 of the General Assembly of the Commonwealth of Pennsylvania approved the 20th day of December, A.D. 1967, except for the exclusion of contracts in amounts less than $5,000.00. Although not attached thereto, this Act shall be considered a part of the Bid Documents on all contracts, regardless of the monetary size of the Contract.

3.9   INSURANCE

The Contractor shall not commence work under this Contract until he has obtained all insurance required hereinafter in this section and not until such insurance has been approved by the Department*, nor shall the Contractor permit a subcontractor, if any, to commence work until all similar insurance has been obtained and approved. Each certificate or policy submitted as evidence of such coverage shall contain a rider that the insurer will notify the Department*, in writing, thirty (30) days prior to cancellation or modification of the policy. All policies shall be issued by insurance companies authorized to conduct such business under the law of the Commonwealth of Pennsylvania.

The required insurances shall be of the Contractural Liability type and the named insured parties shall include the Commonwealth of Pennsylvania or The General State authority, as applicable.

> A   *Workmen's Compensation Insurance*—The Contractor shall take out and maintain during the life of this Contract, Workmen's Compensation Insurance for all of his employees employed on the project and, in case any of the work is sublet, the Contractor shall require the subcontractor similarly to provide Workmen's Compensation Insurance unless the latter's employees are covered by the protection afforded by the Contractor.

* Or Board or The Authority.

In lieu of insurance for this liability, the Contractor may file with the Department* a certificate of exemption from insurance from the Bureau of Workmen's Compensation of the Department of Labor and Industry.

B *Public Liability and Property Damage Insurance*—The Contractor shall take out and maintain for the life of the Contract such Public Liability and Property Damage Insurance as shall protect the Commonwealth, or The Authority, as applicable, the political subdivision(s) where the work is performed, the Contractor, and subcontractor(s), if any, performing work covered by this Contract from claims for damages or personal injury, including accidental death, as well as from claims for property damage which may arise in execution of this Contract, whether such be by the Contractor or by the subcontractor(s) or by anyone directly or indirectly employed by either. The amount of Public Liability Insurance shall be not less than Three Hundred Thousand Dollars ($300,000) per person and Five Hundred Thousand Dollars ($500,000) per accident. The amount of Property Damage Insurance shall not be less than Three Hundred Thousand Dollars ($300,000) per accident and Five Hundred Thousand Dollars ($500,000) aggregate.

C *Automobile Bodily Injury and Property Damage Insurance*—The Contractor shall take out and maintain for the life of the Contract such Automobile Bodily Injury and Property Damage Insurance as shall protect the Commonwealth, the political subdivision(s) in which the work is performed, the Contractor, and subcontractor(s), if any, performing work covered by this Contract, from claims for damages or personal injury, including accidental death, as well as from claims for property damage which may arise in execution of this Contract, whether such be by the Contractor or by the subcontractor(s) or by anyone directly or indirectly employed by either. The amount of the Automobile Bodily Injury Insurance shall be not less than Three Hundred Thousand Dollars ($300,000) per person and Five Hundred Thousand Dollars ($500,000) per accident. The amount of Automobile Property Damage Insurance shall not be less than One Hundred Thousand Dollars (l100,000) per accident and Three Hundred Thousand Dollars ($300,000) per occurrence.

D *Special Hazard*—Special hazards, if there is a possibility of such hazards existing in the work contemplated, shall be covered by separate insurance or by rider(s) to other required policy(ies). Possible hazards, such as blasting, explosion, and fire on insurable items shall be so covered.

* Or Board or The Authority.

E   *Maintenance of Insurance*—Whenever the estimated aggregate of losses covered by the Property Damage Insurance equals or exceeds one-half (½) of the aggregate policy limit as determined by the Department*, the said policy shall, upon fifteen (15) days written notice by the Department*, be endorsed to restore the initial policy limit or replaced by another policy having the same limit.

F   *Accidents and Claims*—The Contractor and his Surety shall indemnify and save harmless the Commonwealth, the local political subdivision(s) in which the work is performed, and all the officers, agents, and employees of both from all suits, actions or claims of any character, name and description brought for or on account of any claims of any injury or damage received or sustained by any person(s) or property on account of any negligence or fault of the Contractor, his agents or employees, in execution of the Contract or from any improper or inferior workmanship or inferior materials used, and the Contractor will be required to pay any judgment, with costs, which may be obtained against the Department* or the local political subdivision(s), growing out of such injury or damage.

SECTION 2
CONDUCT OF WORK

4.1   TIME AND ORDER OF WORK

A   *General*—The Contractor shall commence work within ten (10) days after receipt of the Notice to Proceed and the work shall be carried on at such points and in such order of procedure and such times and seasons as may be necessary in order that all of the Project may be constructed with safety during all stages of construction and completed within the time specified in the Bid Form. If the Contractor does any work or incurs any expense in furtherance of the Contract prior to receipt of Notice to proceed, such action shall be his sole responsibility.

Any shut-down will in no way change the provisions of Section 5.9, "CONTRACTOR'S LIABILITY," of these Standard Specifications. The requirements and responsibilities outlined in that and other pertinent sections shall remain in effect during the period when work has been discontinued.

B   *Field Examination*—Before the Notice to Proceed is given for the Project, the Contractor or his authorized representative shall go over the Project, accompanied by the Engineer or his designated representative, and shall observe for himself, with the Contract Drawings before him,

* Or Board or The Authority.

all pertinent conditions relative to the Contract, including the status of right-of-way, working area, and existing structures and utilities.

C   *Shut-Down Required by Department**—The Department* shall have the right to have the work discontinued for such time as may be necessary, in whole or in part, should the condition of the weather, or of flood, or other contingency make it desirable to do so, in order that the work shall be well and properly executed. Extension of time may be granted the Contractor for discontinuance of work so required, as provided in Section 4.2 of the Specifications titled, "EXTENSION OF TIME."

D   *Winter Shutdown*—Unless otherwise specified, the Contractor may suspend operations for the winter season provided that: (1) progress of the work is such that completion is expected within time specified or there are no items of work which can be satisfactorily and efficiently performed during winter months, and (2) written permission is obtained from the Department* prior to shutdown. Extension of time for winter shut-down will not be considered unless winter season is much longer than could ordinarily be anticipated from a study of local weather conditions, and then only for time in excess of expected winter season duration.

E   *Schedule of Work*—Within fifteen (15) days after receipt of the Notice to Proceed, the Contractor shall submit to the Department* for approval a proposed itemized schedule of work. This itemized schedule shall be submitted on a standard form prescribed by the Department*. The Contractor shall follow this schedule as closely as practical, but shall not delay any portion of the work for the sole purpose of adhering to the approved schedule. The Contractor shall submit revised schedules if he changes his work program, which shall also be subject to the approval of the Department*. Payment on account of progress estimates for the work may be withheld by the Department* unless and until satisfactory itemized schedules of work are submitted as specified herein.

4.2   EXTENSION OF TIME

Delays due to causes beyond the control of the Contractor, other than such as reasonably would be expected to occur in connection with or during the performance of the work, may entitle the Contractor to an extension of time for completing the work sufficient to compensate for such delay. No extension of time shall be granted, however, unless the Contractor shall, within ten (10) days from the initiation of the delay, notify the

* Or Board or The Authority.

Department*, in writing, of such delay and of the time of beginning and the cause of same, and unless he shall, within ten (10) days after the expiration of such delay, notify the Department* in writing, of the extension of time claimed on account thereof and then only to the extent, if any, allowed by the Department*. No extension of time shall operate to release the Surety or Contractor from any of their obligations. The Department* shall be fully authorized and empowered to make such deductions from the final estimate of the amount due the Contractor, as are stipulated in the Bid Form and the Agreement, for each calendar day that the Contractor shall be in default for the completion of the work beyond the date to which the time of completion shall have been extended by the Department*. Should the Contractor be permitted to continue and finish the work, or any part thereof, after the time fixed by the Contract for completion, or as it may have been extended, such permit shall in no way operate as a waiver on the part of the Department* of its right to collect the liquidated damages agreed upon in case of such delay, or of any of its rights under this Contract.

The Contractor declares that he has familiarized himself with the weather, local conditions, and other circumstances which may, or are likely to, affect the performance and completion of the work, and agrees that, taking these conditions and circumstances into account, he will provide adequate equipment and prosecute the work in such manner and with such diligence that the same will be completed within the time specified in the Contract, or as the same may be extended, even though the most adverse conditions which reasonably could be expected to occur during the period of construction do prevail during the performance of the work.

When the work of the Department* is enjoined by legal proceedings which prevent the Contractor from prosecuting any of the work of this Contract, an extension of time may be granted sufficient, in the opinion of the Department*, to compensate for the time lost by such delay.

4.3   INSPECTION AND RIGHT OF ACCESS

The Department* contemplates, and the Contractor hereby agrees to, a thorough inspection by the Engineer or by any of his agents, or by any agents which the Department* may appoint for such purpose, of all work and equipment furnished under this Contract, in order to ascertain whether all workmanship is in strict accordance with the requirements of this Contract.

The Contractor shall furnish to the Department* and any of its agents, access at all times to the work and to the premises used by the Contractor, and shall provide them every reasonable facility as may be desirable, for the purpose of inspection even to

* Or Board or The Authority.

the extent of discontinuing portions of the work temporarily. The Contractor shall make no charge for temporary discontinuance of work for purposes of inspection.

The Contractor shall regard and carry out the directions and instructions of the Engineer, or his agents, and correct any defective work found to be not in accordance with the Specifications and Drawings and in case of dispute the Contractor may appeal to the Department*, whose decision shall be final. The Contractor shall make no claim for damages or delay on this account.

4.4 PROVIDING FOR EMERGENCIES

It is understood by both Parties to this Contract that unusual conditions may arise on the work which will require that immediate and unusual provisions be made to protect the public from danger, loss, or damage due, directly or indirectly, to the prosecution of the work, and that it is part of the service required of the Contractor to make such provisions.

The Contractor shall use such foresight and shall take such steps and precautions as may be necessary to protect the public from danger or damage or loss of life or property, which would result from the interruption of any public service, or from the failure of partly completed work.

Whenever, in the opinion of the Engineer, an emergency exists for which the Contractor has not taken sufficient precaution for the safety of the public or the protection of the work to be performed under this Contract, or of adjacent structures or property which may be damaged by processes of work on account of such neglect; and whenever, in the opinion of the Engineer, immediate action shall be considered necessary in order to protect public or private property interests liable to loss or damage on account of the operations under this Contract, then, and in that event, the Department*, upon giving notice to the Contractor, may provide suitable protection for said interests by causing such work to be done and equipment to be furnished as, in the opinion of the Engineer, may seem reasonable and necessary.

If emergency conditions arise which are due to the lack of foresight or failure to take proper precautionary measures on the part of the Contractor, he shall be solely responsible for the costs of any necessary remedial work, whether incurred by his own forces or by work and equipment provided by the Department*. Cost and expenses for work and equipment provided by the Department* shall be paid for by the Contractor, upon the presentation of the bills therefor, properly certified by the Department*. If said bills are not paid, upon presentation, by the

* Or Board or The Authority.

Contractor, then said cost and expense shall be deducted from any amount due, or which may become due, the Contractor.

In case the Department* shall decide that all or part of the expense incurred in meeting any emergency cannot be justly charged to the Contractor it may compensate the Contractor for all or part of the work done and equipment furnished in meeting such emergency.

4.5   PERSONAL ATTENTION OF CONTRACTOR

The Contractor shall give his personal attention constantly to the faithful prosecution of the work, and shall be present, in person or represented by a qualified and duly authorized agent, on the site of the work, continually during its progress. He shall at all times while the work is in progress keep a complete copy of the Contract, including all Addenda, at the site of the work.

4.6   AGENTS, SUPERINTENDENTS AND FOREMEN

When the Contractor is not present on any part of the work where it may be desired to give directions, orders may be given by the Engineer and shall be received and obeyed by the Superintendents or Foremen who may have charge of the particular part of the work in reference to which orders are given. Superintendents, agents and foremen must be qualified to perform the duties of their position in an orderly and efficient manner. Any superintendent, agent, or foremen who is not qualified or who will not work in a cooperative manner with the Department* representatives shall be discharged from the project at the direction of the Department*.

4.7   LABOR REGULATIONS

A   *Non-discrimination in Hiring*—In hiring of employees for the performance of work under this Contract or any subcontract hereunder, no Contractor, subcontractor, nor any person acting on behalf of such Contractor or subcontractor, shall by reason of race, creed, color, or national origin, discriminate against or intimidate anyone who is qualified and available to perform the work to which this Contract relates.

There may be deducted from the amount payable to the Contractor under this Contract a penalty of Five Dollars ($5.00) for each person for each calendar day during which such person was discriminated against or intimidated in violation of the provisions of the Contract.

This Contract may be cancelled or terminated by the Commonwealth or The Authority and all money due or to become due herewith may be forfeited for a second or any

* Or Board or The Authority.

subsequent violation of the terms or conditions of this portion of this Contract (Act of July 18, 1935, No. 382, P.L. 1173).

B *Preferential Hiring of Veterans*—The Contractor, subcontractor, or any person in his behalf, shall carry out the provisions of the Act of the General Assembly, No. 337, approved the 22nd day of May, A.D. 1945, P.L. 837, which concerns the giving of preferences to honorably discharged persons, who have served in the armed forces of the United States during any way, in determining who shall be employed on public works, which Act in part provides:

> "Whenever the Commonwealth issues specifications for construction, alteration or repair of any public works, such specifications shall include a provision a provision under which the contractors and subcontractors shall agree to give a preferential rating similar to that given by the Commonwealth, as herein provided, to any soldier making application for employment upon such public works."

The word "soldier" as used herein shall be construed to mean a person who served in the armed forces of the United States during any war in which the United States engaged, or as otherwise defined by law, and who has an honorable discharge from such service.

C *Preferential Hiring of Local Labor*—The Contractor shall endeavor to hire, whenever possible, local men living in the vicinity of the work, when such men are qualified, able, and available to perform the work to which the employment relates. The intent is to aid the unemployment situation in the vicinity of the work whenever possible.

D *Character and Residence of Employees*—The Contractor shall employ only competent, skillful, faithful, and orderly men to do the work, and whenever the Department* shall notify the Contractor, in writing, that any man in the work is, in its opinion, incompetent, unfaithful, disorderly, or otherwise unsatisfactory, the Contractor shall discharge such man from the work and shall not again employ his except with the written consent of the Department*.

Laborers and mechanics employed on this project shall have been residents of the Commonwealth for at least ninety (90) days prior to their employment and failure to keep and comply with such provisions shall be sufficient legal reason to refuse payment of the Contract price to the Contractor (Act of July 19, 1935, No. 414, P.L. 1321).

E *Minimum Wage Specification*—In accordance with

* Or Board or The Authority.

the provisions of the Act of June 21, 1937, P.L. 1865, its supplements or amendments (Pennsylvania Laws), the minimum wage requirements as set forth in the Bid Form shall be strictly observed and fulfilled. Failure to comply with the minimum wage specifications shall make the Contractor liable for a penalty of an amount equal to twice the difference between the minimum wage contained in the Specifications and the wage actually paid to any laborer or mechanic for each day during which he has been employed at a wage less than that prescribed therein. The amount of any penalties for which the Contractor is liable as herein provided shall be withheld and deducted for the use of the Commonwealth or The Authority, from any moneys due the Contractor. The authorized representatives of the Department*, acting as inspectors, in accordance with said Act, shall be furnished every facility by the Contractor for determining the wages paid, and such inspectors shall have full and complete access to the records of the Contractor, which records shall be kept accurately and made available at all times on the Project. The Minimum Wage Schedule shall be conspicuously posted at the project site.

In accordance with the provisions of said Act, the Contractor shall submit certified detailed payrolls, giving names, addresses, social security numbers, classifications, hours worked, rates per hour, and total paid on each pay day, and shall also certify that he is not receiving or requiring or will not receive or require, directly or indirectly, from any employee, any refund of any such minimum wage or wages. The amount shown as total paid on each pay day shall include deductions in accordance with Federal and State Laws.

Certified transcripts of labor payrolls shall be submitted to the Department* within ten (10) days after the close of each pay period, which shall be at least twice each month. Payment of estimates may be withheld if certified transcripts of labor payrolls are not submitted in their proper forms within the time limit and as herein specified.

The Contractor and all subcontractors shall keep an accurate record of the information contained in these payrolls for each workman employed in connection with this Contract and such record shall be preserved for two years from date of payment. The record shall be open at all reasonable hours to the inspection of the Department* and to the Secretary of Labor and Industry.

The provisions of Act No. 442, approved August 15, 1961, its supplements and amendments (Pennsylvania Laws), shall be strictly observed and fulfilled. The Contractor and subcontractors, if any, shall file statements certifying to the

* Or Board or The Authority.

amounts due and owing to any workmen for wages, before final payment will be made. Failure to pay the prevailing minimum wages may be cause for termination of the Contractor's right to proceed with the work.

The minimum wages of labor and mechanic positions to be paid on this Contract are given in the Bid Form. Minimum wages for positions not covered therein will be based on the prevailing rate for the particular trade for the locality, subject to the approval of the Secretary of Department of Labor and Industry.

In the event that the Contract award is for less than Twenty-Five Thousand Dollars ($25,000), the wage rates will not apply and can be excluded. Certified transcripts of labor payrolls must be submitted, even if the minimum wage specifications do not apply, in order that compliance with requirements of other legislation may be verified.

4.8 SURVEYS

The Engineer will provide a stationed baseline, centerline, or offset centerline for the entire length of the Project. In addition, bench marks for construction purposes will be located at intervals over the length of the Project.

From the baseline or centerline and bench marks established by the Engineer, the Contractor shall complete the layout of the work and shall be responsible for all measurements that may be required for the execution of the work to the location and limit marks prescribed in the Specifications or on the Contract Drawings, subject to such modifications as the Department* may require to meet changed conditions.

The Contractor shall furnish, at his own expense, such stakes, templates, platforms, equipment, tools and material, and all labor as may be required in laying out any part of the work from the baseline and bench marks established by the Engineer. It shall be the responsibility of the Contractor to maintain and preserve all stakes and other marks established by the Engineer until authorized to remove them, and if such marks are destroyed by the Contractor or through his negligence prior to their authorized removal, the expense of replacement may be deducted from any amounts due or to become due the Contractor. The Department* may require that work be suspended at any time when location and limit marks established by the Contractor are not reasonably adequate to permit checking of the work.

The Contractor shall fabricate for use by the Engineer, all stakes, targets, and supports to be used by the Engineer to establish baselines, ranges, and grids.

The Engineer may check the grade and alignment of concrete

* Or Board or The Authority.

forms prior to the placement of concrete. Any items of work which will be covered or made nonaccessible by subsequent work shall first be checked by the Engineer. When the Contractor covers or makes unaccessible any unchecked work, the Engineer may direct the Contractor to uncover or remove subsequent construction to permit a check of the unchecked work and the costs of uncovering or removing subsequent work and replacement of same will be borne by the Contractor.

It is the intention not to delay the work for the checking of lines or grades, but, if necessary, working operations shall be suspended for such reasonable time as the Engineer may require for this purpose. No special compensation shall be paid for the cost to the Contractor of any of the work or delay occasioned by checking lines and grades, by making other necessary measurement, or by inspection; but such costs, it is agreed, shall be included in the Contract price. The Contractor shall keep the Engineer informed a reasonable time in advance of the times and places at which he intends to do work in order that necessary measurements for record and payment may be made with the minimum of inconvenience to the Engineer or of delay to the Contractor.

4.9   WEATHER PROTECTION

The Contractor shall furnish at his own expense, all equipment, materials, and work necessary to protect the Works from any weather conditions that may prevail. Construction shall be suspended at any time when, in the judgment of the Engineer, the conditions are unsuitable or the proper precautions are not being taken. Apparatus for protection shall be installed and operated in such manner that the finished work will not be damaged thereby.

4.10   LEGAL RELATIONS AND RESPONSIBILITY TO THE PUBLIC

A   *Compliance with Laws*—The Contractor shall keep himself fully informed of all laws, ordinances, and regulations in any manner affecting those engaged or employed in the work, or the equipment and appliances used in the work, or the conduct of the work, and of all orders and decrees of bodies or tribunals having jurisdiction or authority over the same. He shall at all times observe and comply with, and shall cause his agents to observe and comply with, such existing and future laws, ordinances, regulations, orders, and decrees; and shall protect the Department* against any claim or liability arising from or based upon the violation of any such law, ordinance, regulation, order, or decree, whether by

* Or Board or The Authority.

himself or by his employees. He shall procure all permits and licenses, pay all charges and fees, and give all notices necessary and incident to the proper and lawful prosecution of the work.

The Contractor shall accept, insorfar as the work covered by this Contract is concerned, the provisions of the "Pennsylvania Workmen's Compensation Act of 1915," and any supplements or amendments thereto which may hereafter be enacted into law. See paragraph 3.9A for insurance required against this liability.

B   *Police and Sanitary Regulations*—The Contractor and his employees shall promptly and fully carry out the police and sanitary regulations as hereinafter described, or as may from time to time be prescribed by the Engineer, to the end that proper work shall be done, good order shall prevail, and the health of employees, and of the local people using water from the drainage area in which the work is being performed, and of the local communities affected by the operations under this Contract, may be conserved and safeguarded. The Contractor shall summarily dismiss and shall not again engage, except with the written consent of the Department*, any employee who violates the police or sanitary regulations.

C   *Intoxicants*—The Contractor shall not permit or suffer the introduction or use of intoxicating liquor upon the works embraced in this Contract, or upon any of the grounds occupied or controlled.

D   *Department of Labor and Industry*—Special attention is drawn to the regulations of the Department of Labor and Industry covering equipment, materials, labor, safety, sanitation, and other conditions on which the Contractor shall be fully informed and with which he shall fully comply.

The pertinent regulations include but are not necessarily limited to the following:

Construction and Repair (Scaffolding of all types)
Cranes and Hoists
Explosives, Storage, Handling, and Use of (Blasting)
Fire Proofing
Ladders
Machine Guarding
Railings, Toe Boards, Open Sided Floors, Platforms, and Railings
Trenches and Excavations
Unfired Pressure Vessels

E   *Drinking Water Regulations*—In accordance with the regulations of the Department of Labor and Industry for

* Or Board or The Authority.

Industrial Sanitation, cool, pure, and wholesome water of a quality approved by the Department of Health shall be supplied at all times in places acceptable to employees. The common drinking cup for public use is prohibited; either individual drinking vessels or bubbling fountains shall be used in lieu thereof. Bubbling fountains, if used, shall be maintained in a sanitary condition.

Before the Contractor starts work he shall take adequate means to insure provision of a drinking water supply in compliance with the above regulations. Containers in which drinking water is supplied to employees by the Contractor must be maintained in a sanitary condition.

In case of the use of a public water supply, the Contractor shall submit to the Department* a certified statement for the utility showing that the water complies with all requirements of, and has been approved for public use by, The Pennsylvania Department of Health.

In case of the use of a private source of supply, the Contractor shall submit to the Department* the results of laboratory analysis by an approved testing agency indicating the water to be sufficiently pure for potable use.

F   *Medical Service*—The Contractor whall make satisfactory arrangements for medical service and for the proper care of employees who become sick on the job and employees who are injured during the course of the work. If ordered by the Department*, he shall provide, at such places as directed, all articles necessary for giving first-aid to the injured. The Contractor shall remove from the work any employee whose presence is, in the opinion of the Department*, a danger to the health of other persons.

G   *Fish Commission*—Before any work is performed in a fishable stream the Contractor must contact the local State Waterways Patrolman (Fish Warden) and obtain approval of the Patrolman for his proposed operation. The Contractor shall not use explosives in a stream channel without prior approval from the Fish commission.

H   *No Direct Compensation*—No direct payment will be made for any work of materials required to meet the requirements herein before specified, but compensation therefor shall be considered as having been included in the Contract prices stipulated in the Agreement.

4.11   SAFETY PRECAUTIONS

The Contractor at all times throughout the performance of this Contract shall take all precautions necessary effectually to prevent any accident in any place affected by his operations in consequence of the work being done under this Contract and

* Or Board or The Authority.

shall, to this end, put up and maintain suitable and sufficient barriers, signs, lights, or other necessary protections.

Safety precautions will conform to the appropriate and applicable provisions of the "Manual of Accident Prevention in Construction," published by the Associated General Contractors of America (AGC). A copy is on file at the Division of Flood Control, Department of Forests and Waters, Harrisburg, Pennsylvania.

4.12   RIGHT-OF-WAY

The Department* will furnish to the Contractor all rights-of-way which, in its opinion, is necessary for carrying on the work, and for securing access to the site of the work. In some cases the Contractor may be required to obtain rights-of-way for additional spoil areas.

The Contractor shall be responsible for trespassing or injury to private property, and shall conduct his work in accordance with any laws or regulations relating thereto.

The Drawings show the limits of the Right-of-Way and of the Contractor's Working Area. Any buildings or structures within the right-of-way limits which interfere with the permanent features of the Works are to be removed by the Contractor unless designated otherwise on the Drawings. The method of moving or disposal shall be determined by the Engineer. The Contractor's working area is for use by the Contractor and, where so indicated, for spoil disposal. No buildings or structures in this area shall be moved or damaged in any way except by written direction of the Department* or with the written approval of the property owner. The Contractor shall be liable for any property or other damage in the working area. All lands within the contractor's working area must be restored to as good or better than their original condition and left in a sightly state.

4.13   REQUIREMENTS FOR COLLATERAL WORKS

A   *General*—The Department* reserves the right to have such agent or agents as it may elect enter the property or location on which the Works herein contracted for are to be performed for the purpose of constructing or installing such collateral work as the Department* may desire, or for the construction or reconstruction of telephone and telegraph lines, highways, or other such facilities affected by the work. Such collateral works will be constructed or installed with as little hindrance or interference as possible with the Contractor. The Contractor hereby agrees not to interfere with, or prevent the performance of, any collateral work by the agent or agents of the Department*.

* Or Board or The Authority.

B *Protection of Existing Structures*—The Contractor shall carefully protect from injury any existing improvements, property, or structures that may be liable to injury by the work covered by this Contract, except insofar as work of the Contract requires their modification or removal. He shall take all precaution necessary for such protection, and shall be fully responsible for and shall make good any injury to such works, property, or structures, that may occur by reason of his operation.

The Contractor will preserve and protect all existing vegetation such as trees, shrubs, and grass on or adjacent to the site which do not unreasonably interfere with the construction as may be determined by the Department*. The Contractor will be responsible for all unauthorized cutting or damaging of trees and shrubs, including damage due to careless operation of equipment, stockpiling of materials, or tracking of grass areas by equipment.

C *Public and Private Utilities*—The Contractor is required to inform himself fully concerning location of public and private utilities located within the right-of-way which may or may not require removal, resetting, construction and/or reconstruction, and which may interfere with his operations, and shall be assumed to have prepared his bid and entered into the Contract in full contemplation of the conditions to be encountered and his responsibility in connection therewith. The Department* has shown on the Drawings such structures as have been brought to its attention, but such indication on the Drawings shall not be assumed to relieve the Contractor of a y responsibility with respect thereto; neither shall the Department* be held responsible for any omission or failure to give notice to the Contractor of any other utility located within the right-of-way. The Contractor shall take all precautions necessary to protect existing utilities, and shall be fully responsible for and shall make good any injury to such utilities that may occur by reason of his operations.

Necessary relocation or removal of utility structures within the project limits will ordinarily be accomplished by others, but, if so indicated on the Drawings, shall be done by the Contractor. If such work is to be done by others, the Contractor shall give to the Department* sixty (60) days written notice prior to the time such removal or relocations will be necessary in order to enable the owner to complete the work without delay to the Contractor's operations.

D *Work in Vicinity of Railroads*—In accomplishing the work required by the Plans and Specifications adjacent to or on railroad rights-of-way, the Contractor shall make

* Or Board or The Authority.

arrangements with the railroad for all operations on its property for all safety measures such as lights, flares, flagmen, and inspectors as may be required by said railroad for operations by the Contractor on or about its premises. No separate payment will be made for such work and the cost of such work shall be borne entirely by the Contractor, unless the Contractor makes separate arrangements with the Railroad. The Contractor shall indemnify and hold harmless said railroad from and against any loss, damages, or destruction of property, and injury or death of persons, growing out of or occasioned by the operations or presence of the Contractor on or about the Railroad's premises and shall provide insurance coverage satisfactory to said Railroad. Evidence of insurance cover-shall be filed with the Department* before the start of work on or adjacent to the Railroad rights-of-way.

4.14 STREETS AND PUBLIC THOROUGHFARES

A   *Roadways*—The Contractor shall be responsible for the maintenance of streets and public thoroughfares outside the work area used by his vehicles during the progress of the work, to the extent of cleaning up any materials spilled from or otherwise distributed by his vehicles and restoring the said streets and rights-of-way to their original condition, if damaged by him. The cost and expense incidental to the fulfillment of this section shall be borne by the Contractor and should he create any public nuisance, in the opinion of the Engineer, by his failure to fulfill the requirements of this section, then the Department*, upon written notice to the Contractor, may request the appropriate public authority where the nuisance occurs, to correct the damage, and the cost of this work shall be deducted from any amounts due, or to become due, the Contractor under the terms of this Contract.

B   *Maintenance of Traffic*—The Contractor shall conduct the work so as to insure the least obstruction to traffic. He shall provide all necessary barricades, warning signs, lanterns, red flags, torches, and other such items and shall maintain them in operating condition, to the satisfaction of the Department*, Department of Highways, Municipality, or other agency having jurisdiction over affected roads or streets.

4.15 DEPARTMENTAL* REQUIREMENTS

A   *Office Facilities*—The Contractor shall provide a field office at a location approved by the Engineer for the

* Or Board or The Authority.

exclusive use of Department* personnel. The Contractor shall provide a suitable road to the office site, and parking area for a minimum of four (4) cars.

The facilities shall be maintained by the Contractor for the duration of the Contract, and loss or damage by any cause shall be repaired or replaced by the Contractor at no additional cost to the Department*. The facilities shall remain the property of the Contractor and upon completion of the Contract work, shall be removed to the satisfaction of the Engineer.

The field office shall consist of a room having a minimum floor space of three hundred twenty (320) square feet, and be provided with windows to furnish a minimum of sixty (60) square feet of natural light. Each exterior door shall have a cylinder lock, and two (2) keys shall be furnished with each lock. The office shall be entirely closed, waterproof, and provided with suitable artificial light. Screen doors shall be provided for all exterior doors, and screened sash shall be provided for all exterior windows. Prior to construction of the field office, the Contractor shall prepare and submit detailed plans for the approval of the Department*.

The Contractor shall furnish and install an automatic oil-fired, gas-fired, or electric heater in the field office. The heater shall be capable of maintaining a temperature of at least 70°F. throughout the building in the coldest weather. In the event that a fuel oil storage tank is required, the tank shall be located outside the building. Installation shall conform with regulations of the Pennsylvania State Police, Fire Marshal Division.

Interior lighting shall be provided throughout the building, and duplex receptacles shall be provided on approximately ten (10) foot centers along the exterior walls.

The Contractor shall provide a five (5) gallon bottle type drinking fountain with a paper cup dispenser in the office. The fountain shall be cooled by mechanical refrigeration.

The Contractor shall provide a minimum of one (1) desk, in good condition, and sufficient tables and chairs to meet the requirements of the Engineer at the project, and he shall also furnish one (1) four (4) drawer, legal size steel file cabinet, and closet space with shelves, for storage of supplies, in the field office.

A chemical type latrine or better facility shall be provided in the vicinity of the field office.

The Contractor shall provide all fuel oil or gas, electricity, paper cups, drinking water, toilet paper, and

* Or Board or The Authority.

maintenance of the chemical toilet for the life of the Contract.

Subject to the approval of the Department*, the Contractor may furnish space in an existing building near The site of the work, or an office-type trailer, in lieu of the herein described field office. The space, facilities, and service, however, shall be equivalent, in the opinion of the Department*, to that specified for the field office.

No separate payment will be made for the work required by this paragraph. All cost of the work required by this paragraph shall be included in Contract prices for the various items of work included in the Contract.

B *Signs During Construction*—The Contractor shall furnish, erect and maintain, in locations designated by the Engineer, not more than two (2) signs, each being not less than eighteen (18) square feet in area. The wording shall be painted in black on a white background on said signs as directed by the Department*, and shall be similar to the following design:

MODELVILLE FLOOD CONTROL PROJECT	4''
COMMONWEALTH OF PENNSYLVANIA	3''
DEPARTMENT OF ENVIRONMENTAL RESOURCES	3''
JOHN DOE ASSOCIATES—ENGINEERS[†]	2''
RICHARD ROE, INC.—CONTRACTOR	2''

No advertisements will be permitted on any temporary structures, or elsewhere on the work site, excepting signs bearing the names and addresses of the Department*, the consulting engineer and/or architect, if any, and the Contractor. No separate payment will be made for signs during construction specified above, since signs will be considered as incidental to other items of work.

4.16 PUMPS, DRAINS AND WATER SUPPLY

The Contractor shall provide all the necessary pumps, temporary pipes, drains, ditches, and other means for satisfactorily removing water from any part of the work. The Contractor shall provide at convenient points an ample supply of water of proper quality, for all the operations required under this Contract. All compensation for and all expenses incidental to the fulfillment of the provisions of this section, unless otherwise specifically provided, shall be considered as having been included in the prices stipulated in the bid.

* Or Board or The Authority.

4.17   DRAWINGS AND SPECIFICATIONS FURNISHED THE CONTRACTOR

The Department* will furnish free to the Contractor, five (5) complete sets of Contract Drawings, Specifications, and Special Requirements, and if requested, such additional sets as may be available. Copies beyond those immediately available will be furnished to the Contractor at the actual cost to the Department*.

4.18   COMPLETION AND MAINTENANCE

A   *Remedying Damaged Work*—If the work, or any portion thereof, shall be damaged in any way before the final completion and acceptance of the work, the Contractor shall forthwith make good, without compensation, such damage in a manner satisfactory to the Department*.

B   *Clean-up*—Upon completion of the work, the Contractor shall completely remove and satisfactorily dispose of all temporary works, shall remove all plant and equipment, shall satisfactorily dispose of all rubbish and waste material resulting from the operation under this Contract, and shall do all work necessary to restore the territory embraced within the zone of his operation to a sightly condition. Final payment will not be made until the cleanup is satisfactorily completed.

C   *Maintenance of Completed Work*—The Contractor shall maintain all completed work for the duration of the Contract. This shall include any necessary repairs to structures, the removal of accumulations from improved channels, and the reshaping and reseeding of levee and channel slopes. The completed work shall be in accordance with the Contract Plans and Specifications when the work is finally accepted by the Department*.

SECTION 5
CONTROL OF WORK

5.1   DIRECTION OF WORK

It is mutually agreed that the Department* shall have the right to require changes in the Contractor's procedure, to determine the order of precedence and the times and seasons at which the work shall be conducted, insofar as may be necessary, to secure the safe and proper progress and quality of the work, all at no additional cost to the Department*.

Upon all questions concerning the execution of the work and the interpretation of the Drawings and Specifications, and on the

* Or Board or The Authority.

determination of quantitities, the decision of the Department* shall be final and binding on both parties, and its estimates and decisions shall be a condition precedent to the right of the Contractor to recieve any money under this Contract.

The Department* shall especially direct the manner of conducting the work when it is in locations where the Commonwealth is doing other work, either by contract or by its own forces, in order that conflict may be avoided and the work on this Contract be harmonized with that on other Contracts, or with other work being done in connection with, or growing out of, any operations of the Department*.

5.2 DEPARTMENT* CANNOT WAIVE OBLIGATIONS

It is expressly agreed that neither the Department*, nor any of its employees or agents, shall have any power to waive the obligations of this Contract for the performance of good work by the Contractor as herein described. Failure or omission on the part of the Engineer, or any of his assistants or agents to condemn defective or inferior work shall not imply acceptance of the work, or release of the Contractor from obligation to properly replace the same at once without compensation, and at his own cost and expense, at any time upon discovery of said defective work, notwithstanding that such work may have been estimated for payment, or payments may have been made on the same. Neither shall such failure or omission, not any acceptance by the Engineer or by the Department*, be construed as barring the Department*, at any time, from recovery of damages and of such a sum of money as may be needed to build anew all portions of the work in which improper work was done.

5.3 MODIFICATION OF METHODS AND EQUIPMENT

Except where otherwise directly specified in the Contract, the Contractor shall design, lay out, and b   responsible for the methods and equipment used in fulfilling the Contract; but such methods and equipment, when required, shall have the approval of the Department*.

If at any time, the Contractor's methods or equipment appear to the Engineer to be unsafe, inefficient, or inadequate for securing the safety of the workmen, the quality of work, or the rate of progress required, he may order the contractor to increase their safety and efficiency or to improve their character, and the Contractor shall comply with such orders. If at any time, the Contractor's working force, in the opinion of the Department* shall be inadequate for securing the necessary progress, as herein stipulated, the Contractor shall, if so directed, increase the force or equipment to such an extent as to give

* Or Board or The Authority.

reasonable assurance of compliance with the schedule of progress; but the failure of the Department* to make such demand shall not relieve the Contractor of his obligation to secure the quality, the safe conduct of the work, and the rate of progress required by the Contract, and the Contractor alone shall be responsible for the safety, efficiency, and adequacy of his plant, appliances, and methods. All directives issued to comply with this section shall be accomplished without any additional cost to the Department*.

5.4   MINOR CHANGES AND ALTERATIONS

The Department* reserves the right to make such alterations, eliminations, and additions as it may elect in the grade, location, or plan of the work herein contemplated, or any part thereof, either before or after the commencement of work, provided, however, that they are of a character as not to affect materially the unit cost of the work involved. The Contractor will be paid for said work at the Contract unit prices.

5.5   NO WAIVER OF LEGAL RIGHTS

The Department* shall not be precluded or estopped by any measurements, estimate, or certificate, made or given by it or by any agent or employee of the Department*, under any provision or provisions of the Contract at any time, either before or after the completion and acceptance of the work and payment thereof pursuant to any measurement, estimate, or certificate, from showing the true and correct amount and character of the work performed and materials furnished by the Contractor, or from showing at any time that any such measurement, estimate, or certificate, is untrue or incorrectly made in any particular, or that the work or materials, or any part thereof do not conform in fact to the Contract, and the Department* shall have the right to reject the whole or any part of the aforesaid work or materials, should the said measurements, estimate, certificate, or payment be found, or be known to be inconsistent with the terms of the Contract, or otherwise improperly given, and the Department shall not be precluded and estopped, notwithstanding any such measurement, estimate, certificate, or payment in accordance therewith, from demanding and recovering from the Contractor and/or his Surety such damages as it may sustain by reason of his failure to comply with the terms of the Specifications and of the Contract, or on account of any overpayments made on any estimate or certificate. Neither the acceptance of the Department* nor any estimate or certificate by the Department*, for any payment of money nor any payment for, nor acceptance of the whole or any part of the work by the Department*, nor any extension or remission of time, nor any possession taken by

* Or Board or The Authority.

the Department* or its employees, shall operate as a waiver of any portion of the Contract or of any power herein reserved by the Department*, or any right to damages herein provided, nor shall any waiver of any breach of the Contract be held to be a waiver of any other or subsequent breach.

5.6 COMPLETENESS AND INTENT OF SPECIFICATIONS, ESTIMATES, AND DRAWINGS

The Specifications and Drawings, taken in connection with the estimates and other provisions of this Contract, are intended to describe and illustrate the work required to be done. The Specifications and Drawings are to be taken as indicating the approximate amount of work, its approximate nature and position. The work is intended to be performed in accordance with the best practice and with due regard for safety and, in the event of any doubt as to the meanings of any portion of the Contract, supplementary drawings, or instructions of the Engineer, the interpretation adopted shall be understood to call for the best types of workmanship practicable.

The various parts of the Contract are intended to be mutually explanatory, but should any discrepancy appear or any mis-understanding arise as to the import of anything contained in any part of the Contract, the explanation of the Department* shall be final and binding. Correction of an error or omission in the Drawings or Specifications may be made by the Department* when such correction is necessary to bring out clearly the intention which is indicated by a reasonable interpretation of the Drawings and Specifications as a whole.

Whenever in the Specifications or Drawings, or in supplemental drawings which may be furnished to the Contractor for directing his work, the terms or descriptions of various qualities of workmanship, material, structures, processes, plant, or other features of the Contract are described in general terms, the meaning of fulfillment of which must depend upon individual judgment, then, in all cases, the question of the fulfillment of such specifications or requirements shall be decided by the Department*, and said material shall be furnished, said work shall be done, and said structures, processes, plant, or features shall be constructed, furnished, or carried on in full and complete accordance with its interpretation of the same and to its full satisfaction and approval.

It is the intent and purpose of the Specifications and Drawings to include under each item all materials, equipment, apparatus, and labor necessary to properly construct and put into perfect operation all of the various components of the respective items and to interconnect the various equipment, apparatus, or systems to form a complete and properly coordinated whole.

* Or Board or The Authority.

Any material, equipment, apparatus, and labor not hereinafter specifically mentioned or shown on the Drawings, which may be found necessary to complete or perfect the Project in a substantial manner and in compliance with the requirements implied or intended in these Specifications or Drawings, shall be furnished by the Contractor as part of this Contract. The Contract prices shall constitute full payment for all labor, materials, devices, or methods peculiar to the equipment, apparatus or system intended.

5.7   SHOP DRAWINGS

The Contractor shall submit to the Department* for approval ten (10) copies of all shop drawings as called for under the various headings of these Specifications. These shop drawings shall be complete and shall contain all required detailed information. If approved by the Department*, each copy will be identified as having received such approval by being so stamped and dated. The Contractor shall make any corrections required by the Department*. Nine (9) sets of all shop drawings will be retained by the Department*, and one (1) set will be returned to the Contractor. The approval of the shop drawings by the Department* shall not be construed as a complete check, but will indicate only that the general method of construction and detailing is satisfactory. Approval of such shop drawings will not relieve the Contractor of the responsibility for any error which may exist as the Contractor shall be responsible for the dimensions and design of adequate connections, details, and satisfactory construction of all work. The right is reserved to require submission to the Department* of shop drawings for any part of the work not particularly mentioned herein.

5.8   TERMINATION

A   *Termination Due to Nature of Performance by Contractor*—If the work to be done under this Contract shall be abandoned by the Contractor, or if this Contract shall be assigned or placed in bankruptcy, or the work sublet by him otherwise than as herein specified, or if at any time the Engineer shall be of the opinion and shall so certify in writing to the Department* that the performance of the Contract is unnecessarily or unreasonably delayed, or that the Contractor is violating any of the conditions or agreements of the Contract, or is executing the same in bad faith or not in accordance with the terms thereof, or is not making such progress in the execution of the work as to indicate its completion within the time specified in this Contract or within the time to which the completion of the Contract may have been extended by the Department*, the

* Or Board or The Authority.

Department* may notify the Contractor to discontinue all work or any part thereof under this Contract by a written notice to be served upon the Contractor, as hereinbefore provided, and a copy of said notice may be served upon his Surety, or its authorized agent. Within two (2) weeks from the date of such notice, the Contractor shall discontinue the work or such part thereof as the Department* shall designate, whereupon the Surety may, at its option, assume this Contract, or that portion thereof on which the Department* has ordered the Contractor to discontinue the work, and proceed to perform the same and may, with the written consent of the Department*, sublet the work so taken over; provided, however, that the Surety shall exercise its option, if at all, within two (2) weeks after written notice to discontinue the work has been served upon the Contractor and upon the Surety or its authorized agent. The Surety, in such event, shall take the Contractor's place in all respects, and shall be paid by the Commonwealth for all work performed by it in accordance with the terms of this Contract and if the Surety, under the provisions hereof, shall assume said entire Contract, all moneys remaining due the Contractor at the time of his default shall thereupon become due and payable to the Surety as the work progresses, subject to all of the terms of this Contract.

In case the Surety does not, within the hereinbefore specified time, exercise its right and option to assume this Contract, or that portion thereof on which the Department* has ordered the Contractor to discontinue work, then the Department* shall have the power to complete, by contract or otherwise as it may determine, the work herein described or such part thereof as it may deem necessary, and the Contractor agrees that the Department* shall have the right to take possession of and use any of the materials, plant, tools, equipment, supplies, and property of every kind provided by the Contractor for the purpose of his work, and to procure other tools, equipment, and materials for the completion of the same, and to charge to the Contractor the expense of said contracts, labor, materials, tools and equipment, and expenses incident thereto.

The expense so charged shall be deducted by the Department* out of such moneys as may be due or may at any time become due the Contractor under any by virtue of the Contract or any part thereof. The Department* shall not be required to obtain the lowest figures for the work of completing the contract, but the expense to be deducted shall be the actual cost of such work. In case such expense is less than the sum which would have been payable under

* Or Board or The Authority.

this Contract if the same had been completed by the Contractor, then the Contractor shall be entitled to receive the difference; and in case such expense shall exceed the amount which would have been payable under the Contract if the same had been completed by the Contractor, then the Contractor shall pay the amount of such excess to the Department* on notice from the Department* of the excess so due, but such excess shall not exceed the amount due under this Contract at the time the Contractor is notified to discontinue said work or any part thereof, plus the amount of the Bond(s) executed by the Contractor for the performance of this Contract. When any particular part of the work is being carried on by the Department*, by contract or otherwise under the provisions of this section, the Contractor shall continue the remainder of the work in conformity with the terms of this Contract and in such manner as in no way to hinder or interfere with the persons or workmen employed, as above provided by the Department*.

B   *Termination for Convenience of the Commonwealth*—It is understood and agreed that the Department* may, at any time during the term hereof, cancel and terminate this Contract in whole or in part, and award such compensation as in the Department's* best judgment is fair and reasonable; subject, however, to appeal by the Contractor to the Board of Arbitration of Claims as provided in paragraph 6.12.

5.9   CONTRACTOR'S LIABILITY

The work in every respect, from the execution of the Contract and during its progress until final acceptance, shall be under the charge and in care of the Contractor and at his risk. The foregoing sentence is intended to include risks of every kind and description, including fire and flood risks.

He shall properly safeguard against any or all injury or damage to the public, or to property of any kind, and shall alone be responsible for any such damage or injury.

The Contractor shall save harmless the political subdivision(s) concerned, the Department*, the Commonwealth, and all their officers, agents, and employees, from any suits or claims of every name or description brought against them for and on account of any injury or damage to person or property received or sustained by any person or persons, by or from the Contractor, or any duly authorized subcontractor, or any agent, employee or workman by or on account of work done under this Contract, or any extensions or additions thereto, whether caused by negligence

* Or Board or The Authority.

or not, or by or in consequence of any negligence in guarding the same, or by its construction, or by or on account of any accident, or of any act of omission of the Contractor, or any duly authorized subcontractor or any agent, employee or workman.

The Contractor agrees that so much of the money due him under this Contract as shall be considered necessary by the Department* may be retained until all suits or claims for damages, as aforesaid, have been settled and evidence to this effect has been furnished to the Department*.

5.10   HINDRANCES AND DELAYS

The risks and uncertainties in connection with the work are assumed by the Contractor as a part of this Contract, and are compensated for in the Contract price for the work. The Contractor, except as otherwise definitely specified in this Contract, shall bear all loss or damage from hindrances or delays from any cause during the progress of any portion of the work embraced in this Contract, including all loss or damage arising out of the nature of the work to be done, or from the action of the elements, inclement weather, and floods, or from any unforeseen and unexpected conditions or circumstances encountered in connection with the work, or from any cause whatever, and except as otherwise definitely specified in this Contract, no charge other than that included in the Contract price for the work shall be made by the Contractor against the Department* for such loss or damage.

Should the work be stopped by order of the Department* for any cause other than those authorized in this Contract, then and in that event, such expense as, in the opinion of the Department*, is caused to the Contractor hereby other than the legitimate cost of carrying on this contract shall be paid by the Commonwealth.

5.11   PURCHASE AND DELIVERY OF SUPPLIES, EQUIPMENT, AND MATERIALS

The Contractor shall not purchase any supplies, equipment, or materials manufactured in any State which prohibits the specification of or use in or on its public buildings or other works, or the purchase of supplies, equipment, or materials not manufactured in such State. Materials to be used in the permanent portion of the work shall have been produced in the United States unless specifically otherwise approved. Materials to be used for work under this Contract shall be delivered sufficiently in advance of their proposed use to prevent delays, and they shall be delivered approximately in the order required.

---

* Or Board or The Authority.

5.12   INFRINGEMENTS OF PATENTS

The Contractor shall be held responsible for any claims made against the Department* or the Commonwealth for any infringement of patents by his use of patented articles or methods in the performance and completion of the work, or any patented process connected with the work agreed to be performed under the Contract, or of any patented materials used upon the said work, and shall save harmless the Department* and the Commonwealth from all claims against them, by reason of any infringement or alleged infringement of patents used in the construction and completion of the work.

5.13   PROTECTION AGAINST CLAIMS FOR LABOR AND MATERIALS

The Contractor agrees that he will save harmless the Department* and the Commonwealth, from all claims against them for material furnished or work done under this Contract.

It is further agreed by the Contractor that he shall, if so requested, furnish the Department* with satisfactory evidence that all persons, who have done work or furnished material under this Contract have been duly paid for such work or material and, in case such evidence is demanded and not furnished as aforesaid, such amount as may, in the opinion of the Department*, be necessary to meet the claim of the persons aforesaid, may be retained from the money due the Contractor under this Contract, until satisfactory evidence be furnished that all liabilities have been fully discharged.

When required by the laws of Pennsylvania, moneys due the Contractor shall be retained for protection against claims.

5.14   MATERIAL SAMPLES REQUIRING LABORATORY TESTS

Where required in the Specifications or on the Drawings, tests which are to be performed at the expense of the Contractor shall be conducted by a material supplier or by an independent testing laboratory, either or both of which shall be subject to the approval of the Department*. The test results shall be forwarded in duplicate directly to the Department*. The Contractor shall pay all costs of the tests for which he is responsible including sampling, packing, shipping, and laboratory fees. No separate payment will be made for the cost of testing, which shall be included in the appropriate Contract unit price. The Department* reserves the right to perform additional tests at its own expense and to use such tests as a basis of approval or rejection regardless of previous decisions.

* Or Board or The Authority.

5.15   REMEDY GUARANTEE PERIOD

The Contractor shall remedy, without cost to the Department*, any defects which may develop within one year from date of completion and acceptance of the work performed under this Contract, provided said defects, in the judgment of the Department*, are caused by defective or inferior materials or workmanship.

SECTION 6
PAYMENT

6.1   PAYMENT COVERAGE

The Contractor agrees to accept as full compensation, satisfaction, and discharge for all work done and all materials furnished, whether mentioned in the Proposal and Specifications or not, and for all costs and expenses incurred and damages sustained, and for each and every matter, thing, or act performed, furnished, or suffered in the full and complete performance and completion of the work of the Contract in accordance with terms, conditions, and provisions thereof and of the instructions, orders, and directions of the Engineer thereunder, except extra work which shall be paid for as provided in Section 6.7 of these Specifications and except as in the Contract otherwise specifically provided, the unit or lump sum prices stated in the Agreement.

6.2   PAYMENT ONLY IN ACCORDANCE WITH CONTRACT

The Contractor shall not demand, nor be entitled to receive, payment for the work or materials, or any portion thereof, except in the manner set forth in the Contract and after the Engineer shall have given a certificate for such payment.

6.3   DELAYED PAYMENTS

Should any payments due the Contractor on any Estimate be delayed beyond the time stipulated, such delay shall not constitute a breach of Contract, or be the basis of a claim for damages.

6.4   PROGRESS ESTIMATES

A   (1) The Engineer shall, from time to time during the active progress of the work, at intervals of approximately once a month, make a determination of all work done and materials incorporated into the work by the Contractor up to that time, and shall prepare a Progress Estimate, in writing, showing the value of such work.

* Or Board or The Authority.

(2) In addition, the Engineer may, at his discretion, make an estimate, based upon invoices or delivery tickets, of the amount of money represented by the materials so delivered, in storage on the job site but not incorporated in the work. This payment shall not exceed 75% of the material cost.

(3) The Engineer will determine any other amounts due the Contractor.

(4) The Engineer will enumerate all deductions to be charged against the Contract in accordance with the provisions of the Contract.

(5) The Engineer will then compute the resulting Balance from amounts derived as directed above.

B   From this Balance will be deducted ten percent (10%) of such Balance up and including the time when fifty percent (50%) of the Contract shall have been completed; this deduction will remain in possession of the Commonwealth until the project shall have been completed and accepted, at which time the amount previously deducted and retained shall then be five percent (5%) of the Contract price.

C   After fifty percent (50%) of the work shall have been completed, Progress Estimates will continue to be made, and payments will continue to be made to the Contractor at the proper times, but with no further deductions from any Balance, except as provided in 6.4A foregoing and 6.4D below.

D   However, the Department* reserves the right to revise the percentages to be retained subject to the following conditions:

(1) If, in the opinion of the Department*, a larger or additional percentage is required to be retained to protect its interests, the Department* shall be authorized to make such additional deduction.

(2) If, in the opinion of the Department*, a smaller percentage will be sufficient to protect its interests and provided that the Contract has been at least ninety percent (90%) completed, the retained percentage may be reduced but shall in no case be less than two percent (2%) of the total Contract amount.

E   Such Progress Estimates shall not be required to be made by strict measurements, but they may be made either by measurements or by approximations. Progress Estimates may at any time be omitted if, in the opinion of the Engineer, the protection of the Department* so requires.

F   In case work is nearly suspended, or in case only unimportant progress is being made, the Engineer may, at

* Or Board or The Authority.

his discretion, make Progress Estimates at longer intervals than once a month.

G   Upon such Progress Estimate being made and certified by the Contractor in writing to the Department*, the Department* shall certify to the Auditor General for payment, the amount due the Contractor under such estimate, provided, however, that the Department* may at all times reserve and retain from such amount, in addition to the amount retained under paragraph 6.4B foregoing, any sum or sums which, by the terms hereof or of any law of the Commonwealth of Pennsylvania, it is, or may be, authorized to reserve or retain.

H   It is specifically understood and agreed that protection of any materials in storage on the job site on which payments have been made in accordance with paragraph 6.4A(2) shall be the sole responsibility of the Contractor. Should the materials be pilfered, damaged, or removed from the job site in any manner, subsequent deductions shall be appropriately made by the Engineer and computed in said Balance. The Contractor shall not incorporate in the work, any materials damaged during storage or in any other manner.

6.5   DETERMINATION OF QUANTITIES

The Engineer shall make all measurements and determine all quantities and amounts of work and materials done or furnished under this Contract.

6.6   MODIFICATION OF SPECIFICATIONS AND DRAWINGS BY WRITTEN AGREEMENT

Subject to the provisions of subsection 5.6, the Specifications and Drawings herein referred to may be modified and changed from time to time as may be agreed to in writing between the Department* and the Contractor in a manner not materially affecting the substance thereof, if such changes are necessary to carry out and complete more fully and perfectly the work agreed to be done and performed. If such changes and modifications materially increase the unit cost of the work, the increased expense will be paid by the Department*, as provided herein.

   If such modifications and changes diminish the unit cost of the work, the amount of said diminution may be retained or withheld by the Department*. No consequent loss of anticipated profit on work not executed will be paid to the Contractor.

6.7   EXTRA WORK

If, during the performance of this Contract, it shall become necessary or desirable for the proper completion of the work

* Or Board or The Authority.

under this Contract to order additional work done or materials furnished which, in the opinion of the Department*, are not included in the original Contract, the Contractor shall, if ordered in writing by the Department*, do and perform such work and furnish such materials. Any such additional work will be done as Extra Work at a price to be previously agreed upon in writing by the Contractor and the Department*. Where a lump sum or a unit price cannot be agreed upon by both parties, or where this method of payment is impracticable, the Engineer may order the Contractor to do such Extra Work on a "Force Account" basis.

All Extra Work done on a "Force Account" basis will be paid for in the following manner:

A *Labor*—For all labor, including equipment operators and foreman in direct charge of the specific operation, the Contractor shall receive the current local rate of wage per hour, to be agreed upon in writing before starting such work, for each and every hour that said labor and foreman area actually engaged in such work, plus fifteen percent (15%) in addition thereto.

The Contractor will also be allowed to add to such direct labor and foreman costs the percentage rates paid for the following items:

Social Security Tax at the percentage legally required.
Unemployment Tax at the percentage legally required.
Workman's Compensation Insurance at the policy percentage rate.
Contractor's Public Liability Insurance at the policy percentage rate.
Contractor's Property Damage Liability Insurance at the policy percentage rate, including coverage for damage due to blasting and explosions when such additional coverage is secured on projects where blasting is required.

The 15% hereinbefore noted shall not be added to these tax and insurance items.

B *Materials*—For all materials furnished and used the Contractor shall receive the actual cost of such materials, including freight charges, as shown by original receipted bills, to which cost shall be added a sum equal to ten percent (10%).

C *Equipment*—For any machinery, trucks or equipment (exclusive of operators), except small tools and equipment for which no rental is allowed, which it may be deemed necessary or desirable to use, the Engineer shall allow the Contractor a reasonable rate of hire for rental prices for machinery, trucks, or equipment, which shall include fuel and lubricants, to be agreed upon in writing before such work is begun, for each and every hour that such ma-

* Or Board or The Authority.

chinery, truck, or equipment is in use on such work, and to which sum no percentage shall be added.

The compensation as herein provided shall be received by the Contractor as payment in full for Extra Work done on a "Force Account" basis, the fifteen percent (15%) which is allowed on the working force and the ten percent (10%) which is allowed on materials being made and accepted to cover all general superintendence, use of small tools and equipment for which no rental is allowed, camp, job, and general overhead, bonding, expenses, and anticipated profit. The Contractor's representative and the Engineer shall compare records of Extra Work done on a "Force Account" basis at the end of each day. All claims for Extra Work done on a "Force Account" basis shall be submitted to the Engineer by the Contractor upon certified triplicate statements to which shall be attached original receipted bills covering the cost of, and the freight charges on, all materials furnished and used in such work, and said statement shall be filed during the month following that in which the work is actually performed. Should the Contractor refuse to prosecute the work as directed or should he refuse to submit his claim as required, then the Department* may withhold payment of all estimates until the Contractor's refusal or failure is eliminated.

D   *Subcontracts*—Force account work may be performed by a subcontractor only when the type of work involved is specialized and is deemed, in the opinion of the Department*, outside the scope of work normally performed under general construction contracts.

Subcontractors for force account work will be approved only when specifically authorized in writing by the Department*. The work performed by the subcontractor shall conform to Contract requirements.

Payment for work performed by subcontractors will be based upon actual labor, materials, and equipment supplied. Subcontracts on a lump sum basis will not be accepted as a component of force account work. Payment to the Contractor will be made only as specified in subsections A, B and C above. No additional allowance or mark-up will be paid on a percentage basis and the ten percent (10%) for materials and fifteen percent (15%) for labor which includes overhead, profit, etc., will be paid only once and will include overhead, profit, etc. for both subcontractor and prime contractor.

6.8   FINAL EXAMINATION AND ACCEPTANCE

As soon as practicable after the completion of the entire project, a thorough examination thereof will be made by the Engineer at

* Or Board or The Authority.

the site of the work. If such work is found to comply fully with the requirements of the Contract, it will be accepted and final payment therefore will be made in accordance with paragraph 6.9 of the Specifications.

6.9 FINAL PAYMENT

Whenever, in the opinion of the Engineer, the work covered by this Contract has been completed, the Engineer shall so certify in writing to the Department* and shall submit a final estimate showing the total amount of work done by the Contractor and its value under and according to the terms of this Contract; any other amounts due the Contractor; all deductions made in accordance under such provisions of the Contract; and the amount due the Contractor on the final estimate. Provided, however, that before the Contractor shall be entitled to payment of such amount, the Contractor shall execute and file with the Department* a release, in proper form, of all claims against the Department* on account of this Contract, except for the Contractor's equity in the amounts kept or retained under the terms of this Contract; and except any other claims that have theretofore been filed in accordance with the provisions of the Contract, which are listed and itemized in detail in a statement attached to and made a part of such release, giving reasons for, nature of, and amount of, each claim so listed.

6.10 MONEY RETAINED FOR DEFECTS AND DAMAGES

The Contractor shall pay to the Department*, all expenses, losses and damages, as determined by the Department*, incurred in consequence of any defect, omission, or mistake of the Contractor or his employees, of the making good thereof, and the Department* may apply any moneys which otherwise would be payable at any time under this Contract to the payment thereof.

Imperfect or damaged work shall be repaired or replaced where feasible, but if the imperfection in the opinion of the Department* shall not be of such magnitude or importance as to necessitate, or be of such nature as to make impracticable or dangerous or undesirable the re-execution of the imperfect part, then the Department* shall have the right to make such reduction as may be just and reasonable from the amounts due or to become due the Contractor, instead of requiring the imperfect work to be redone.

6.11 CLAIMS FOR DAMAGES

It is agreed that if the Contractor shall claim compensation for any alleged damage by reason of the acts or omissions of the

* Or Board or The Authority.

Department* or its agents, he shall, within ten (10) days after sustaining of such damage make a written statement to the Department* of the nature of the alleged damage. On or before the last day of the month succeeding that in which any such damage is claimed to have been sustained, the Contractor shall file with the Department* an itemized statement of the details and amound of such damage and, upon request of the Department*, shall give access to all books of account, receipts, vouchers, bills of lading, and other books or papers containing any evidence of the amount of such damage. Unless such statement shall be filed as thus required, his claim for compensation shall be forfeited and invalidated, and he shall not be entitled to payment on account of any such damage.

6.12 BOARD OF ARBITRATION OF CLAIMS

"WHEREAS, Act No. 193, of the General Assembly, approved May 20, 1937, creates a Board of Arbitration of Claims which shall have exclusive power to dispose of all final claims involving contracts between the Commonwealth and all persons who furnish any labor, material, supplies, furniture, books, stationery, or any other personal effects or services whatsoever, and whose awards shall be final and without right of appeal, it is hereby further agreed that this Contract is executed with full knowledge, accord, and binding force of all the provisions of the above stated act."

GENERAL CONDITIONS
ADDENDA

INSURANCE

PUBLIC LIABILITY AND PROPERTY DAMAGE INSURANCE

1.   The CONTRACTOR shall take out and maintain during the life of this Contract or extension thereof, such Public Liability and Property Damage Insurance as shall protect him, and any subcontractor performing work covered by this Contract, from claims for damage for personal injury, including wrongful death, as well from claims for property damages, which may arise from operations under this Contract, whether such operation by himself or by any subcontractor or anyone directly or indirectly employed by either of them.

2.   The CONTRACTOR by his execution of this Contract, does certify that he has taken out sufficient Public Liability and Property Damage Insurance, to protect himself or any

* Or Board or The Authority.

subcontractor or anyone directly or indirectly employed by either of them, against claims as set forth above.

3.   The CONTRACTOR by his execution of this Contract, does certify that he has furnished and paid for all insurance on all work included in the Contract, in the total amount of the Contract Price, against loss or damage by fire and lightning and the extended coverages, in the names of the COMMONWEALTH OF PENNSYLVANIA and the CONTRACTOR as their respective interests may appear.

4.   All policies shall be issued by the Insurance Companies authorized to conduct such business under the laws of the COMMONWEALTH OF PENNSYLVANIA, and shall run until date of final acceptance of the work. Policies expiring at a fixed date before final acceptance of the work must be renewed and refiled before such date.

OBSERVANCE OF LAWS AND REGULATIONS

The CONTRACTOR shall observe all laws and regulations pertaining to his work, including regulations of the DEPARTMENT OF LABOR AND INDUSTRY, the DEPARTMENT OF HEALTH, and any other local laws and ordinances, and shall furnish, as required, any permits, licenses and certificates and pay any fees incidental thereto.

INSPECTION, CHANGE AND PAYMENT

All work shall be subject to inspection and acceptance by the DEPARTMENT. The DEPARTMENT shall have the right to make changes in the quantities and character of the work involved, adjustments of the Contract Amount to be on the basis of agreed Unit Price, Lump Sum Price or Force Account.

Upon completion, final inspection and acceptance of the work, the CONTRACTOR will be paid the total amount of the Contract, subject to any authorized additions to or deductions from the amount.

ARBITRATION

All questions or disputes arising between the parties hereto respecting any matter pertaining to this Contract or any part thereof, or any breach of said Contract arising thereunder, shall be referred to the Attorney General of the COMMONWEALTH OF PENNSYLVANIA (under Section 2408, of the Administrative Code of 1929) the Board of Arbitration of Claims (as set forth in Act of May 20, 1937, P.L. 728, whichever the claimant shall elect, whose decision and award shall be final, binding and conclusive upon all parties hereto, without exception or appeal, and all rights or any action at alw or in equity and by virtue of this

* Or Board or The Authority.

Contract, and all matters connected with and relative thereto are hereby expressly waived. Reference to questions under this Arbitration Provision must be prior to the final payment to the CONTRACTOR or CONTRACTORS.

APPROVALS

The CONTRACTOR shall not sublet any part of this Contract without written approval of the COMMONWEALTH. He shall also submit for written approval, a list of all materials and equipment he proposes to use.

RECIPROCAL LIMITATIONS UPON USE OF SUPPLIES AND MATERIALS

The CONTRACTOR shall not use any supplies, equipment, or materials manufactured in any State which prohibits the specification for, or in or on its public buildings or other works, of supplies, equipment or materials not manufactured in such State.

LABOR REQUIREMENTS

All laws of the COMMONWEALTH pertaining to regulations and conditions of employment shall be observed, including Labor Discrimination Act 382, approved July 18, 1935, Act No. 414, approved July 19, 1935 (requiring ninety (90) days residence of labor within the State) applicable to building construction.

PREVAILING MINIMUM WAGE

The CONTRACTOR is hereby notified that this Contract is subject to the provisions, duties, obligations, remedies and penalties of the Pennsylvania Prevailing Wage Act No. 442, August 15, 1961, P.L. 987, as amended August 9, 1963, under Act 342; and the said Act is incorporated herein by reference thereto as if fully set forth herein.

In compliance with said Pennsylvania Prevailing Wage Act, the Prevailing Minimum Wage Predetermination is hereto attached and made part hereof as approved by the SECRETARY, of the PENNSYLVANIA DEPARTMENT OF LABOR AND INDUSTRY. If estimated bid is less than $25,000, this predetermination does not apply and will not be attached.

WITHDRAWAL OF BIDS

Bids may be withdrawn on written or telegraphic request received from bidders prior to the time fixed for opening.

* Or Board or The Authority.

appendix 6
examples of standard reference specifications

* Guide Specifications for Construction of Hot Plant Mix
Tennis Courts
* Standard Specification for One Type of Road Surface
Course

GUIDE SPECIFICATIONS FOR CONSTRUCTION OF HOT PLANT MIX TENNIS COURTS*

NOTICE: These proposed specifications are merely guides for use by architects, engineers, contractors, and potential tennis court and track owners. It is hoped that these specifications will be of particular value to those who do not have a detailed knowledge cf the construction of tennis court and tract facilities and that they will aid in maintaining high construction standards. U.S. Tennis Court and Track Builders Association and its members and employees do not warrant the specifications as proper under all conditions.

1. GENERAL REQUIREMENTS
    a. *Scope of Work to be Done.*   The contract work to be performed under these specifications consists of furnishing all of the required labor, materials, equipment, implements, parts, and supplies necessary for, or appurtenant to, the installation of tennis court(s) at (insert street address of the construction site), (insert names of city and state), for (insert name of Owner) in accordance with the drawings appearing hereinafter or annexed hereto and as further elaborated in these specifications.

    b. *Standards.*   The work hereunder shall be done in a thorough, workmanlike manner and conform to standards for tennis court construction as prescribed or approved by the U.S. Tennis Court Builders Association. Any reference to a specification or designation of the American Society for Testing and Materials, Federal Specifications, or other standards, codes, or orders refers to the most recent or latest specification or designation. Where names of specific products may be designated in these specifications or in the details appearing on the drawings the intent is to state the general type and quality of product desired without ruling out use of other products of equal type and quality provided that use of such other products of equal type and quality has been approved in writing by the Owner or his representative.
    c. *Layout of Work.*   The work shall be laid out to true lines and grades in full accord with the drawings. Surveying of lines and grades from a base line and bench mark established by the Owner at the construction site, and staking therefore shall be accomplished by the Contractor. Monuments shall be

substantially established, protected, and maintained in place by the Contractor for the duration of the contract or until such other time as their removal may be authorized by the Owner or his representative.

d. *Electrical Power and Water.*   The Owner shall furnish adequate electrical power and water at and upon the construction site for the performance of this work. The Contractor shall furnish, install, maintain, and remove any temporary lines of wiring or any temporary piping that additionally may be required.

e. *Protection of the Public.*   The Contractor shall erect the maintain barricades, canopies, guards, lights, and warning signs to the extent required by law for protection of the public.

f. *Permits and Taxes.*   The Owner shall obtain and pay for all construction permits, fees, licenses, etc. as may be required by law. The Contractor's contract sum shall include such federal, state, and local taxes as may be applicable to the performance of the contract.

g. *Insurance.*   The Contractor shall provide reasonable and adequate casualty insurance including employer's liability and public liability insurance and include the cost thereof in the contract sum.

h. *Guarantee.*   The Contractor and any subcontractors hereunder guarantee their respective work against defective materials or workmanship for a period of (   ) from date of filing notice of completion by the Contractor and acceptance by the Owner.

2. SITE INSPECTION AND PREPARATION

a. *Inspection and Selection.*   The site shall have een inspected by the Owner or his representative and determined by them to be suitable for construction of the tennis court(s) specified herein. Inspection shall include examination of the soil by a professional soil engineer to establish its suitability as a foundation for the court(s).

b. *Clearing and Grubbing.*   Trees and other vegetation including their root systems to a depth of not less than twelve inches (12″) shall be removed from the site and the soil treated with a sterilant that will effectively inhibit future growth of flora.

c. *Excavation and Filling.*   The site shall be excavated and filled so as to provide the finished grades shown on drawings for the tennis court areas. Excavated areas occurring directly under and adjacent to tennis court areas shall be compacted to the same density required for the fill material specified hereinbelow.

d. *Fill Material.*   Fill material where required shall be as approved by the Owner or his representative and shall

(Continued)

be placed in layers not exceeding six inches (6″) each in thickness and compacted to 95 per cent standard density at optimum moisture in accordance with ASTM D698.

    e. *Subgrade.* The subgrade shall be shaped to true and even lines so as to assure a uniform thickness of the base course required under paved areas as shown on the drawings. Surface of the subgrade shall not be more than three-fourths inch (¾″) above or below the subgrade elevation shown on drawings.

3. STORM DRAINAGE PROVISIONS

    a. *Local Ordinances and Regulations.* Work hereunder shall conform to applicable local ordinances and regulations respecting storm drain specifications or special provisions therefor.

    b. *Interceptor Drainage System.* A peripheral drainage system shall be installed as may be necessary and detailed on drawings to intercept and drain either surface or subsurface water that would otherwise drain over or under the court(s).

    c. *Trench Backfills.* Any trench backfill areas occurring under or adjacent to tennis court areas shall be composed of a suitable earth material compacted to the same density as the surrounding soil.

4. SLOPE REQUIREMENT

    a. *Slope Requirement.* All excavating, filling, compacting, grading, and leveling work required hereunder shall be performed so that the finished court surface slopes one inch (1″) in each ten feet (10′) on a true plane from side to side, end to end, or corner to corner as indicated on the drawings.

5. PERIMETER EDGING

        (Optional—but RECOMMENDED)

    a. *Curb Wall.* An edging of (specify one: brick, concrete, steel, or treated wood) as detailed on drawings shall be installed around entire perimeter of the court area. Sections may be left open to allow trucks and other equipment to enter and leave the court area until other work specified herein has been completed. Top elevation of the edging shall be exactly one-half inch (½″) below the finished grade level and the court's surface course shall be tapered from six inches (6″) out to meet it.

6. BASE CONSTRUCTION

    a. *Material.* A base course of (specify one: bituminous asphaltic mixture, crushed aggregate; hot-mixed, hot-laid asphaltic concrete; or penetration macadam) as indicated on drawings shall be installed over the subgrade detailed hereinbefore. The specified material shall meet applicable ASTM specifications. Compacted thickness shall be as shown on drawings to satisfy local soil and climatic conditions but in no case shall the thickness be less than the equivalent of four inches (4″) of thoroughly compacted crushed rock.

b. *Spreading.* The material shall be spread by methods and in a manner proposed by the Contractor to produce a uniform density and thickness and the grades and dimensions shown on drawings and elaborated hereinafter.

c. *Compaction.* The material as thus spread shall be compacted by rolling with a powered steel wheel tandem roller weighing not less than eight (8) nor more than ten (10) tons or by other equipment producing equivalent density. Surface of the base course as thus compacted shall not vary from the specified grade more than one-half inch (½″) in ten feet (10′) measured in any direction.

7. LEVELING COURSE

a. *General Description.* A leveling course of hot plant mix having a maximum aggregate size of three-eighths inch (⅜″) to three-fourths inch (¾″) in accordance with specifications of the Asphalt Institute shall be constructed over the base course to a compacted thickness of not less than one inch (1″) as indicated on drawings.

b. *Spreading.* This hot plant mix shall be spread by methods and in manner proposed by the Contractor to meet the tolerances specified herein.

c. *Compaction.* The mix as thus spread shall be thoroughly compacted by rolling with a powered steel wheel tandem roller weighing not less than two (2) nor more than six (6) tons. The finished surface of the leveling course shall not vary from the specified grade more than one-fourth inch (¼″)in ten feet (10′) when measured in any direction.

8. SURFACE COURSE

a. *General Description.* A surface course of a hot plant mix having a maximum aggregate size of three-eighths inch (⅜″) in accordance with specifications of the Asphalt Institute shall be constructed over the leveling course to a compacted thickness of not less than one-half inch (½″) as shown on the drawings.

b. *Spreading.* This hot plant mix shall be spread by methods and in a manner proposed by the Contractor to meet the tolerances specified herein.

c. *Compacting.* The mix as thus laid shall be thoroughly compacted by rolling with a powered steel wheel tandem roller weighing not less than two (2) nor more

(Continued)

than six (6) tons. The finished surface of the surface course shall not vary from the specified grade more than one-eighth inch (⅛″) in ten feet (10′) when measured in any direction.

9.   NET AND EQUIPMENT

    a.   *Post Foundations.*   Post foundations shall be not less than twenty-four inches (24″) in diameter at the top, not less than thirty inches (30″) in diameter at the bottom, and not less than thirty-six inches (36″) in depth. Foundations shall be so situated as to provide a clear distance between posts of thirty-three feet (33′) on single courts and forty-two feet (42′) on double courts. Concrete for foundations shall be mixed in ratios of six (6) standard 94-pound sacks of cement per cubic yard of concrete, with one (1) such sack of cement to not more than six (6) U.S. gallons of water, attaining a compressive strength of not less than three thousand five hundred (3,500) pounds per square inch at the twenty-eighth (28th) day after pouring. Foundations shall be so designed and poured and the posts so set as not to cause cracking or other damage to the finished court surface.

    b.   *Net Posts and Sleeves.*   Net posts shall be galvanized steel having an outside diameter of not less than two and seven-eighths inches (2⅞″) and shall be equipped with lever- or ratchet-type net tightening devices for nonmetallic nets. Posts and the sleeves therefore shall be set where indicated on drawings. Posts shall be set plumb and true so as to support the net at a height of forty-two inches (42″) above the court surface at the net posts.

    c.   *Center Strap Anchor.*   A center strap anchor shall be positioned as shown on the drawings and set in concrete footings measuring twelve inches by twelve inches by twelve inches (12″ × 12″ × 12″).

    d.   *Net.*   A tennis net measuring forty-two feet (42′) long and three and one-fourth feet (3¼″) wide and otherwise conforming to regulations of the United States Lawn Tennis Association shall be provided for each court. Netting portion of net shall be synthetic netting material treated by a black synthetic treatment to maintain a tensile strength of not less than two hundred seventy-five (275) pounds. Top binding of net shall have a double thickness and the outer thickness thereof shall be fabricated of a white synthetic material treated for resistance to sunlight and mildew. Bottom and end tapes of net shall be fabricated of a black synthetic material treated to prevent deterioration from sunlight. Net when erected shall be suspended from its top binding upon a vinyl-coated wire cable having a diameter of seven thirty-seconds inch ($\frac{7}{32}''$), measuring forty-seven (47') feet in length, and having a tensile strength of not less than one thousand three hundred (1,300) pounds. Each corner of net shall have a tie string for securing net to posts. Tie strings shall be synthetic material having a tensile strength of not less than one thousand seven hundred (1,700) pounds.

10. COLOR FINISH COURSE
   a. *Final Surface Inspection.* Prior to application of a color finish system the court surface shall be flooded with water and allowed to drain. Any depressions thereupon holding water deeper than one-sixteenth inch ($\frac{1}{16}''$) shall be patched and leveled in accordance with recommendations of the manufacturer of the color finish material specified hereinafter.
   b. *Color Finish Material.* Color finish material for the surface course shall be (insert name of preferred material) as manufactured by (insert name of manufacturer), (insert street address), (insert names of city and state). The color finish material shall be compatible with the surface course material. The manufacturer shall guarantee the material for one (1) year from date of finished application against chalking, checking, fading, discoloration, or other adverse effects from ultra violet rays of the sun, from weather moisture, or from weather temperatures. The material shall be devlivered to the construction site in its original unopened containers clearly labeled with trade name and name of manufacturer.
   c. *Application.* The color finish course shall be applied only after the surface course is thoroughly dry. The color finish material shall be applied to the surface course areas in multiple applications in the selected and approved colors as shown on the drawings so as to form a true, uniform texture and color. Applications work shall be performed by skilled mechanics in a workmanlike manner in accordance with the manufacturer's standard printed instructions; however, no work shall be performed when rain is imminent or when the temperature is below 55 degrees Farenheit.

11. PLAYING LINES
   a. *Playing Lines.* Base lines shall not be more than four inches (4'') wide and playing lines not more than two inches (2'') wide, accurately located and marked in accordance with rules of the United States Tennis Association, and painted with a paint recommended or

(Continued)

approved by the manufacturer of the color finish material; however, use of traffic, oil, alkyd, or solvent-vehicle type paints is prohibited. The painting shall be done by skilled mechanics in a workmanlike manner in accordance with the manufacturer's standard printed instructions.

STANDARD SPECIFICATION FOR ONE TYPE OF ROAD SURFACE COURSE*

SECTION 430   BITUMINOUS SURFACE COURSE FB-2

430.1   DESCRIPTION   This work shall consist of constructing two courses of plant-mixed bituminous concrete on a prepared base course in ccordance with these specifications and within reasonably close conformity to the lines, grades, width, and depth shown on the drawings and as specified.

The two courses of plant-mixed bituminous concrete shall consist of wearing course having a depth of 1 inch and a binder course having a depth of 2 inches.

430.2   MATERIALS

(a)   Bituminous Material.   The bituminous material shall conform to the applicable requirements of Bulletin No. 25 and shall be one of the following:

1.   Class of Bituminous Material and Mixing Temperatures

Class of Material	Type of Material	Mixing Temperature °F Minimum	Maximum
AC-2000	Asphalt cement	265	300
RC-250	Cut-back asphalt	150	190
RC-800	Cut-back asphalt	175	210
NRC-250	Cut-back native asphalt	150	190
NRC-800	Cut-back native asphalt	170	210
E-5	Cationic emulsified asphalt	100	160
E-6	Emulsified asphalt	70	150
RCE-250	Emulsified cut-back asphalt		175
RCE-800	Emulsified cut-back asphalt		175
RT-6-C	Coal tar cut-back	130	175
TR-6-W	Water gas tar cut-back	130	175
RT-9-W	Water gas tar cement	175	220
RT-10-C	Coal tar cement	200	240
RT-10-W	Water gas tar cement	200	240

Extreme precaution must be taken to avoid all possibility of fire when any of the cut-back asphalts are used in the mixture or when raw naphtha is used with asphalt cement.

Cut-back asphalt or emulsified cut-back asphalt shall be chemically treated with a prepared additive as specified in Bulletin No. 25. All bituminous material shall be heated within the required temperature range, but not in excess of the maximum temperature specified for the class of material used.

2.   Petroleum Naphtha.   The naphtha shall be an asphalt base petroleum distillate, which, when distilled in accordance with

* Department of Transportation, Commonwealth of Pennsylvania. *Form 408 Specifications,* Harrisburg, Pa., 1973, pp. 273–277.

(Continued)

ASTM Designation D86, shall comply with the following:

DISTILLATION REQUIREMENTS

Distillation	Minimum	Maximum
10% by volume		300F
50% by volume	280F	350F
95% by volume		435F
Residue by volume		2.0%

Petroleum naphtha shall be used only in conjunction with asphalt cement Class AC-2000. It shall be accurately measured by volume by an approved gaging or metering device, and the additions of the naphtha shall be on the basis of volume-weight relationship.

(b)   Aggregates.

1.   Fine Aggregate.   The fine aggregate shall meet the requirements of Section 703.2.

2.   Course Aggregate.   The coarse aggregate in the wearing and binder courses shall be Type A stone, gravel, or slag, meeting the requirements of Section 703.3 for No. 1B and No. 2B material, modified as follows:

The No. 1B coarse aggregate shall have a minimum of 20% passing the No. 4 sieve and the No. 2B coarse aggregate shall have a minimum of 40% passing the ½ inch sieve.

(c)   Composition of Mixtures.   The quantity of bituminous residue on the coarse aggregate shall conform to the following table:

BITUMINOUS RESIDUE, PERCENT BY WEIGHT (Minimum)

Wearing Course		Binder Course	
No. 1B Stone or Gravel	Slag	No. 2B Stone or Gravel	Slag
4.2	5.7	3.0	3.5

The bituminous material shall thoroughly coat the aggregate, and shall form a film of sufficient thickness to furnish the desired binding properties and meet with the approval of the engineer. When necessary to dry the aggregate, the temperature of the aggregate prior to its mixing with the bituminous materials shall not exceed 110F.

The fine aggregate used with all classes of bituminous material shall be dry. The addition of 6% to 12% by weight of fine aggregate, within the range designated by the engineer, shall be made to both the binder and wearing courses and shall be introduced uniformly into the mix after the other aggregates and bituminous materials have been combined.

The coarse aggregate used in the mixture shall be dry when asphalt cement is used and surface-dry when cut-back asphalt or emulsified cut-back asphalt is used. Damp coarse aggregate can be used only with emulsified asphalt or tar or with cut-back asphalt or emulsified cut-back asphalt chemically treated as specified in Subsection (a)1.

430.3 CONSTRUCTION REQUIREMENTS   The construction requirements shall conform to Section 401.3, except as follows:

(d)   Bituminous Mixing Plant.

1.   Plant Requirements.   The approved equipment for developing the design and conducting control tests in accordance with the Department's Marshall method, will not be required.

4.   Preparation of Mixtures.

4a.   Bituminous Material.   When asphalt cement Class AC-2000 is used, it shall be heated at the plant and shall be brought to a temperature of not less than 265F nor more than 300F, as directed. The mineral aggregates shall be dried, and the maximum permissible temperature of the aggregate as determined at the mixer shall not exceed 100F.

4c.   Mixing.   Mixing shall be accomplished in an approved twin pugmill type mixer. The mixture shall be such that it may be handled, placed, and finished without stripping the bituminous material from the aggregate.

When asphalt cement and naphtha are used with stone or gravel coarse aggregate, the materials shall, unless otherwise directed, be introduced into the mixer in the following order: coarse aggregate, naphtha, asphalt cement, and fine aggregate. When slag is used as a coarse aggregate, the sequence of addition of the ingredients shall be as follows: coarse aggregate, asphalt cement, naphtha, and fine aggregate.

After the required quantities of aggregate and bituminous material have been introduced into the mixer, unless otherwise specified, the materials shall be mixed until a uniform coating of the particles and a thorough distribution of the bituminous material throughout the aggregate is secured. Wet mixing time shall be determined for the aggregate used.

A sufficient interval of time shall be allowed to elapse after the addition of each material to permit its thorough incorporation into the mixture prior to the introduction of the next ingredient.

(e)   Rollers. Rollers shall be of the steel-wheel types as specified in Sections 108.05(c)3.a and 3.b.

(f)   Conditioning of Existing Surface.   Prior to placing the surface course, the existing surface shall be prepared as specified in Section 401.3(f), except that the requirements for prime coat or tack coat shall apply only when indicated on the drawings or specified in the proposal.

(g)   Spreading and Finishing.   The requirements of Section 401.3(g) are supplemented as follows:

If an emulsified asphalt is used, the coated aggregate shall be

(Continued)

spread in a manner to avoid stripping the asphalt from the aggregate.

The wearing course shall not be placed until the binder course is satisfactorily cured. In no case shall this period of time be less than 60 hours when Class RCE-250 or RCE-800 bituminous material is used, or less than 24 hours when any other specified bituminous materials are used.

(h) Compaction.   Section 401.3(h) is modified as follows:

After each course has been uniformly spread, it shall be allowed to cure as previously specified or until the surface becomes tacky, then compacted with an approved power roller until it is compressed to a firm even surface, true to grade and cross section.

The intermediate rolling with a pneumatic-tired roller will not be required.

The Marshall density requirements will be waived.

(i)   Joints.   Section 401.3(i) is modified to eliminate the requirement for an infrared heater.

(j)   Pavement Samples.   Section 401.3(j) is modified to eliminate the requirements for density samples.

430.4   METHOD OF MEASUREMENT   This work will be measured in accordance with the method specified in Section 401.4.

430.5   BASIS OF PAYMENT   Bituminous Surface Course FB-2 will be paid for at the contract unit price per square yard or contract unit price per ton as specified in Section 401.5.

appendix 7
advertisements for competitive-bid park development contracts

* Example of Advertisement for a Municipal Park Development, Published in a Local Newspaper

* Example of Advertisement for a State Park Development, Published in an Official State Gazette

* Example of Advertisement for a Federal Park Development, Published in an Official Federal Gazette

* Example of Bid Notification for Recreational Projects, Published by a Construction News Subscription Service

EXAMPLE OF ADVERTISEMENT FOR A MUNICIPAL PARK DEVELOPMENT, PUBLISHED IN A LOCAL NEWSPAPER*

LEGAL NOTICE
NOTICE TO CONTRACTORS

Town of Natick
Massachusetts

Separate sealed bids for furnishing and installing floodlights at Memorial School Softball Field, Eliot Street—Rt. 16, in the Town of Natick will be received by the Town of Natick, Massachusetts, acting by and through the Recreation Commission at 5 Summer Street, Rm. 9, Natick, Massachusetts, until 10:00 A.M., D.S.T., September 4, 1975 and then at said time and place publicly opened and read aloud.

The Information for Bidders, Form of Bid, Form of Contract, Plans Specifications and Forms may be examined at the Natick Recreation and Park Office by depositing Twenty Dollars in cash or check payable to the Town of Natick for each complete set of plans and specifications. No plans will be mailed. Telephone orders will not be accepted.

Plan deposits will be returned after the bid opening provided that documents are returned unmarked, complete and in good condition.

The Town of Natick, Massachusetts, reserves the right to waive any informalities in or to reject any, any part of, or all bids.

Each general bidder must deposit with his bid, security in the amount of Two Thousand Dollars ($2,000.00) in the form and subject to the conditions provided in the Information for Bidders.

No bidder may withdraw his bid within thirty (30) days after the actual date of the opening thereof.

All contracts executed for the various portions and whole of the work shall contain the significant words: "The undersigned as bidder declares that he has carefully examined the location of the proposed work, the annexed proposed form of contract, and the plans and specifications therein referred to; and he proposes and agrees if his proposal is accepted, that he will contract with the Town, in the A.I.A. Form of Contract A-107 1966 which will state that all plans, general and detailed, all specifications, the information for bidders, and the proposal of the Contractor are hereby made part of this contract."

The Town of Natick, Massachusetts, reserves the right to waive any informalities in or to reject any, any part of, or all bids.

Each general bidder must deposit with his bid, security in the amount of Two Thousand Dollars ($2,000.00) in the form and

* Published in the *Suburban Press and Recorder,* August 20, 1975 and the *Natick Bulletin,* August 21, 1975.

subject to the conditions provided in the Information for Bidders.

No bidder may withdraw his bid within thirty (30) days after the actual date of the opening thereof.

All contracts executed for the various portions and whole of the work shall contain the significant words: "The undersigned as bidder declares that he has carefully examined the location of the proposed work, the annexed proposed form of contract, and the plans and specifications therein referred to; and he proposes and agrees if his proposal is accepted, that he will contract with the Town, in the A.I.A. Form of Contract A-107 1966 which will state that all plans, general and detailed, all specifications, the information for bidders, and the proposal of the Contractor are hereby made part of this contract."

Town of Natick, Massachusetts
by
Recreation Commission
   Patrick Moynihan, Chairman
   James Webb
   Paul Bregoli
   Ronald Ordway
   Betty O'Brian

EXAMPLE OF ADVERTISEMENT FOR A STATE PARK DEVELOPMENT, PUBLISHED IN AN OFFICIAL STATE GAZETTE*

Construction of Day Use Facilities, North
Side Park Development, Phase III,
Moraine State Park, Butler County

Sealed bids for the construction of day use facilities, North Side Park Development, Phase III, Moraine State Park, Butler County, Pa., Contract No. SP-0101-500-210-6.1, will be received by the Department of Environmental Resources in Room 518, Executive House, 101 South Second Street, Harrisburg, Pa. 17101, until 2 p.m., March 6, 1975, at which time said proposals will be publicly opened and read at the same location.

The principal items of work and approximate quantities are:

(a)   Maintenance Buildings
(b)   Bathhouse Complex
(c)   Three (3) Comfort Stations
(d)   Paved Access Roads   3300 L.F.
(e)   Parking Areas
(f)   Storm Sewers   3300 L.F.
(g)   Sanitary Sewers Laterals   605 L.F.
(h)   Waterlines Extensions   945 L.F.
(i)   Swimming Beach Extension
(j)   Two (2) Launch Ramps
(k)   Floating Wooden Boat Docks

Each bidder must submit a bid deposit of 10 percent of the amount bid.

Bid documents may be examined during office hours in the office of the Bureau of Operations, Department of Environmental Resources, Room 210, Evangelical Press Building, Third and Reily Streets, Harrisburg, Pa., or the office of Michael Baker, Jr., Inc., Consulting Engineers, P. O. Box 280, 4301 Dutch Ridge Road, Beaver, Pa. 15009. Bid documents will be furnished upon application to the Bureau of Operations, P. O. Box 1467, Harrisburg, Pa. 17120, accompanied by check payable to the Commonwealth of Pennsylvania in the amount of $42.40, per set, which includes sales tax. Bid documents need not be returned and payment *will not* be refunded.

MAURICE K. GODDARD,
Secretary

(Pa. B. Doc. No. 75-234. Filed February 7, 1975, 9:00 a.m.)

EXAMPLE OF ADVERTISEMENT FOR A FEDERAL PARK
DEVELOPMENT, PUBLISHED IN AN OFFICIAL
FEDERAL GAZETTE*

(1) Y—CONSTRUCTION OF RECREATIONAL BUILDINGS
AND SHELTERS—Group VI, West Pont Project, Chattahooche
River, AL and GA. The construction is located in Veasey Creek
and State Line Recreational Areas, in the vicinity and north of
West Point, GA. The work is located in Chambers County, AL,
and Troup County, GA, and includes approx 2 shower wash
houses with disposal systems, 2 flush toilet buildings with
disposal systems, 5 picnic shelters, 7 chlorinator houses, and 9
vault latrines. The contract will also include the construction of
the water and electrical systems for the above mentioned
recreational areas. Network Analysis System will not be required.
– Est cost is between $500,000 and $1,000,000 – IFB DACW21-76-B-
0003 – will be issued o/a 8 Aug 75. Bid opening o/a 11 Sep 75.
Contract time will be about 36 days. Sets of specs and plans cost
$10. Remittance to be made payable to "Treasurer of the U.S."
No refund will be made and material need not be returned.
Material requested after 1 Aug 75 will be supplied if available.
(P205)

Savannah District, Corps of Engineers
P. O. Box 889, Savannah GA 31402

* *Commerce Business Daily,* Issue No. PSA-6373, July 28, 1975.

EXAMPLE OF BID NOTIFICATION FOR RECREATIONAL PROJECTS, PUBLISHED BY A CONSTRUCTION NEWS SUBSCRIPTION SERVICE*

PGH 18 173 932G   BID(S) 10-14
1ST REPT 11-13-74   9-23-75

2 PARKLETS & OUTSIDE LIGHTING $116,000

CHARLEROI PA (WASHINGTON CO) (A) CREST AVE (B) WOODLAND AVE
    (CHAMBER OF COMMERCE PK-RIVER FRONT)
BIDS TO OWNER OCT 14 AT 7:30 PM (EDT)
OWNER—BOR OF CHARLEROI—KATHRENE PATRILAK (SECY) BOR BLDG
    325-27 MC KEAN AVE CHARLEROI PA
ENGR—MC DONALD & ASSOC—BILL DEICAS (IN CHG) 325 MC KEAN AVE
    CHARLEROI PA
ENGR (STR—MECH—ELEC) BY ENGR
    TOT LOTS—4 WD PAVILLONS—PLAYGROUND EQPT—BIT PAV
    WALKWAYS—3 DRINKING FOUNTAINS—3 TENNIS CTS—REPR TO
    EXIST BALL FIELDS—FENCING—LANDSCAPING CONC STAIRWAY—
    OUTSIDE LTG
PLANS FROM ENGR *$50 DEP—NON REF
BID BOND OR CERT CK 10%—PERF BOND 100%
*CHANGED DATA

PGH 9-14 182 568   O-A BID 9-29
                                                    9-23-75

3 TENNIS COURTS & SITE GRADING RH

WESTMORELAND CO PA—ALLEGHENY TWP—MELWOOD MANOR &
    BAGDAD PKS
BIDS TO OWNER SEPT 29 AT 7 PM (EDT)
    (TO BE OPENED IN THE BSMT LEVEL OF KISKI PK PLAZA R D #2
    LEECHBURG PA)
ONWER-SUPVR OF ALLEGHENY TWP—EDWARD S OSHESKIE (SECY) BOX
    152—R D #5 APOLLO PA
ARCH (LANDSCAPING)—ROBERT MUELLER 1415 MT ROYAL BLVD
    GLENSHAW PA
    SITE GRDG & CONST 3 BIT TENNIS CTS (1 SINGLE & 1 DOUBLE)
    INCL DRAINING & FENCING
SPECS FROM ARCH $15 DEP
10% BID BOND—CERT CK

---

* *Dodge Reports*, published by F.W. Dodge Division of McGraw-Hill Information Systems Company.

appendix 8

example of a standardized instructions to bidders

EXAMPLE OF STANDARDIZED INSTRUCTIONS TO BIDDERS*

WORK TO BE PERFORMED

1.   The work to be performed is described in plans and specifications for the project which are on file and may be inspected during business hours at the office of The Authority, 18th and Herr Streets, Harrisburg, Pennsylvania or at the office of the Architect/Engineer. Copies may be secured upon application to the Architect/Engineer by making a deposit in the amount stipulated in the "Notice to Contractors" for each set of plans, specifications and proposal forms. This deposit will be refunded upon the receipt of a bonafide bid, or a list of bidders to whom prices were forwarded, and the return of the plans and specifications in good order within ten (10) days after the opening of bids, otherwise the deposit will be forfeited.

FAMILIARITY WITH PROPOSED WORK

2.   It is the responsibility of the bidder by careful personal examination of the site to satisfy himself as to the nature and location of the work, the conformation of the ground, the soil and rock conditions, and the character, quality and quantity of the materials which will be required. The bidder shall examine carefully the proposed contract, the plans, specifications and all other documents and data pertaining to the project. The bidder shall not at any time after the execution of the contract, make any claims whatsoever alleging insufficient data or incorrectly assumed conditions, nor shall he claim any misunderstanding with regard to the nature, conditions or character of the work to be done under the contract, and he shall assume all risks resulting from any changes in the conditions which may occur during the progress of the work.

METHOD FOR SUBMITTING BIDS

3.   No proposal will be considered unless upon the proposal form for the project. Proposal forms are supplied in duplicate, one of which is to be submitted to The Authority and the other is for bidder's use. The blank spaces in the proposal form shall be filled in correctly, where indicated, for each and every item for which a description is given, and the bidder must state the prices (which should be written in ink, in words and numerals) for which he proposes to do each part of the work contemplated, and the total amount for all the parts included in any or all of the combinations of the work. In case of discrepancy, the written words shall be considered as being the bid price.

* Standard Form 194(2) 10/67, used by the General State Authority of Pennsylvania.

The bidder shall sign his proposal correctly. If the proposal is made by an individual, in addition to his signature his complete post office address should be given. If made by a firm or partnership, the complete post office address of each member of the firm or partnership must be given. If made by a corporation, the person signing the proposal should be the President or Vice President AND the Secretary or Treasurer of the corporation; otherwise, the signing individual's certificate or authority to execute such papers should accompany the proposal.

If bidder has been incorporated in some state other than Pennsylvania, bidder shall state whether the corporation is registered to do business in Pennsylvania. If bidder operates under an assumed or fictitious name, he shall state whether such name has been registered in Pennsylvania.

No contract will be awarded to a bidder who is a foreign corporation or operating under a fictitious or assumed name unless he has complied or agreed to comply with the proper registration under the laws of this Commonwealth.

PROPOSAL GUARANTY

4.   No proposal for any contract shall be considered unless accompanied by a certified check, bank cashiers check or bid bond on the form provided by The General State Authority, payable to The General State Authority in the amount specified in the proposal. All checks or bid bonds not forfeited under the terms of bidding except for the two lowest responsible bidders, shall be returned on or before the sixth day subsequent to the bid opening. The security of the two lowest responsible bidders, except where forfeiture of security is required, shall be returned upon the execution of the Contract Bond by the lowest responsible bidder. In the event the contract is not awarded by The Authority, the checks or bid bonds of the two lowest bidders, will be returned on or about forty-five (45) days after the date of the bid opening, unless an extension is granted by them.

DELIVERY OF PROPOSALS

5.   It is the responsibility of the bidder to deliver his bid to The Authority prior to the time of opening, regardless of what medium he uses to deliver it, whether by mail or otherwise. No bid shall be considered if it arrives after the time set for the bid opening. Each proposal should be submitted in a special envelope furnished by The Authority, 18th and Herr Streets, Harrisburg, Pennsylvania. If forwarded by mail, the above mentioned envelope shall be addressed to The General State Authority, 18th and Herr Streets, Harrisburg, Pennsylvania, preferably by registered mail. If forwarded otherwise than by mail, it shall be delivered at the office of The Authority, 18th and Herr Streets, Harrisburg, Pennsylvania, prior to the time stated in the "Notice to Contractors."

WITHDRAWAL OF PROPOSALS

6.   Bidders may withdraw any proposal after it has been received by The Authority provided the bidder makes his request in writing. The request must be received prior to the time of the bid opening. At the bid opening the low bidder on one contract may withdraw his bid or bids on subsequent contracts before such subsequent bids are read, if and only if, the representative of the bidder at the bid opening has with him a letter of authority executed by the persons who have executed the bid or bids to be withdrawn. Such letter of authority shall be given to the representative of The Authority prior to the time of the reading of the bids.

BID OPENING PROCEDURE

7.   Sealed proposals on projects, the plans and specifications for which were prepared by the Architect or Engineer names in the request for proposals, will be received by The General State Authority at its office, 18th and Herr Streets, Harrisburg, Pennsylvania, until the time stated in the "Notice to Contractors" at which time all proposals will be publicly opened, read, tabulated and the tabulations made public. All such proposals shall be enclosed in a sealed envelope and marked palinly on the outside with the contract number, bid opening date and time.

REJECTION OF PROPOSALS

8.   The right is reserved to The Authority in its discretion to reject any or all bids or parts thereof. Proposals may be rejected if they show any omission, alterations of form, additions or deductions not called for, conditional or uninvited alternate bids, or irregularities of any kind, but The Authority reserves the right to waive defects or irregularities on proposals.

PROOF OF BIDDER'S RESPONSIBILITY

9.   On request, or is specifically required by the terms of the proposal, bidders shall file an experience questionnaire and financial statement with The Authority, 18th and Herr Streets, Harrisburg, Pennsylvania, on the form of The Authority. The questionnaire and statement shall be certified to be true and correct by an affidavit sworn to or affirmed before a notary public, or other officer empowered to administer oaths or affirmations.

   If required, bidder shall prove ownership of current assets over and above the current liabilities in an amount equal to at least 20% of the bid price. No asset will be considered current unless there is reasonable expectation that it will be realized within a period of one year; nor will any liability be considered current that will not be liquidated within one year.

In addition to the financial qualifications, the bidder may be required to prove to the satisfaction of The Authority that he has successfully completed a contract for similar work in amount of not less than seventy-five percentum (75%) of the amount of the proposed contract.

The foregoing will guide The Authority in determining the responsibility of the bidder, but additional information may be requested by The Authority whenever in its judgment such information is necessary to determine the responsibility of the bidder.

In the event the bidder fails, refuses or neglects to submit any required information within the reasonable time stated in any request therefor or fails to qualify as a responsible bidder, his proposal guaranty shall be forfeited to the use of The Authority, not as a penalty, but as liquidated damages.

UNIT PRICES

10.   Where the proposal is based on unit prices for estimated quantities the unit prices control and not the totals or extensions.

COLLUSIVE BIDS WILL BE REJECTED

11.   The proposals of any bidder or bidders who engage in collusive bidding shall be rejected. Any bidder who submits more than one proposal in such manner as to make it appear that the proposals submitted are on a competitive basis from different parties shall be considered a collusive bidder. The Authority may reject the bid proposals of any collusive bidder upon bid openings of future projects. Nothing in this section shall prevent a bidder from superseding a bid proposal by a subsequent proposal delivered prior to bid opening which expressly revokes the previous bid.

AWARD OF CONTRACT

12.   The Authority shall have the right to reject any or all proposals or any parts thereof or items therein. The Counsel for The Authority shall have the right to waive technicalities for the best interests of The Authority. If an award of contract is made, it will be made to the lowest responsible bidder within forty-five (45) days from the date of bid opening. This time may be extended by written consent of either of the two lowest responsible bidders. Award will be made by letter mailed to the contractor and shall be effective the date of mailing. If the lowest bidder withdraws his bid, refuses award of contract or refuses to

grant an extension of time to award contract, The Authority shall have the right to award the contract to the next lowest responsible bidder or to reject all bids and rebid the contract.

EXECUTION OF CONTRACT AND CONTRACT BOND

13.   The individual, firm of corporation to who or to which the contract has been awarded must, within ten (10) days after receipt of the documents, sign and return to The Authority, 18th and Herr Streets, Harrisburg, Pennsylvania, the said contract documents, and a contract bond, or bonds, on the form provided by The Authority, in the penal sum equal to the amount of the awarded contract, for the faithful performance of the contract, and to cover the prompt payment in full for all materials furnished and labor supplied or performed and equipment actually rented (but not sold); and a bond in the penal sum of ten percentum (10%) of the contract amount, covering the correction of defective workmanship and material for one year after the completion and acceptance of the work, said bond or bonds to be executed by a surety company or companies qualified to do business in the Commonwealth. Failure or refusal of contractor to properly execute the contract documents or furnish said bonds shall be considered a refusal to accept the award or a default of contract at The Authority's discretion.

FAILURE TO EXECUTE CONTRACT

14.   If the lowest responsible bidder to whom the contract is awarded fails to give bonds or execute the contract within the time specified, the amount of the proposal guaranty shall be paid to The Authority as liquidated damages. In such cases The Authority, in its discretion, may award the contract to the next lowest responsible bidder, or reject all bids.

DETAILED BREAKDOWN SHEET AND SCHEDULE OF PRICES

15.   The successful bidder shall submit, on forms furnished by The Authority, a detailed, balanced breakdown sheet and schedule of the true prices of the proposed construction work. Until The Authority approves the breakdown, The Authority will not be obliged to make any payments to the bidder.

VETERAN'S PREFERENCE

16.   The Authority strongly recommends that, all things being equal, Contractors give preference in   mployment on projects of

The Authority to veterans of the Armed Services of the United States of America.

PROOF OF SURETY'S RESPONSIBILITY ON CONTRACT BOND

17.   The Surety Company, which is designated by the lowest responsible bidder for the faithful performance of the contract and prompt payment of materials and labor, shall with its contract bond furnish The Authority with a certificate showing that the amount of the bond is within the limit of net retention, or evidence that appropriate reinsurance or other security has been obtained in conformance with Section 661 of the Pennsylvania Insurance Code, 40 P.S., Sec. 832.

If the Surety has entered into an arrangement for reinsurance under the foregoing section of the law, the bond shall be supported by a duplicate original of the reinsurance agreement which shall contain a "direct liability to insured" clause, enabling The Authority to maintain an action against the company reinsured jointly with the reinsurer and, upon recovering judgment against such reinsured, to have recovery against such reinsurer, for payment to the extent in which it is liable under such reinsurance and in discharge thereof.

appendix 9
example of a bid tabulation form for a park construction project

EXAMPLE OF A BID TABULATION FORM FOR A PARK CONSTRUCTION PROJECT*

BID TABULATION SHEET   Page 1 of 3

WASHINGTON STATE PARKS AND RECREATION COMMISSION

LOCATION: Lake Easton State Park

PROJECT: Campground and Day Use Development

BID OPENING: 3:00 p.m., Wednesday, November 22, 1972

QUAN.	ITEM NO.	DESCRIPTION	Engineer's Estimate $210,258.00 UNIT PRICE	Bidder 1 $229,466.41 UNIT PRICE	Bidder 2 $231,699.40 UNIT PRICE	Bidder 3 $258,720.00 UNIT PRICE
L.S.	1	Clearing, grubbing, and grading for roadways, parking areas, and trails, at:	9,895.00	10,727.00	36,500.00	$
3000 CY	2	Gravel base, Class B, in place, at:	3.36	4.10	6.90	
1200 CY	3	Crushed surfacing top course, in place, at:	6.53	4.50	10.00	
1350 T.	4	Asphalt concrete payment, Class B, in place, at:	28.20	17.75	19.75	
45 Only	5	Campsite construction, at:	225.00	200.00	225.00	
L.S.	6	Installation of day use area equipment, at:	2,524.00	4,500.00	3,375.00	$
L.S.	7	Playground area, in place, at:	4,130.00	6,500.00	4,750.00	
8 Only	8	Bench, in place, at:	114.75	115.00	125.00	
L.S.	9	Remove existing roadway for lawn, at:	1,349.00	1,525.00	437.50	$
350 CY	10	Topsoil, in place, at:	10.54	6.00	4.75	
0.3 Acre	11	Lawn, in place, at:	4,543.00	5,968.00	1,000.00	
L.S.	12	Clear, grub, and grade swimming beach, at:	6,121.00	5,000.00	8,700.00	$
550 CY	13	Beach and playground sand, in place, at:	5.84	5.45	8.15	
180 LF	14	Cement concrete curb, in place, at:	3.89	3.00	5.00	
L.S.	15	Boat launch improvements, at:	4,652.00	5,110.00	10,250.00	$

Qty/Unit	Description	No.				$
860 LF	3'' diameter PVC plastic pipe, in place, at:	16	1.19	2.40	1.65	
960 LF	2'' diameter PVC plastic pipe, in place, at:	17		1.20	1.35	$
1800 LF	1½'' diameter PVC plastic pipe, in place, at:	18	0.46	1.00	1.20	
2700 LF	1'' diameter PVC plastic pipe, in place, at:	19		0.90	1.05	
2 only	3'' diameter gate valve with valve box, in place:	20	250.00	185.00	162.50	
2 only	2'' diameter gate valve with valve box, in place, at:	21	225.00	150.00	135.00	$
3 only	1½'' diameter gate valve with valve box in place at:	22	187.33	130.00	120.00	
2 only	1'' diameter gate valve with valve box, in place, at:	23	265.00	100.00	69.00	
2 only	1'' diameter stop and waste valve with valve box, in place, at:	24	160.00	100.00	69.00	$
3 only	¾'' diameter stop and waste valve with valve box, in place, at:	25	133.33	90.00	50.00	
13 only	1'' riser with quick coupling valve, in place, at	26	42.31	19.00	20.00	$
6 only	Fountain, in place, at:	27	87.00	90.00	148.00	
1 only	2'' vacuum breaker, in place, at:	28	999.00	570.00	390.00	
L.S.	Pumping station, in place, at:	29	8,490.00	17,145.00	12,950.00	$
L.S.	Additional irrigation equipment, at:	30	229.00	290.00	350.00	
3000 LF	4'' diameter plastic sewer pipe, in place, at:	31	1.73	1.69	2.10	
4 only	1000-gallon pre-cast concrete septic tank, in place, at:	32	250.00	275.00	350.00	$
400 LF	Drainfield (Type A), in place, at:	33	7.50	2.70	3.95	
1900 LF	3-#2/0 direct burial aluminum conductors, in place, at:	34	1.93	1.09	1.70	
400 LF	3-#4/0 direct burial aluminum conductors, in place, at:	35	2.77	2.46	1.90	$
1800 LF	2-#6/0 direct burial aluminum conductors, in place, at:	36	1.06	0.73	1.00	
2 only	Electrical panel, in place, at:	37	453.00	426.00	210.00	
45 only	Utility hook-ups, in place, at:	38	183.58	210.00	45.00	$
500 CY	Bedding material, in place, at:	39	10.10	4.25	10.00	
LS	Camp comfort station, in place, at:	40	42,883.00	44,355.00	35,750.00	
LS	Bathhouse, in place, at:	41	34,851.00	43,058.00	34,750.00	

* Standard form used by the Washington State Parks and Recreation Commission

appendix 10
example of a periodic partial payment form and invoice voucher for a park construction project

EXAMPLE OF A PARTIAL PAYMENT FORM FOR A PARK CONSTRUCTION PROJECT*

LAKE EASTON STATE PARK ESTIMATE NUMBER Three (3)
STATE PARKS AND RECREATION COMMISSION, CHARLES H. ODEGAARD, DIRECTOR
CONTRACTOR Nittany Contracting Company ADDRESS 1155 Smithfield Street, Seattle
PROJECT #371-19 Campground Development CONTRACT DATED November 22, 1972
DATE June 1, 19 73

ITEM NO.	UNIT	UNIT PRICES	QUANTITY	TOTAL	PREVIOUS	PRESENT
1. Clear/Grubb/Grade	L.S.	9,895.00	100%	9,895.00	9.796.05	98.95
2. Gravel Base	C.Y.	3.36	3420	11,491.20	403.20	11,088.00
3. Crushed Surfacing T.C.	C.Y.	6.53	—	—	—	—
4. A.C. Class B	Ton	28.20	—	—	—	—
5. Campsite Construction	Each	225.00	22	4,950.00	—	4,950.00
6. Day Use Area	L.S.	2,524.00	50%	1,262.00	—	1,262.00
7. Playground Area	L.S.	4,130.00	100%	4,130.00	—	4,130.00
8. Bench	Each	114.75	—	—	—	—
9. Remove Existing Roadway	L.S.	1,349.00	100%	1,349.00	—	1,349.00
10. Topsoil	C.Y.	10.54	—	—	—	—
11. Lawn, in place	Acre	4,543.00	—	—	—	—
12. Clear/Grubb Beach	L.S.	6,121.00	100%	6,121.00	—	—
13. Beach & Playground Sand	C.Y.	5.84	475	2,774.00	2,277.60	496.40
14. Concrete Curb	L.F.	3.89	168	653.52	653.52	—
15. Boat Launch Improvements	L.S.	4,652.00	90%	4,186.80	4,186.80	—
16. 3″ Dia. PVC	L.F.	1.19	953	1,134.07	1,134.07	—
17. 2″ Dia. PVC	L.F.	0.865	938	811.37	811.37	—
18. 1 ″ Dia. PVC	L.F.	0.46	1872	861.12	109.02	752.10
19. 1″ Dia. PVC	L.F.	0.374	2289	856.09	253.20	602.89
20. 3″ Dia. Gate Valve	Each	250.00	2	500.00	500.00	—
21. 2″ Dia. Gate Valve	Each	225.00	2	450.00	450.00	—
22. 1 ″ Dia. Gate Valve	Each	187.33	3	562.00	562.00	—
23. 1″ Dia. Gate Valve	Each	265.00	1	265.00	265.00	—
24. 1″ Dia. Stop & Waste Valve	Each	160.00	2	320.00	320.00	—
25. ″ Dia. Stop & Waste Valve	Each	133.33	3	400.00	400.00	—
26. 1″ Riser with Quick Coupl. Valve	Each	42.31	13	550.03	550.00	0.03
27. Fountain	Each	87.00	6	522.00	522.00	—

___LAKE EASTON___ STATE PARK   ESTIMATE NUMBER _____Three (3)_____
STATE PARKS AND RECREATION COMMISSION, CHARLES H. ODEGAARD, DIRECTOR
CONTRACTOR Nittany Contracting Company   ADDRESS 1155 Smithfield Street, Seattle
PROJECT #371-19 Campground Development   CONTRACT DATED   November 22, 1972
DATE _____June 1,_____ 19 __73__

ITEM NO.	UNIT	UNIT PRICES	QUANTITY	TOTAL	PREVIOUS	PRESENT
28. 2'' Vaccum Breaker	Each	999.00	1	999.00	999.00	—
29. Pumping Station	L.S.	8,490.00	95%	8,065.50	6,792.00	1,273.50
30. Add. Irrigation Equipm.	L.S.	229.00	100%	229.00	229.00	—
31. 4'' Dia. Plastic Sew. Pipe	L.F.	1.73	3500	6,055.00	—	6,055.00
32. 1000 Gal. Septic Tank	Each	250.00	4	1.000.00	1,000.00	—
33. Drainfield Type A	L.F.	7.50	400	3,000.00	1,500.00	1,500.00
34. 3-#2/0 Aluminum Conductor	L.F.	1.93	1633	3,151.69	—	3,151.69
35. 3-#4/0 Aluminum Conductor	L.F.	2.77	888	2,459.76	2,459.76	—
36. 2-#6/ Aluminum Conductors	L.F.	1.06	1000	1,060.00	—	1,060.00
37. Electrical Panel	Each	453.00	2	906.00	906.00	—
38. Utility Hook-ups	Each	183.58	23	4,222.34	—	4,222.34
39. Bedding Material	C.Y.	10.10	—	—	—	—
40. Comfort Station	L.S.	42,883.00	90%	38,594.70	32,162.25	6,432.45
41. Bathhouse	L.S.	34,851.00	90%	31,365.90	26,138.25	5,227.65
42. Modified #36	L.F.	1.44	1050	1,512.00	—	1,512.00
43. Modified #38	Each	195.38	22	4,298.36	—	4,298.36
SUB TOTAL				160,963.45	101,501.09	59,462.36
APPLICABLE SALES TAX				8,048.17	5,075.05	2,973.12
TOTAL			5%	169,001.62	106.576.14	62,435.18
10% RETAINED AS PER CONTRACT				16,901.16	10,657.61	6,243.55
TO BE PAID				152,110.46	95,918.53	56,191.93

APPROVED_____

* Standard form used by the Washington State Parks and Recreation Commission

EXAMPLE OF AN INVOICE VOUCHER FOR A PARK CONSTRUCTION PROJECT*

FORM A19 REV. 11-72	STATE OF WASHINGTON **INVOICE VOUCHER**

AGENCY NAME
State Parks and Recreation Commission
P. O. Box 1128
Olympia, Washington 98504

INSTRUCTIONS TO VENDOR OR CLAIMANT. SUBMIT THIS FORM IN TRIPLICATE TO CLAIM PAYMENT FOR MATERIALS, MERCHANDISE OR SERVICES. SHOW COMPLETE DETAIL FOR EACH ITEM.

INVOICE VOUCHER DATE 6/1/76 Contract # 676-BL

Blue Lake Campground Development
Payment #3

VENDOR OR CLAIMANT
Nittany Contracting Company
Blue Lake Project Office
Olympia, Washington 98504

VENDOR'S CERTIFICATE. I HEREBY CERTIFY, UNDER PENALTY OF PERJURY THAT THE ITEMS AND TOTALS LISTED HEREIN ARE PROPER CHARGES FOR MATERIALS, MERCHANDISE OR SERVICES FURNISHED TO THE STATE OF WASHINGTON, AND THAT ALL GOODS FURNISHED AND/OR SERVICES RENDERED HAVE BEEN PROVIDED WITHOUT DISCRIMINATION ON THE GROUNDS OF RACE, CREED, COLOR, NATIONAL ORIGIN, SEX, OR AGE.

D. Johnson (SIGN IN INK) President (TITLE)

DATE	DESCRIPTION	QUANTITY	UNIT	UNIT PRICE	AMOUNT	FOR AGENCY USE
6/1/76	Payment for work completed to date:					
	Original Contract				$ 229,466.61	
	5% Sales Tax				11,473.32	
	Subtotal				$ 240,939.73	
	Less 10% Retainage				24,093.97	
	TOTAL				$ 216,845.76	
	Amount Due to Date				$ 152,110.46	
	Less Previous Payments				95,918.53	
	PLEASE PAY THIS AMOUNT				$ 56,191.93	

ACCOUNT CODE						AMOUNT	
FUND	APPROP.	PROGRAM	OBJECT	SUB.		LIQUIDATION	NET INVOICE
070	T-5	052	40	03			

BUS.	AUTO FR.	P.P.	EX.	RAIL
CARRIER				

SHIPPING DOC. NO. COLL. PPD. NO. OF PC'S

CENTRAL RECEIVING BY BLUE LAKE, STATE PARK

DIV. OR UNIT RECEIVED FOR Johnson

DIV. OR UNIT RECEIVED BY

DATE OF RECEIPT FRT. CHARGE

	TOTAL			
CHECKED AND APPROVED FOR PAYMENT	AUTHORIZATION NO.	DATE 6/19/76	AMOUNT	DISCOUNT
BY				
BY			INVOICE VOUCHER	

VOUCHER NO. WARRANT NO. MLC-6174

* Standard form used by the Washington State Parks and Reaction Commission

appendix 11
park safety activity standards

PARK SAFETY ACTIVITY STANDARDS*

The Safety Program of a park shall be considered satisfactory when:

1.   The Employee Injury Frequency Rate of the park is below 10.0 injuries requiring medical treatment and/or involving lost workdays per million employee-hours of exposure.

2.   The Employee Disabling Injury Frequency Rate of the park is below 5.0 disabling injuries per million employee-hours of exposure.

3.   There have been no work-connected park employee fatalities.

4.   The Motor Vehicle Accident Frequency Rate of the park is below 5.0 chargeable motor vehicle accidents per million miles traveled.

5.   No structural fire loss occurs from a cause which could have been prevented by timely and appropriate action.

6.   The Visitor Injury Rate of the park is below 10.0 visitor injuries (medical treatment cases) per million visits.

7.   There have been no resource-related† visitor fatalities and the overall Visitor Fatality Rate of the park is below 0.5 visitor fatalities per million visits.

8.   There have been no work-connected Concessioner/Permittee Employee Fatalities in the park.

9.   There have been no work-connected Contractor Employee Fatalities in the park.

10.   All applicable provisions of Federal, State, and local safety, health, and sanitation statues and codes are complied with.

11.   A Safety Committee, the chairman of which shall be the superintendent or his principal assistant, has been established and is active.

12.   The Safety Program is understood by each employee in the park.

13.   The Safety Program is implemented, as appropriate, by each employee in the park.

14.   All tort claims are investigated and handled promptly. . . .

15.   All Liquefied Petroleum Gas installations and appliances are in compliance with the following standards as each may be applicable to the installation or facility involved‡:

  NFPA No. 37   Stationary Combustion Engines and Gas Turbines

* Source: USDI National Park Service, *Safety Management—Guidelines Requirements and Responsibilities,* USGPO, Washington, D.C., 1973, pp. 67–70.
† Resource-Related Fatality—any fatality resulting directly from the use of the resource(s) of the park, attributable to design and/or maintenance, which could have been prevented by timely and appropriate action.
‡ NFPA Standards are available from National Fire Protection Association, 60 Batterymarch Street, Boston, Massachusetts 02110.

NFPA No. 54   Installation of Gas Appliances and Gas Piping
NFPA No. 58   Storage and Handling Liquefied Petroleum
   Gases
NFPA No. 501B   Standard for Mobile Homes

16.   An up-to-date "Documented Safety Program" is on file in the park . . . which provides for:

   1.   Top management's leadership and participation in the development and operation of the safety program.
   b.   The assignment of full responsibility for the safety activities to one responsible individual.
   c.   A safety committee comprised of at least one member from each major park activity.
   d.   Periodic hazard detection inspections, by qualified personnel, coupled with a provision for corrective action.
   e.   The orientation and training of all employees (permanent, temporary, and seasonal) in safety attitudes, job skills, and their public safety responsibility.
   f.   The safety and health of all park employees.
   g.   The safety and well-being of concessioner/permittee employees (when applicable).
   h.   The safety and well-being of contractor employees (when applicable).
   i.   The safety and well-being of visitors.
   j.   Safety messages, when appropriate, are included in all interpretive talks.
   k.   All park literature and trail guides, including those sold by associations, contain appropriate safety messages.
   l.   Prompt and efficient first aid and medical care of injured persons.
   m.   A documented "Fire Prevention/Protection Plan" including a written procedure of what to do and who is to do it, in case of a building fire.
   n.   The furnishing and required use of personal protective clothing and equipment, when its use is clearly necessary.
   o.   Prompt investigation and reporting of all personal injury and/or property damage accidents along with all fire losses, ...
   p.   Review and analysis of the park's accident experience and the implementation of appropriate preventive measures.
   q.   Compliance with all applicable provisions of Federal, State, and local safety, health, sanitation, and fire statutes, codes, and standards.
   r.   The availability of all applicable statutes, codes, standards, publications, and manuals referred to in this standard.

appendix 12
information sources for specific activities: nongovernment organizations

INFORMATION SOURCES FOR SPECIFIC ACTIVITIES: NONGOVERNMENT ORGANIZATIONS

Archery

NATIONAL ARCHERY ASSOCIATION OF THE UNITED STATES (NAA)
1951 Geraldson Drive
Lancaster, Pennsylvania 17601

NATIONAL FIELD ARCHERY ASSOCIATION (NFAA)
Route 2, Box 514
Redlands, California 92373

Badminton

AMERICAN BADMINTON ASSOCIATION (ABA)
1330 Alexandria Drive
San Diego, California 92107

Ballooning

BALLOON FEDERATION OF AMERICAN (BFA)
806 15th Street, N.W., Suite 610
Washington, D.C. 18940

BALLOON PLATOON OF AMERICA (BPA)
Box 272
Bloomfield Hills, Michigan 48013

Baseball

AMERICAN AMATEUR BASEBALL CONGRESS (AABC)
212 Plaza Building
2855 West Market Street
P. O. Box 5332
Akron, Ohio 44313

BABE RUTH LEAGUE
P. O. Box 5000
Trenton, New Jersey 08638

BOYS BASEBALL
P. O. Box 225
Washington, Pennsylvania 15301

LITTLE LEAGUE BASEBALL
P. O. Box 809
Williamsport, Pennsylvania 17701

NATIONAL AMATEUR BASEBALL FEDERATION (NABF)
Route 1, Box 280B
Rose City, Michigan 48654

Basketball

BASKETBALL FEDERATION OF THE UNITED STATES OF
AMERICAN (BFUSA)
4215 Tallwood Drive
Greensboro, North Carolina 27410

Bicycling

AMATEUR BICYCLE LEAGUE OF AMERICA (ABLA)
P. O. Box 699
Wall Street Station
New York, New York 10005

BICYCLE INSTITUTE OF AMERICA (BIA)
122 East 42nd Street
New York, New York 10017

LEAGUE OF AMERICAN WHEELMEN (LAW)
19 South Bothwell Street
Palatine, Illinois 60067

Boating

AMERICAN POWER BOAT ASSOCIATION (APBA)
22811 Greater Mack
St. Clair Shores, Michigan 48080

BOAT OWNERS ASSOCIATION OF THE UNITED STATES
(BOAT/US)
8111 Gatehouse Road
Falls Church, Virginia 22042

BOAT OWNERS COUNCIL OF AMERICA (BOCA)
401 North Michigan Avenue
Chicago, Illinois 60611

NATIONAL BOATING FEDERATION (NBF)
629 Waverly Lane
Bryn Athyn, Pennsylvania 19009

OUTBOARD BOATING CLUB OF AMERICA (OBC)
401 North Michigan Avenue
Chicago, Illinois 60611

UNITED STATES COAST GUARD AUXILIARY (USCGAUX)
Commandant (G-BAU) U.S. Coast Guard
Washington, D.C. 20590

Bowling

AMERICAN BOWLING CONGRESS (ABC)
5301 South 76th Street
Greendale, Wisconsin 53129

AMERICAN JUNIOR BOWLING CONGRESS (AJBC)
5301 South 76th Street
Greendale, Wisconsin 53129

AMERICAN RUBBERBAND DUCKPIN BOWLING CONGRESS (ARDBC)
124 Odette Street
Pittsburgh, Pennsylvania 15227

NATIONAL BOWLING ASSOCIATION (NBA)
1806 Madison Avenue
Suite 407-08
Toledo, Ohio 43624

NATIONAL DUCK PIN BOWLING CONGRESS (NDPBC)
711 14th Street, N.W.
Washington, D.C. 20005

WOMEN'S INTERNATIONAL BOWLING CONGRESS (WIBC)
5301 South 76th Street
Greendale, Wisconsin 53129

Camping

AMERICAN CAMPING ASSOCIATION (ACA)
Bradford Woods
Martinsville, Indiana 46151

ASSOCIATION OF JEWISH SPONSORED CAMPS (AJSC)
130 East 59th Street
New York, New York 10036

FAMILY CAMPING FEDERATION OF AMERICA (FCFA)
Bradford Woods
Martinsville, Indiana 46151

NATIONAL CAMPERS AND HIKERS ASSOCIATION (NCHA)
7172 Transit Road
Buffalo, New York 14221

NATIONAL CAMPGROUND OWNERS ASSOCIATION (NCOA)
Box 366
Mill Valley, California 94941

NATIONAL CAMPING ASSOCIATION (NCA)
353 West 56th Street
New York, New York 10019

NORTH AMERICAN FAMILY CAMPERS ASSOCIATION (NAFCA)
P. O. Box 552
Newburyport, Maryland 01950

Canoeing

AMERICAN CANOE ASSOCIATION (ACA)
4260 East Evans Avenue
Denver, Colorado 80222

AMERICAN WHITEWATER AFFILIATION (AWA)
Box 1584
San Bruno, California 94066

Cross Country Skiing

SKI TOURING COUNCIL (STC)
c/o Rudolf F. Mattesich
West Hill Road
Troy, Vermont 05868

Field Hockey

FIELD HOCKEY ASSOCIATION OF AMERICA (FHAA)
1160 Third Avenue
New York, New York 10021

UNITED STATES FIELD HOCKEY ASSOCIATION (USFHA)
107 School House Lane
Philadelphia, Pennsylvania 19144

Fishing

BASS ANGLERS SPORTSMAN SOCIETY (BASS)
P. O. Box 3044
Montgomery, Alabama 36109

FEDERATION OF FLY FISHERMEN
4500 Beach Drive, S.W.
Seattle, Washington 98116

SPORT FISHING INSTITUTE (SFI)
608 Thirteenth Street, N.W.
Washington, D.C. 20005

Football

POP WARNER JUNIOR LEAGUE FOOTBALL
1315 Walnut Street, Suite 606
Philadelphia, Pennsylvania 19107

Golf

UNITED STATES DUFFER'S ASSOCIATION (Golf) (USDA)
P. O. Box 283
Newport, Kentucky 41072

UNITED STATES GOLF ASSOCIATIONS (USGA)
Golf House
Far Hills, New Jersey 07931

Handball

UNITED STATES HANDBALL ASSOCIATION (USHA)
4101 Dempster Street
Skokie, Illinois 60076

UNITED STATES TEAM HANDBALL FEDERATION (USTHF)
10 Nottingham Road
Short Hills, New Jersey 07078

Hiking

ADIRONDACK MOUNTAIN CLUB (ADK)
R. D. #1, Ridge Road
Glen Falls, New York 12801

Hockey

AMATEUR HOCKEY ASSOCIATION OF THE UNITED STATES
(AHAUS)
7901 Cedar Avenue
Bloomington, Minnesota 55420

Horseshoe

NATIONAL HORSESHOE PITCHERS ASSOCIATION OF
AMERICA (NHPAA)
c/o Lt. Ray Williams
P. O. Box 3150
Eureka, California 95501

Jogging

NATIONAL JOGGING ASSOCIATION (NJA)
1910 K Street, N.W., Suite 202
Washington, D.C. 20006

Lawn Bowls

AMERICAN LAWN BOWLS ASSOCIATION (ALBA)
10337 Cheryl Drive
Sun City, Arizona 85351

Orienteering

UNITED STATES ORIENTEERING FEDERATION (USOF)
P. O. Box 1081
Athens, Ohio 45701

Parachuting

UNITED STATES PARACHUTE ASSOCIATION (USPA)
P. O. Box 109
Monterey, California 93940

Platform Tennis

AMERICAN PLATFORM TENNIS ASSOCIATION (APTA)
c/o Fox Meadow Tennis Club
Wayside Lane
Scarsdale, New York 10583

Polo

UNITED STATES POLO ASSOCIATION (USPA)
1301 West 22nd Street
Executive Plaza, Suite 706
Oak Brook, Illinois 60521

Racquetball

INTERNATIONAL RACQUETBALL ASSOCIATION (IRA)
P. O. Box 1016
Stillwater, Oklahoma 74074

NATIONAL RACQUETBALL CLUB (NRC)
4101 Dempster Street
Skokie, Illinois 60076

Rodeo

NATIONAL LITTLE BRITCHES RODEO ASSOCIATION
(NLBRA)
P. O. Box 651
Littleton, Colorado 80120

Rowing

AMERICAN ROWING ASSOCIATION
4 Boat House Road
Fairmount Park
Philadelphia, Pennsylvania 19130

NATIONAL ASSOCIATION OF AMATEUR OARSMEN
(NAAO)
31552 Waltham Road
Birmingham, Michigan 48009

UNITED STATES ROWING SOCIETY (USRS)
4 East River Drive
Philadelphia, Pennsylvania 19130

Shooting, Firearms

AMATEUR TRAPSHOOTING ASSOCIATION (ATA)
P. O. Box 246, West National Road
Vandalia, Ohio 45377

AMERICAN SINGLE SHOT RIFLE ASSOCIATION (ASSRA)
11439 Wicker Avenue
Cedar Lake, Indiana 46303

NATIONAL BENCH REST SHOOTERS ASSOCIATION (NBRSA)
607 West Line Street
Minerva, Ohio 44657

NATIONAL MUZZLE LOADING RIFLE ASSOCIATION
(NMLRA)
Friendship, Indiana 47021

NATIONAL RIFLE ASSOCIATION OF AMERICA (NRA)
1600 Rhode Island Avenue, N.W.
Washington, D.C. 20036

NATIONAL SHOOTING SPORTS FOUNDATION (NSSF)
1075 Post Road
Riverside, Connecticut 06878

NATIONAL SKEET SHOOTING ASSOCIATION (NSSA)
P. O. Box 28188
San Antonia, Texas 78228

UNITED STATES REVOLVER ASSOCIATION (USRA)
59 Alvin Street
Springfield, Maine 01104

Shuffleboard

NATIONAL SHUFFLEBOARD ASSOCIATION (NSA)
10418 N.E. 2nd Avenue
Miami, Florida 33138

Skating, Ice

ICE SKATING INSTITUTE OF AMERICA (ISIA)
P. O. Drawer 2506
Fort Myers, Florida 33902

UNITED STATES FIGURE SKATING ASSOCIATION (USFSA)
178 Tremont Street
Boston, Massachusetts 02111

Skating, Roller

AMATEUR SKATING UNION OF THE UNITED STATES
Route 2, Box 464
Kenisha, Wisconsin 63126

ROLLER SKATING FOUNDATION OF AMERICA (RSFA)
515 Madison Avenue
New York, New York 10022

ROLLER SKATING RINK OPERATORS ASSOCIATION OF
AMERICA (RSROA)
7700 A Street
Lincoln, Nebraska 68510

SOCIETY OF ROLLER SKATING TEACHERS OF AMERICA
(SRSTA)
7700 A Street
Lincoln, Nebraska 68510

UNITED STATES OF AMERICA CONFEDERATION (Skating)
(USAC)
7700 A Street
Lincoln, Nebraska 68510

Skiing, Downhill

EASTERN SKI ASSOCIATION (ESA)
22 High Street
Brattleboro, Vermont 05301

NATIONAL SKI PATROL SYSTEM (NSPS)
2901 Sheridan Boulevard
Denver, Colorado 80214

PACIFIC NORTHWESTERN SKI ASSOCIATION (PNSA)
P. O. Box 6228
Seattle, Washington 98188

UNITED STATES SKI ASSOCIATION (USSA)
1726 Champa Street, Suite 300
Denver, Colorado 80202

Snowmobiling

AMERICAN SNOWMOBILE ASSOCIATION (ASA)
13104 Crooked Lake Boulevard
Anoka, Minnesota 55303

Soaring

SOARING SOCIETY OF AMERICA (SSA)
Box 66071
Los Angeles, California 90066

Soccer

UNITED STATES SOCCER FOOTBALL ASSOCIATION (USSFA)
350 Fifth Avenue, Room 4010
New York, New York 10001

Softball

AMATEUR SOFTBALL ASSOCIATION OF AMERICA (ASA)
P. O. Box 11437
Oklahoma City, Oklahoma 73111

Surfing

WESTERN SURFING ASSOCIATION (WSA)
c/o Jack Flanagan
2024 West Cliff Drive
Santa Curz, California 95060

Swimming

COUNCIL FOR NATIONAL COOPERATION IN AQUATICS
(CNCA)
51 Clifford Avenue
Pelham, New York 10803

NATIONAL SWIMMING POOL INSTITUTE (NSPI)
2000 K Street, N.W.
Washington, D.C. 20006

Tennis

AMERICAN TENNIS ASSOCIATION
P. O. Box 1139
Danville, Virginia 24541

NATIONAL PUBLIC PARKS TENNIS ASSOCIATION (NPPTA)
155 West Washington Boulevard
Los Angeles, California 90015

UNITED STATES TENNIS ASSOCIATION (USTA)
51 East 42nd Street
New York, New York 10017

U.S. TENNIS COURT AND TRACK BUILDERS ASSOCIATION
(USTCTBA)
1201 Waukegan Road
Glenview, Illinois 60025

Track

UNITED STATES TRACK AND FIELD FEDERATION (USTFF)
1226 North 10th Avenue
Tucson, Arizona 85705

Trapping

NATIONAL TRAPPERS ASSOCIATION (NTA)
c/o Gerald Walkup
Route 2
Iowa City, Iowa 52240

Volleyball

UNITED STATES VOLLEYBALL ASSOCIATION (USVBA)
P. O. Box 554
Encino, California 91316

Waterskiing

AMERICAN WATER SKI ASSOCIATION (AWSA)
Seventh Street and G Avenue, S.W.
Winter Haven, Florida 33880

appendix 13
periodicals devoted to specific types of activities

PERIODICALS DEVOTED TO SPECIFIC TYPES OF ACTIVITIES

CATEGORY 1: PERIODICALS DEVOTED TO SPECIAL SURFACE SPORTS

Bowling
American Bowling Congress, Inc.
5301 S. 76th Street
Greendale, Wisconsin
monthly
$4.00

Handball
U.S. Handball Assoc.
4101 Dempster St., Skokie, Illinois 60076
bimonthly
$3.00

Paddle World
Racquett Paddle Publications, Inc.
370 7th Avenue, New York, New York 10001
quarterly
$3.95

Racquetball
Int. Racketball Assn.
4101 Dempster Street, Skokie, Illinois 60076
bimonthly
$3.00

Skate
Roller Skating Rink Operators Assn. of America
7700 A Street, Lincoln, Nebraska 68510
quarterly
$2.00

Skating
U.S. Figure Skating Assoc.
178 Tremont Street, Boston, Massachusetts 02111
8/yr
$3.50

Tennis Industry
Industry Publishers, Inc.
14965 N.E. 6th Ave., N. Miami, Florida 33161
monthly except Jan.
free to qualified individuals or $15.00/yr.

Tennis, Magazine of the Racquet Sports
Tennis Features, Inc.
297 Westport Ave., Norwalk, Connecticut 06854
monthly
$7.00

Tennis Trade
Hoffman Press
3000 France Avenue, South Minneapolis, Minnesota 55416
bimonthly
$4.50

Tennis USA
Steele Publications Inc.
420 Lexington Avenue, New York, New York 10017
monthly
$5.00

U.S. Hockey Arena Biz
U.S. Hockey Biz, Suite 12, 2038 Penn. Ave.,
   Madison, Wisconsin 53704
monthly
free to qualified individuals or $9.00 annually

U.S. Hockey/Arena Biz
Suite 12, 2038 Penn. Ave., Madison, Wisconsin 53704
monthly
$9.00

World Tennis
8100 Westglen, Houston, Texas 77042
monthly
$7.00

CATEGORY 2: PERIODICALS
DEVOTED TO TEAM TURF SPORTS

Sportscope (Newsletter)
The Athletic Institute
705 Merchandise Mart, Chicago, Illinois 60654
monthly
free

CATEGORY 3: PERIODICALS
DEVOTED TO INDIVIDUAL OR
SPECIAL TURF SPORTS

The Jogger
National Jogging Assoc.
1832 K St., N.W., Washington, D.C. 20006
monthly
membership to NJA $8.00

Runner's World
World Publications
Box 366, Mountain View, California 94040
monthly
$7.00

Skeet Shooting Review
National Skeet Shooting Assn.
Linwood Bldg., 2608 Inwood Rd., Dallas, Texas 75235
monthly
$1.00

USGA Green Section Record
U.S. Golf Assn.
Far Hills, New Jersey 07931
6/yr.
$2.00

CATEGORY 4: PERIODICALS DEVOTED TO AERIAL ACTIVITIES

Parachutist
United States Parachute Assoc.
P. O. Box 109, Monterey, California 93940
monthly
$7.00 (to U.S. nonmembers)

Sky Diver
Box 1024 La Habra, California 90631
monthly
$5.00

CATEGORY 5: PERIODICALS DEVOTED TO WATER RELATED ACTIVITIES

American Canoeist
A.C.A. Publications
6104 Vineland Ave., N. Hollywood, California 91606
bimonthly
$3.50

Canoe
The Webb Company, Inc.
1999 Sheppard Road
St. Paul, Minnesota 55116
bimonthly
$6.00

Fly Fisherman Magazine
Dorset, Vermont 05251
7 issues/year
$10.00

Lake and Boating
Boating Publications, Inc.
412 Longshore Dr., Ann Arbor, Michigan 48107
monthly
$5.00

Marine and Recreation News
27601 Little Mack, St. Clair Shores, Michigan 48081
weekly
$5.00

Ocean Lifeguard
Nat'l Surf Life Saving Assoc.
NSLA of America
P. O. Box 366, Huntington Beach, California 92648
twice yearly
$2.50

Pool News
Leisure Publications, Inc.
3923 W. 6th St., Los Angeles, California 90020
twice monthly
$5.00

Powerboat
Nordco Pub., Inc.
16216 Raymer St., Van Nuys, California 91406
monthly
$6.00

Reaching for Life
Nat. Surf Life Saving Assoc. (NSLSA) of America
P. O. Box 366, Huntington Beach, California 92648

Safety Standards for Small Craft
American Boat and Yacht Council, Inc.
15 East 26th St., New York, New York 10010
continuous
initial cost $35.00 plus $10.00 annually

Salt Water Sportsman
Salt Water Sportsman, Inc.
10 High Street, Boston, Massachusetts 02110
monthly
$5.00

Surfing
Petersen Publishing Co.
8490 Sunset Blvd., Los Angeles, California 90069
bimonthly
$3.00

Surfing East
Richard S. Van Winkle
244 Highland Ave., Ridgewood, New Jersey 07450
bimonthly
$5.00

Swimming Pool Weekly and Swimming Pool Age
Hoffman Publications, Inc.
Box 11299, Fort Lauderdale, Florida 33306
3/mo.
$8.00

Swimming Technique
Swimming World
5507 Laurel Canyon Blvd., N. Hollywood, California 91607
quarterly
$4.50

Swimming World and Junior Swimmer
Swimming World Publications
5507 Laurel Canyon Blvd., N. Hollywood, California 91607
monthly
$9.00

U.S. Coast Guard Boating Safety Newsletter
U.S. Coast Guard Comdt. (G-BBE-1),
U.S. Coast Guard, Washington, D.C. 20590
quarterly
free

Water Skier, The
American Water Ski Assoc.
P. O. Box 191, Winter Haven, Florida 33880
7 issues/year
$3.00

Watersport, Boat Owners Council of America
Market Communications, Inc.
534 N. Broadway, Milwaukee, Wisconsin 53202
quarterly
$5.00

CATEGORY 6: PERIODICALS DEVOTED TO LAND OUTING ACTIVITIES

Adirondack
Adirondack Mountain Club, Inc.
172 Ridge St., Glens Falls, New York 12801
bimonthly
$3.00 (nonmembers)

American Hiker
2236 Mimosa, Houston, Texas 77019
monthly
$5.00

Forest User
American Forest Institute
9711 S. W. Corbett St., Portland, Oregon 97219
quarterly
free

Long Trail News
Green Mountain Club
45 Part St., Rutland, Vermont 05701
quarterly

Mountain Gazette
Write On Publishing House
1801 York St., Denver, Colorado 80206
monthly
$5.00

Outdoor America
Izaak Walton League of America
1800 North Kent St., Suite 806, Arlington, Virginia 22209
monthly
$5.00

Outdoor Press
Fred L. Peterson
W. 2205 Longfellow, Spokane, Washington 99205
weekly (tabloid)
$9.00

Outdoors Unlimited
Outdoor Writers Assn. of America
Brown Deere Professional Bldg., Suite 110, 4141 W. Bradley Road,
    Milwaukee, Wisconsin 55416
monthly
membership

Outdoor Times
M. L. Harrell
4515 Prentice, Dallas, Texas 7506
weekly (tabloid)
$6.00

Potomac Appalachian
Potomac Appalachian Trail Club
1718 N. St., N.W. Washington, D.C. 20036
monthly
$3.00

Social Agency Management including *Better Camp Management*
Galloway Publications
5 Mountain Ave., N. Plainfield, New Jersey 07060
quarterly
$10.00/2 yrs. $8.00/1 yr.

Wilderness Camping
Fitzgerald Communications Inc.
1255 Portalnd Pl., Boulder, Colorado 80302
Jan., March, May, July, Sept., Nov.
$4.00

CATEGORY 7: PERIODICALS
DEVOTED TO RECREATIONAL VEHICLES

American Bicyclist and Motorcyclist
National Bicycle Dealers Assn.
Cycling Press Inc.
461 8th Ave., New York, New York 10001
$6.00

Mobile Home/Recreational Vehicle Dealer
J. Brown Hardison
6229 Northwest Hwy., Chicago, Illinois 60631
Twice monthly
$7.00

Recreational Industry
Conover Mast (Cahners Pub. Co.)
205 E. 42 St., New York, New York 10017
8 issues/year

Recreational Vehicle Retailer
Trailer Life Publishing Co., Inc.
23945 Craftsman Rd., Calabasas, California 91302
monthly
$8.00

RV Business
Hoffman Press
3000 France Ave., South, Minneapolis, Minnesota 55416
6/yr.
$4.50

Snotrack
United States Snowmobile Assn.
534 N. Broadway, Minneapolis, Minnesota 53202
6/yr. (winter)
$3.00

Snowmobiler's Race & Rally Magazine
Box 182, Alexandria, Minnesota 56308
3/yr.
$3.00

Snowsports Dealer News
Snowsport's Publications Inc.
1500 E. 79th St., Minneapolis, Minnesota 55420
monthly
$5.00

Wheels Afield
Petersen Publishing Co.
8490 Sunset Blvd., Los Angeles, California 90069
monthly
$7.50

CATEGORY 8: PERIODICALS DEVOTED TO WINTER ACTIVITIES

National Ski Area News
Ziff-Davis Publishing Co.
1 Park Ave., New York, New York 10016
quarterly
free to qualified individuals

Nordic World
World Publications
Box 366, Mountain View, California 94040
bimonthly
$4.00

NSAA Newsletter
National Ski Areas Assoc.
99 Park Ave., New York, New York 10016
twice monthly

Ski
Popular Science Pub. Co.
235 E. 45th St., New York, New York 10017
7/yr.
$5.00

Ski Area Management
Beardsley Publishing Corp.
Box 242, N. Salem, New York 10560
quarterly
free to qualified individuals

Ski Business
Popular Science Pub. Co.
335 Lexington Ave., New York, New York 10017
bimonthly
$6.00

Skiing
Ziff-Davis Publishing Co.
1 Park Ave., New York, New York 10016
7/yr. (Sept.–March)
$4.00

United States Ski News
U.S. Ski Assoc.
1726 Champa St., Suite 300, Denver, Colorado 80082
4/yr.
membership

CATEGORY 9: PERIODICALS DEVOTED TO EMPHASES USEFUL TO PARK PLANNERS AND ADMINISTRATORS

American City, The
Buttenheim Publishing Corp.
Berkshire Common, Pittsfield, Maine 01201
monthly
$15.00

American County Government
The National Association of Counties
1001 Connecticut Ave., N.W., Washington, D.C. 20036
monthly
$10.00

Fund Development and Technical Assistance Report
Leisure Information Service
729 Delaware Ave., S.W. Washington, D.C. 20024
biweekly
$45.00

Human Resource Management
Office of Publications, Graduate School of Administration
The University of Michigan, Ann Arbor, Michigan 48104
quarterly
$6.50

Journal of Environmental Education, The
Dembar Educational Research Service
Box 1605, Madison, Wisconsin 53701
quarterly
$10.00

Journal of Physical Education and Recreation
1201 16th St., N.W., Washington, D.C. 20036
monthly except for July and August
$25.00

Journal of Physical Education
Physical Education Society of the YMCA of North Am.
c/o Douglas Boyea, 105 Black Rock Ave., New Britain,
   Connecticut 06052
bimonthly
$5.00/nonmembers

Journal of Leisure Research
National Recreation and Park Assoc.
1601 N. Kent St., Arlington, Virginia 22209
quarterly
$10.00

Journal of Safety Research
425 N. Michigan Ave., Chicago, Illinois 60611
quarterly
$15.00

Journal of Travel Research
Travel Research Assoc.
University of Color., Business Research Div.,
   Boulder, Colorado 80302
quarterly
membership ($25.00 non-members)

Land and Water Development
Cummins Publishing Co.
21590 Greenfield Rd., Oak Park, Michigan 48237
quarterly
$8.00

Land Economics
University of Wisconsin
Social Science Building, Madison, Wisconsin 53706
quarterly
$10.00

Landscape Architecture
American Society of Landscape Architects
Schuster Bldg., 1500 Bardstown Rd., Louisville, Kentucky 40205
6/yr.
$8.50

Land Use Digest
Urban Land Institute
1200 18th St. N.W., Washington, D.C. 20036
monthly
$15.00

Land Use Planning Reports
Plus Publications, Inc.
2814 Pennsylvania Ave., N.W., Washington, D.C. 20007
weekly
$115

Leisurability (Journal of Leisurability)
Leisure and Disability Publications
Steering Committee, Box 281, Station A, Ottawa, Canada
quarterly
$9.00

Leisure Today
American Alliance for Health, Physical Education and Recreation
1201 16th St., N.W., Washington, D.C. 20036
3 times/yr.

Leisure Time
Leisure Time Institute
Box 721, New Rochelle, New York 10802
bimonthly
$1.50

National Civic Review
National Municipal League
Carl H. Pforzheimer Building, 47 E. 68th Street,
  New York, New York 10021
monthly
$7.50

National Parks and Conservation Magazine
National Parks and Conservation Assoc.
monthly
$10.00

National Safety News
National Safety Council
425 N. Michigan Ave., Chicago, Illinois 60611
monthly
$9.25

Nation's Cities
National League of Cities
1620 Eye St., N.W., Washington, D.C. 20006
monthly
$10.00

Natural Resources Journal
Univ. New Mexico School of Law
1117 Stanford N.E. Albequerque, New Mexico 87131
quarterly
$12.00

NRPA: Washington Action Report
National Recreation and Park Association
1601 N. Kent St., Arlington, Virginia 22209
biweekly
$20/yr. for members

Occupational Hazards Magazine
Industrial Publishing Co.
614 Superior Ave., W. Cleveland, Ohio 44113
monthly
$9.25

Park Maintenance
Madisen Publishing Div.
P. O. Box 409, Appleton, Wisconsin 54911
monthly
$5.00

Park Practice Program, The
3 publications: 1. *Trends* incorporating *Guideline*
                2. *Design*
                3. *Grist*
National Society for Park Resources
National Park and Recreation Assn.
1601 N. Kent St., Arlington, Virginia 22209
Initial membership of $80.00 plus $20.00 annually

Parks and Recreation
National Recreation and Park Association
1601 N. Kent St., Arlington, Virginia 22209
monthly
$10.00

Planning
American Society of Planning Officials
1313 East 60th St., Chicago, Illinois 60637
monthly
membership

Public Administration Review
American Society for Public Administration
1225 Connecticut Ave., N.W., Washington, D.C. 20036
bimonthly
$25.00

Public Management
International City Management Association
1140 Connecticut Ave., N.W., Washington, D.C. 20036
monthly
$8.00

Public Personnel Management
International Personnel Management Association
Rm. 240, 1313 East 60th St., Chicago, Illinois 60637
quarterly
$12.00

Recreation Management
National Industrial Recreation Association
20 N. Walker Dr., Chicago, Illinois 60606
10/yr.
$5.00

Recreation Management
Inst. of Recreation Management (British)
Kernan Pub. Co., Box 9095, College Station, Texas 77840
bimonthly
£4.50 U.K.

Recreation Review
Ontario Research Council on Leisure
400 University Ave., 23rd Floor, Toronto, Ontario M7A 149
quarterly

Research Quarterly
American Alliance for Health, Physical Education,
   and Recreation
1201 16th St., N.W., Washington, D.C. 20036
quarterly
$15.00

Tab
The American Society of Planning Officials
1313 East 60th., Chicago, Illinois 60637
semimonthly
membership

Urban Affairs Quarterly
Sage Publications
275 South Beverly Drive, Beverly Hills, California 90212
quarterly
institutions—$15.00/yr. Professionals and Teachers—$10.00/yr.
    Students—$9.00/yr.

Urban Research News
Sage Publications Inc.
275 South Beverly Drive, Beverly Hills, California 90212
biweekly
$30.00/yr.—institutional; $20.00/yr—professional & teacher

Washington Action Report
National Recreation and Park Assoc.
Division of Special Programs
1601 N. Kent St., Arlington, Virginia 22209
biweekly
$10.00/yr. NRPA members
$15.00/yr. nonmembers

Weeds, Trees and Turf
Harvest Publishing Company
9800 Detroit Ave., Cleveland, Ohio 44102
monthly
$10.00

appendix 14
periodicals published by federal agencies useful to park planners

PERIODICALS PUBLISHED BY FEDERAL AGENCIES USEFUL TO PARK PLANNERS

Aging
U.S. Department of Health, Education and Welfare
   Office of Human Development
   Administration on Aging
monthly

American Rehabilitation
Rehabilitation Service Administration
   Department of Health, Education and Welfare
   Washington, D.C.
6/yr.
$11.75

Average Monthly Weather Outlook
U.S. Department of Commerce
   National Oceanic and Atmospheric Administration
   National Weather Service
monthly
$3.50

Data User News
U.S. Department of Commerce
   Bureau of the Census
   Subscriber Services Section
   Social and Economics Statistics Administration
   Washington, D.C. 20233
monthly
$4.00

Dimensions
U.S. Department of Commerce
   National Bureau of Standards
monthly
$9.45

Exponent (Publication of Planning and Design Activities)
National Park Service
   U.S. Department of Interior
quarterly

Extension Service Review
Cooperative Extension Service USDA
   Official Monthly Publication
monthly
$3.60

Fire Management
USDA Forest Service
quarterly
$3.00

HUD Challenge
Housing and Urban Development Department
    U.S. Superintendent of Documents
monthly
$15.90

HUD Newsletter
Housing and Urban Development Department
    U.S. Superintendent of Documents
weekly
$12.50

In Touch
National Park Service
    Division of Interpretation and Visitor Services
    1100 L Street NPS Bldg.
    Washington, D.C. 20240
monthly

Job Safety and Health
U.S. Department of Labor
    Occupational Safety and Health Administration
    U.S. Superintendent of Documents
monthly
$13.60

Monthly Catalog—U.S. Government Publications
U.S. Superintendent of Documents
monthly

NEISS News
National Electronic Injury Surveillance System
    U.S. Consumer Products Safety Commission
    Room 323, 5401 Westbard Ave.
    Bethesda, Maryland 20207
monthly

Newsletter
National Park Service
    Department of Interior
    Washington, D.C. 20240
biweekly (for service employees)

Newsletter
President's Council on Physical Fitness and Sports
    Executive Office of the President
irregular

Newsletter—Committee on Barrier Free Design
The President's Committee on Employment of the Handicapped
    Washington, D.C. 20210
monthly

Northeast Outdoor Memo
Bureau of Outdoor Recreation
  Northeast Regional Office
  600 Arch Street
  Philadelphia, Pa. 19106
monthly

NTIS Weekly Government Abstracts: Administration
U.S. Department of Commerce
  National Technical Information Service
  5285 Port Royal Road
  Springfield, Virginia 22160
weekly
$40

NTIS Weekly Government Abstracts: Behavior and Society
U.S. Department of Commerce
  National Technical Information Service
  5285 Port Royal Road
  Springfield, Virginia 22160
weekly
$40

*NTIS Weekly Government Abstracts: Environmental Pollution
  and Control*
U.S. Department of Commerce
  National Technical Information Service
  5285 Port Royal Road
  Springfield, Virginia 22160
weekly
$40

*NTIS Weekly Government Abstracts: NASA Earth Resources
  Survey Program*
U.S. Department of Commerce
  National Technical Information Service
  5285 Port Royal Road
  Springfield, Virginia 22160
weekly
$40

NTIS Weekly Government Abstracts: Natural Resources
U.S. Department of Commerce
  National Technical Information Service
  5285 Port Royal Road
  Springfield, Virginia 22160
weekly
$40

*NTIS Weekly Government Abstracts: Problem-Solving
  Information for State and Local Governments*

U.S. Department of Commerce
  National Technical Information Service
  5285 Port Royal Road
  Springfield, Virginia 22160
weekly
$60

NTIS Weekly Government Abstracts: Transportation
U.S. Department of Commerce
  National Technical Information Service
  5285 Port Royal Road
Springfield, Virginia 22160
weekly
$40

NTIS Weekly Government Abstracts: Urban Technology
U.S. Department of Commerce
  National Technical Information Service
  5285 Port Royal Road
  Springfield, Virginia 22160
weekly
$40

Our Public Lands
Land Management Bureau, Interior Department
  U.S. Superintendent of Documents
quarterly
$3.00

Outdoor Recreation Action
Outdoor Recreation Bureau
  Interior Department
  U.S. Superintendent of Documents
quarterly
$4.15

Programs for the Handicapped
Department of Health, Education and Welfare
  Office of the Assistant Secretary for Human Development
  Office for Handicapped Individuals
  Washington, D.C. 20201
8/yr.

Public Roads, Journal of Highway Research
Federal Highway Administration
  Department of Transportation
  Washington, D.C. 20591
quarterly
$4.50

Reclamation Era
Reclamation Bureau, Interior Department
  U.S. Superintendent of Reclamation
quarterly
$4.00

Reclamation Safety News
Department of Interior
  Bureau of Reclamation
  Washington, D.C. 20240
quarterly

Safety News Letter
Federal Safety Council Department of Labor
  Office of Information
  Fourteenth Street and Constitution Ave., N.W.
  Washington, D.C. 20210

Selected U.S. Government Publications Catalog
Superintendent of Documents
  U.S. Government Printing Office
  Washington, D.C. 20402
monthly

Selected Water Resources Abstracts
Water Resources Scientific Information Service
  National Technical Information Service
  U.S. Dept. of Comm., Springfield, Virginia 22151
semimonthly
$45.00

Soil Conservation
Agriculture Department, Soil Conservation Service
  U.S. Superintendent of Documents
monthly
$6.85

Tree Planter's Notes
Agriculture Department, Forest Service
  Division of Information and Education
  Washington, D.C. 20250
quarterly
$1.00

Water Resources Review
Department of Interior
  Geological Survey
  Reston, Virginia 22090
monthly

Water Spectrum, Issues, Choices, Actions
Defense Department, Army Department, Corps of Engineers
  U.S. Superintendent of Documents
quarterly
$6.20

Wildlife Review
Fish and Wildlife Service
  Department of Interior
  Washington, D.C. 20240
quarterly

index

Page numbers in *italics* refer to definitions.